THE ALEVIS IN MODERN TURKEY AND
THE DIASPORA

Edinburgh Studies on Modern Turkey

Series Editors: Alpaslan Özerdem and Ahmet Erdi Öztürk

International Advisory Board
- Sinem Akgül Açıkmeşe
- Samim Akgönül
- Rebecca Bryant
- Mehmet Gurses
- Gareth Jenkins
- Ayşe Kadıoğlu
- Stephen Karam
- Paul Kubicek
- Peter Mandaville
- Nukhet Ahu Sandal
- M. Hakan Yavuz

Books in the series (published and forthcoming)

Islamic Theology in the Turkish Republic
Philip Dorroll

Turkish–Greek Relations: Foreign Policy in a Securitisation Framework
Cihan Dizdaroglu

Policing Slums in Turkey: Crime, Resistance and the Republic on the Margin
Çağlar Dölek

The Kurds in Erdoğan's Turkey: Balancing Identity, Resistance and Citizenship
William Gourlay

The Politics of Culture in Contemporary Turkey
Edited by Pierre Hecker, Ivo Furman and Kaya Akyıldız

Peace Processes in Northern Ireland and Turkey: Rethinking Conflict Resolution
İ. Aytaç Kadioğlu

The British and the Turks: A History of Animosity, 1893–1923
Justin McCarthy

The Alevis in Modern Turkey and the Diaspora: Recognition, Mobilisation and Transformation
Edited by Derya Özkul and Hege Markussen

Religion, Identity and Power: Turkey and the Balkans in the Twenty-first Century
Ahmet Erdi Öztürk

A Companion to Modern Turkey
Edited by Alpaslan Özerdem and Ahmet Erdi Öztürk

The Decline of the Ottoman Empire and the Rise of the Turkish Republic: Observations of an American Diplomat, 1919–1927
Hakan Özoğlu

Turkish-German Belonging: Ethnonational and Transnational Homelands, 2000–2020
Özgür Özvatan

Contesting Gender and Sexuality through Performance: Sacrifice, Modernity and Islam in Contemporary Turkey
Eser Selen

Turkish Politics and 'The People': Mass Mobilisation and Populism
Spyros A. Sofos

Electoral Integrity in Turkey
Emre Toros

Erdoğan: The Making of an Autocrat
M. Hakan Yavuz

edinburghuniversitypress.com/series/esmt

THE ALEVIS IN MODERN TURKEY AND THE DIASPORA

Recognition, Mobilisation and Transformation

Edited by Derya Özkul and Hege Markussen

EDINBURGH
University Press

Edinburgh University Press is one of the leading university presses in the UK. We publish academic books and journals in our selected subject areas across the humanities and social sciences, combining cutting-edge scholarship with high editorial and production values to produce academic works of lasting importance. For more information visit our website: edinburghuniversitypress.com

Edinburgh University Press Ltd
The Tun – Holyrood Road
12 (2f) Jackson's Entry
Edinburgh EH8 8PJ

Typeset in 11/15 Adobe Garamond by
IDSUK (DataConnection) Ltd

A CIP record for this book is available from the British Library

ISBN 978 1 4744 9202 7 (hardback)
ISBN 978 1 4744 9205 8 (webready PDF)
ISBN 978 1 4744 9204 1 (epub)

CONTENTS

TABLES, FIGURES AND MAPS

Tables

Figures

Maps

NOTES ON CONTRIBUTORS

Ayşegül Akdemir is an Assistant Professor in Sociology at Bahçeşehir University in Istanbul. She earned her BA degree in Sociology from Boğaziçi University in 2009, her MA degree in Conflict Studies from the University of Augsburg and her PhD in Sociology from the University of Essex in 2016. Her research interests include social identity, transnational migration, gender and qualitative research methods.

Ayca Arkilic is a Lecturer in Comparative Politics at Victoria University of Wellington. She received her PhD from the Department of Government at the University of Texas at Austin in 2016. Between 2013 and 2014, she was a Chateaubriand Fellow at Sciences Po-Paris and a visiting researcher at the WZB Berlin Social Science Research Centre's Migration, Integration and Transnationalisation research unit. She was an Imam Tirmizi Research Fellow at the Oxford Centre for Islamic Studies during the spring term of 2015.

Murat Borovalı is a Professor in Political Science and International Relations at Izmir University of Economics. He holds a PhD degree in Political Philosophy from the University of Manchester and a BA degree from Boğaziçi University. Among his publications are *Turkish Secularism and Islam: A Difficult Dialogue with the Alevis* (2014) and *Turkey's 'Liberal' Liberals* (2017). He is currently working on contemporary Turkish politics.

Cemil Boyraz is an Associate Professor in International Relations at Istanbul Bilgi University. He holds a PhD degree in Political Science. His research interests are Turkish politics and foreign policy, nationalism, international political economy and labour movements. He has published various articles on the Alevi and Kurdish questions, political Islam, neo-Kemalism and the global political economy, and he has edited an anthology on the political participation of youth in Turkey. He is currently working on post-colonial critique in international relations, democratic autonomy, (con)federalism and the changing structure of global labour.

Eray Çaylı, PhD (University College London, 2015), is Leverhulme Early Career Fellow (2018–22) at London School of Economics and Political Science. He has taught and published widely on the spatial and visual politics of violence and disasters, including in his monographs *Victims of Commemoration: The Architecture and Violence of 'Confronting the Past' in Turkey* (2021) and *İklimin Estetiği: Antroposen Sanatı ve Mimarlığı Üzerine Denemeler* (Climate Aesthetics: Essays on Anthropocene Art and Architecture, 2020). For more, see eraycayli.com.

Markus Dressler has taught at universities in the United States, Turkey and Germany. He is Professor in Modern Turkish Studies at the Institute for the Study of Religions, Leipzig University. He has published extensively on Alevism and questions of inner-Islamic difference and the politics of secularism and religion, with an empirical focus on Turkey. Dressler's publications include the monographs *Writing Religion: The Making of Turkish Alevi Islam* (2013), *Die Alevitische Religion: Traditionslinien und Neubestimmungen* (2002), as well as the edited volumes *Secularism and Religion-Making* (2011) and *Sufis in Western Society: Global Networking and Locality* (2009).

Ahmet Kerim Gültekin is an exiled ethnologist (PhD) in Germany. He was an assistant professor at the Sociology Department of Munzur University (Dersim, Turkey) when he was dismissed because of signing the declaration by 'Academics for Peace'. He was also sentenced to imprisonment due to his academic studies. Gültekin received his doctorate in Ethnology from Ankara University (2013). His areas of interest are Kurdish Alevism Studies, anthropology of religion, sacred places, pilgrimage studies, and ethnography. He is the author of the books *Tunceli'de Kutsal Mekân Kültü* (Sacred Place Cults in Tuncel, 2004), *Tunceli' de Sünni Olmak* (Being Sunni in Tunceli, 2010) and *Kutsal Mekanın Yeniden Üretimi* (Reproduction of Sacred Place, 2020), and co-editor of *Kurdish Alevis and the Case of Dersim* (2019) and *Ethno-Cultural Others of Turkey: Contemporary Reflections* (2021).

Erhan Kurtarır is Assistant Professor in the Department of City and Regional Planning at Yıldız Technical University (YTU) since 2005. He graduated from Middle East Technical University in 2003. He received his PhD in 2012 from YTU. His PhD research addressed an unstudied aspect of urban planning: what is the role of place and urban planning in the process of sustaining the cultural identity of minorities and disadvantaged faith groups in Turkey and UK? His research interests include: cultural geography (geography of religion); local democracy and participation in planning, urban sociology; migration studies (urban refugees), planning theory and ethics, human rights and inclusive planning. See https://avesis.yildiz.edu.tr/kurtarir.

Hege Markussen is a researcher in the History of Religions at Lund University, Sweden. She is the author of the book *Teaching History, Learning Piety: An Alevi Foundation in Contemporary Turkey* (2012) and the editor of *Alevis and Alevism: Transformed Identities* (2005). She is a member of the Editorial Committee of the Swedish Research Institute in Istanbul.

Ulaş Özdemir earned his PhD in Ethnomusicology from Yıldız Technical University in 2015. He specialises in ethnomusicology, organology and film music in Turkey. He is the author of the books *Şu Diyar-ı Gurbet Elde – Âşık Mücrimi'nin Yaşamı ve Şiirleri* (2007), *Kimlik, Ritüel, Müzik İcrası: İstanbul Cemevlerinde Zakirlik Hizmeti* (2016) and *Senden Gayrı Âşık mı Yoktur: 20. Yüzyıl Âşık Portreleri* (2017), as well as several scholarly articles. As a musician, he has recorded albums, compilations and soundtracks; he has participated in various concerts, festivals and lectures around the world. Currently, he works in the Musicology Department at the Istanbul University State Conservatory.

Nazlı Özkan is an Assistant Professor in the Department of Media and Visual Arts at Koç University, Istanbul. She received her PhD in Cultural Anthropology from Northwestern University. Her research received support from several institutions such as the Wenner-Gren Foundation, Fulbright Foreign Student Program, and Henry R. Luce Initiative of Religious and International Affairs. Özkan's publications on journalism, digital media, religious difference, and the state appeared in journals such as *PoLAR: Political and Legal Anthropology Review*, *Visual Anthropology Review*, and *META: Middle East Topics and Arguments*. Her current project about the history of new media technologies in Turkey is funded by the Horizon 2020 Marie Sklodowska-Curie Actions (MSCA) Widening Fellowship.

Derya Özkul is a Senior Research Fellow at the Refugee Studies Centre, University of Oxford. She previously taught sociological theory, sociology of terrorism, human rights and social protest at the University of Sydney. Her doctoral research examined the impact of changing diversity and immigration policies on Alevis' struggle for recognition and diaspora mobilisation in Germany and Australia. She has published extensively on transnationalism, refugee settlement, immigration and diversity policies in Turkey, Germany and Australia. She is a co-editor of *Social Transformation and International Migration* (2015), as well as of a volume on *Precarious Lives and Syrian Refugees in Turkey* (2016).

David Shankland is the Director of the Royal Anthropological Institute. As a social anthropologist, he has spent many years working and conducting fieldwork in Anatolia on questions of religion, politics, the state and social change. Among his various publications is *The Alevis in Turkey* (2001). He is formerly Reader in Social Anthropology at the University of Bristol and an Honorary Professor of Anthropology at University College London.

Meral Salman Yıkmış is an Assistant Professor in Sociology at Izmir University of Democracy. Salman holds a BA degree in Sociology from Hacettepe University and MA and PhD degrees in Sociology from the Middle East Technical University. Her research areas are anthropology of religion, qualitative research and gender.

Martin Sökefeld is a Professor of Social Anthropology at Ludwig-Maximilians-University Munich, Germany. Before he taught at Hamburg University, Germany, and the University of Bern, Switzerland. In 1997, he received his PhD degree from the University of Tübingen and, in 2005, his Habilitation from Hamburg University. Sökefeld has also worked on ethnicity, conflicts and disasters in Northern Pakistan.

Besim Can Zırh is an Assistant Professor of Sociology at the Middle East Technical University, where he also received his BA degree in Sociology in 2002 and his MSc degree in Political Science in 2005. He received his PhD degree in Social Anthropology from University College London in 2012. His doctoral thesis was a multi-sited ethnographic study focusing on Alevis' migration experiences and their transnational networks in Europe.

PREFACE

With this book we have aimed to gather an international community of researchers in Alevi studies to critically reflect on the conditions of Alevis in Turkey and the diaspora. This idea was born after an international conference, titled *Alevi Identity Revisited: Cultural, Religious, Social and Political Perspectives*, which took place at the Swedish Research Institute in Istanbul (SFII) on 21 and 22 February 2014. This conference was organised against the backdrop of one of the earliest international conferences on Alevism in 1996, also held at the SFII, resulting in the publication *Alevi Identity: Cultural, Religious and Social Perspectives*. At the time, Alevi studies as an international academic discipline were still nascent; yet, Alevi communities in both Turkey and the diaspora were in the midst of what scholars then coined a period of 'Alevi revival'. The revival referred to the rapid increase in the number of Alevi associations and Alevi publications on the nature and history of Alevism, which vastly increased the visibility of Alevi communities in Turkey and the diaspora.

Since then, as this book demonstrates, Alevi communities have experienced continuities and changes in their practices and rituals, in line with broader processes of social transformation in their surroundings. These include the rise of authoritarianism, discrimination and violence towards Alevis in Turkey, as well as growing Islamophobia and demands for recognition by minority communities in Western countries. Alevi studies have grown accordingly, and today researchers from different disciplines within the humanities and social sciences find interest in the developments of Alevi identity, beliefs and practices. The chapters in this book reflect the multiplicity of experiences among Alevi communities, with a particular emphasis on the past two decades.

We are grateful for the funding we received from the Swedish Consulate General and the Swedish Research Institute in Istanbul, which facilitated the organisation of the conference in Istanbul. The strategic research area 'The Middle East in the Contemporary World' at the Centre for Middle Eastern Studies and the Centre for Theology and Religious Studies, both at Lund University, funded the proof-reading costs of the manuscript. Cemil Boyraz and Besim Can Zırh contributed to the editing of some of the earlier chapters. We are thankful to them for all their work and support. We thank Kay Hutchings-Olsson for her careful proof-reading of the text. We acknowledge the very helpful comments of the anonymous reviewers in improving the quality of this work.

Finally, we are grateful to the authors who remained with us throughout the numerous phases of editing. Their endurance facilitated the intellectual coherence of this work. Some had to continue working on this book under extremely difficult conditions. Academia in Turkey, in particular, has suffered tremendously, with extremely high numbers of dismissals by the Turkish state. Many scholars either suffered immediate mental and financial consequences after losing their employment, or spent their time and energy seeking truth and supporting those who were persecuted in trials. This book is one of the products of this era and shows that scholars working under oppressive regimes continue to theorise and share their analyses. We hope that this book will constitute a reference work, not only for Alevi studies, but also for the unjust period we are experiencing.

Derya Özkul and Hege Markussen
Oxford and Lund, March 2021

INTRODUCTION

1

ALEVI AGENCY IN CHANGING POLITICAL CONTEXTS

DERYA ÖZKUL AND HEGE MARKUSSEN

Introduction

Readers not acquainted with the topic may first want to know what
Alevism (in Turkish, *Alevilik*) is and who the Alevis are. The definition of Alevism is subject to both internal (that is, within and across Alevi
communities) and external controversies (namely, in relation to surrounding
forces such as the state, media and society questioning or defining Alevism).
Some consider Alevism to be the essence or the true, unadulterated form of
Islam. Others would say that Alevism contains some Islamic traditions, be it
Shi'a-oriented or a mystical Islamic approach, while yet another group does
not acknowledge it as a religion and instead perceives it as a philosophy, a
set of ethics, a worldview, or a continuous struggle for justice and equality.
Recently, and especially in European countries, there is also a call for Alevism
to be recognised as a unique religion in its own right. As this volume will
show, Alevi communities are also varied and may have different definitions
according to their histories, own sources of knowledge and experiences of
living Alevism.

Despite the variety of explanations, most Alevis emphasise what Sökefeld
(2008, p. 94) calls the 'master differences' – that is, the differences between
Sunni Islam and Alevism. The major dissimilarities include conducting *cem*
gatherings, respecting *dede*s for their spiritual and social guidance, fasting

during the month of Muharrem and going to *cemevis* (especially in cities), as opposed to performing the *namaz* (prayers prescribed by Islam to be conducted five times a day), going to mosques, following Sunni leaders and fasting during the month of Ramadan. Moreover, Alevis' demands from the Turkish state are fairly coherent. They demand to be treated as 'equal citizens', ending the discrimination that they face at political and social levels. This involves abolishing or reforming the Presidency of Religious Affairs in Turkey (*Diyanet*), recognizing the *cemevis* (Houses of Communion) as the official place of worship for Alevis and abolishing compulsory religious classes in schools, which teach students Sunni Islam and ignore Alevi teachings, if not denigrate them. Yet, since its establishment, the Turkish state has disregarded Alevi communities' requests, at least until recent times, when the state started to lead a strategy of double-sided politics. As will be shown in Chapter 3 in this volume, the ruling Justice and Development Party (*Adalet ve Kalkınma Partisi*, AKP) administration 'opened' the Alevi question to public discussion, for it then to be shown as unworthy of agreement. Since the end of what has been called 'Alevi Openings', the AKP has taken an even more inattentive approach to Alevis' demands.

The Turkish state officially sees Alevism as part of Islam, albeit of a lesser-valued, culturally infused and almost non-acceptable form of Islam. For example, the *Diyanet* (2014) defines Alevism merely as a concept rather than an integrated belief system:

> It is not correct to perceive some cultural values that have historically entered Alevism in various ways as Alevism's faith principals. [. . .] The concepts of Alevi and Sunni, which are commonly used today, do not contradict each other. On the contrary, these concepts' supra-identity or their common ground is Islam and being Muslim. Therefore, it is not possible to make a distinction between Alevis and Muslims in terms of religion, history, logic and science.[1]

As such, the *Diyanet* ignores the differences between Alevis and Sunnis, rendering them mere concepts and obliterating the former's peculiarities to the advantage of the latter. Later, the *Diyanet* removed this definition from its

---

[1] Translation from Turkish by the authors.

website and currently has no distinct definition for Alevism, but its approach to Alevis has hardly changed (see Lord 2018 and, in particular, Chapter 3 for an analysis of the *Diyanet*'s interventions).

The descriptions and analyses presented within the academic field of Alevi studies are not detached from such debates. When international scholarship became interested in Alevism and Alevi communities during the 1980s and 1990s, Alevis had already started to organise in Turkey and Europe, establishing cultural associations, publishing literature on the nature and history of Alevism, and increasingly rendering their Alevi identity publicly visible. Associations that were established in the urban centres of Turkey and Germany and their new social movements were the driving forces behind what is often called the 'Alevi revival' or 'Alevi renaissance' (Özyürek 2009, Şahin 2005, Erdemir 2005, Çamuroğlu 1998, van Bruinessen 1996; see also Part Four in White and Jongerden 2003). These associations consisted of Alevis from various geographical areas of Turkey and Alevis who had migrated to larger cities in Turkey or Germany and other countries in Europe (see Issa 2019, Massicard 2013). Claiming the right to define, describe and historically contextualise Alevism was a central part of their quest for recognition and visibility. Naturally, how to define Alevism became a central question while they sought to represent their history and religious and cultural traditions. The academic field of Alevi studies that developed during the 1980s and 1990s also focused on these issues.

The way in which Alevis and Alevism are defined and legitimised today is still an integral part of this ever-growing and contested body of knowledge. Scholars have been interested in the historical contextualisation of Alevism and examined it in relation to Shi'a Islam (Tambar 2011), in relation to efforts to create a Turkish version of Islam (Dressler 2013), as a 'folk Islam' (Aktay 2011) and with a focus on Turkic elements from Central Asia (Mèlikoff 1996), as well as pre-Islamic elements (Kehl-Bodrogi 1997, Ocak 2013). Some scholars approach the term 'Alevi' as a modern creation comprising and homogenising several Anatolian groups (such as *Kızılbaş*, *Alawis*, *Çepni*, *Abdal* and *Tahtacı*) living in different regions and under different socio-political conditions (see Shankland 2003, Dressler 2013).

One of the strategies used by the state to ensure that Alevis are not too visible – at least to the extent that it becomes possible to ignore them – is simply not counting them as Alevis in official statistics. Hence, estimates on the number of Alevis in Turkey range from 10 to 30 per cent of the national population (Dressler 2013, Erman and Göker 2000, Şirin 2013). In Europe, the majority of Alevis reside in Germany (estimates go up to 700,000); in smaller numbers, they also live in other European countries such as France, Britain and the Netherlands. In the Scandinavian countries, the Alevis are estimated to number around 20,000, with the majority living in Denmark and Sweden. There are also ethnic differences among Alevis. Approximately two-thirds of Alevis today are Turkish, and the second-largest groups are *Kurmanji-* and *Zazaki*-speaking Alevis. There also exists a smaller group of Arabic-speaking Alevis living, or having lived, mostly in areas near the Syrian border. Recent research emphasises the role of ethnic identification and how Alevis from different ethnicities have experienced Alevism and participated in political life (see Cetin et al. 2020, Gezik and Gültekin 2019, Jenkins et al. 2018; see also Part Five in White and Jongerden 2003).

This book resulted from the desire to re-think Alevi studies because of two significant processes of transformation. First, ongoing processes of urbanisation and internal and international migration have significantly transformed Alevis' daily life, rituals, internal authority and external representations (see Aktürk 2020). As much as Alevi communities are varied, the need (and, at times, the agency) to express what Alevism is for non-Alevis in cities and the need to perform it in Alevi organisations established in cities, particularly in the diaspora, have inevitably led to the standardisation of some practices and to a shift in leadership roles.

Second, the changes in the political landscape of Turkey, most prominently the rise in authoritarianism and Islamist politics, have had significant implications for Alevis. To clarify, Islamist politics was not an entirely new threat to Alevis. Although founded as a secular state, the Republic of Turkey was established by privileging Sunni Turks over non-Sunni groups and Sunni Kurds. Sunni Islam has been organised by the state through the Presidency of Religious Affairs in Turkey, the *Diyanet* (see Lord 2018), which is funded compulsorily by all citizens but provides services only to adherents of Sunni Islam. In contrast, Alevis' problems and demands from the state have long been ignored (Boyraz 2019), or at best tolerated, to the extent that Alevis' claims resonated with the Turkish state's historical ideology (Kambar 2014).

This discriminatory tolerance has become even more problematic under the AKP administration, resulting in the Alevis' growing reactions and demands for equal citizenship rights (Boyraz 2019, Karakaya-Stump 2018).

It is crucial to understand these structural changes in order to comprehend the way in which Alevis navigate their path, while also re-shaping and transforming Alevism itself. As this volume shows, these changes are often influenced by dynamics at local, national and transnational levels. We suggest that Alevi studies can benefit from exploring these structural factors and the agency of actors, together with and in relation to each other at different levels of analysis. Below we provide an overview of the changes that we find significant for re-assessing Alevi studies.

Changes in the Political Landscape and in Alevi Rituals, Representation and Authority

Following the economic crisis in Turkey in 2001–2, the newly established AKP, led by the former Mayor of Istanbul, Recep Tayyip Erdoğan, rapidly rose to power based on its promise to transform the economy and bring stability to the country. Given the AKP's acknowledged Islamist roots and previous links to the Welfare Party (*Refah Partisi*), there were drawbacks to Erdoğan's success, particularly in secularist circles. However, the AKP's promise to establish a democratic state, along with its 'conservative globalist' economic model (Öniş 2012), at least initially attracted those who were disadvantaged by the secularist Kemalist regime, such as businesspersons who benefitted from its economic policies and some liberals who argued that the AKP was, in fact, a democratic party.

Indeed, the first years of the AKP administration opened up new forms of visibility for disadvantaged groups in the public sphere, and Alevis counted among them. Several laws were amended in the context of accession to the European Union, and it became legally possible to establish associations with the term 'Alevi' in its name. The visibility of *cemevi*s obtained a *de facto* legitimacy in the public sphere. After their second victory in the 2007 general elections, the AKP government intensified the so-called democratisation processes. It adopted various initiatives (often referred to as 'openings' in the popular media) that brought into the public domain unresolved issues related to Alevis, Kurds, Armenians, Greek-Orthodox and Assyrian communities.

For the Alevis, a series of workshops was initiated as a platform for dialogue with Alevi associations. Therefore, ironically and for the first time, an Islamist party publicly included Alevis' long-standing demands in official discussions (see Chapter 3 in this volume).

However, these initial seemingly opportunistic democratisation attempts were followed by a top-down approach towards Alevis (Goner 2016). It was soon clear that the Alevi workshops were not organised to respond to the demands of major Alevi associations, but to build a platform where they had to define themselves in front of the state and disagree with each other in the process (see Özkul 2015). The 'openings' came to a standstill in March 2012, when the AKP government decided that the charges against the five remaining suspects of the Sivas massacre should be dropped due to the statute of limitations, despite activists' persistent appeals for the massacre to be considered a crime against humanity. The Office of the Prosecutor in Sivas also introduced restrictions on the commemoration of the Sivas massacre (see Kaleli 2011, Radikal 2011). Similarly, the Alevi workshops concluded that the Madımak Hotel's transformation into a 'museum of shame', as most Alevi participants had requested, would sow new seeds of hatred (Subaşı 2010, pp. 179–85). In late 2010, the hotel became a public entity and was later turned into the Sivas Science and Culture Centre, with no mention of the massacre itself (see Chapter 4 in this volume).

Following the *de facto* end of the 'openings', the AKP administration moved towards rising authoritarianism and deliberate political polarisation. In the face of growing threats, Alevis initiated protests demanding 'equal citizenship' rights (Açıkel and Ateş 2011). Due to the increasing politicisation of the dominant Turkish Sunni Islam and the redistribution of more power to religious institutions, including the *Diyanet*, Alevis – along with some secularists – claimed that these state practices violated Article 136 of the 1982/2010 Constitution. This article requires the *Diyanet* to act based on the principle of secularism and, therefore, neutrality towards all views. Yet, in practice, it was clear that the state favoured certain groups over others. Although the protests on equal citizenship rights attracted thousands of advocates, in the end no major changes were undertaken to meet the demands.

In present-day Turkey, Alevis are visible in the public sphere. They take their concerns to the streets to demand change. They engage in local and national politics, often through centre-left parties (on Alevi Kurds' representation in parties, see Ertan 2019, Gunes 2020). However, their demands remain unmet. The Turkish state's role in the political and otherwise societal discrimination of Alevis needs to be examined in greater detail. The first section of this book, therefore, discusses the relationship between the Turkish state and Alevis, as well as their struggles for recognition.

In contrast, European and English-speaking countries, where some Alevis emigrated, have provided entirely different conditions for Alevis (Issa 2019, Massicard 2013) whereby they could freely establish Alevi associations and practise their beliefs and rituals without restrictions from state officials. Recently, these countries have increasingly securitised their immigration policies and targeted Muslim immigrants as potential sources of threat (Cesari 2010, Kaya 2009). The denigration of Islam, Islamophobia, has had implications for all Muslim immigrants, including, albeit to a lesser extent, those who are not practising the Islamic requirements or following understandings alternative to mediatised Islam. The relationship between immigration states' changing diversity policies and Alevis' claims and practices in these contexts is notably interesting. The second section of this book, therefore, examines the relationship between immigration countries and Alevis, as well as the emergence of Alevi diasporas, considering the conditions in these countries and prospects for recognition.

While struggling for 'equal citizenship' in Turkey as well as political and social recognition in the countries where they have migrated, Alevis' rituals have also changed in line with their new political, economic and social conditions. Continuing changes in the organisation of daily life seem to have accelerated these conditions. Rapid urbanisation, migration to cities and later neoliberalisation have profoundly affected work-life dynamics, the focus on the individual and self-reliance, and community dynamics, for all groups. Against this background, the third section of this book examines the transformation of rituals, authority and representation – in other words, the processes beyond the struggle for recognition. Some of the examples in this volume include the construction of *cemevi*s in cities, changes in Alevi ritual (such as the role of the *zakir*), the mediatisation of Alevis through modern means of communication and changes to sacred authorities. To analyse the change in Alevis' practices and rituals, we entirely agree with

David Shankland's call to turn to ethnographic studies on villages in order to understand the way in which traditional forms of Alevism have been practised (see the Epilogue in this volume). We also suggest that these changes need to be theorised within broader transformations at the local, national and transnational levels in those places where Alevis have lived for decades. We believe that these empirical studies help us understand the conditions that Alevis face in Turkey and elsewhere, and how they actively respond to the changing political, economic and social structures within which they are located. In what follows, we outline how we explore these issues in this book.

Three Strands of Recognition: Contentions, Prospects and Internal Changes beyond Recognition

This book is divided into three strands, reflected in Parts I, II and III. Each part captures the central actors and their strategies in their struggle for recognition and rights in Turkey and abroad. We are particularly interested in how Alevis have made their claims and how their claim-making practices have changed over time in various contexts. As they are struggling for rights and recognition, we can also observe profound changes in institutions of ritual and spiritual authority.

In the first part, *The Turkish State and Alevis: Contentions over Recognition*, the questions guiding the chapters are not so much about what Alevism is or how Alevis identify themselves, but rather how we can explore the tensions between the Turkish state and Alevis' agency. The chapters in this section introduce discussions about recognition, including Markus Dressler's examination of the debates around the definition of Alevism, Murat Borovalı and Cemil Boyraz's study of the 'Alevi Openings', Eray Çaylı and Besim Can Zırh's analyses of the politics of collective memory based on the examples of the Sivas and Dersim massacres and, finally, Ahmet Kerim Gültekin's examination of the social dynamics in Dersim where Alevis constitute a majority. We identify these contentions over recognition from the Turkish state with limited success in the face of an insincere and reluctant political leadership in Turkey.

In the second part, *Alevis in the Diaspora: Prospects for Recognition*, we turn to the processes in countries abroad, where Alevis have lived for almost six decades and where they have organised around Alevi associations. We track changes over this period with a closer look at how they organise and make their claims *vis-à-vis* their new states and societies. With a particular focus on Germany, Australia, France and the United Kingdom, the chapters in this section – authored by Martin Sökefeld, Derya Özkul, Ayca Arkilic and Ayşegül Akdemir – build on Sökefeld's (2006) leading theoretical model on social movements and diaspora mobilisation. These chapters show that, when compared to their situation in their homeland, Alevis have gained greater social and political recognition in those countries where they have migrated. For example, in Germany, where the largest numbers of Alevi immigrants live, the Alevi movement for the first time managed to acquire the official recognition of Alevism as a distinct religion separate from Islam. These attempts were later followed by ideas about establishing a World Alevi Union (see Özkul 2019). The implications of the official recognition of Alevism as a distinct religion by some Western states and these newly formed transnational movements to build and strengthen Alevi networks are yet to be seen.

The third and final part, *Beyond Recognition: Changes in Alevi Rituals, Representation and Authority*, gathers empirical examples of changes in sacred and ritual authority, as well as contemporary forms of performance, distribution and representation of Alevism. The chapters demonstrate how changing state policies and transnational contexts contribute to changes in Alevi practices, rituals and authorities. Meral Salman Yıkmış examines newly emerging forms of the sacred and political power of the traditionally inherited authority of the Çelebi family. Ulaş Özdemir studies the adaptation of the ritual musical performance of the *zakir* to contemporary and international forms of recognition. Erhan Kurtarır maps the contemporary cultural geography of Alevis in Istanbul through the establishment of *cemevi*s, and Nazlı Özkan examines the representation of Alevism as mediatised through transnational Alevi television networks. In the epilogue, David Shankland calls for further research on Alevism in Anatolian villages, which can provide an excellent case to compare and understand how Alevi practices and rituals have changed (or resisted change) over time. In the final concluding remarks, Hege Markussen revisits central themes in the development of Alevi mobilisation from the perspective of societal visibility and points out achievements and blind spots in research on Alevis and Alevism.

Bibliography

Açıkel, F., and Ateş, K. (2011). Ambivalent Citizens: The Alevi as the 'Authentic Self' and the 'Stigmatized Other' of Turkish Nationalism. *European Societies* [online]. 13(5), 713–33. [Viewed 29 March 2021]. Available from: doi: 10.1080/14616696.201.597968

Aktay, Y. (2011). *Türk Dininin Sosyolojik İmkanı: İslam Protestanlığı ve Alevilik*. 4th ed. Istanbul: İletişim.

Aktürk, H. (2020). *Modern Alevi Ekolleri*. Istanbul: İletişim.

Boyraz, C. (2019). The Alevi Question and the Limits of Citizenship in Turkey. *British Journal of Middle Eastern Studies* [online]. 46(5), 767–80. [Viewed 29 March 2021]. Available from: doi: 10.1080/13530194.2019.1634396

Cesari, J. (2010). *Muslims in the West after 9/11: Religion, Politics and Law*. London: Routledge.

Cetin, U., Jenkins, C., and Aydin, S., eds (2020). Special Issue: Alevi Kurds: History, Politics and Identity. *Kurdish Studies* [online]. 8(1). [Viewed 29 March 2021]. Available from: https://kurdishstudies.net/journal/ks/issue/view/57

Çamuroğlu, R. (1998). Alevi Revivalism in Turkey. In: Olsson, T., Özdalga, E., and Raudvere, C., eds, *Alevi Identity: Cultural Religious and Social Perspectives*. Istanbul: Swedish Research Institute. pp. 79–84.

Diyanet İşleri Başkanlığı (2014). *Dini Kavramlar Sözlüğü: Alevi(lik)*. [Viewed 27 October 2018]. Available from https://kurul.diyanet.gov.tr

Dressler, M. (2013). *Writing Religion: The Making of Turkish Alevi Islam*. Oxford: Oxford University Press.

Erdemir, A. (2005). Tradition and Modernity: Alevis' Ambiguous Terms and Turkey's Ambivalent Subjects. *Middle Eastern Studies* [online]. 41(6), 937–51. [Viewed 29 March 2021]. Available from: doi: 10.1080/00263200500262033

Erman, T., and Göker, E. (2000). Alevi Politics in Contemporary Turkey. *Middle Eastern Studies* [online]. 36(4), 99–118. [Viewed 29 March 2021]. Available from: doi: 10.1080/00263200008701334

Ertan, M. (2019). The Latent Politicization of Alevism: The Affiliation between Alevis and Leftist Politics (1960–1980). *Middle Eastern Studies* [online]. 55(6), 932–44. [Viewed 29 March 2021]. Available from: doi: 10.1080/00263206.2019.1591276

Gezik, E., and Gültekin, A. K., eds (2019). *Kurdish Alevis and the Case of Dersim*. New York: Lexington Books.

Goner, O. (2016). Recognition as a Relationship of Power and Struggle: The Governing of Kurds and Alevis in Turkey. In: Stokes-DuPass, N., and Fruja, R., eds, *Citizenship, Belonging, and Nation-States in the Twenty-First Century*. New York: Palgrave. pp. 163–94.

Gunes, C. (2020). Political Representation of Alevi Kurds in Turkey: Historical Trends and Main Transformations. *Kurdish Studies* [online]. 8(1), 71–90. [Viewed 29 March 2021]. Available from: doi: 10.33182/ks.v81.522

Issa, T. ed. (2019). *Alevis in Europe: Voices of Migration, Culture and Identity*. London: Routledge.

İnalcık, H. (1994). *The Ottoman Empire: The Classical Age, 1300–1600*. London: Phoenix.

Jenkins, C., Aydin, S., and Cetin, U., eds (2018). *Alevism as an Ethno-Religious Identity: Contested Boundaries*. London: Routledge.

Kaleli, I. (2011). Sivas Katliamı'nın Anılması Yasaklanıyor. *Biyanet* [online]. 11 October. [Viewed 14 March 2021]. Available from: http://goo.gl/me5lTo

Karakaya-Stump, A. (2018). The AKP, Sectarianism, and the Alevis' Struggle for Equal Rights in Turkey. *National Identities* [online]. 20(1), 53–67. [Viewed 29 March 2021]. Available from: doi: 10.1080/14608944.2016.1244935

Kaya, A. (2009). *Islam, Migration and Integration: The Age of Securitization*. London: Palgrave.

Kehl-Bodrogi, K. (1997). Introduction. In: Kehl-Bodrogi, K., Kellner-Heinkele, B., and Otter-Beaujean, A., eds, *Syncretistic Religious Communities in the Near East*. Leiden: Brill. pp. xi–xvii.

Lord, C. (2018). *Religious Politics in Turkey: From the Birth of the Republic to the AKP* [online]. Cambridge: Cambridge University Press. [Viewed 29 March 2021]. Available from: doi: 10.1017/9781108638906

Massicard, E. (2013). *The Alevis in Turkey and Europe: Identity and Managing Territorial Diversity*. London: Routledge.

Mélikoff, I. (1996). From God of Heaven to King of Men: Popular Islam among Turkic Tribes from Central Asia to Anatolia. *Religion, State and Society* [online]. 24(2–3), 133–38. [Viewed 29 March 2021]. Available from: doi: 10.1080/09637499608431734

Mélikoff, I., and İlber, O., eds (1999). *Tarihi ve Külütürel Boyutlarıyla Türkiye'de Aleviler Bektaşiler ve Nusayriler*. Istanbul: Ensar Neşriyat.

Ocak, A. Y. (2019). Alevi. In: Türkiye Diyanet Vakfı, İslâm Araştırmaları Merkezi. *Islam Ansiklopedisi*. [Viewed 29 March 2021]. Available from: https://islamansiklopedisi.org.tr/alevi

Ocak, A. Y. (2013). *Alevi ve Bektaşi İnançlarının İslâm öncesi Temelleri*. 10th ed. Istanbul: İletişim.

Öniş, Z. (2012). The Triumph of Conservative Globalism: The Political Economy of the AKP Era. *Turkish Studies* [online]. 13(2), 135–52. [Viewed 29 March 2021]. Available from: doi: 10.1080/14683849.2012.685252

Özkul, D. (2019). The Making of a Transnational Religion: Alevi Movement in Germany and the World Alevi Union. *British Journal of Middle Eastern Studies* [online]. 46(2), 259–73. [Viewed 29 March 2021]. Available from: doi: 10.1080/13530194.2019.1569304

Özkul, D. (2015). Alevi 'Openings' and Politicization of the 'Alevi Issue' during the AKP Rule. *Turkish Studies* [online]. 16(1), 80–96. [Viewed 29 March 2021]. Available from: doi: 10.1080/14683849.2015.1022722

Özyürek, E. (2009). 'The Light of the Alevi Fire Was Lit in Germany and Then Spread to Turkey': A Transnational Debate on the Boundaries of Islam. *Turkish Studies* [online]. 10(2), 233–53. [Viewed 29 March 2021]. Available from: doi: 10.1080/14683840902864028

Radikal (2011). Sivas Katliamı Anmasına Yasak. *Radikal* [online]. 30 June. [Viewed 14 March 2021]. Available from: http://goo.gl/zeMGNr

Shankland, D. (2003). *The Alevis in Turkey: The Emergence of a Secular Islamic Tradition*. London: Routledge.

Sökefeld, M. (2006). Mobilizing in Transnational Space: A Social Movement Approach to the Formation of Diaspora. *Global Networks* [online]. 6(3), 265–84. [Viewed 29 March 2021]. Available from: doi: 10.11/j.1471-0374.2006.00144.x

Sökefeld, M. (2008). *Struggling for Recognition: The Alevi Movement in Germany and in Transnational Space*. New York: Berghahn Books.

Subaşı, N. (2010). *Alevi Çalıştayları Nihai Rapor*. Ankara. [Viewed 29 March 2021]. Available from: https://serdargunes.files.wordpress.com/2013/08/alevi-c3a7al-c4b1c59ftaylarc4b1-nihai-rapor-2010.pdf

Şahin, Ş. (2005). The Rise of Alevism as a Public Religion. *Current Sociology* [online]. 53(3), 465–85. [Viewed 29 March 2021]. Available from: doi: 10.1177/0011392105051336

Şirin, Ç. V. (2013). Analyzing the Determinants of Group Identity among Alevis in Turkey: A National Survey Study. *Turkish Studies* [online]. 14(1), 74–91. [Viewed 29 March 2021]. Available from: doi: 10.1080/14683849.2013.766983

Tambar, K. (2014). *The Reckoning of Pluralism: Political Belonging and the Demands of History in Turkey*. Stanford: Stanford University Press.

Tambar, K. (2011). Iterations of Lament: Anachronism and Affect in a Shi'i Islamic Revival in Turkey. *American Ethnologist* [online]. 38(3), 484–500. [Viewed 29 March 2021]. Available from: doi: 10.1111/j.1548-1425.2011.01318.x

van Bruinessen, M. (1996). Kurd, Turks, and the Alevi Revival in Turkey. *Middle East Report* [online]. 200. [Viewed 29 March 2021]. Available from: https://merip.org/1996/09/kurds-turks-and-the-alevi-revival-in-turkey/

White, P. J., and Jongerden, J., eds (2003). *Turkey's Alevi Enigma: A Comprehensive Overview*. Leiden: Brill.

Part I

THE TURKISH STATE AND ALEVIS: CONTENTIONS OVER RECOGNITION

2

WHAT IS ALEVISM? CONTEMPORARY DEBATES *VIS-À-VIS* HISTORICAL AND SYSTEMATIC CONSIDERATIONS

MARKUS DRESSLER

Introduction: Defining Alevism

Since 1998, the Commission of the European Union (EU) has published annual reports on Turkey's progress towards fulfilling the EU accession criteria. In the negotiations between the EU and the Republic of Turkey, the Alevis' situation plays an important role, albeit a secondary one. The question of the definition of Alevism in the Commission's official reports has often caused heated discussions, especially when the Alevis were therein labelled a 'Muslim minority' (Commission of the European Communities 2004, p. 172), a 'non-Sunni Muslim community' (Commission of the European Communities 2005, p. 29) and an 'officially not recognized Muslim community' (Commission of the European Communities 2006, p. 60). From 2004 onwards, the definition of Alevism in the EU Commission's reports has become less specific, and this is in direct proportion to the indignant reactions that the respective ascriptions provoked among the Turkish public (Dressler 2014, pp. 145–49). In other words, the EU Commission has come to realise how highly politicised the question of Alevism is. Accordingly, from 2007 until today (2020), the annual EU Progress Reports on Turkey avoid positioning Alevism in relation to Islam.

The 2007 report confined itself to the observation that there is no real progress on the Alevi question and that the Alevis continue to encounter difficulties when wanting to establish *cemevis* (Houses of Communion), where they conduct their major rituals (Commission of the European Communities 2007, pp. 17–18). It further referred to a thus far contested ruling by the European Court of Human Rights (ECHR) on compulsory religious instruction in Turkey (Hasan and Eylem Zengin v. Turkey 2007). The claims that are made about Alevism in the course of this legal conflict are highly illuminating in regard to the politics of definition involved. In 2004, an Alevi plaintiff had lodged a complaint concerning the insufficient regard for Alevism in the religious education provided by state schools, arguing that, contrary to the state's assertions, its curriculum is *de facto* Sunni-oriented and therefore violates the principle of religious freedom of non-Sunni Muslim students. He, therefore, demanded that his daughter be exempted from religious instruction. In October 2007, the ECHR ruled in the plaintiff's favour (Council of Europe 2007). Attorney Kazım Genç, the then President of the (Alevi) Pir Sultan Abdal Cultural Association, counselled the plaintiff. Genç based his case on the opinion that Alevism 'differs completely from and is independent of Islam in both its teaching and philosophy, as well as in its religious practices' (Aleviyol 2006). Genç's argumentation caused strong reactions among other Alevis. For instance, Ali Çoban, the president of a local Alevi association from Elazığ, announced that he would sue Alevi representatives who maintained that Alevism stands apart from Islam (Alatürk 2006).

Unlike the EU Commission, the ECHR was compelled to define Alevism, since the complaint required clarification as to whether the religious instruction provided by Turkey conformed with the religious convictions of the Alevi students. The ECHR was therefore forced to specify the relation of Alevism to Sunni Islam. The ECHR defined Alevism as follows:

> Alevism originated in central Asia but developed largely in Turkey. Two important Sufis had a considerable impact on the emergence of this religious movement: Hoca Ahmet Yesevi (12th century) and Haci Bektaşi Veli (14th century). This belief system, which has deep roots in Turkish society and history, is generally considered as one of the branches of Islam, influenced in particular by Sufism and by certain pre-Islamic beliefs. Its religious practices differ from those of the Sunni schools of law in certain aspects such as prayer, fasting and pilgrimage (Hasan and Eylem Zengin v. Turkey 2007, p. 2).

It is noticeable that this definition broadly reflects the position of the French historian of religion Irène Mélikoff (1917–2009), who participated in the hearing as an adviser to the Alevi plaintiff. As within Mélikoff's scholarly work, Alevism is in the ECHR's ruling firmly situated within a Turco-centric framework, reflective of the continuity of Turkish culture from Central Asian pasts to modern Anatolia – a *longue durée* in the course of which its pre-Islamic core received imprints from certain branches of libertarian Sufism, while remaining distant to Sunnism (Mélikoff 1998; cf. Dressler 2013, pp. 256–59).

This short excursion into transnational and judicial arenas was meant to show how controversial and highly politicised the question of defining Alevism is, especially in terms of its relationship to Islam. Situating the historical and religious roots of Alevism is relevant today, not only for theologians and historians specialising in religion, but also for secular law experts and political and administrative institutions (Dressler 2011, Hurd 2014). As a matter of fact, contemporary discourses on Alevism are extremely diverse and present us with a variety of understandings of Alevism that can be categorised in the following manner:

1. The hegemonic state-loyal or Turkist-Islamic position presents Alevism as a 'Turkish heterodox' form of Islam – 'heterodox' since it carries elements of pre-Islamic Turkish religious traditions such as Shamanism. This position is embraced mainly by Turkish Alevis, by non-Alevi Turks with a nationalist inclination and by scholars who are somehow invested in the idea of a *longue durée* of Turkish culture or Turkish nationhood and for whom Alevism is a token of this assumed continuity.
2. Similar in its attempt to define Alevism through a particular reading of its cultural and religious essence is the Kurdish nationalist position, which connects Alevi roots to Kurdish-Iranian religious traditions. Espoused by Kurdish Alevis and Kurdish nationalists, this position is diametrically opposed, but structurally similar to the Turkish nationalist position.
3. Very common are interpretations of Alevism as a legitimate Islamic form beside the Sunni and Shi'a mainstream, sometimes describing it as a mystical form of Islam or as 'real Shi'a'.

4. Interpretations of Alevism as a religion in its own right tend to reject nationalist readings of Alevism and rather argue for its universal nature. This is a minority position among Alevis, however articulated much more fervently in Germany and Europe than in Turkey.

5. Another position presents Alevism as a humanist worldview that connects universal philosophical (and especially ethical) principles with a Turkish-Anatolian cultural substratum. For proponents of this reading of Alevism, the Alevi tradition's socio-religious institutions are secondary to the universal values that it espouses, such as brotherhood, democracy, equality of the sexes and, above all, tolerance.

6. The revolutionary political position understands Alevism as a tradition of struggle for justice in the name of the oppressed. This is a worldly reading of Alevi tradition in which salvation is conceived in entirely immanent terms, as the overcoming of social and political exploitation.

Contrary to the first two nationalism-inspired conceptualisations of Alevism, which insist on an implicit ethnic bond, the fourth and even more so the fifth and sixth of the ideal-typical interpretations of Alevism presented above transcend the traditionally tight social boundaries of Alevism by emphasising its universal features.[1]

What all these interpretations have in common is that they are deeply influenced by a modern worldview. Categories such as religion, nation and ethnicity, which are constitutive of the secular nation-state and have greatly impacted modern identities, have become important coordinates for most of these defining efforts.[2] Since these categories are constitutive for the modern nation-state, the latter has, especially in its more state-centric and authoritarian varieties such as in Turkey, an interest in controlling them.

In Turkey, the state controls Islam through the Directorate of Religious Affairs (*Diyanet İşleri Başkanlığı*, Diyanet) (Gözaydın 2009). Well-staffed

---

[1] For overviews on competing interpretations of Alevism, see Vorhoff (1998) and Gorzewski (2010).

[2] For the impact of these categories on modern Alevi subjectivities, see Vorhoff (1995), Bruinessen (1997), Dressler (2008), Mandel (2008, pp. 272–76), White and Jongerden (2003) and Jenkins, Aydın and Cetin (2018).

and well-endowed, this still growing institution defines and organises legitimate forms of public Islam, oversees religious services, mosques' maintenance, the issuing of *fatwa*s (Islamic legal opinions) and the organisation of the pilgrimage to Mecca. While the *Diyanet* claims to represent all Muslims of Turkey, including the Alevis, Alevi concerns are *de facto* hardly taken into account in the *Diyanet*'s activities. If Alevi issues are addressed at all in the *Diyanet*'s discourse, then it is usually within an apologetic rationale. According to Ali Bardakoğlu, president of the *Diyanet* from 2003 to 2010, the *Diyanet* represents no specific – for example, Sunni – position, but treats all Islamic groups equally. It concerns itself only with aspects of faith common to all Muslims – and what is common for all Muslims, 'the scientific and authentic form of Islam', could be clearly ascertained (Gültekin and Işık 2005, p. 13). The *Diyanet* presents itself as standing above all Islamic sub-groups and claims authority to interpret in an objective manner what is Islamic and what is not. According to Bardakoğlu, the Alevis are Muslims. Some of their practices, however, such as the *cem* ritual, are of a cultural, not religious nature, and the *cemevi* is not a 'house of prayer' (*ibadet yeri*) in the Islamic sense (Gültekin and Işık 2005, pp. 5–6).[3] The *Diyanet*'s position within the political system was reinvented after Bardakoğlu. With the AKP consolidating its power over state institutions, the *Diyanet*'s role began to change during the Presidency of Mehmet Görmez (2010–17), when it started to interpret its position in line with AKP politics of piety, a development that continued under its current President Ali Erbaş (2017–present). Despite the new, more assertive role of the *Diyanet* as agent of Islamisation of Turkish society, its position on Alevism has remained astonishingly constant.[4] This points to continuities between Kemalism and AKP Islamism, both of which have little tolerance for a plural conception of Islam that could integrate Alevism as a legitimate religious tradition.

[3] For a more comprehensive treatment of the *Diyanet*'s position on Alevism, see Gözaydın (2009, pp. 289–99), Zengin Arslan (2015) and Lord (2017a).
[4] Created originally to contain Islam, fight political Islam and spread a secular, state-loyal Sunnism, it has now been turned into an instrument of the AKP's project of forming a 'New Turkey' based on a 'Pious Generation'. See The Economist (2018).

Since in Turkey mainstream Sunni Islam is regarded as benchmark for legitimate Islamic practices, Alevi religious sites and practices are not subsidised by the state in the same way as those of Sunni Islam. Initially, the AKP had shown a more accommodating approach towards the Alevis. Prior to AKP rule, when Alevis qualified certain practices or spaces in terms perceived in the secularist discourse as 'religious', this could be regarded as 'religious separatism'. Accordingly, Alevi associations that used Alevi-specific terms in their names or in their statutes were regularly persecuted. In order to avoid direct confrontation with the state, they used to refer to *cemevis* as 'cultural' sites. In 2003, the first AKP government abolished the law that justified this practice (Soner and Toktaş 2011, p. 422). However, the traditional reservation of the state and the political establishment against the Alevis remained intact. This has been reflected in the refusal to recognise *cemevis* as places of worship (*ibadethane*) on par with mosques and places of worship of recognised non-Muslim religious communities – that is, churches and synagogues. The status of *ibadethane* comes with state support and thus signals a certain state recognition. This is why the *ibadethane* status of Alevi *cemevis* has remained fiercely contested, although the ECHR already in 2014 ruled that the Turkish state had to grant the *cemevis* this status and although the AKP in the past repeatedly announced that it would move towards some form of recognition of the *cemevi*. Clearly, the AKP inherited the fear of the Turkish state tradition that recognition of the Alevis as different from Sunnis on religious grounds would harm the national unity of the country. As illustrated in Chapter 3 in this volume, the AKP's several 'Alevi Openings' have not led to any substantial change in the state's approach to the question of how to accommodate Alevi difference (see also Özkul 2015, Lord 2017b). Alevis still face concrete disadvantages, as the annual EU Commission Reports and other human rights and religious freedom monitors regularly point out. Moreover, the AKP's turn towards authoritarian politics since the Gezi uprising of 2013, the doubt raised occasionally by AKP politicians concerning Alevi loyalty to the Turkish state in light of the conflict with Syria and its Alawite leadership, as well as the continuing Islamisation of the public sphere following a Sunni Muslim model have all contributed to an increased sense of threat among the Alevi population (Karakaya-Stump 2017).

The public discourse on religion in Turkey is imbued with Islamic semantics. Religious belonging is negotiated through Islamic concepts, such as *din* (religion) and *mezhep* (a recognised school of law or legitimate religious group). Within Turkey, the chances of recognizing the independent religious and cultural identity of the Alevis and their group-specific practices are therefore higher if the Islamic frame of reference is maintained. Accordingly, most Alevi representatives in Turkey display in public appearances, in principle, a positive attitude to Islam. In Germany, by contrast, Alevis are less exposed to such pressure; therefore, positioning Alevism outside Islam is discussed more openly here. Adjusting to the semantics that structure German religion discourse, Alevis have gained important rights: recognised as a religious community, they began to offer Alevi religious education in the public school system in 2002 (initially in Berlin), and in 2020 the Federation of the Alevi Communities in Germany was even recognised as a corporation under public law (in the state of North Rhine Westphalia) – the highest formal recognition a religious community can achieve in the country (Sökefeld 2008, see also Chapters 7 and 8 in this volume).

This brief survey shows how the question of Alevi difference is marked by specific political contexts. Academic papers on Alevism, such as those collected in this volume, partake in the complex politics of situating and defining Alevism – firstly, because academic work can be utilised for political ends; secondly, because academic reflections on Alevism are themselves situated in specific social, historical and political contexts. This deserves more attention than is generally granted.

Modern Transformations

It is usually claimed that about 10 to 30 per cent of the Turkish population has Alevi roots. Of these, 70 to 80 per cent are estimated to be Turkish-speakers (Shankland 2003, p. 20). Smaller sections speak the Kurdish dialect Kurmanci or Zazaki (also Dımıli or Kırmancki). Both are counted among the Northwestern Iranian languages, but the relation of Zazaki to Kurdish is highly contested.[5] The difficulty in determining the percentage of the Alevi

---

[5] The contestation appears to be guided by political as much as linguistic concerns; for a competent discussion of their intersection, see Gezik (2012, pp. 26–32). In recent decades a – however marginal – discourse of Zaza nationalism has developed, which claims that both the language and the culture of the Zaza are different from Kurdish culture and language. This idea is also supported by some academics – for example, Paul J. White (2003).

population in Turkey results primarily from the fact that 'Alevism' (*Alevilik*) is not a nationally recognised category of identity and therefore not recorded in official statistics. Furthermore, as with other 'we-group' identities, an individual relationship to Alevism is often situational. Alevism can denote socio-cultural, religious, ethnic, as well as political registers of belonging. Alevi organisations, which only represent a minority of the population with Alevi background, differ with respect to these orientations, to which they tend to subscribe in more static ways than individual Alevis.

The increasing positioning of Alevism within a religious framework that can be observed since the 1990s needs to be understood in the context of Turkey's socio-economic and political developments over the twentieth century. We can distinguish three major transformative processes that had an impact on Alevism over roughly the last hundred years. The first of these processes began with the reconceptualisation of the concept of 'Alevism' (*Alevilik*) in the context of Turkish nation-building, when Alevism became related to notions of Turkishness, Anatolian culture and 'heterodox' Islam (Dressler 2013). Although there are modern examples of the use of '*Alevi*' as a self-characterisation dating back to the 1880s (see Dressler 2013, p. 1), the oldest example of the abstract noun '*Alevilik*' that I am aware of dates from 1898, from the pen of an Ottoman provincial governor (Karaca 1993, p. 128). In the first half of the twentieth century, *Alevilik* gradually came to be used as umbrella term for the social forms, rituals and beliefs of those socio-religious communities that the Ottomans, up to that time, had called by the derogatory name *Kızılbaş* ('Redheads', a designation that goes back to the Ottoman–Safavid conflict; see below). The use of the term Alevi by the Turkish public and among Alevis themselves steadily increased throughout the twentieth century.

The second transformation, which began in the mid-twentieth century, can be described in terms of 'urbanisation' and 'secularisation'. Socio-economic changes resulted in many Alevis leaving behind their villages and their traditional ways of life. With the rural exodus, the social and ritual practices that had marked Aleviness thus far and that could have very specific local colourings, were largely abandoned, contributing to a secularisation of Alevi identities. Aleviness was politically re-signified in the 1960s and 1970s when many Alevis – especially the younger generation – turned to leftist political ideologies and started to interpret Alevism based on this new political frame of reference (Bumke 1979).

A third and more recent phase of transformation occurred with the revitalisation of Alevi traditions in the late twentieth century (Ellington 2004). Until the 1980s, Alevi cultural and/or religious concerns were, with few exceptions, hardly noticed in the Turkish public sphere. In the late 1980s, however, the Alevis became more publicly visible and vocal. They began to speak out against discrimination and demanded recognition as a cultural and religious tradition outside of the Sunni Islamic fold (Kehl 1993, Vorhoff 1995). This development needs to be situated within the context of the political changes in the aftermath of the military *coup* of 1980, a renaissance in which the religious dimensions of Alevism were highlighted. The emergence of an active Alevi public and a reinvigorated Alevi identity discourse accelerated following the Sivas massacre of 1993, during which a hotel hosting an Alevi festival in the provincial town of Sivas was set ablaze by a fanaticised mob.[6] Thirty-seven people, most of them Alevis, died as consequence of this tragic incident. The Alevi sense of threat increased even more when anti-Alevi violence entered the metropolis of Istanbul in March 1995. Following a drive-by shooting targeting customers of several Alevi teahouses in the neighbourhood of Gaziosmanpaşa, angry protests by the local Alevi population were met with violent police interference that left twenty-two people dead (Massicard 2005, pp. 70–73).[7]

Alevis then increased their efforts to organise themselves and thus needed to further position themselves in relation to various religious and political discourses (Vorhoff 1995, Dressler 2002, Massicard 2012). The opening and repositioning of Alevi identity over the last decades are in continuity with earlier developments in the twentieth century, which can be described in terms of a religio-secularisation of Alevism.[8] One example is the differentiation of

---

[6] The remains of the hotel are now a Science and Culture Centre. For an interesting analysis of the controversies between Alevis and the Turkish state regarding the use of this centre, see Chapter 4 in this volume.

[7] For a discussion of the relationship between physical and epistemic violence experienced by the Alevis of Turkey, see Dressler (2021).

[8] The term religio-secularisation points to the parallelism of secularisation and religionisation (Dressler 2019, pp. 6–8).

authority into religious/ritual and public/secular areas of competence (Dressler 2008). The drawing of explicit distinctions between religious and secular Alevi practices and spaces can be employed to either reify Alevism as religion or to secularise it as folklore (Dressler 2013, pp. 84–87, cf. Tambar 2014). The qualitative change in the authority of the office of the *dede*, *dedelik*, is a good example of this development. Traditionally, *dedelik* united ritual, social and legal skills in the person of the *dede*, whose authority was based on his sacred lineage (*ocak*, literally 'hearth'). The *ocak* system is the social backbone of Alevism. Traditionally, non-*ocak* Alevi families were as *talip*s ('students') associated with specific *ocak*s and their acting *dede*s (Yaman 2004). By contrast, in the contemporary urbanised *Alevilik*, the authority of the *dede* is largely limited to ritual and, in a narrower sense, 'religious' competence. Alevi associations have taken over the public representation of Alevism. The judicial/arbitrating role of the *dede* in the *cem* has greatly diminished. Even in the interpretation of Alevi faith and history today, he plays only a minor role. Consequently, the previously stark hierarchies between *talip* and *dede* among Alevis have been flattened. The question of the role of the *dede* in contemporary and future Alevism is one of the major issues for all those Alevis who insist on continuing it as a religious practice (Karolewski et al. 2013).

Babai, Bektaşi and Kızılbaş

Even though the term *Alevilik* is historically relatively young, this does not mean that Alevism as a social phenomenon is a twentieth-century invention. The historical name for those groups today called Alevis, *Kızılbaş*, dates back to the late fifteenth century. Originally, the term was used for the Anatolian and Iranian followers of the Safevi Order, pointing to their red headgear.[9] Coined during the Ottoman-Safavid conflict, it was from the outset a term with strongly pejorative connotations (of immorality, sexual debauchery and political subversion) that it still carries to this day (Dressler 2005, pp. 154–56).

---

[9] In the second half of the fifteenth century, the Safevi Order gained influence with mainly Turkmen but also Kurdish populations in Central and Southeastern Anatolia. The order was originally Sunni, but in the fifteenth century acquired an Alid orientation. In 1501, its young leader, İsmail, much venerated among his Anatolian *Kızılbaş* followers, declared himself Shah of Iran. On the Safevi Order, see Sohrweide (1965) and Babayan (2002).

Another term often associated with Alevism is *Bektaşi*. It relates to the Sufi order of the Bektaşiye. Today, it is often appended to *Alevi*, creating the neologism *Alevi-Bektaşi* that is used in the names of a number of Alevi associations. Beyond this hyphenated designation, the terms Alevi and Bektaşi, even when they stand alone, are often understood to be mutually inclusive. However, from historical and sociological perspectives, this is clearly misleading.

The Bektaşiye in a narrower sense is a Sufi order (*tarikat*) formed in the early sixteenth century. In the Ottoman historiography of Aşıkpaşazade (fifteenth century), Hacı Bektaş Veli, the order's patron saint, is presented as being close to the Babai movement that in 1240 rebelled against the Rum-Seljuk Sultanate (Mélikoff 1982, p. 148). In all likelihood, this revolt had mainly socio-economic reasons but was legitimised by a religious messianism, at the centre of which stood a certain Baba Ilyas from Khorasan, who was revered as a saviour (Ocak 1989). The insurgents' social and cultural environment differed significantly from the urban centres of the Rum-Seljuk Empire. In contrast to the Persianate urban culture of the Rum-Seljuk capital Konya – where Hacı Bektaş's coeval, the patron saint of the Mevlevi Order, Celaleddin Rumi, lived – the Babai movement originated in a rural Turkic cultural context that was strongly influenced by pre/non-Islamic Turkmen traditions and connected to the charismatic Sufism of the ghazis and dervishes of the borderlands (Ocak 1989). According to legend, after the suppression of the Babai revolt, Hacı Bektaş Veli settled in a small place in Central Anatolia, which today is named after him and which hosts his mausoleum in the Bektaşi mother lodge. Admirers of Hacı Bektaş can be found in Ottoman sources from the late thirteenth through fifteenth centuries as members of various loosely organised dervish groups, such as the Vefai, Kalender, Haydari and Yesevi. It deserves to be noted that the early leaders of the Ottoman dynasty came from a socio-religious milieu that was very close to this Turkmen dervish milieu (Ocak 1989, Zarcone 2014).

At the beginning of the sixteenth century, Balım Sultan (d. 1519), the principal of the dervish lodge of Seyyid Ali Sultan at Dimetoka (modern-day Didymóteicho in Greece), was appointed by Sultan Bayezid II (reigned 1481–1512) as headmaster (*postnişin*) of the dervish convent in Hacıbektaş. Due to his important role in organising the Bektaşiye, he is revered by the

Bektaşis as 'Second Master' (*ikinci pir*) (Mélikoff 1998, pp. 154–57). The reorganisation of the *tarikat* was in line with Bayezid's interest in a more streamlined organisation and centralisation of the Bektaşi milieu (Zarcone 2014). This clearly had political reasons. With the establishment of the Safavid Empire in the immediate vicinity of the Ottomans, the influence of the Safevi Order in Anatolia was growing to become a threat to Ottoman sovereignty. The Anatolian Kızılbaş venerated Shah Ismail (reigned 1501–24) as their religious leader (*pir*); some glorified him, and also his heirs, as Mahdi.[10] We find evidence of this in the orally transmitted poems and hymns of the Kızılbaş (see Dressler 2005, pp. 158–59). In the first decades of the sixteenth century, Anatolia became the scene of several riots, which Ottoman chroniclers explained in reference to Safavid propaganda; in history, they were recorded as 'Kızılbaş uprisings' (Sohrweide 1965). One of these uprisings was initiated in 1527 by Kalender Çelebi, headmaster of the Bektaşi dervish convent of Hacıbektaş, suggesting a closeness between parts of the Bektaşi-milieu and the Kızılbaş. The militancy of the Kızılbaş fed on economic discontent, coupled with messianic expectations projected onto the Safavid Shah. Even though the Ottomans suppressed the Kızılbaş revolts, coercive measures against the Kızılbaş did not lead to their complete assimilation. Considering that the social milieus of the Bektaşis and Kızılbaş overlapped, it is not surprising that the Ottomans sought more influence with the Bektaşi order so as to curb the political resistance of the Kızılbaş.

The social formations referred to by the term *Bektaşilik* (Bektaşism) are complex (Yıldırım 2010). Today we encounter the Bektaşiye in two separate lines of tradition, the *baba-* and the *çelebi*-Bektaşis. The *baba*-Bektaşis are organised as *tarikat*, into which in principle every Muslim can be initiated. The *dede/baba* acts as its headmaster, elected by the most senior dervishes (*halife baba*). *Baba*-Bektaşis claim that the patron of the order, Hacı Bektaş, was childless. In contrast, the *çelebi*-Bektaşis believe that Hacı Bektaş did have offspring and that only his direct descendants are entitled to lead and represent the Bektaşi tradition (Mélikoff 1998, pp. 197–98).

Both historians of religion and those Alevis who identify with Bektaşism point to the large number of shared ritual practices and beliefs, as well as the

---

[10] Belief in the Mahdi as a messianic saviour is a central doctrine of Shi'a faith.

common historical roots of Alevis and Bektaşis. Some postulate that Alevis and Bektaşis should be regarded as one tradition – namely, as *Alevi-Bektaşilik* (for example, Mélikoff 1998). This makes sense if one considers Bektaşis primarily as comprised of the *çelebi*-Bektaşis, whose authority is based on their alleged descent from Hacı Bektaş Veli, and who today are considered by many Alevis as their highest religious authority. However, this prominent position of the *çelebi*-Bektaşis is a product of relatively new developments that have taken place since the nineteenth century – even if institutional links of individual Alevi sacred lineages (*ocak*) to the Bektaşi order can be traced as far back as the sixteenth century (Karakaya-Stump 2007, 2011).[11]

For Alevis and for *çelebi*-Bektaşis, religious authority is bound to biological lineage. Membership in the *baba*-Bektaşiye, in contrast, is based on initiation independent of descent. The Kızılbaş, too, were originally integrated in a *tarikat*-like structure. However, with the separation of the Anatolian Kızılbaş from the Safavids began the transformation of the former into an endogamous community that constituted itself by means of socio-religious boundaries against non-Kızılbaş. A catalyst of this process probably consisted of the Ottoman punitive anti-Kızılbaş measures in the early sixteenth century that made many of them retreat to remote areas and reduce, to the extent that this was feasible, contact with the non-Kızılbaş outside world. However, the popular narrative of the Kızılbashes withdrawal and isolation seems exaggerated.[12]

The picture already gets more complex when we compare Bektaşis and Kızılbaş in terms of their social position in the Ottoman Empire. The *çelebi*-Bektaşis were the official administrators of the convent (*zaviye*) in Hacıbektaş, which as a religious foundation (*vakıf*) was incorporated into the Ottoman administration. The *baba*-Bektaşis, on the other hand, had a close connection to the Janissaries. Accordingly, both Bektaşi branches were institutionally linked to the Ottomans, whereas the Kızılbaş apparently remained marginalised – particularly those who were not affiliated with the Bektaşiye.

In the context of the modern nation-state, the Bektaşis have drifted further away from the Kızılbaş-Alevis insofar as they absorbed Turkish

---

[11] For an analysis of the changes in the authority of the *çelebi*-Bektaşis between the Ottoman and Republican periods, see Chapter 11 in this volume.

[12] For a recent historical study that problematises this narrative and suggests more complicated relations between Kızılbaş and non-Kızılbaş, as well as the Ottoman state, see Weineck (2020).

nationalist ideas to a greater extent than the latter (Bahadır 2005). In particular, Alevis of Kurdish and Zaza origin are, due to their negative experiences with centralising and homogenising policies since the nineteenth century, often rather critical of the (Turkish) state and its nationalist ideology. Moreover, historically, there seem to have been relatively few connections between the Kurdish Kızılbaş-Alevis of the eastern provinces of Anatolia and the Turkish Kızılbaş-Alevis of Central and Western Anatolia, as well as the Balkans (Kieser 2003).

To summarise, for a discussion of the relationship between Kızılbaş-Alevis and Bektaşis we need to distinguish (1) between the Bektaşiye order (*baba-*Bektaşis*)* and the *çelebi*-Bektaşi lineage, (2) between the *Kızılbaş*-Alevi *ocak*s and their followers connected with the *çelebiyan* and those independent of the *çelebiyan*, and (3) between Kurdish- or Zazaki-speaking and Turkish-speaking Kızılbaş-Alevis. The term *Alevi-Bektaşi*, which appeared initially in the context of Turkish nationalist discourse in the early 1920s, can be seen as an attempt to relativise these existing socio-cultural divides in the service of a homogenising nationalist discourse (Dressler 2013, pp. 259–60). Supporters of the term may rightly point out that the beliefs and rituals of the Alevis and the Bektaşis considerably overlap in their basic features, that there exist institutional links and that their histories show numerous points of contact. In this sense, the term can be viewed as an umbrella term that highlights elements common to both traditions. However, the hyphenated term 'Alevi-Bektaşi' obscures sociological (initiation versus ethnic community), socio-regional (urban-literate versus rural-oral), linguistic-cultural (Turkish versus Kurmanci and Zazaki) and, last but not least, ritual and religious differences for the purpose of a nationalist rhetoric of homogeneity. It is not coincidental that the term is mainly used by Turkish-speaking Alevis, who generally feel closer to Bektaşism than Kurdish Alevis.

Beliefs and Practices

The practices and beliefs of Bektaşis and Alevis overlap to a large extent, despite regional and lineage-related particularities. Bektaşism and Alevism are more influenced by Sufism's charismatic and mystical traditions than by the law-oriented normativity of mainstream Islam of either Sunni or Shi'a variety. They connect Sufi concepts and practices that are not recognised by the legalist traditions of Islam with Shi'ite mythology. It is certainly true that in the Bektaşi tradition scripturalised texts are more important than in Alevism, which is based strongly, though not exclusively, on oral traditions. However, in Alevism the transition from oral to written tradition is fluid; thus, this differentiation should not be taken too categorically (Otter-Beaujean 1995, Karolewski 2014). In the Alevi tradition, the lower level of literacy and the multitude of competing *dede* lineages (*ocak*s) contributed to a pluralistic religious culture. In contrast, the Bektaşiye is organised hierarchically, and its practices and beliefs are therefore standardised to a larger extent.

Historical reconstructions of Alevism as a religious tradition since the late nineteenth century have painted extremely different pictures. Some – mainly Western – observers find Christian traces in Bektaşism and Alevism.[13] Others emphasise pre-Islamic Turkish beliefs and practices, often interpreted as being of shamanic origin. Mélikoff (1998) has described Alevism as 'Islamized shamanism'; her scholarship, in the footsteps of the eminent Turkish historian Mehmed Fuad Köprülü (1890–1966), has provided further legitimacy to this perspective. Others, such as Ahmet Yaşar Ocak, consider marginalised Islamic traditions of Sufi and Shi'a inclination to have been of greater importance in the formation of Alevism (Ocak 1997; cf. Dressler 2013, pp. 256–68; Karakaya-Stump 2020). Both perspectives focus on the thirteenth century as a formative period for the Alevi and Bektaşi traditions. The Babai milieu, to which Hacı Bektaş belonged, and related currents were, however, not yet Shi'ite in a doctrinal sense. Veneration of the *ehlibeyt* ('people of the abode') or close circle of the Prophet's family – Muhammad, Ali, Fatima, Hasan and Hüseyin – is no prerogative of Alevi and Bektaşi groups. We encounter it among Sufis and in Sufism-influenced rural Islam, as well as among the Ottoman *ahi*-guilds of the thirteenth and fourteenth centuries, which revered Ali as their patron saint.[14] Moreover, while many Islamic and also pre-Islamic elements of Central Asian Turkic origin can be

---

[13] This trope was developed by Protestant American missionaries in the mid-nineteenth century. See, for example, 'Letter from Mr. Nutting, July 30, 1850', in the *Missionary Herald*. This approach was already criticised by Hasluck (1921); see also Dressler (2013, Chapter 1).

[14] See Mélikoff (1962, pp. 63–66). The Turkish Ahi tradition (*ahilik*) constituted a regional form of the Arab tradition of chivalry that was organised in fraternities (*futuwwa*) and strove for an extension of the faith (*cihad*) (Taeschner 1979, pp. 13–19, 277–87).

found in the *Vilayetname* (hagiography) of Hacı Bektaş Veli, it contains only a few Shi'ite traces. The Bektaşi tradition adopted more comprehensive Shi'ite traits only over the course of the sixteenth and seventeenth centuries (Yıldırım 2010, p. 34; Kafadar 1995, pp. 75–76). The *Buyruk* texts of the Kızılbaş are, on the other hand, imbued with Shi'a motifs, but contain hardly any elements that can be linked to pre-Islamic Central Asian Turkic religiosity.[15]

The increasing Shi'ite imprint on Bektaşism over time appears to be connected to the Safavid influence on the fluid boundaries between the Kızılbaş and Bektaşi milieus of Anatolia. Given that the *Buyruk* texts and the *Vilayetname* of Hacı Bektaş Veli both originated in the sixteenth century, but display remarkably different religious textures, it can be argued that the symbiosis of Shi'ite religiosity and Bektaşi-style charismatic Sufism was not yet completed at that time. While there were contact points between the religious milieus of the Kızılbaş and Bektaşi, they still need to be seen as two strands of tradition that began to overlap and connect during that period (Karakaya-Stump 2008, 2020). With the help of poetry that can be ascribed to early Kızılbaş and Bektaşi milieus, respectively, one can try to retrace this development. The popular poems from the late sixteenth and early seventeenth centuries attributed to the famous Bektaşi poet Kul Himmet from Tokat and Pir Sultan Abdal from Sivas, who reputedly had close ties with Kul Himmet, adumbrate the beginnings of a symbiosis between Bektaşi and Shi'ite symbolism. Thus, Kul Himmet describes Hacı Bektaş as embodying the essence of Ali:

> Your outside is Hacı Bektaş Veli,
> Your inside is Ali, the head of the Forty.[16]
> You possess all knowledge, everywhere,
> Hünkar Hacı Bektaş, do come to [our] rescue.[17]

---

[15] The *Buyruk* texts probably originated as epistles sent by the Safavids to their Kızılbaş followers. They contain moral prescriptions, dogmatic teachings, rules for the religious path and aspects of Shi'ite mythology.

[16] A reference to the mythological first *cem*, conducted by forty saints and led by Ali.

[17] Zâhirinde Hacı Bektaş Veli'sin
Bâtınında kırklar başı Ali'sin
Dört köşede cümle ilmin varısın
Hünkâr Hacı Bektaş sen imdat eyle.

As quoted in Aslanoğlu (1997, p. 45).

In the following verse of the Kızılbaş rebel poet Pir Sultan Abdal, Hacı Bektaş is similarly positioned in a Shi'ite framework:

> Why does the nightingale complain?
> The King of Sainthood[18] is guidance for all
> We hope for help from Bektaş Veli
> For the sake of Karbala, we hurried to rescue.[19]

The symbiosis of charismatic Anatolian dervish piety and Kızılbaş Shi'ite mythology would become a characteristic feature of both Kızılbaş-Alevism and Bektaşism. At the same time, the social organisation of the Bektaşis and the Kızılbaş developed, as described above, in different directions – towards a Sufi order in the case of the Bektaşis and toward ethnic religion in the case of the Kızılbaş-Alevis.

Alevis and Islam

The Islam of the Anatolian periphery encountered in the Kızılbaş-Alevi tradition comprises a unique set of religious practices and ideas. What marks Alevism as Islamic is the Islamicate context of its historical formation and its terminology, which is markedly Sufi and Twelver Shi'ite. Alevis, as well as Bektaşis, venerate the first Shi'ite Imam Ali and his descendants. Like Twelver Shi'ites, Alevis remember their own history as a history of suffering, for which the tragedy of Karbala has remained the symbolic and emotional anchor point until today. According to the Shi'ite tradition, the third Imam Hüseyin, the sole legitimate leader of the Muslim community, and most of his closest relatives were massacred by Umayyad troops in the desert near the Iraqi settlement of Karbala in AD 680. Despite the importance of remembering the tragedy of Karbala, the Alevis have, however, little in common with the mainstream of Twelver Shi'ism. Traditional Orientalist scholarship

---

[18] A metaphor for Ali.
[19] Can bülbülü neden ediyor feryat
Şah-ı velâyettir cümleye irşat
Bektaş-ı Veli'den umarız imdat
Kerbelâ aşkına imdada geldik.

As quoted in Öztelli (1996, p. 272).

has argued that their creed has been affected by certain elements of *ghuluw* ('exaggeration' in the veneration of the Imams) – a term used in early Shi'ite apologetics and heresiography to condemn individuals and groups as heretics (Moosa 1988). These apologetics contributed to the formation of Shi'ite orthodoxy. The veneration of Ali as divine, the idea of the incarnation of the divinity in human form (*hulul*) and the idea of the transmigration of souls (*tanasukh*) were branded as *ghuluw* (Asatryan 2017). For Alevis (as well as Bektaşis), God is not only transcendent, but also manifest in the immanent world, especially in humans (Tiraz 2021, pp. 135–42). The shari'a plays at best a minor role in this system; it is interpreted – in particular by Alevis – in an allegoric sense, as an initial step on the mystical path that is of only limited importance for the initiated. Mainstream Islamic authorities regularly condemned such interpretations and the resulting negligence of shari'a prescriptions in practice as unacceptable 'libertinism' (Ocak 1998). For both Bektaşis and Alevis, shari'a has a different meaning. It is integrated into their interpretation of the *tasawwuf* teaching of the 'four gates and forty stations' (*dört kapı, kırk makam*) that functions as a metaphor for and normative orientation on the mystical path. The four gates and the forty stations (ten per gate) associated with them consists of ethical and spiritual rules that structure that path. They advance from more practical and social responsibilities (the first gates of *shari'a* and *tarikat*) to the spiritual and mystical stages of the third and fourth gates (*marifet* and *hakikat*). The goal of the mystical path is to advance to the last gate and turn into a 'perfect human being' (*insan-ı kamil*) (Birge 1937, pp. 104–9; Tiraz 2021, pp. 139–42).

The central ritual of the Alevis, as well as the Bektaşis, is the *ayin-i cem* (ceremony of unity). While the remembrance of Shi'ite mythological events has a prominent place in the ritual, another sequence of the *cem* celebration re-enacts the mythical '*Cem* of the Forty' (*kırklar cemi*), in which forty saints participated. It took place in mythical time, during Muhammad's nocturnal ascension to the heavens, and is interpreted by the Alevis as allegoric proof of Ali's spiritual superiority over Muhammad (Mélikoff 1998, pp. 204–10). The *cem* ritual is structured by lamenting hymns that are accompanied by the weeping sound of the *saz* or *bağlama* (long-necked lute), the traditional musical instrument of the Alevis. As in the mythical '*Cem* of the Forty', men and women celebrate the *cem* together and join the *semah* ritual dance. This has led outsiders, for whom participation in the ritual used to be strictly forbidden, to the false notion that Alevis conducted wild orgies.[20]

What is Alevism?

Historians of religion often describe Alevism as syncretism (Kehl-Bodrogi et al. 1997). Syncretism refers to processes by which practices and ideas formerly independent of each other are drawn together in a new form. Thus, the concept focuses not on the continuity of religions, but on their dynamic nature, in response to changing environments. It carries, however, the risk of an implicit hierarchisation of different religions according to the extent of their mixing and the respective degree of 'purity'. Engrained in the concept is an implicit conceptualisation of religions as being distinct from each other and their respective 'non-religious' environments, as being differentiated and bounded entities with clearly traceable origins. Such normative assumptions, combined with the insight that every historical religion as such is necessarily a product of mingling and differentiation processes of various earlier cultural elements, put the heuristic usefulness of the concept into doubt.[21]

The socio-religious traditions known since the early twentieth century under the label Alevism share practices and beliefs that bear points of contact with charismatic Sufism, a Shi'ite mythological orientation and Turkish, Kurdish-Iranian, as well as Anatolian non-Islamic cultural and religious traditions. Over the course of the twentieth century, these traditions were reinterpreted in the light of modern ideals and values. The Alevism that emerges as a product of such processes of reinterpretation may look very different from imaginations of 'traditional Alevism' (*geleneksel Alevilik*) but is certainly no less real and authentic. The notion of a 'traditional Alevism' as the core tradition of Alevism is itself a product of modern longings for authenticity and clearly definable origins. Like other living religious traditions, Alevism should not be understood as a fixed entity with clearly

---

[20] For descriptions of the Alevi *cem* ritual, see Karolewski (2005) and Langer (2008).

[21] For a critical discussion of the concept of syncretism as well as of other taxonomic instruments (such as 'heterodoxy') conveniently deployed to position Alevism in relation to Islam, see Dressler (2013, Chapter 5).

definable origins and boundaries, but as a set of historical traditions, constantly adjusting and rejuvenating themselves, thereby drawing on a multitude of sources and inspirations and in dynamic contact with their various environments.

Pragmatically, one may regard the Alevi tradition as part of the Islamic discourse, to the extent that the carriers of this tradition relate themselves to Islam and are regarded by Muslims as part of the Islamic fold. Even the accusation of heresy marks the Alevis as part of the Islamic tradition, since someone accused of transgressing a religion's limits is *a priori* perceived as being part of it. The way in which the discussion about Alevism in relation to Islam is led is in itself very modern: it is concerned with origins along imaginations of national, ethnic and religious purity, postulates singularity and historical continuity, and emphasises clear demarcations between different religious formations.

Processes of objectifying religion have long been present in the Ottoman Empire, intensifying since the sixteenth century when the Ottomans began to more explicitly turn to Sunni Islam as the basis of their religious authority (Krstic 2011, Terzioğlu 2012). It is in the sixteenth century that we find in Ottoman administrative and court records many examples of the accusation of heresy directed against the Kızılbaş and other non-Sunni groups (Imber 1979). Such accusations contributed to the historical constitution of a Sunni-Ottoman identity. In the Turkish republic, too, the Turkish national subject has often been marked as Sunni and Turkish, thus positioned against Alevis and Kurds (see Gezik and Gültekin 2019). Hence, in the state-centric, nationalist discourse of Turkey, similar to the way in which the demands of the Kurds for ethnic recognition and autonomy can be interpreted as ethnic separatism, the call of the Alevis for the recognition of their difference from Sunni Islam is perceived as dividing the nation by some of those participating in the nationalist discourse.[22] Both Kurdish and Alevi identities challenge homogenising ethnic and religious interpretations of Turkish nationhood in the Kemalist tradition of 'unity and togetherness' (*birlik ve beraberlik*) (Dressler 2014). This hegemonic religious discourse

---

[22] In hegemonic nationalist discourse, the boundaries of the nation are defined by religion, and divisions within the Muslim nation are perceived as dangerous.

of Turkey presents the Alevis with four main alternatives to strengthen their position:

1. Some argue for the inclusion of Alevism into an explicitly Islamic frame of reference and into the existing state structures. This is the strategy of the Alevi CEM Foundation (*CEM Vakfı*), founded and for a long time led by İzzettin Doğan, who speaks of 'Alevi Islam' and is principally inclined to cooperate with the state.

2. The radical alternative to this is locating Alevism outside of Islam in order to entirely avoid the pressure to assimilate, which is exerted by the Islamic discourse. This position is primarily represented by Alevis who are critical of the Turkish state. It is more developed among Alevis living in Western Europe (represented, for example, by the Federation of Alevi Communities in Germany, see Chapters 7 and 8 in this volume) and among Kurdish Alevis who locate the origins of Alevism in pre-Islamic Kurdish and Iranian traditions.

3. The probably most popular position challenges both of these options. It rejects both assimilation into the existing religious discourse and an explicit distinction from Islam. It demands the right to determine the meaning of Alevism independent of state interests as well as the semantics of mainstream Islamic discourse. The Federation of the Alevi-Bektaşi (*Alevi Bektaşi Federasyonu*) is a prominent representative of this position.

4. Less popular is the by far most liberal proposal that calls for a secularisation of the Turkish discourse on religion, in the sense of an abolishment of the laicist system of control of religion by the government: it demands religious freedom for all, without state patronage and sponsorship. It, therefore, demands the abolition of the *Diyanet* (positions 2 and 3 above concur with that demand). Such a liberal reorganisation of religious institutions following the US-American model is, however, considered rather dangerous by most Alevis. Fear of discrimination and attacks by Sunni Muslims is deeply anchored in the Alevis' collective memory. It corresponds to a Kemalist discourse that sees political Islam as a threat to the secular orientation of the state. With the undoing of Kemalist secularism and the Islamisation of Turkish society in the later period of the AKP rule, such fears have increased in recent years.

Common to almost all Alevis beyond these four ideal-typical positions is that they demand social and legal recognition, as well as equal rights for the Alevi population.

Alevis today face the immense task of maintaining a pluralist tradition while adapting to a political context that strives for religious homogeneity through assimilation/'return' of the Alevis into the Sunni mainstream. They often find themselves in very ambivalent situations, for example, when they, for the sake of preserving their tradition, embark on *dede* training programmes, even though the homogenisation that this entails harbours the danger of further undermining traditional Alevi plurality. Reservations among Alevis also exist with regard to the efforts by Alevi umbrella organisations toward a certain standardisation of Alevi practices. While Alevis are unanimous in their principal demand for acknowledgement of their difference from Sunni Islam, the political, religious and cultural differences among the various Alevi currents make it difficult for them to unite. Therefore, the plurality within the Alevi tradition is likely to endure, even if the grounds for inner-Alevi pluralism have changed considerably. Today, dividing lines are based less on lineage and traditional affiliations than on political and cultural preferences, economic opportunities, as well as practical considerations.

Acknowledgements

This text is an extensively revised translation of 'Was ist das Alevitum? Die aktuelle Diskussion und historische Traditionslinien'. In: Karolewski, J., Langer, R., and Motika, R., eds, *Ocak und Dedelik: Institutionen religiösen Spezialistentums bei den Aleviten*. Frankfurt a. M.: PL Acad. Research, 2013, pp. 13–35. I thank the editors of the current volume, as well as Ahmet Kerim Gültekin and Benjamin Raßbach, for helpful suggestions in the last stages of completing this chapter.

Bibliography

Alatürk, E. (2006). Alevileri İslam Dışı Gösterenlere Dava Açacağız. *Zaman*. 24 November.

Aleviyol (2006). Tarihi Hata: AIHM'de 'Alevilik, Ayrı bir Dindir' Görüşü Savunulmuş! *Aleviyol* [online]. [Viewed 20 January 2021]. Available from: http://aleviyol. blogcu.com/kutsal-ittifak-yine-isbasinda/693488

Asatryan, M. (2017). *Controversies in Formative Shi'i Islam: The Ghulat Muslims and their Beliefs*. London: Shi'i Heritage.

Aslanoğlu, İ. (1997). *Kul Himmet: Yaşamı, Kişiliği ve Şiirleri*. Istanbul: Ekin.

Babayan, K. (2002). *Mystics, Monarchs, and Messiahs: Cultural Landscapes of Early Modern Iran*. Cambridge, MA: Harvard University Press.

Bahadır, İ. (2005). Türk Milliyetçi Söyleminde Şamanizm ve Alevilik. *Kırkbudak*, 1(4), 5–26.

Birge, J. K. (1937). *The Bektashi Order of Dervishes*. London: Luzac.

Bumke, P. J. (1979). Kızılbaş-Kurden in Dersim (Tunceli, Türkei): Marginalität und Häresie. *Anthropos Freiburg*, 74, 3–4, 530–48.

Commission of the European Communities (2004). *Regelmässiger Bericht über die Fortschritte der Türkei auf dem Weg zum Beitritt* [online]. Brussels, 6 October 2004. [Viewed 20 January 2021]. Available from: www.libertas-institut.com/de/Mittel-Osteuropa/rr_tr_2004_de.pdf

Commission of the European Communities (2005). *Turkey 2005 Progress Report* [online]. Brussels, 9 November 2005. [Viewed 20 January 2021]. Available from: https://ec.europa.eu/neighbourhood-enlargement/sites/near/files/archives/pdf/key_documents/2005/package/sec_1426_final_progress_report_tr_en.pdf

Commission of the European Communities (2006). *Turkey 2006 Progress Report* [online]. Brussels, 8 November 2006. [Viewed 13 February 2017]. Available from: http://ec.europa.eu/enlargement/pdf/key_documents/2006/nov/tr_sec_1390_en.pdf

Commission of the European Communities (2007). *Turkey 2007 Progress Report* [online]. Brussels, 6 November 2007. [Viewed 20 January 2021]. Available from: https://www.refworld.org/docid/47382d392.html

Dressler, M. (2002). *Die Alevitische Religion: Traditionslinien und Neubestimmungen*. Würzburg: Ergon.

Dressler, M. (2005). Inventing Orthodoxy: Competing Claims for Authority and Legitimacy in the Ottoman-Safavid Conflict. In: Karateke, H. T., and Reinkowski, M., eds, *Legitimizing the Order: The Ottoman Rhetoric of the State Power*. Leiden: Brill. pp. 161–73.

Dressler, M. (2008). Religio-Secular Metamorphoses: The Re-making of Modern Alevism. *Journal of the American Academy of Religion* [online]. 76(2), 280–311. [Viewed 29 March 2021]. Available from: https://jstor.org/stable/25484003

Dressler, M. (2011). Making Religion through Secularist Legal Discourse: The Case of Turkish Alevism. In: Dressler, M., and Mandair, A-P. S., eds, *Secularism and Religion-Making*. Oxford: Oxford University Press. pp. 187–208.

Dressler, M. (2013). *Writing Religion: The Making of Turkish Alevi Islam*. Oxford: Oxford University Press.

Dressler, M. (2014). 'Our Alevi and Kurdish Brothers': Some Remarks on Nationalism and Minority Politics in Turkey. In: Omarkhali, K., ed., *Religious Minorities in Kurdistan: Beyond the Mainstream*. Wiesbaden: Harrassowitz Verlag. pp. 139–57.

Dressler, M. (2017). Erdoğan und die fromme Generation: Religion und Politik in der Türkei. *Aus Politik und Zeitgeschichte* [online], 24 February 2017. [Viewed 30 March 2021]. Available from: https://www.bpb.de/apuz/243029/erdoan-und-die-fromme-generation-religion-und-politik-in-der-tuerkei

Dressler, M. (2019). Modes of Religionization: A Constructivist Approach to Secularity. *Working Paper Series of the HCAS 'Multiple Secularities: Beyond the West, Beyond Modernities'* 7. Leipzig.

Dressler, M. (2021). Physical and Epistemic Violence against Alevis in Modern Turkey. In: Astourian, St. H., and Kévorkian, R. H., eds, *Collective and State Violence in Turkey. The Construction of a National Identity from Empire to Nation-state*. New York: Berghahn. pp. 347–71.

Ellington, G. (2004). Urbanisation and the Alevi Religious Revival in the Republic of Turkey. In: Shankland, D., ed., *Archaeology, Anthropology, and Heritage in the Balkans and Anatolia: The Life and Times of F. W. Hasluck, 1878–1920*. Istanbul: Gorias Pr Llc. pp. 369–401.

Gezik, E. (2012). *Dinsel, Etnik ve Politik Sorunlar Bağlamında Alevi Kürtler*. Istanbul: İletişim.

Gezik, E. and Gültekin, A. K., eds (2019). *Kurdish Alevis and the Case of Dersim: Historical and Contemporary Insights*. New York: Lexington Books.

Gözaydın, İ. (2009). *Diyanet: Türkiye Cumhuriyeti'nde Dinin Tanzimi*. Istanbul: İletişim.

Gorzewski, A. (2010). *Das Alevitentum in seinen divergierenden Verhältnisbestimmungen zum Islam*. Berlin: EB-Verlag.

Gültekin, A. K., and Işık, Y. (2005). Diyanet İşleri Başkanı Prof. Dr. Ali Bardakoğlu'yla Söyleşi. *Kırkbudak*, 1(3), 4–23.

Hasan and Eylem Zengin v. Turkey, [2007]. ECHR 1448/04 [online]. [Viewed 31 March 2021]. Available from: https://hudoc.echr.coe.int/fre#{"itemid":["001-82580"]}

Hasluck, F. W. (1921). Heterodox Tribes of Asia Minor. *Journal of the Royal Anthropological Institute of Great Britain and Ireland*, 51, 310–42.

Hurd, E. S. (2014). Alevis under the Law: The Politics of Religious Freedom in Turkey. *Journal of Law and Religion*, 29(3), 1–20.

Imber, C. (1979). The Persecution of the Ottoman Shi'ites according to the Mühimme Defterleri, 1565–1585. *Der Islam*, 56, 245–73.

Jenkins, C., Aydın, S., and Cetin, U., eds. (2018). *Alevism as an Ethno-Religious Identity: Contested Boundaries.* London and New York: Routledge.

Kafadar, C. (1996). *Between Two Worlds: The Construction of the Ottoman State.* Berkeley: University of California Press.

Karaca, A. (1993). *Anadolu İslahatı ve Ahmet Şakir Paşa, 1839–1899.* Istanbul: Eren.

Karakaya-Stump, A. (2007). 16. Yüzyıldan bir Ziyaretname (Yazı Çevirimli Metin-Günümüz Türkçesine Çeviri-Tıpkıbasım). *Türklük Bilgisi Araştırmaları*, 31, 67–79.

Karakaya-Stump, A. (2008). *Subjects of the Sultan, Disciples of the Shah: Formation and Transformation of the Kizilbash/Alevi Communities in Ottoman Anatolia.* Unpubl. doctoral dissertation, Harvard University.

Karakaya-Stump, A. (2011). The Forgotten Dervishes: The Bektashi Convents in Iraq and their Kizilbash Visitors. *International Journal of Turkish Studies*, 16(1–2), 1–24.

Karakaya-Stump, A. (2017). The AKP, Sectarianism, and the Alevis' Struggle for Equal Rights in Turkey. *National Identities*, 9, 1–15.

Karakaya-Stump, A. (2020). *The Kizilbash-Alevis in Ottoman Anatolia: Sufism, Politics and Community.* Edinburgh: Edinburgh University Press.

Karolewski, J. (2005). *Ayin-i Cem, das Alevitische Kongregationsritual: Idealtypische Beschreibung des Ibadet ve Öğreti Cemi.* In: Langer, R., Motika, R., and Ursinus, M., eds, *Migration und Ritualtransfer: Religiöse Praxis der Aleviten, Jesiden und Nusairier zwischen Vorderem Orient und Westeuropa.* Frankfurt: Lang. pp. 109–31.

Karolewski, J. (2014). Manuskripte, gesungene Dichtung und Langhalslaute als Aufbewahrungsorte: Vermittlung und Vergegenwärtigung von Wissen im Anatolischen Alevitentum. In: Hoins, K., Kühn, Th., and Müske, J., eds, *Schnittstellen: Die Gegenwart des Abwesenden.* Berlin: Reimer. pp. 172–94.

Karolewski, J., Langer, R., and Motika, R., eds (2013). *Ocak und Dedelik: Institutionen Religiösen Spezialistentums bei den Aleviten.* Frankfurt: Lang.

Kehl, K. (1993). Die 'Wiederfindung' des Alevitums in der Türkei: Geschichtsmythos und Kollektive Identität. *Orient*, 34(2), 267–82.

Kehl-Bodrogi, K., Kellner-Heinkele, B., and Otter-Beaujean, A., eds (1997). *Syncretistic Religious Communities in the Near East: Collected Papers of the International Symposium 'Alevism in Turkey and Comparable Syncretistic Religious Communities in the Near East in the Past and Present', Berlin, 14–17 April 1995.* Leiden: Brill.

Kieser, H.-L. (2003). Die Aleviten im Wandel der Neuzeit. In: Tamcke, M., ed., *Orient am Scheideweg*. Hamburg: Kovac. pp. 35–61.

Krstic, T. (2011). *Contested Conversions to Islam: Narratives of Religious Change in the Early Modern Ottoman Empire*. Stanford: Stanford University Press.

Langer, R. (2008). Alevitische Rituale. In: Sökefeld, M., ed., *Aleviten in Deutschland: Identitätsprozesse einer Religionsgemeinschaft in der Diaspora*. Berlin: Transcript. pp. 65–108.

Lord, C. (2017a). Between Islam and the Nation: Nation-Building, the Ulama and Alevi Identity in Turkey. *Nations and Nationalism*, 23(1), 48–67.

Lord, C. (2017b). Rethinking the Justice and Development Party's 'Alevi Openings'. *Turkish Studies*, 18(2), 278–96.

Mandel, R. E. (2008). *Cosmopolitan Anxieties: Turkish Challenges to Citizenship and Belonging in Germany*. Durham, NC: Duke University Press.

Massicard, É. (2005). *L'autre Turquie: Le Mouvement Aléviste et ses Territoires*. Paris: Presses Universitaires de France.

Massicard, É. (2012). *The Alevis in Turkey and Europe: Identity and Managing Territorial Diversity*. London: Routledge.

Mélikoff, I. (1962). *Abu Muslim: Le 'porte-hache' du Khorassan dans la Tradition Épique Turco-iranienne*. Paris: Maisonneuve.

Mélikoff, I. (1982). L'Islam hétérodoxe en Anatolie. *Turcica*, 14, 142–54.

Mélikoff, I. (1998). *Haji Bektach: Un myth et ses Avatars. Genèse et Évolution du Soufisme en Turquie*. Leiden: Brill.

Missionary Herald (November 1860). Letter from Mr. Nutting, 30 July 1850. *Missionary Herald*, 56, 345–47.

Moosa, M. (1988). *Extremist Shiites: The Ghulat Sects*. Syracuse: Syracuse University Press.

Ocak, A. Y. (1989). *La Révolt de Baba Resul ou la Formation de l'hétérodoxie Musulmane en Anatolie au XIIIe Siècle*. Ankara: Türk Tarih Kurumu.

Ocak, A. Y. (1997). Un Aperçu Général sur l'hétérodoxie Musulmane en Turquie: Réflexions sur les Origines et les Caractéristiques du Kızılbachisme (Alévisme) dans la Pérspective de l'histoire. In: Kehl-Bodrogi, K., Kellner-Heinkele, B., and Otter-Beaujean, A., eds, *Syncretistic Religious Communities in the Near East: Collected Papers of the International Symposium 'Alevism in Turkey and Comparable Syncretistic Religious Communities in the Near East in the Past and Present', Berlin, 14–17 April 1995*. Leiden: Brill. pp. 195–204.

Ocak, A. Y. (1998). *Osmanlı Toplumunda Zındıklar ve Mülhidler: Yahut Dairenin Dışına Çıkanlar (15–17 Yüzyıllar)*. Istanbul: Türkiye Ekonomik ve Toplumsal Tarih Vakfı.

Otter-Beaujean, A. (1997). Schriftliche Überlieferung versus mündliche Tradition: Zum Stellenwert der Buyruk-Handschriften im Alevitum. In: Kehl-Bodrogi, K., Kellner-Heinkele, B., and Otter-Beaujean, A., eds, *Syncretistic Religious Communities in the Near East: Collected Papers of the International Symposium 'Alevism in Turkey and Comparable Syncretistic Religious Communities in the Near East in the Past and Present', Berlin, 14–17 April 1995*. Leiden: Brill. pp. 213–26.

Özkul, D. (2015). Alevi 'Openings' and Politicization of the 'Alevi Issue' During the AKP Rule. *Turkish Studies*, 16(1), 80–96.

Öztelli, C. (1996). *Pir Sultan Abdal: Bütün Şiirleri*. Istanbul: Özgür.

Shankland, D. (2003). *The Alevis in Turkey: The Emergence of a Secular Islamic Tradition*. London: Routledge Curzon.

Sohrweide, H. (1965). Der Sieg der Safaviden in Persien und seine Rückwirkungen auf die Schiiten Anatoliens im 16. Jahrhundert, *Der Islam*, 41, 95–223.

Soner, A. B., and Toktaş, Ş. (2011). Alevis and Alevism in the Changing Context of Turkish Politics: The Justice and Development Party's Alevi Opening. *Turkish Studies*, 12(3), 419–34.

Sökefeld, M., ed. (2008). *Aleviten in Deutschland: Identitätsprozesse einer Religionsgemeinschaft in der Diaspora*. Bielefeld: Transcript.

Taeschner, F. (1979). *Zünfte und Bruderschaften im Islam: Texte zur Geschichte der Futuwwa*. Zürich: Artemis-Verlag.

Tambar, K. (2014). *The Reckoning of Pluralism: Political Belonging and the Demands of History in Turkey*. Palo Alto: Stanford University Press.

Terzioğlu, D. (2012). How to Conceptualize Ottoman Sunnitization. *Turcica*, 44(3), 301–38.

The Economist (2018). Turkey's Religious Authority Surrenders to Political Islam. *The Economist* [online]. 18 January 2018. [Viewed 31 March 2021]. Available from: https://www.economist.com/europe/2018/01/18/turkeys-religious-authority-surrenders-to-political-islam

Tiraz, H. (2021). Poetische Widerklänge des Alevitischen Menschenbildes. In: Alevitische Gemeinde Deutschland, ed., *Dokumentation des Projekts 'Vom Streiten der Kulturen zu Streitkulturen: Für eine demokratische Gesellschaft der Vielfalt streiten!'* Köln: [n. p.]. pp. 130–44.

van Bruinessen, M. (1997). 'Aslını Inkar Eden Haramzadedir!' The Debate on the Ethnic Identity of the Kurdish Alevis. In: Kehl-Bodrogi, K., Kellner-Heinkele, B., and Otter-Beaujean, A., eds, *Syncretistic Religious Communities in the Near East: Collected Papers of the International Symposium 'Alevism in Turkey and*

Comparable Syncretistic Religious Communities in the Near East in the Past and Present', Berlin, 14–17 April 1995. Leiden: Brill. pp. 1–23.

Vorhoff, K. (1995). *Zwischen Glaube, Nation und Neuer Gemeinschaft: Alevitische Identität in der Türkei der Gegenwart*. Berlin: Klaus Schwarz.

Vorhoff, K. (1998). 'Let's Reclaim our History and Culture!' Imagining Alevi Community in Contemporary Turkey. *Die Welt des Islam*, 38, 220–52.

Weineck, B. (2020). *Zwischen Verfolgung und Eingliederung: Kızılbaş-Aleviten im Osmanischen Staat (16–18. Jahrhundert)*. Baden-Baden: Ergon Verlag.

White, P. J. (2003). The Debate on the Identity of 'Alevi Kurds'. In: White, P. J., and Jongerden, J., eds, *Turkey's Alevi Enigma: A Comprehensive Overview*. Leiden: Brill. pp. 17–29.

White, P. J., and Jongerden, J., eds. (2003). *Turkey's Alevi Enigma: A Comprehensive Overview*. Leiden: Brill.

Yaman, A. (2004). *Alevilik'te Dedelik ve Ocaklar*. Istanbul: Ufuk.

Yıldırım, R. (2010). Bektaşi Kime Derler? 'Bektaşi' Kavramının Kapsamı ve Sınırları üzerine Tarihsel bir Analiz Denemesi. *Türk Kültürü ve Hacı Bektaş Veli Araştırma Dergisi*, 55, 23–58.

Zarcone, T. (2014). Bektaşiyye. In: Fleet, K., et al., eds, *Encyclopaedia of Islam, THREE* [online]. [Viewed 28 November 2018]. Available from: http://dx.doi.org/10.1163/1573-3912_ei3_COM_24010.

Zengin A. B. (2015). Aleviliği Tanımlamak: Türkiye'de Dinin Yönetimi, Sekülerlik ve Diyanet. *Mülkiye Dergisi*, 39(1), 135–58.

3

THE 'ALEVI OPENING' OF THE JUSTICE AND DEVELOPMENT PARTY

MURAT BOROVALI AND CEMİL BOYRAZ

Introduction

Alevis have always had an uneasy presence in Turkey. Subject to differing degrees of social exclusion and religious discrimination during Ottoman times, the situation of Alevis did not improve markedly under the republican regime of the twentieth century (see Chapter 2 in this volume). Particularly important to note for our discussion below, incorporative policies through different state apparatuses to assimilate Alevis into the dominant (Sunni) interpretation of Islam accelerated during the 1980s. Partly as a result of this, Alevis' reactions against state policies and processes of social exclusion began to be increasingly visible by the end of that decade. As Erman and Göker (2000, p. 112) argue, by the 1990s, a distinctive 'Alevi politics' would manifest itself through a demand for recognition. This Alevi quest needs to be evaluated within the broader context of the post-Cold War era, during which claims of identity, ethnicity and culture came to the fore almost universally. Moreover, thanks to the greater tendency of political issues to no longer remain 'internal', an increasing number of Alevi organisations in Europe, not to mention their significant political gains, especially in Germany, also contributed to the revitalisation of Alevi politics in Turkey.[1] With the emergence of diverse Alevi

[1] See Özyürek (2009), Massicard (2013) and Issa (2017). See also Chapters 7, 8, 9 and 10 in this volume.

organisations and associations as well as the mushrooming of *cemevis* in big cities as centres of Alevi belief and culture, the conditions materialised for what scholars have called the 'Alevi revival', 'Alevi enlightenment', or even 'the explosion of Aleviness' (Erdemir 2005, pp. 939–40). However, this forceful presence on the public stage was to be met mostly by the pragmatic and symbolic gestures of the weak and short-lived coalition governments of the 1990s.

The Justice and Development Party (*Adalet ve Kalkınma Partisi*, AKP) was set up by the moderate wing of the Welfare Party, which was known for its detachment from the Alevi cause. Therefore, Alevis largely received the AKP's electoral victory in 2002 with caution, even though this period brought an end to the turbulent times of the previous decade. The AKP started off with the promise of much-needed and long-overdue democratisation reforms in Turkey. While these reforms received acknowledgment from some groups in Turkey and the European Union, it is important to note that the AKP's first period of rule (2002–7) did not attempt to address any of the Alevis' concerns and demands from the state.[2]

Following a resounding electoral victory in July 2007, the new AKP government expressed its will to address the problems of Alevis in a serious manner. Consequently, in November 2007 the Minister for Religious Affairs, Sait Yazıcıoglu, who himself was the head of the state-controlled Directorate of Religious Affairs (*Diyanet İşleri Başkanlığı*, in short *Diyanet*) between 1987 and 1992, and the Alevi deputy of the AKP, Reha Çamuroğlu, led an initiative. The stated aim of this initiative was to engage with Alevi citizens' demands, such as representation in the *Diyanet*, granting legal status to *cemevis* as Alevi places of worship and the introduction of sections on Alevi belief in the compulsory religious courses in schools (Bozkurt 2007). To initiate a rapprochement, a dinner attended by representatives of Alevi organisations as well as the prime minister, several ministers and deputies from the AKP was arranged. The government thus set the stage for the 'Alevi Opening' in the following years.

---

[2] The only notable improvements were limited to the legal recognition of Alevi associations and the broadcasting of programmes on Alevi culture and tradition by the Turkish Radio-Television Corporation (TRT). See Soner and Toktaş (2011). See also Chapter 14 in this volume, on the impact of this period on Alevi television.

The Alevi Opening was part of the larger 'Project for National Unity and Brotherhood' (*Milli Birlik ve Kardeşlik Projesi*, the 'democratic opening' process) that also included dialogue with the Kurds and the Roma population in Turkey. What made the Alevi Opening particularly different and interesting was that it was carried out in the form of seven workshops organised by the government on a monthly basis between June 2009 and January 2010. These workshops were arranged and run by the minister in charge, Faruk Çelik, and the moderator Necdet Subaşı. Despite certain misgivings about this initiative, major Alevi organisations participated in the process, as it represented an end to earlier practices of (mostly) personal and informal negotiations behind closed doors.

In the following, we will analyse the dialogue between the political authority and the Alevis in Turkey. Although there exist comprehensive studies on the revitalisation of the Alevi question and its impact on the relations between Turkey and the EU, the major contribution of this chapter is to highlight the sources of the tension during the Alevi Opening workshops and the following inaction of the state authorities to bring a concrete solution to the problems, which resulted in the successive judiciary processes. The problematic relationship between Alevis and state authorities in Turkey also portrays one of the most interesting cases on how to manage (or mismanage) diversity in divided societies.

The Organisation and Composition of Alevi Workshops

Interestingly, the Alevi opening was not necessary for the AKP in terms of its electoral success. It was generally accepted that Alevis had been voting for the main opposition Republican People's Party (CHP) for decades. It was not at all realistic to expect this pattern to change drastically.[3] Moreover, an attempt to accommodate the demands of Alevis who interpreted and practised Islam differently from the Sunni majority carried for the ruling party the political risk of alienating its pious Sunni electoral base. Nonetheless, it was also increasingly clear that the reinforcement of the democratic credentials of the government and the credibility of the overall reform process would require the inclusion of a proper consideration of Alevi grievances.

---

[3] For a study on the impact of religious affiliation on party preferences, see Çarkoğlu (2005).

First of all, the growing dynamism of the Alevi diaspora in Europe (see Part II on Alevis in the Diaspora in this volume) and the close scrutiny entailed in the EU Accession Process helped to keep the problems of freedom of conscience in Turkey on the agenda. Secondly, the mushrooming of Alevi organisations in the big cities and their ability to make their mark on the domestic political and social landscape rendered it less possible for political authority to ignore their demands. Therefore, despite the immediate political uncertainty, internal and external dynamics made it politically and morally impossible for the government to ignore the Alevi issue in Turkey. Thus, facing uncertain political benefits, but finding it increasingly necessary to address Alevi demands, the ruling party can then be said to have chosen a relatively 'costless' strategy. Starting a dialogue with the Alevis in the form of workshops brought the government credit for having taken an unprecedented step in the Alevi question, without creating an immediate commitment to making any specific promises for reform.

Therefore, it seems that a proper evaluation of the Alevi Opening will need to focus on the workshops, and more particularly on their organisation and composition.[4] In this respect, what needs to be pointed out first is that the workshops were decided upon, organised and run exclusively according to the government's priorities. The list of participants, the number and frequency of workshops, and the topic of each meeting were all unilaterally decided by the political authority. The government's wish to closely control the process had important consequences. For instance, despite having organisations in thirteen European countries and encompassing 250 Alevi cultural centres, the main representative body of the Alevi diaspora in Europe, the Confederation of Alevi Unions, were not invited to any of the workshops. Similarly, a Turkey-based organisation such as the Pir Sultan Abdal Cultural Foundation, while present during the first workshop, was not invited to the last one. Moreover, with the number of total participants reaching 300, and with only one (the first) out of seven workshops having a dominant Alevi presence, carrying out well-defined discussions in order to produce concrete solutions to specific Alevi problems became much more difficult. The government's

---

[4] For a comprehensive and detailed analysis of the workshop debates, see Borovalı and Boyraz (2015), Lord (2017) and Özkul (2015).

wish to consult widely on the Alevi issue had already produced a broad range of (mostly Sunni) participants from many segments of the population: academics (second), (Sunni) theologians (third), labour union leaders and representatives of civil society organisations (fourth), media representatives (fifth) and politicians (sixth workshop). Finally, the seventh workshop comprised Alevi and Sunni participants in roughly equal numbers. The failure of this last workshop to carry out what it initially promised – that is, to produce a 'road map' for solutions – was emblematic of the whole process: an Alevi Opening with 'Alevi' workshops mostly conducted without consultation or in certain instances even participation by Alevis.[5]

Despite the unmistakable government dominance in the whole process, it must still be pointed out that the workshops succeeded in providing a transparent platform, which openly brought the Alevi issue to the public domain. For the first time in the history of the Turkish Republic, Alevis had the opportunity to communicate with the state as represented by the government and discuss their problems with many representatives of the larger society. This is indeed why the Alevi workshops can be said to represent a historic step in state–Alevi relations in Turkey. Despite certain misgivings and objections, this is also why many Alevi organisations decided to participate, with an (albeit cautious) optimism about the Alevi opening.

Contentious Issues and Debates during Alevi Workshops

The historic nature of the Alevi Opening was not sufficient to bridge the considerable distance between the expectations of the Alevi organisations, on the one hand, and the intentions and ability of the government, on the other. Alevi representatives were expecting the workshops to constitute the final step towards finding specific ways to redress what they saw to be a significant injustice. For the government, as well as for many Sunni participants, however, issues such as defining Alevism, specifying its place in Islam and scrutinising its rituals were important pre-requisites to identifying the true nature of the 'Alevi problem'. Accordingly, it seemed that, while Alevi

---

[5] Indeed, in protest against the government's handling of the workshops, the Alevi Bektaşi Foundation, despite participating in the first meeting, decided to decline an invitation to the seventh workshop.

representatives were asking for immediate and concrete steps to be taken by the political authority, for many other participants in the workshops and the government the issue first needed to be discussed thoroughly from a theological perspective. In the words of the workshop moderator, Alevi participants were wrong to present a 'catalog of demands' and expect these demands to be hastily met.[6] It was therefore clear that the nature of the Alevi 'problem' was not at all agreed upon by the workshop participants: was it a political problem to be addressed solely by reference to a discourse of equal citizenship rights, or a theological problem with a long and disputed history? The answer to this question undeniably informed the choice underlying the path of progress on the Alevi issue. Despite the overwhelming Alevi tendency to see the matter in political terms, it was clear that the government and the Sunni establishment as represented by the workshop participants were not inclined to discard theological concerns. It seemed that the nature of the Sunni-based 'conservative democratic' ideology of the ruling party, together with its concerns about alienating its pious electoral base, could not allow the Alevi issue to be treated simply as a political problem. Consequently, Alevi objections to debates about the definition, history and features of Alevism as irrelevant to their claims, or as matters internal to the Alevi community, would by and large be ineffective.[7] Any discussion of Alevi problems would have to be carried out intelligibly, if not acceptable, to the Sunni perspective.

Before examining how such a discussion presented significant bottlenecks in the debate on Alevis' problems, it may be necessary to mention briefly one other remark concerning the 'Alevi position'. A familiar comment, also frequently voiced during the workshops, had been that the Alevi community was too divided to come forward with a solid consensus on key demands. The complaint was that different Alevi organisations, with competing claims and different priorities, were unable to form a unified position in their dialogue

---

[6] All workshop transcripts and the final report are available online. See Subaşı (2010, 5th workshop, p. 132).

[7] Indeed, one of the Alevi participants claimed that these discussions on the theological content of Alevism reminded her of the Council of Nicea. See Subaşı (2010, 1st and 2nd workshops).

with the state.[8] However, while an undeniably wide spectrum of organisations represented the Alevi community, this diversity did not render a political solution impossible. As exemplified by the 1998 declaration by more than 2,000 Alevi representatives,[9] whatever the 'fractured nature' of the Alevi community, one could point to many instances of consensus and unity among Alevi organisations. Of course, the three decades since the 'Alevi revival' of the 1990s have also seen a process of increasing Alevi socialisation and awareness, resulting in reformulation, clarification and sharper demands. Yet, it is also clear that underlying all these demands has been the desire for recognition as equal citizens and an end to many forms of discrimination (see Tol 2005).

In light of this, one route that the political authority could take was to acknowledge this legitimate desire and to initiate a process by satisfying demands (such as the legal recognition of *cemevis*) over which there was almost unanimous Alevi agreement. Alternatively, as it continually chose to do, the government could portray the existing diversity within the Alevi community as a 'serious division', which in turn would be used to characterise any steps for reform as 'premature'. At any rate, as demonstrated in the discussions during the workshops, the facts that certain Alevi demands commanded broad consensus within their community and that these demands were clearly formulated and presented were not sufficient for ensuring a positive reception. Even when the Alevis presented a somewhat unified and coherent set of demands, the common reaction was that many of these demands were (1) 'manufactured' and, hence, 'not genuine'; (2) 'irresponsible and divisive'; (3) 'utopian'; (4) embodying unwelcome implications for 'Sunni freedoms'; and (5) opening the way to the much-feared 'slippery slope'. Let us now turn to a brief discussion of each of these five charges.

A very familiar objection to the Alevi demand for the legal recognition of *cemevis* as places of worship questions the very 'genuineness' of this demand. Overlooking the effects of migration and urbanisation on Alevi communities, this objection focuses on the relatively new and rapid emergence of *cemevis*

---

[8] Özkul (2015, p. 86) argues that, by forcing Alevis to discuss their views on Alevism in public, the government deliberately presented Alevis as irreconcilable.

[9] For the declaration in the first Congress of Leaders of Alevi Belief, organised by the Cem Foundation in Istanbul, see Cem Vakfı (2000).

in cities (see Chapter 13 in this volume). Accordingly, the demand for the recognition of *cemevi*s has been seen as a 'suspiciously new' development, backed essentially by the overly politicised Alevi organisations, not to mention the increasingly aggressive Alevi diaspora in Europe. Even the intervention in the seventh workshop by a well-respected (Sunni) scholar of Alevism, Ahmet Yaşar Ocak, who stated that 'for centuries *cem* sessions have been the fundamental form of worship in Alevism',[10] could not calm suspicions over the somewhat 'manufactured' nature of this demand. Despite its long history as an institution, the undisputable fact that the name '*cemevi*' itself was new seemed sufficient for many to doubt the genuineness of this quest for recognition. For an audience that was broadly sceptical of the rise of identity politics and discussions about 'multiculturalism', this demand merely exemplified another one of the mostly 'imported' and fashionable claims for recognition. What is more, the fact that until the 1990s a significant majority of Alevis had been of social democratic and secular orientation only reinforced suspicions about their 'newly discovered' religious sensibilities.

A second familiar reaction to Alevi demands, again best exemplified by the question of the *cemevi*s' status, was an expression of concern about the implications of this demand for 'Islamic unity'. In view of the argument that Islam had only one universally acknowledged place of worship, the mosque, it was feared that the legal recognition of *cemevi*s would bring about serious religious discord. Therefore, the Alevi representatives' insistence on this item was seen to be irresponsible and 'divisive'. Particularly interesting about this reaction was that, rather than there being any attempt to think about ways to accommodate a demand considered to be very important by the Alevis, there was an uncompromising assessment of this demand from within the dominant (Sunni) perspective. To the extent that it risked causing disunity, any claim for recognition was to be discarded. In other words, without questioning the very dominance of this Sunni perspective, the onus was put on the proponents of the Alevi quest to adjust to it. Considering the overwhelming presence of Sunni Islam in the religious and (more recently) political landscape in Turkey, it would perhaps be naïve to expect a dialogue between a relatively weak religious minority group and the one recognised

---

[10] See Subaşı (2010, 7th workshop, p. 416).

and supported by the establishment to be any different. However, what also needs to be considered are the radicalising implications of the persistent denial of claims of justice. In this regard, the frustration over the debates concerning the acknowledged place of worship in Islam surely is not unrelated to certain groups within the Alevi community being now ready to define Alevism as an independent religion, different from Islam.[11]

A third reaction to Alevi objections revealed an interesting aspect of the current practices and institutions of the secular regime in Turkey. Alevis have long demanded that the fully state-funded Directorate of Religious Affairs (*Diyanet*) be either abolished or radically transformed to accommodate Alevis' needs and that the compulsory religious courses in secondary education be eliminated or once again thoroughly reformed. These demands were mostly met with criticisms that these objections overlooked the 'existing realities of the country' and were therefore 'utopian'. Accordingly, it was argued that Alevis were basing their demands on a conception of secularism which 'set the bar too high', and that this 'too ideal' framework was impossible to implement. Throughout the Turkish Republic's history, a common and justified complaint among the pious Sunni citizens was that the staunchly secularist regime was using the *Diyanet* to control religion. Ironically, however, now that the directorate under the AKP government had become much more sensitive to the Sunni majority's religious sensibilities, the impulse to reform the *Diyanet* or the secular regime in Turkey subsided. Therefore, it seemed that, once the institutions and the current practices of the regime were under the control of the new political authority, any calls for the reform of equal citizenship rights or the freedom of conscience were deemed 'utopian'. In the name of being 'realistic', Alevis would need to accept the state's demands. In other words, they had to continue funding the *Diyanet*, even though they would not benefit from its services. They also had to accept that their children would attend compulsory religious courses in which their belief would receive cursory treatment at best.

Fourthly, and somewhat related to the objection above, Alevis were also seen to be making demands that carried the potential to diminish 'Sunni gains and freedoms'. Now that, as a result of 'the victory of democracy', Sunnis

---

[11] For a review of the different understandings of Alevism, see Chapter 2 in this volume.

were finally able to enjoy greater religious freedoms, newly emerging Alevi demands were thought to have the consequence of undermining these (Sunni) gains.[12] Yet, it was not clear why demands based on equal citizenship needed to interfere with the legitimate freedoms of the majority. Surely, a reform of the *Diyanet* or of the compulsory religious courses could have been carried out in a way that respected the legitimate rights of the (Sunni) majority while ensuring the treatment of Alevis as equal citizens. However, if the current *status quo* embodied freedoms unfairly enjoyed by the majority, the satisfaction of minority claims based on equal treatment was a requirement of justice. Any gain, if unfairly enjoyed, could not be defended on morally legitimate grounds. In this respect, it was the democratic duty of the government to demonstrate the political will to implement reforms for the rectification of an important injustice, while certainly safeguarding the legitimate rights of others. What seemed to be the case, however, as demonstrated throughout the workshop debates, was that the authorities put the onus on the representatives of the Alevi community to convince the Sunni establishment that their demands would not make the rest of the population 'worse off'. It seemed that, in the eyes of the government, convincing the majority to rectify an injustice was the duty of the very minority suffering from that injustice.

The final reaction to Alevi demands to be discussed here is a concern very familiar to close observers of Turkish politics. Frequently displayed by state authorities, this concern is based on what can be called 'slippery slope reasoning'. When evaluating demands from groups in the country, one standard reflex of the state is to think that, when satisfied, a certain demand will trigger other, more aggressive demands from that group or, indeed, new requests from other segments of society. Accordingly, the settlement of a political or social problem is rarely evaluated on its own merits, but mostly with respect to its potential to constitute a precursor to other, presumably much less desirable, demands. Therefore, in the case of the Alevis, one concern seemed to be that, once some of their demands are satisfied, the Alevi community would become emboldened by its political success and forcefully press for other measures deemed much less 'reasonable'. The endemic anxiety of Turkish decision-makers – that is, the fear of weakening 'national

---

[12] See Subaşı (2010, 2nd workshop, p. 187).

unity' – then becomes prominent. Yet another possible development, voiced especially in the seventh workshop, also fuelled that anxiety: if Alevi demands are satisfied, then other religious groups may come forward with their own demands. Seeing this eventuality also as highly undesirable, the displayed attitude becomes one of always favouring the *status quo*. The result then often is a situation where any desire for reform becomes entangled in arguments about hypothetical future events deemed undesirable. This then inevitably hampers many efforts to embrace social and cultural diversity in the country. It seems tragic but not wholly unsurprising that Alevi demands have also fallen prey to the 'slippery slope' logic of the authorities.

The Post-workshop Period: Towards The 'Alevi Closing'

Following the workshop-dominated opening process between June 2009 and January 2010, it is almost impossible to note any progress concerning the demands presented by the Alevis. As a matter of fact, it is not unreasonable to argue that for many Alevis the situation is now worse than in the period of 'neglect by the government' between 2002 and 2007. Increasingly disillusioned with the situation in Turkey, one avenue for Alevis seeking justice has consisted of recourse to the European Court of Human Rights (ECHR). In light of the existing relevant Case Law, Alevis correctly foresaw that their complaints about being subject to discrimination and violation of religious freedoms would be received positively. Indeed, as demonstrated in the recent verdicts by the ECHR in the case of *Mansur Yalçın and Others* v. *Turkey* and *Cumhuriyetçi Eğitim ve Kültür Merkezi Vakfı* v. *Turkey*, this Alevi strategy of appealing to the European Court of Human Rights seems to have produced positive results. A brief discussion of these cases will be necessary to assess their impact on Alevis demands.

As stated above, one long-standing Alevi complaint against the Turkish state concerns the compulsory religious courses in the Turkish primary and secondary education system. The main objection regarding these courses was that they ignored Alevi convictions and were designed to teach the students the dominant Sunni interpretation of Islam. In a case brought before the ECHR back in 2004 (*Hasan and Eylem Zengin* v. *Turkey*), Alevi applicants had claimed that there was an infringement of their rights protected by Article 2 of Protocol 1 of the Convention. In its 2007 decision on the case, the ECHR ruled that the Turkish state had indeed failed to respect the 'religious and philosophical convictions' of the parent of the Alevi student under consideration.[13] Subsequently, Turkey had to remedy the situation, either by making the course optional in an appropriate manner or by ensuring that the content of the course was modified to satisfactorily include the Alevi faith. However, many Alevi groups deemed the curriculum changes in the wake of the ECHR's decision cursory and unsatisfactory. In the following case of *Mansur Yalçın and Others* v. *Turkey*, the ECHR's decision would prove to leave less room for the Turkish state. Following the observation that the 'main aspects of the curriculum had not really been overhauled' and that the courses 'still predominantly focused on knowledge of Islam as practised and interpreted by the majority of the Turkish population', the ECHR this time ruled that Turkey must install without delay a system whereby students could be exempted from these courses, without their parents needing to disclose their own religious or philosophical convictions.[14] This decision became final in February 2015, but since then the Turkish state has not taken any substantial steps. What is certain, however, is that Alevi interests are finding significant support in the ECHR, an important ally for the group in its current domestic struggle.

Another decision by the ECHR with potentially far-reaching consequences concerns the case of *Cumhuriyetçi Eğitim ve Kültür Merkezi Vakfı* v. *Turkey*. As mentioned earlier, acquiring legal recognition for *cemevi*s as places of worship has been perhaps the single most important demand by Alevis in their quest for equal citizenship. In that regard, the *Cem Vakfı* operating the Yenibosna Cultural Centre in Istanbul lodged a complaint with the ECHR that it was subject to discrimination by the state. The applicant foundation argued that the *cemevi* within the centre, as place of worship, held a status similar to mosques in Turkey. Consequently, it should be entitled to receive the same financial help as mosques, in the form of having its electricity costs covered by the state, through the budget of the Directorate of Religious Affairs (*Diyanet*). The ECHR rejected the state's defence that Alevism was one of many formations within the Sufi tradition in Islam and that therefore the *cemevi* could not be treated as a place of worship on par with mosques. Trying to steer clear of theological arguments, the ECHR nevertheless clearly recognised the *cemevi*

---

[13] Hasan and Eylem Zengin v. Turkey (2007).
[14] Mansur Yalçın and Others v. Turkey (2014).

as place of worship.[15] The ECHR then referred to the state's duty of neutrality and impartiality, well entrenched in the Case Law of the ECHR, and claimed that the Turkish state had not advanced an objective and reasonable justification for differential treatment of *cemevi*s. Consequently, it ruled that the applicant foundation suffered from discrimination on the grounds of religion.

This ruling, which became final in April 2015, already seems to embody important implications for Alevis in Turkey. One immediate outcome has been the decision by many municipalities, especially those overwhelmingly but not exclusively controlled by the main opposition party, to recognise *cemevi*s as places of worship and to extend financial support (see Chapter 13 in this volume). Another significant consequence has been a judgment by the Supreme Court of Appeals in Ankara in August 2015. In this instance, the Court of Appeals specifically cited the ECHR ruling and ruled in favour of the applicant Alevi association.[16] As part of an initiative possibly not independent of these Alevi legal achievements, the government made public in December 2015 its project of presenting a reform package on the Alevi issue. However, the details of the package remained ambiguous, especially the leaked proposals about giving an unspecified 'status' to *cemevi*s being too vague to soothe Alevis' concerns, much like the similarly vague projections in the following years. Whether this latest promise of reform produces concrete and satisfactory results is unclear. Yet, it is safe to assume that any status short of full legal recognition of *cemevi*s, with all the rights and privileges that it entails, is bound to leave Alevis dissatisfied. Clearly, obtaining legal recognition for *cemevi*s has become an absolutely necessary, if not fully sufficient, step for many Alevis in their quest for equal citizenship.[17]

Viewed from a broader perspective, however, it is still correct to argue that, in the Turkish authority's oscillating treatment of Alevis, the current weakening of the democratisation process in the country will unavoidably negatively affect Alevi demands. To give one significant example, the Democratisation Package of 2013, which had introduced promising measures for a peaceful settlement of the Kurdish problem, is now stalled and remains uncertain, with an ensuing escalation of violence. Therefore, in an atmosphere dominated by

[15] Cumhuriyetçi Eğitim ve Kültür Merkezi Vakfı v. Turkey (2014).

[16] For the decision of the Supreme Court of Appeals in Turkey, see Hürriyet (2015).

[17] On the development of *cemevi*s in Istanbul, see Chapter 13 in this volume.

state security concerns, it seems unlikely that Alevi interests will find sympathetic consideration by the government.

Moreover, as we are currently observing, facing greater domestic political problems and a more hostile international environment, the ruling party has decided to fortify its electoral base by relying more on its self-declared 'conservative democratic' ideology. If this continues to be the case, Alevis will be one of the main groups to face the reforming limits of this ideology. In this regard, the experience of recent years already bears signs that bode ill for Alevi aspirations. Recurring remarks about the Alevi origins of the leader of the main opposition party,[18] the official naming of the third inter-continental bridge in Istanbul after the (for Alevis very controversial) Ottoman Sultan Selim the Grim (reigned 1512–20; in Turkish, Yavuz Sultan Selim) and perceptions of a (Sunni) identity-based foreign policy approach towards the events unfolding in Syria[19] all stoke uneasiness among the Alevis in Turkey. In this sense, we can argue that what started as a so-called 'opening' ended with a clear 'closing' that proved even more dangerous for Alevis in Turkey (see also Yilmaz and Barry 2020).

Conclusion

In light of the domestic difficulties that the country is currently experiencing, the Alevi issue seems to have lost its priority for the ruling party. What is more, the escalating antagonism between Turkey and the European Union is also bound to have a negative impact on how the government views the rulings of the ECHR. The 2020 Report of the European Commission still notes Alevis' problems in Turkey, from the discriminative aspects of official practices to the non-recognised status of *cemevis* as places of religious worship, conflicting with the respective judgments of the ECHR (European Commission 2020). Due to the increasing alienation from many European institutions and the observable decrease in the pressure emanating from Alevi transnational advocacy networks,[20] a hostile domestic reaction to such Alevi gains is likely to occur.

---

[18] For a critical view, see Sedat Ergin (2011).

[19] For criticism of the AKP's anti-Alevi discourse during the Syrian crisis, see Çandar (2013).

[20] See Arkilic and Gurcan (2020), as well as Chapter 9 in this volume.

Yet, whatever the current domestic and international conditions, it will surely be a mistake to assume that the broader Alevi question will lose its significance and can henceforth be ignored. However fragile it may be at the moment, the democratisation process in Turkey will never be complete as long as it overlooks the need to redress the injustices faced by Alevis. Initiatives such as drawing up a new constitution, addressing the problematic nature of secularism in the country, or introducing reforms to safeguard the equal freedoms of all citizens cannot be fully successful if they ignore legitimate Alevi demands. However, considering that Turkey is still technically a candidate for EU membership, it is also reasonable to assume that the existing relations between Turkey and the EU, once they are settled in some form, will necessitate addressing the Alevi issue.

It seems to be the case that Alevis, with their religious heritage creating a sense of unease for the ruling party and with their votes neither numerous nor safe enough for electoral success, do not command the immediate attention of the government. However, a continuous denial of their grievances will alienate many Alevis from the state, leading them to be a forceful and persistent part of any opposition movement. Regardless of the international dimension, this surely is cause for concern for those who desire a robust democracy and equal citizenship in Turkey.

Bibliography

Arkilic, A., and Gurcan, A. E. (2020). The Political Participation of Alevis: A Comparative Analysis of the Turkish Alevi Opening and the German Islam Conference. *Nationalities Papers* [online]. 1–18. [Viewed 31 March 2021]. Available from: doi: 10.1017/nps.2020.49

Borovalı, M., and Boyraz, C. (2015). The Alevi Workshops: An Opening without an Outcome? *Turkish Studies*, 16(2), 145–60.

Bozkurt, G. (2007). EU Monitors Alevi Reform. *Hürriyet Daily News*. 29 December.

Cem Vakfı (2000). *Alevi İslam İnancının Öncüleri Dedeler, Babalar, Ozanlar Ne Düşünüyor?* Istanbul: Cem Vakfı.

Commission of the European Communities (2007). *Turkey 2007 Progress Report* [online]. Brussels 6 November 2007. [Viewed 20 January 2021]. Available from: https://www.refworld.org/docid/47382d392.html

Cumhuriyetçi Eğitim ve Kültür Merkezi Vakfı v. Turkey [2014]. ECHR 32093/10 [online]. [Viewed 31 March 2021]. Available from: http://hudoc.echr.coe.int/sites/eng/pages/search.aspx?i=001-148609

Çandar, C. (2013). Is Syria War Additional Spark to Alevi Protests in Turkey? *Al-Monitor* [online]. 16 September. [Viewed 14 February 2021]. Available from: http://www.al-monitor.com/pulse/originals/2013/09/turkish-alevis-protest-syria-war.html

Çarkoglu, A. (2005). Political Preferences of the Turkish Electorate: Reflections of an Alevi-Sunni Cleavage. *Turkish Studies*, 6(2), 273–92.

Erdemir, A. (2005). Tradition and Modernity: Alevis' Ambiguous Terms and Turkey's Ambivalent Subjects. *Middle Eastern Studies*, 41(6), 937–51.

Ergin, S. (2011). Erdoğan and the CHP Leader's Alevi Origin. *Hürriyet Daily News* [online]. 18 May. [Viewed 31 March 2021]. Available from: http://www.hurriyetdailynews.com/erdogan-and-the-chp-leaders-alevi-origin.aspx?pageID=438&n=erdogan-and-the-chp-leader8217s-alevi-origin-2011-05-18

Erman, T., and Göker, E. (2000). Alevi Politics in Contemporary Turkey. *Middle Eastern Studies*, 36(4), 99–118.

Hasan and Eylem Zengin v. Turkey, [2007]. ECHR 1448/04 [online]. [Viewed 31 March 2021]. Available from: https://hudoc.echr.coe.int/fre#{"itemid":["001-82580"]}

Hürriyet (2015). Turkey's Top Court Rules in Favor of Covering Expenses of Alevi Houses of Worship. *Hürriyet* [online]. 17 August. [Viewed 14 February 2021]. Available from: https://www.hurriyetdailynews.com/turkeys-top-court-rules-in-favor-of-covering-expenses-of-alevi-houses-of-worship-87092

Hürriyet (2007). AKP'nin Alevi Açılımı Tartışılıyor. *Hürriyet* [online]. 23 November. [Viewed 31 March 2021]. Available from: http://www.hurriyet.com.tr/akpnin-alevi-acilimi-tartisiliyor-7746376

Lord, C. (2017). Rethinking the Justice and Development Party's 'Alevi Openings'. *Turkish Studies*, 18(2), 278–96.

Mansur Yalçın and Others v. Turkey, [2014]. ECHR 257 [online]. [Viewed 31 March 2021]. Available from: http://hudoc.echr.coe.int/sites/eng-press/pages/search.aspx?i=003-4868983-5948734

Massicard, E. (2013). *The Alevis in Turkey and Europe: Identity and Managing Territorial Diversity*. London: Routledge.

NHC and İÖG. (2013). *The Right to Freedom of Religion or Belief in Turkey: Monitoring Report January-June 2013*. Istanbul: NHC and İÖG.

Özkul, D. (2015). Alevi 'Openings' and Politicization of the 'Alevi Issue' During the AKP Rule. *Turkish Studies*, 16(1), 80–96.

Özyürek, E. (2009). 'The Light of the Alevi Fire Was Lit in Germany and Then Spread to Turkey': A Transnational Debate on the Boundaries of Islam. *Turkish Studies*, 10(2), 233–53.

Soner, B. A., and Toktaş, Ş. (2011). Alevis and Alevism in the Changing Context of Turkish Politics: The Justice and Development Party's Alevi Opening. *Turkish Studies*, 12(3), 419–34.

Subaşı, N. (2010). *Alevi Çalıştayları* [online]. [Viewed 31 March 2021]. Available from: http://www.necdetsubasi.com/alevi-calistaylar

Tol, U. U., ed. (2005). *Alevi Olmak: Alevilerin Dilinden Ayrımcılık Hikayeleri*. Ankara: Özdoğan.

Yalçınkaya, A., and Ecevitoğlu, P. (2013). *Aleviler Artık Burada Oturmuyor*. Ankara: Dipnot.

Yilmaz, I., and Barry, J. (2020). The AKP's De-Securitization and Re-Securitization of a Minority Community: The Alevi Opening and Closing. *Turkish Studies*, 21(2), 231–53.

4

'MADIMAK SHALL BE TURNED INTO A MUSEUM': NEGOTIATING THE SIVAS MASSACRE THROUGH THE BUILT ENVIRONMENT

ERAY ÇAYLI

Introduction

On 2 July 1993, the city of Sivas in Central Eastern Turkey witnessed hundreds of rioters take to the streets in protest against a culture festival. The festival was organised by an association representing Turkey's Alevis and named after the sixteenth-century minstrel Pir Sultan Abdal, who is revered by members of this community. The rioters first spent about four hours shuttling between and attempting to storm various sites significant to the administration of Sivas and/or the culture festival. They ultimately converged outside the Madımak Hotel where the festival's guests were accommodated and set it alight in front of inactive law enforcement, thousands of onlookers and TV cameras. Thirty-three guests died as a result of this chain of events; many who identify with the victims have since then called this event the Sivas massacre. Soon after the arson attack, the Madımak Hotel was renovated in order to continue serving commercial purposes. Over the years, it has become host to commemorations held and attended by those who identify with the victims. The participants and organisers of these annual gatherings have called upon state authorities to admit their culpability and take the steps necessary to find out who exactly was behind the attack. This call has also involved an architectural component: the demand that the hotel be turned into a museum in memory of the victims. Although the authorities for many years refused to engage with the call, the gradually accumulating pressure led the state to expropriate the hotel in December 2010. Concurrently, an architectural transformation project was launched at the site, which preserved much of the superstructure but involved a complete overhaul of the interiors and the façade. After a secretive process in which the public remained largely uninformed about the site's forthcoming function, the building was inaugurated in May 2011 as the Science and Culture Centre. Although the centre's program is largely unrelated to the Sivas massacre, the building still involves a significant commemorative aspect as it hosts an entire section dedicated to the 1993 arson attack, called the Memory Corner.

Until recently, the concept of memory has featured in scholarly work on Turkey predominantly as an object of deprivation. The relationship between the country's successive governments and the difficult chapters of its twentieth-century history has been perceived as characterised by amnesia (Mills 2010, p. 211). The perception is so widespread that it is even considered an integral part of public opinion (Ahıska and Kırlı 2006, p. 5). Forgetting the episodes of past violence in which governing authorities were implicated was indeed constitutive of the Republic of Turkey at its outset (Göçek 2011, p. 53; Özyürek 2007, p. 3), and this continued to be so for many decades afterwards (Üngör 2011, p. 247).[1] It is tempting to place the transformation of the former Madımak Hotel within this binary framework of forgetting versus remembering, where the former is identified as the state's strategy of dealing with Turkey's difficult past.[2] However, in what follows, I argue that the Science and Culture Centre signals a change in strategy. I suggest that it indicates a managing of the difficult past by its inclusion within, rather than exclusion from, official policies and historical narratives.

---

[1] With the processes of the 'Democratic Openings' and the so-called 'Dersim Apology', the early reign of the AKP government seemed to break with this pattern. However, as Borovalı and Boyraz illustrate in Chapter 3 in this volume, the Alevi workshops yielded no results, and, as Zırh demonstrates in Chapter 5 in this volume, the history of Dersim is still a controversial issue in Turkey. See also Göner (2017) for the continuous processes of recognition and re-marginalisation in Alevi–state relations in Turkey.

[2] For an analysis that places the arson attack within such a framework, see Ersoy (2012, pp. 221–47).

Acknowledging this change brings up a number of inquiries, beyond those governed by the diametric opposition of remembering versus forgetting. The first such inquiry concerns the demand that the state turn the Madımak Hotel into a memorial museum. Note that much of Western literature on the topic considers museums and memorials as modern inventions through which the sovereign has sought to break with the past and deprive it of its potential to directly influence everyday life in the present.[3] How and why, then, has the struggle to keep alive the Sivas victims' legacy, as well as the related pursuits of justice, turned into demands for an on-site memorial museum? Secondly, what are the implications of the state's intervention into the realm of remembering difficult pasts, from which it had until recently shied away? How could the present-day contestation prompted by the legacy of Turkey's complicated past be better understood if not as an opposition between remembering and forgetting?

The Science and Culture Centre: Narratives of Objectivity and Political Teleology

The above-mentioned questions guided my doctoral research on the Science and Culture Centre project between 2011 and 2013. Throughout this period, I paid repeated visits to the building, carried out research in municipal and national archives, and interviewed the state officials and the architect involved in the project. I talked to the latter about, for instance, the Memory Corner, which presents a list of thirty-seven names, including the two people known to be members of the crowd that surrounded the hotel during the arson attack. The names are written in alphabetical order, which means that one of

---

[3] Critics have argued that memorials, monuments and/or museums render invisible what they are meant to accentuate (Musil 1986, p. 320) and 'cannot be integrated into the present, because they fail to participate in history as it unfolds' (Maleuvre 1999, p. 60); they conflate events in an essentialist and exclusive way with particular physical places and thus relieve societies of the responsibility for a kind of remembering that is more individuated and widespread (Young 1993, Nora 1996). According to Paul Connerton (2009, p. 29), 'the relationship between memorials and forgetting is reciprocal: the threat of forgetting begets memorials and the construction of memorials begets forgetting'. Similarly, David Harvey has suggested that '[a]uthorities want to corral memory into a monument', because 'they don't want it to be alive, they want it to be dead' (quoted in Stephen Pender 2007, p. 21).

the arsonists tops the list. There are two statements displayed in the Memory Corner. One is attributed to Mustafa Kemal Atatürk and reads: 'Whatever be the different ideas, different beliefs in society, there is no task that cannot be fulfilled, no obstacle that cannot be overcome for a nation which knows how to act in national unity and togetherness'.[4] Mustafa Kemal's iconic signature and a golden mask portraying his face accompany this statement. The second statement is a synopsis of the speech that the then Minister of State, Faruk Çelik, delivered in 2010 when he became the first government representative to visit the site; it reads: 'In the deplorable incident that took place on 2 July 1993, our 37 people have lost their lives. With the wish that such pains are not experienced again . . .'[5]

Regarding the Science and Culture Centre project, state authorities have publicly proclaimed to follow a 'human-centric' approach in that they 'do not distinguish between the people who died in the incident' (Bia Haber Merkezi 2011). The deputy governor in charge of the project and the state-employed engineer who supervised it also frequently deployed this rhetoric of objectivity when I interviewed them in the summer of 2011. This was how they explained the reason why the name list is inclusive of the two members

---

[4] My translation from the following original Turkish: '*Toplumun içindeki farklı düşünceler, farklı inanışlar ne olursa olsun, milli birlik ve beraberlik içerisinde hareket etmesini bilen bir milletin başaramayacağı iş, aşamayacağı engel yoktur*'.

[5] My translation from the following original Turkish: '*2 Temmuz 1993 tarihinde meydana gelen elim olayda 37 insanımız hayatını kaybetmiştir. Böyle acıların bir daha yaşanmaması dileğiyle . . .*' My abridged translation of Faruk Çelik's original statement dating to his 2010 visit to the site of the Sivas massacre is as follows: '2 July 1993 is one of the painful days of our history . . . Insidious power groups sought to stage dark scenarios . . . to destroy our fraternity by way of manipulating our differences . . . The pain that the Madımak Hotel bears is ours altogether; it is the pain of the whole of Turkey. There can be no sides in this incident; to take a side in this incident means to not extinguish the fire . . . I vehemently condemn those who hatched this event . . . Nothing was able to ruin our unity and togetherness and will not be able to do so unless we allow it. We will not forget this event which took place seventeen years ago but will also remember our fraternity and will embrace each other tighter than ever. The screen of fog surrounding this incident has not yet been parted . . . I say that we should take the necessary steps to advance our unity and togetherness in spite of those who are disturbed by our unity, and that I remember with grace and respect our thirty-seven citizens who lost their lives on 2 July 1993' (Aytekin et al. 2010).

of the crowd who surrounded the hotel during the arson attack, why the list is in alphabetical order, why the statements in the Memory Corner say what they say and why the very name of the institution merely reads 'Science and Culture Centre' rather than referencing historical events or people. In addition to these remarks, I observed that certain physical aspects of the Science and Culture Centre were also intended to reinforce the rhetoric of objectivity in question. Noteworthy in this respect is the Memory Corner's appropriation of a design that is familiar to citizens of Turkey across the socio-political spectrum. It draws on an interior architectural element characteristic of state buildings, which is known as the Atatürk Corner and dedicated to the Turkish leader's cult (Özyürek 2004).[6]

The physical and discursive aspects of the Science and Culture Centre, therefore, demonstrate that understanding the socio-political work done by this transformation project requires thinking beyond a diametrical opposition between remembering and forgetting. Or, if the language of that opposition is to be preserved, I would argue that the statements and the design employed in the Memory Corner do indeed remember the arson attack, but in doing so embed it within the nation's teleology, by advancing a rhetoric of objectivity that seeks to break with the difficult past.

Challenges to the Science and Culture Centre: Grassroots Commemorations, Visitors' Inquiries and *in Situ* Research

The Science and Culture Centre's rhetoric of objectivity and its teleological underpinnings are not without their challenges. Consider the memorial gatherings held in Sivas every year on the anniversary of the arson attack. They typically proceed along a two-kilometre route stretching from Alibaba, the famous Alevi neighbourhood of central Sivas, down to the former hotel, culminating in the laying of flowers.[7] Commemorative events of this sort are often taken to have their own stable rhythm and involve a linear structuring of

[6] For an ethnographic study of the 'Cult of Atatürk', see also Navaro-Yashin (2002). See also Çaymaz (2019) for the formation of this myth and Şenay (2012) for its implications in the diaspora.

[7] Although the neighbourhood in question is officially called Seyrantepe, here I have chosen to refer to it as 'Alibaba', since this is the name by which those originally hailing from Sivas or those who are familiar with it have historically (and colloquially) called it.

time. However, the gatherings I attended in 2011 and 2012, which were held after the site's transformation, challenged that impression. The state authorities had set up barricades *en route* to the site of the arson attack, which disrupted both gatherings. The commemoration participants with whom I spoke perceived this as result of the authorities' unfounded belief that the Science and Culture Centre was at risk of vandalism by activists protesting against the building being turned into something other than a memorial museum.

The first, and perhaps obvious, way in which the barricades disrupt linear time concerns the unexpected interruptions they cause to the route of the march. But there is another such disruption, which emerged during my interviews with some of the activists. Although the authorities may have presented the barricades as an anti-vandalism measure, these objects served to remind the activists of the lack of such protection at that very same place on 2 July 1993. This disturbing contrast was especially evident after a brief confrontation at the barricades set up during the 2011 commemoration, when the police reacted by using tear gas. Fearing that this reaction could incite a violent backlash by activists, leading figures of the community addressed the crowd while strongly emphasising peacefulness and non-violence, notions they spoke of as integral to the Alevi faith. Directly referencing historic events and personas significant to the faith, the leaders cautioned the activists to remain calm *vis-à-vis* the law enforcement's measures. When the minor physical confrontation finally came to an end, concluding speeches by the leaders commented on the law enforcement's attitude as 'a continuation of previous massacres and of the centuries-long tyranny of hegemonic powers'.[8]

The overarching theme that characterised these speeches is one which scholars of Alevism have called passive or non-violent martyrdom (Hess 2007, p. 281).[9] Central to the Alevi faith is a martyrology, a lineage of sanctity whose links consist not of birth but of tragic death during acts of non-violent dissidence against the perceived oppressor. One of the most prominent martyrs venerated in Alevism is Pir Sultan Abdal, after whom the 1993 culture festival was named. Many followers of the faith consider each of the Sivas

---

[8] On some of these previous massacres, see Korkmaz (1997).

[9] On the historical distinction between martyrology and hagiography, especially in Islam, see Ernst (1985). For a study of Turkish nationalism and the commemoration of Mevlana Celaleddin Rumi, Hacı Bektaş Veli and Yunus Emre, see Soileau (2018).

arson attack victims also to be such a martyr, regardless of whether s/he was actually Alevi.[10] The latter's legacy has reverberated across a series of memorials in provincial Sivas, each of which is dedicated to an individual victim of the arson attack, located in the village from where he or she originally hailed, and funded by members of the association representing that village. Those who identify with the victims refer to these commemorative artifacts as martyrs' memorials (*şehitlerin anıtları*). Also reflecting this martyrology is a memorial located in London and dedicated to the 1993 arson attack. Situated in an area that is home to a significant Alevi population, this memorial was built in 1997 but fell into neglect for many years, only to be rediscovered in September 2011. Upon its rediscovery, directors of the local Alevi organisation immediately re-inaugurated the memorial under the new name 'The Memorial to Pir Sultan Abdal and the Sivas Martyrs' (*Pir Sultan Abdal ve Sivas Şehitleri Anıtı*).[11] The reference to martyrdom was enhanced not only thanks to this new name, but also due to a series of proposed extensions to the memorial, which include a sculpture depicting Pir Sultan Abdal, the prominent figure of Alevi martyrology. Such emphases on martyrdom throw teleological narratives into disarray by drawing direct links between different points along the calendrical timeline that may otherwise seem irreconcilably separated (Çaylı 2020).

In Sivas, linear temporalities are undermined not just outside the site of the arson attack, but also inside it, in spite of the teleology that underpins the Science and Culture Centre project. Consider the relations that unfold around the building's staircase. The memorial significance of the staircase originates in numbered photographs of the atrocity, which portray victims sheltering, held captive by the crowd outside. These widely circulated photos have lent this otherwise insignificant space an important commemorative function. This is evidenced by various cultural works on the arson attack, such as two well-known theatre plays that revolve around the element of stairs (*Sivas'93* and *Simurg*), a documentary in which survivors are interviewed on staircases (*Menekşe'den Önce*) and a memorial project dedicated to the Sivas victim Murat Gündüz, which incorporates stairs as a central element and

---

[10] Ali A. Yildiz and Maykel Verkuyten (2011, pp. 243–69) have called this 'inclusive victimhood'. See also Zırh (2014).

[11] See Salman (2020) for a study of commemoration in the British Alevi Festival.

whose architects told me that the intention of the design was to remind visitors of what the Sivas victims and survivors experienced on 2 July 1993.[12]

The Science and Culture Centre project has not imbued the building's staircase with commemorative purposes. But the memorial significance of this element continues to strongly resonate with visitors. Many demand to see the original staircase where people were waiting. These demands cause significant frustration and unease among staff members. In the words of the centre's director:

> How am I supposed to know where the staircase is, where the air well is? Can a staircase from 1993 remain intact and survive until today? If anyone asks about the stairs, we tell them that we do not know anything, that this is a Science and Culture Centre, and that kids are being educated here! Otherwise, there is no way out of it.[13]

The visitors' quests for the original staircase and the resulting tensions therefore constitute important challenges to the teleology that governs the Science and Culture Centre project.

Importantly, such challenges to linear temporalities have come up in my research not only as a theoretical conclusion, but also as part and parcel of its methodological engagements. This has to do with the fact that, at the end of the first phase of my research, I envisaged a reconsideration of my methods. In addition to archival research, visual analysis and an ethnography of life outside the Science and Culture Centre, I also wanted to conduct an ethnography of life inside it and do so in late summer and early autumn 2012. At that point, I had already been visiting Sivas for research for more than a year and therefore had established a certain rapport with the state officials involved in the Science and Culture Centre project. For instance, I had introduced myself openly and talked to the deputy governor about my research, which helped me obtain the necessary permits and authorisations for more than a year when I went to Sivas for only short periods.

When I returned to the city in August 2012, the first person I met with was once again the deputy governor. He welcomed me warmly. I told him

---

[12] Personal interview, 6 September 2011, Istanbul. Further, mainly text-based works of cultural production that bear the legacy of the staircase include a book titled *Three Poets on the Stairs* (Tüleylioğlu 2012) and an article titled 'Three Poets Lined up on the Stairs' (Aysan 2003).

[13] Personal interview, 28 August 2012, Sivas.

that I would like to spend more time inside the Science and Culture Centre in order to study how visitors experienced the building and its services on a daily basis. I asked if I would need to submit a written application to secure a permit. He said that written applications were not necessary and immediately approved my request, phoning the director of the Science and Culture Centre to tell him to expect me. I thus began my research inside the building. But, one afternoon, not very long after the beginning of this second period of research at the building, I found the director peeking over my shoulder at my notes. He suddenly grabbed my notebook and ordered me to join him in his office so that he could interrogate me. A detailed discussion of the ensuing chain of events are beyond the scope of this chapter; suffice it to say that the predicament resulted in my being held by the police in front of the Science and Culture Centre for three quarters of an hour, the confiscation of my notes and eventually the deputy governor threatening me with prosecution.

The whole story can be considered a sort of initiation into the harsh realities of fieldwork; such expulsions from the field are not uncommon, especially for anthropologists.[14] But I would like to insist that there is something else about this experience that makes it directly pertinent to the subject of the research itself. First, the open threat that I faced and the confiscation of my notes clearly throw narratives of political teleology into disarray. Secondly, the arguments that both the deputy governor and the director presented as to why they wanted me gone were very much underpinned by the rhetoric of objectivity that characterises the Science and Culture Centre project at large. These arguments were based on the two officials' notions of science and architecture, as they both suggested that 'what you are doing has nothing to do with scientific research' and that, in fact, 'this building itself has nothing to do with architecture; what are you going to study here that is architectural anyway?' Moreover, the director and deputy governor both concluded that 'this [the Science and Culture Centre] is a public space (*kamusal alan*), you cannot conduct this kind of research here'.[15] Indeed, since the transformation of the Madımak Hotel into the Science and Culture Centre, organisers of the annual on-site commemorations have also been told by the authorities that in 2011

[14] For a number of relevant cases, see Geertz (2005, pp. 58–59), Herzfeld (2008, p. 32) and Borneman (2009, p. 241).

[15] Personal conversation, 8 and 9 September 2012, Sivas.

the building was made a public space and that, thus, it is no longer possible to hold such gatherings in front of it (Yıldız 2011). This conception of public-space-as-state-prescribed-space has therefore provided the legal basis for the particular rhetoric of objectivity that the state authorities involved in the Science and Culture Centre project deployed from the outset (Çaylı 2019).

Solingen: A Reference Case Idealised through Years of Comparison

Further challenges to this rhetoric of objectivity are rooted in comparisons with the aftermath of another arson attack that occurred a few weeks before 2 July 1993, in another part of the world. This was the Solingen arson attack that took place in Germany on the night from 28 to 29 May 1993, when four young Neo-Nazi men set fire to a house hosting a family of Turkish background. Immediately after the Sivas arson attack, Solingen emerged in Turkey as a reference case for the debate around the Madımak Hotel. Key to this emergence was Germany's significance as an epicentre for both the memorialisation of World War II atrocities and social organisations representing followers of the Alevi faith. Indeed, it was representatives from these organisations and relevant publications such as *Alevilerin Sesi* that made repeated references to Solingen in order to render more visible the demand for the Madımak Hotel's conversion into a museum. Many of these references have displayed a celebratory tone as far as the commemorative aftermath of the Solingen arson attack is concerned; the site of the arson attack is spoken of as having been turned into a memorial museum and the authorities who have governed Germany over the years are spoken of as having led several other related memorial projects.[16]

---

[16] In an issue that included special reports about this visit, *Alevilerin Sesi* published several articles whose authors stated that 'in Solingen the site where people were set ablaze has become a memorial' (Gül 2005), 'a museum' (Seyman 2005, Kaya 2005) and 'a mausoleum' (Kaya 2005). Moreover, the articles highlighted the similarities between 'Germany's Nazis' and 'Sivas' bigots' (Aydın 2005), as well as the differences between the state officials of Turkey and of Germany (Aktaş 2005, Demirtaş 2005, Günel 2005), demanding that 'those in Turkey follow the example of humanity set by the local authorities in Solingen, and learn from the sensitivity of the German state' (Gül 2005). These visits, reports, articles and programmes caused a snowball effect as far-reaching as the Grand National Assembly of Turkey, where references to 'the on-site museum' in Solingen were made (Büyük Millet Meclisi Tutanak Dergisi 2005); the snowball effect has lasted up to this day (Özdemir 2011, Harmancı 2009, Eser 2009, Kırkaya and Demirkaya 2008).

In order to investigate the Solingen case more closely, I spent the spring of 2013 in Germany. I attended memorial gatherings and events, visited related sites and interviewed various people involved in commemorations of the arson attack. I observed that many of the Sivas-related references to Germany, and especially the idea that the site of the Solingen arson attack has been turned into a memorial museum, lacked factual and material basis (Çaylı 2021). But this is not to say that the currency of Solingen in Turkey is unworthy of consideration. My conversations with individuals who have worked in or on Alevi organisations in Germany demonstrated that this currency has less to do with the German authorities' involvement in memorialising the arson attack there, than with the Turkish authorities' simultaneous involvement in Solingen and lack of engagement with Sivas. What underpins the belief that there is an on-site memorial museum in Solingen is the fact that, throughout the 1990s and 2000s, Turkey's state representatives consistently participated in on-site commemorations of the Solingen arson attack but refused to engage with the legacy of the Sivas massacre. The idea of this museum, in other words, has been mobilised to highlight the contrast between the two approaches displayed by the same set of actors. It could be argued that the Turkish authorities' absence in Sivas has rendered their presence in Solingen as fictitious as the idea that there is an on-site museum in the latter city.

What it may mean to insist on a museum-based memorialisation of the Sivas massacre follows from this. Rather than indicate the top-down imposition of a break with the past, it seeks to make publicly known and render visible the subjective positions that self-proclamations of objectivity seek to conceal. As leading Alevi figures have highlighted over and over again, what is at stake is not that the former Madımak Hotel becomes a museum, but that the state converts it into a museum:

> To accept a memorial museum that is not endorsed by state officials would mean to unjustly claim the responsibility of the Sivas massacre. [For] the state authorities, both past and present, are responsible for and guilty of the Sivas massacre (Kaplan 2008, p. 52).

The concept of a memorial museum thus emerges as a mechanism through which social justice in the aftermath of Sivas is pursued and the elucidation of related questions of culpability is sought. Be that as it may, the recent transformation of the site of the arson attack indicates the flip side of an emphasis on state-prescribed measures as mechanisms for resolving socio-judicial questions. The transformation is in many ways the end point of a trajectory stretching from the insistence that the state ought to turn the Madımak Hotel into a museum, through the site's expropriation (*kamulaştırma*; in Turkish, to make something *kamu*, public) in 2010, to the building's current status of public-space-as-state-prescribed-space that is presented as a hindrance to research activity and grassroots commemoration.

Concluding Remarks

This chapter has argued that the contestation surrounding the site of the Sivas massacre has more to do with conflicting experiences of historical time than with a diametric opposition between remembering and forgetting. It has demonstrated that the Science and Culture Centre project mobilises a teleological rhetoric of objectivity. The spatial outcome of this rhetoric is a particular idea of the building as public space, which is presented by the authorities as an obstacle to those who attempt to trace the past's contemporary presence in and through the site of the 1993 arson attack. But the annual commemorative gatherings that take place at the site lead, if inadvertently, to the conflation of historical moments that may otherwise seem separated by temporal gaps. Such moments include 2 July 1993, the execution of Pir Sultan and present-day ordeals such as those triggered by barricades and tear gas. Moreover, it is not just intra-community references, such as those concerning martyrdom, that give substance to this conflation. There are also other phenomena, such as *in situ* research, which trigger processes resulting in challenges to discourses of social and political teleology.

Importantly, if public space is the spatial notion that corresponds to the site of the Sivas massacre as state-prescribed-space, there is also one that accounts for the challenges facing that prescription. Condemning the lapsing of a related court case due to the statute of limitations, the chairperson of a prominent Alevi organisation remarked during the 2012 demonstration outside the Science and Culture Centre that 'it is not the palaces of justice but this very *meydan* where the Sivas court case is being held!' This reference to the concept of *meydan* is significant in at least two ways. First, *meydan* is the name given to the socio-judicial and spiritual platform in Alevism where intra-community problems are resolved and misdoings penalised (*düşkünlük meydanı*; literally, *meydan* of fallenness). Secondly, the word also means 'town square' in many Eastern European, West Asian, and North African countries and languages, including in Turkey and Turkish; it is a geography that has recently witnessed numerous waves of mass protest in its *meydan*s.[17] In contrast to the attempts to render the former Madımak Hotel a public space and the past a bygone temporality, such references to the *meydan*ness of the site of the arson attack seek to reclaim it as a place for the grassroots expression of dissent and the pursuit of social justice.

Bibliography

Ahıska, M., and Kırlı, K. B. (2006). Editors' Introduction. *New Perspectives on Turkey*, 34, 5–8.

Aktaş, Ö. (2005). Solingen Başka, Sivas Başka. *Alevilerin Sesi*, 85, 10.

Aydın, H. (2005). Almanya'da Naziler, Sivas'ta Yobazlar. *Alevilerin Sesi* 85, 16.

Aysan, E. (2003). Merdivende Dizilmiş Üç Şair . . . *Cumhuriyet*, July 2.

Aytekin, E., et al. (2010). Devlet İlk Kez Madımak'ta. *Posta* [online]. 2 July. [Viewed 6 February 2021]. Available from: http://www.posta.com.tr/devlet-ilk-kez-madimakta-haberi-35394

Bevan, R. (2006). *The Destruction of Memory: Architecture at War*. London: Reaktion Books.

---

[17] These countries, more specifically, span the geographical triangle demarcated by (and inclusive of) the countries of Libya, Ukraine and India. Although each case of mass protest that the region witnessed was unique in regard to the social make-up of protesters and their political motivations, the protests have all shared a spatial characteristic in that each has seen civilians take to the central square of their city to express their dissent and in some cases also demonstrate alternative socio-political models. One of the most recent instances of such mass protests took place in the Ukraine; it has been dubbed *Euro-maidan* (where *Euro* indicates the protesters' alleged pro-EU stance). Turkey also witnessed a wave of protests that began in summer 2013 and originated in the area in and around Taksim Square (*Taksim Meydanı*) in Istanbul. An important link between the latter and the Sivas massacre came about when a form of anti-violence activism emerged spontaneously, as people started standing motionless in Turkey's town squares. Among the sites where this form of activist performance took place was the Science and Culture Centre, providing further substance to its associations with the concept of *meydan* (Hürriyet 2013).

BİA Haber Merkezi (2011). Saldıran ve Öldürülen Aynı Yerde, *Bianet* [online]. July 1. [Viewed 6 February 2021]. Available from: http://bianet.org/biamag/bianet/131188-saldiran-ve-oldurulen-ayni-yerde

Borneman, J. (2009). Fieldwork Experience, Collaboration, Interlocution: The 'Metaphysics of Presence' in Encounters with the Syrian Mukhabarat. In: Borneman, J., and Hammoudi, A., eds, *Being There: The Fieldwork Encounter and the Making of Truth*. Berkeley: University of California Press. pp. 237–58.

Connerton, P. (2009). *How Modernity Forgets*. Cambridge: Cambridge University Press.

Çaylı, E. (2019). Making Violence Public: Spatializing (Counter) Publicness through the 1993 Sivas Arson Attack, Turkey. *The International Journal of Urban and Regional Research*, 43(6), 1106–22.

Çaylı, E. (2020). The Politics of Spatial Testimony: The Role of Space in Witnessing Martyrdom and Shame During and After a Widely Televised and Collectively Perpetrated Arson Attack in Turkey. *Space and Culture* [online]. February. [Viewed 31 March 2021]. Available from: doi: 10.1177/1206331220906090

Çaylı, E. (2021). The Aesthetics and Publics of Testimony: Participation and Agency in Architectural Memorialisations of the 1993 Solingen Arson Attack. *The Cambridge Journal of Anthropology*, 39(1), 72–92.

Çaymaz, B. (2019). The Construction and Re-Construction of the Civil Religion around the Cult of Atatürk. *Middle Eastern Studies*, 55(6), 945–57.

Demirtaş, H. (2005). Solingen'in Özürü, Sivas'ı Niye Yener? *Alevilerin Sesi*, 85, 14–15.

Ernst, W. C. (1985). From Hagiography to Martyrology: Conflicting Testimonies to a Sufi Martyr of the Delhi Sultanate. *History of Religions*, 24, 308–27.

Ersoy, D. (2012). 'Madımak Oteli Müze Olsun': Talebi Çerçevesinde Bir Kimlik ve Bellek Siyaseti Olarak Alevilik. In: Parmaksız, P. M. Y., ed., *Neye Yarar Hatıralar?* Istanbul: Phoenix. pp. 221–47.

Eser, T. (2009). Söze Ne Hacet Var? *Sacayak*, 4(9).

Geertz, C. (2005). Deep Play: Notes on the Balinese Cockfight. *Daedalus*, 134, 56–86.

Göner, Ö. (2017). Alevi-State Relations in Turkey: Recognition and Re-Marginalisation. In: Issa, T., ed., *Alevis in Europe: Voices of Migration, Culture and Identity*. London: Routledge.

Göçek, F. M. (2011). *The Transformation of Turkey: Redefining State and Society from the Ottoman Empire to the Modern Era*. New York: I. B. Tauris.

Gül, Z. (2005). Madımak Müze Olmalı. *Alevilerin Sesi*, 85, 19.

Günel, M. (2005). Suistimal ve Devlet Büyükleri. *Alevilerin Sesi*, 85, 16.

Harmancı, H. (2009). Katliam Sayıklaması. *Sacayak*, 4, 4.

Herzfeld, M. (2008). Looking Both Ways: The Ethnographer in the Text. In: Atkinson, P., and Delamont, S., eds, *Representing Ethnography: Reading, Writing and Rhetoric in Qualitative Research, vol. 1: Contexts and Controversies*. Los Angeles: Sage Publications. pp. 26–42.

Hess, R. (2007). Alevi Martyr Figures. *Turcica*, 39, 253–90.

Hürriyet (2013). Standing Man Inspires a New Type of Civil Disobedience in Turkey. *Hürriyet* [online]. 18 June. [Viewed 5 February 2021]. Available from: http://www.hurriyetdailynews.com/standing-man-inspires-a-new-type-of-civil-disobedience-in-turkey-.aspx?pageID=238&nID=48999&NewsCatID=339

Kaya, H. (2005). Solingen'den Sivas'a. *Alevilerin Sesi*, 85, 18.

Kırkaya, K., and Demirkaya, R. (2008). Küllenmeyen Yangın: Sivas Katliamı. *Birgün*, 2 July.

Korkmaz, E. (1997). *Alevilere Saldırılar*. Istanbul: Pencere.

Maleuvre, D. (1999). *Museum Memories: History, Technology, Art*. Palo Alto: Stanford University Press.

Mills, A. (2010). *Streets of Memory: Landscape, Tolerance, and National Identity in Istanbul*. Athens: University of Georgia Press.

Musil, R. (1986). Monuments. In: Pike, B., ed., *Robert Musil: Selected Writings*. New York: Continuum. pp. 320–23.

Navaro-Yashin, Y. (2002). *Faces of the State: Secularism and Public Life in Turkey*. Princeton: Princeton University Press.

Neyzi, L. (1999). *İstanbul'da Hatırlamak ve Unutmak*. Istanbul: Türk Tarih Vakfı.

Neyzi, L. (2010). Oral History and Memory Studies in Turkey. In: Kerslake, C., Öktem, K., and Robbins, P., eds, *Turkey's Engagement with Modernity: Conflict and Change in the Twentieth Century*. New York: Palgrave Macmillan. pp 443–59.

Nora, P. (1996). General Introduction: Between Memory and History. In: Nora, P., ed., *Realms of Memory, Volume I: Conflicts and Divisions*. New York: Columbia University Press. pp. 1–20.

Özdemir, Y. (2011). Solingen Halkaları ve Irkçılığa Nefret. *Yeni Hayat*, May 29.

Özyürek, E. (2004). Miniaturizing Atatürk: Privatization of State Imagery and Ideology in Turkey. *American Ethnologist*, 31, 374–91.

Özyürek, E. (2007). *The Politics of Public Memory in Turkey*. Syracuse: Syracuse University Press.

Pender, S. (2007). An Interview with David Harvey. *Studies in Social Justice*, 1, 14–22.

Ricoeur, P. (2004). *Memory, History, Forgetting*. London and Chicago: University of Chicago Press.

Salman, C. (2020). Diasporic Homeland, Rise of Identity and New Traditionalism: The Case of the British Alevi Festival, *Kurdish Studies*, 8(1), 113–32.

Seyman, Y. (2005). Solingen-Sivas Sızısı Sökülmeli! *Alevilerin Sesi*, 85: 17.

Şenay, B. (2012). *Beyond Turkey's Borders: Long Distance Kemalism, State Politics and the Turkish Diaspora*. London: I. B. Tauris.

Tüleylioğlu, O. (2012). *Merdivende Üç Şair*. Istanbul: Kırmızı Kedi.

Türkiye Büyük Millet Meclisi (2005). 121'inci Birleşim. *Türkiye Büyük Millet Meclisi Tutanak Dergisi*, June 29.

Soileau, M. (2018). *Human Mystics: Nationalism and the Commemoration of Saints in Turkey*. Salt Lake City: University of Utah Press.

Üngör, U. Ü. (2011). *The Making of Modern Turkey: Nation and State in Eastern Anatolia, 1913–1950*. Oxford: Oxford University Press.

Yıldız, M. (2011). Olaylı Anma. *Takvim* [online]. July 2. [Viewed 5 February 2021]. Available from: www.takvim.com.tr/Siyaset/2011/07/03/olayli-anma

Yildiz, A. A., and Verkuyten, M. (2011). Inclusive Victimhood: Social Identity and the Politicization of Collective Trauma among Turkey's Alevis in Western Europe. *Peace and Conflict: Journal of Peace Psychology*, 17, 243–69.

Young, J. E. (1993). *The Texture of Memory: Holocaust Memorials and Meaning*. London and New Haven: Yale University Press.

Zırh, B. C. (2014). Alevilikte Şehadet: Kerbela'dan Gezi'ye Hüseyin'in Tarih Dışına Taşan Nefesi. In: Değirmencioğlu, S. M., ed., *'Öl Dediler Öldüm': Türkiye'de Şehitlik Mitleri* Istanbul: İletişim. pp. 89–110.

5

DERSIM: THE PARADOX OF DISCLOSING 'AN OPEN SECRET'

BESIM CAN ZIRH

Introduction

On 25 December 2014, Mehmet Fatih Maçoğlu, the mayor of the Ovacık district, was invited by socialist students to give a speech at Middle East Technical University. The audience waiting for him in the largest conference hall on campus was greeted with a short video clip. This clip, titled 'Tayyip [the then Prime Minister], When He Learns that Ovacık is Won by the Communists', was the first Turkish version of an internationally famous viral parody video, specifically made for this occasion. The clip, originally titled 'Hitler's Outrage', contained a scene from the film *Downfall* (*Der Untergang*, 2004, directed by Oliver Hirschbiegel) and depicted the tense meeting between Hitler and his subordinate officers in his bunker in Berlin when he learned that the Soviet advance could not be stopped. This scene had inexplicably turned into a famous Internet meme and become a parody for expressing political issues all around the world.

After the Gezi Park protests in 2013, the question of how to intervene in politics had become an important discussion agenda among opponents (see Bakıner 2014). It was proposed that municipalities should serve as one of the best channels for achieving this goal. Some leftist circles suggested that the political mobilisation created during the Gezi Park protests should be directed towards the March 2014 local elections. The Communist Party of Turkey

(*Türkiye Kommünist Partisi*, TKP), one of the minor parties, won the elections in Ovacık, which is one of the smallest election districts in the country, by receiving 656 (36.1 per cent) of 1,819 votes and outperforming the republican People's Party (*Cumhuriyet Halk Partisi*, CHP) and the People's Democratic Party (*Halkların Demokratik Partisi*, HDP), which both have very strong support in the region. Hence, for the first time in the political history of Turkey, a communist party won a district. Ovacık is located in the province of Tunceli, which has a population consisting of communities mostly Alevi by faith and Kurdish/Zazaki by ethnicity/language, and it has faced discrimination on both counts throughout the history of the Republic. Hence, regardless of the number of its electorate, the TKP's victory in this province gained significant symbolic value in Turkish politics (see Doğancan 2019).

The parody clip aimed to play on this symbolic value by depicting this particular electoral success of a small political party as a significant loss for Erdoğan, the then Prime Minister and leader of the ruling Justice and Development Party (*Adalet ve Kalkınma Partisi*, AKP). Since the introduction of a series of political reforms called 'Democratic Openings' in 2007, the issue of Dersim,[1] which has constituted one of the political taboos in Turkey (see Goner 2017), has also become publicly debatable. Moreover, despite being the second-smallest electoral region, the question of which parties would win the election in Tunceli and its districts inevitably gained symbolic importance for all parties. In my opinion, this anecdote indicates how the issue of Dersim had broad repercussions in public life during the 2000s. In this article, I aim to discuss this period during which 'Dersim' came out of the shadows, by focusing on a political controversy surrounding an interview given by Hüseyin Aygün, then CHP's Tunceli MP, to the newspaper *Zaman* in 2011. I argue that, regarding the Alevi question in Turkey, the growing

---

[1] Dersim is the historical name given to the cultural and geographical region where ethno-linguistically distinctive communities of Alevi-Kızılbaş faith have been living throughout history. See Jenkins, Aydin and Cetin (2018) for an analysis of the ethno-religious components of Alevi identity and Chapter 6 in this volume for an analysis of the compositions of Alevis and Sunnis in the area. After a law enacted in 1935, Dersim was converted into the province of Tunceli, and most parts of the geographical region of Dersim remained within the boundaries of this province. With the Dersim revival, using the name Dersim instead of Tunceli has become a political reference challenging the official historicisation of this particular region.

visibility of Dersim Alevism in Turkish politics was one of the most important developments in the 2000s.

Dersim: A Spectre is Haunting the Prospects of Democratisation in Turkey

In the wake of the interview with CHP's Tunceli MP Hüseyin Aygün, printed in *Zaman* on 10 November 2011, we witnessed an interesting media debate that is rare in Turkish media history. From 10 November to 29 December, 535 columns in twenty national newspapers addressed the issue of Dersim. Dersim – which, in the words of Dr Şükrü Aslan (2010), remained the 'secret that everyone knows' – was now suddenly and extensively talked about, in line with the political struggles around the opening processes at the time. Through the statements of politicians from almost all political parties and campaigns organised by civic associations, it became apparent that the military operations conducted in Dersim in 1937–38[2] regained their relevance during the 'Democratic Openings' (see Ayata and Hakyemez 2013, Cansun 2013, Dilşa 2020). This was a reformation process initiated in 2007, when most of the taboo issues of the republican period became subjects of public concern.[3] Before this process was initiated, it was not very common to hear the name Dersim publicly. Now, however, Dersim gained a very sharp political visibility with three significant incidents: the Öymen incident (2009), the Constitutional Referendum of 12 September (2010) and Hüseyin Aygün's interview with *Zaman* (2011).

In the AKP group meeting on 1 June 2010, then Prime Minister Erdoğan stated: 'We have started the process for the opening, national unity, and brotherhood project and put it in a schedule so that mothers will no longer cry, and there will be no more bloodshed'. Since then, the expression 'mothers will no

---

[2] The name of the operation known as *Tertelêin Zazaki* means 'great turmoil' and was popularised by the European Federation of Dersim Associations as reference for this military campaign. Instead of employing previously used concepts such as *katliam* (massacre) or *soykırım* (genocide), Dersim Alevis prefer to employ this term as a reminder that this incident specifically targeted them.

[3] For the series of workshops called 'Alevi Openings', see Lord (2017), Özkul (2015) and Chapter 3 in this volume.

longer cry' has become the official motto of the openings (Hürriyet 2010). This statement received a response from Onur Öymen (then Vice Chair of the main opposition party, CHP), who made the following statement in the General Assembly of the Parliament on 10 October 2010 (Birgün 2009):

Unfortunately, the mothers of this country have cried a lot. Many of our people have been martyred throughout our history. We had 200,000 martyrs in the Battle of Çanakkale, and all of their mothers cried. Nobody came out and said, 'Let's end this war'. Didn't mothers cry during the War of Independence, Şeyh Said uprising, Dersim uprising, or in Cyprus? Did anyone say, 'Let's give up the struggle, so mothers don't cry anymore'? You are the first one to say this, because you have no courage to fight against terrorism.

Reactions soon followed Öymen's statement. Dersim and Alevi federations organised demonstrations throughout Turkey and Europe. The most striking images from these demonstrations were posters depicting Öymen with a Hitler moustache. The most meaningful reaction was the rally organised by the European Federation of Dersim Associations (*Avrupa Dersim Dernekleri Federasyonu*, ADDF) on 15 November 2010 in Buğday Square in Elazığ, where Seyyid Rıza, a local religious and political leader, had been executed in 1938. In this 2010 rally, which was organised for the first time that year but with the intention of repeating it every year, the demands of Dersim people were openly voiced with regards to the incident of 1937–38. Kemal Kılıçdaroğlu, rising within the party and elected as CHP leader in May 2010, asked for Öymen's resignation and gave the following statement while repeating this demand in his visit to Tunceli on 11 November 2010:

I would like to emphasise this specifically. The incident that took place in the Dersim region is a human tragedy. To this day, the people living in this region have been listening to the grievances of that period, the lost lives of that period and the laments of that period (Hürriyet 2009).

Although contrary to his intention, being born in Tunceli inevitably signifies Kılıçdaroğlu's Dersim origin, and therefore his request for Öymen to resign came to mean a crucial political gesture for everyone. However, Öymen refused to resign and continued making statements that backed his initial words, which in turn deepened the crisis, as well as the reactions to

Kılıçdaroğlu. Alevi organisations in Europe protested against Öymen during his visit to Vienna on 21 November 2010.

This issue had not only become a hot topic within Alevi and Dersim circles, but Öymen's statements also received significant attention from the then pro-AKP newspapers, such as *Yeni Şafak* and *Zaman*. Although Alevis regarded the silence from the CHP as anticipated and unfortunate, the support from the pro-AKP media was unexpected and surprising. Also, the fact that these articles handled the issue as a 'deep crack in the CHP' and targeted the historical relations between Alevis and the CHP was equally suspicious. For example, one of the columns featured the striking title 'Dersim: Stockholm Syndrome of Alevis' (Albayrak 2010). This whole 'Dersim earthquake' continued its course until the referendum on 12 September 2010, with small aftershocks. One of the most important incidents in this period was that Erdoğan referred to the events in Dersim as a 'massacre' and put the blame on the CHP, which at that time had been the single ruling party. Speaking at a rally in Sakarya on 14 August 2010, Erdoğan said the following:

> You know what they say about Dersim, right? Who bombed the villages of Dersim because they did not pay their taxes? On the direct order of the President at the time . . . Who was it? İsmet İnönü was the CHP's leader at the time. So, the CHP bombed it. It is said that 20,000, 30,000, 40,000 people were executed without due process of law (Hürriyet 2010b).

The pro-AKP media presented this statement as an official recognition that the military operations in 1937–38 had resulted in a massacre; however, no legislative actions were taken in this regard. Despite being the second-smallest electoral region (see Hürriyet 2010a), Tunceli had unexpectedly gained politically symbolic significance during the March 2009 local elections. Hence, it also became a place where various political movements such as major parties – including the AKP, CHP and the Peace and Democracy Party (*Barış ve Demokrasi Partisi*, BDP, the predecessor of HDP), as well as small socialist parties – competed against each other during the 2010 referendum campaigns. Opposition parties and anti-AKP political circles had strong doubts about the referendum, which was designed to make significant changes to the 1982 constitution written by the military regime of the 1980 coup. Therefore, the CHP called for a 'no' vote for the referendum, and the BDP stated that they would boycott the referendum. The symbolic importance of Tunceli in this referendum was heightened because it was the birthplace of Kılıçdaroğlu, now chairing the CHP. I would like to point out a column text by Erdoğan that indicated this aspect. In this column, Erdoğan (2010) used the title 'Seyyid Rıza of Dersim was captured on 12 September' and wrote the following:

> Another hot topic. The spectre of Dersim is out again. In fact, almost all of our recent history has become a spooky forest of spectres because it was not properly left behind; it did not receive a proper funeral. This is the reason why they appear in unexpected places . . . The CHP's mindset at the time saw Dersim as a point of resistance against the Republic and branded it as a 'reactionary movement'. Although current Tunceli people do not accept this fact, the real crime of Dersim was being 'reactionist'. How strange! Since the term reactionary has been associated with Sunni Islam and used as an excuse for ideological agendas, its meaning was distorted over time.

That is, government representatives and pro-AKP journalists were inviting the people of Dersim to place themselves on the right side by reminding them of the 1937–38 incident. However, the results were not satisfactory for pro-AKP circles because 33.28 per cent of the voters did not participate in the referendum, 53.09 per cent voted 'no' and only 12.59 per cent voted 'yes'.

The referendum results gave the impression that the people of Dersim shared common ground against the AKP but were divided between the CHP as the representative of the republican tradition, which the Alevis had heavily supported since the 1960s, and the BDP as the representative of the Kurdish movement. Pro-AKP circles soon reacted against this situation, and Dersim gained controversial visibility in public debates on the process of openings. However, this time, those who had sided with the Alevis in the Öymen incident now turned against them. After the publication of columns with titles such as 'Falling in love with the executioner' (Kamış 2010) and 'Simons who reside in the CHP!' (Tuna 2010) during the referendum period, Hakan Albayrak (2010) wrote the following in his column in *Yeni Şafak*, under the title 'We thought it was Dersim, but it turned out to be Tunceli!':

> You try to eliminate the remains of the single-party dictatorship or its projections who cannot tolerate the existence of Kurds with their Kurdish

identity, who destroyed Dersim, who stated that 'There's no place for Alevis here' when establishing the Directorate of Religious Affairs, but the grandchildren respond as 'no' with an 80 per cent landslide majority . . . Good old Dersim . . . You really became Tunceli. So, if there was a referendum tomorrow that said 'Should the name of Sabiha Gökçen Airport be changed?' you would say 'no' to that, too, you would embrace Sabiha Gökçen who was commended because she participated in the Dersim massacre with air bombardment.

Aygün: The Man Walking the Red Line

Hüseyin Aygün's interview with *Zaman* should be understood against this historical background. I argue that Aygün's nomination by the CHP under Kılıçdaroğlu, as the Tunceli MP candidate, in 2011 has a deeper meaning. Alevis had already been alienated from the CHP during the years of Deniz Baykal's party leadership in the 1990s and 2000s. With the Öymen incident, their feeling of 'political abandonment' had grown deeper, and Alevis had started to withdraw their political support from the CHP. During this period, the long-time unvoiced idea of establishing a new party was put forth as the 'Joint Party Initiative' during the Hacı Bektaş Festival on 15 August 2009, in a meeting with a large audience. Leftist political parties, political organisations, non-governmental organisations and syndicates hosted by Alevi organisations came together during this festival around the question 'How do we want Turkey to be?' However, before this new party was initiated, Kılıçdaroğlu became the CHP leader in May 2010, when Deniz Baykal was forced to resign due to a personal scandal. The Alevis, who were suffering from 'political abandonment' and discrimination during the opening process, welcomed this development with great enthusiasm. I was in London when this unexpected incident happened and I had the chance to observe how some Alevis, once highly critical of the CHP, instantly became CHP supporters.

While Turkey prepared for the June 2011 general elections, the CHP was trying to complete its reconstruction with the slogan 'the new CHP for everyone'. Simultaneously, its leader was constantly targeted by the ruling party for his Dersim origins, indicating his Alevi background. Therefore, during this period, MP candidates became much more important, and all eyes were once again set on Tunceli. Tunceli, as one of the smallest electoral regions in Turkey with a voter population of around 40,000, sent two independent members to parliament in the July 2007 general elections. Along with Kamer Genç, the longest-serving MP for Tunceli, Şerafettin Halis, one of the independent candidates of the Kurdish movement called 'Thousand Hopes Candidates', entered parliament after winning 27.14 per cent of the votes, and during his service in parliament he presented, both orally and in writing, many parliamentary questions regarding the problems of the region.[4]

In the June 2011 general elections, the BDP attempted to continue its presence in Tunceli with Ferhat Tunç, a famous political singer from the region. In contrast, the CHP nominated Kamer Genç and Hüseyin Aygün, who were lawyers and not much recognised outside the region. Hence, the local fault lines, which are hard to understand without knowing the region's political history, were drawn, and the CHP-BDP rivalry became a more important issue than the AKP-CHP contest. As the result of the elections, Genç and Aygün brought 56.2 per cent of the votes to the CHP, securing the only electoral victory for the CHP outside of Turkey's western parts. The

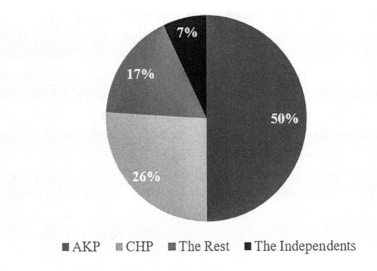

■ AKP   ■ CHP   ■ The Rest   ■ The Independents

Figure 5.1   Turkish General Election 2011 – Turkey

[4] Aygün (n. d.a and b).

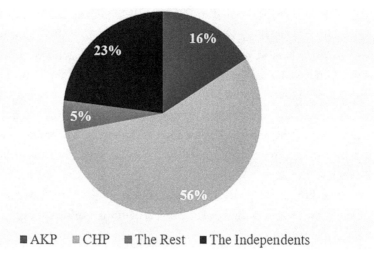

■ AKP   ▧ CHP   ■ The Rest   ■ The Independents

Figure 5.2   Turkish General Election 2011 – Tunceli

BDP's independent candidate, Tunç, obtained only 22.9 per cent of the votes and could not enter parliament. The election results became a topic of discussion within the BDP. Ahmet Türk, a prominent representative of the Kurdish movement in Turkey, stated that they realised how the results in Tunceli indicated that they could not reach the Alevi citizens when necessary.

Hüseyin Aygün unexpectedly gained important symbolic status in Turkish politics. Born in 1970, Aygün practised law in Tunceli after he had graduated from Ankara University's Faculty of Law in the early 1990s and engaged in legal practices regarding current and past human rights violations in the region, especially regarding the operations of 1937–38. Moreover, Aygün wrote three books on the issue of Dersim: the first one in his native language, *Eve Tarixê Ho Têri Amaene* (Confronting Our Own history, 2007), then *Dersim 1938 ve Zorunlu İskan* (Dersim 1938 and the Forced Resettlement, 2009) and *0.0.1938: Resmiyet ve Hakikat* (0.0.1938: the Official and the Truth, 2011), both in Turkish. Moreover, he addressed the general public with a series of columns concerning local issues, which he wrote for he wrote for the leftist newspaper *Birgün* (Aygün 2006a-b; 2007b-g; 2009b). Aygün continued working on the campaigns he had initiated as a lawyer during his time in parliament. In addition to his reports and press statements about various subjects, he also voiced many sensitive issues in the parliamentary minutes – such as environmental problems, the planned building of dams in Dersim and the call for an investigation of mass graves from the years 1937–38 – by presenting four legislative proposals and twelve written parliamentary inquiries.[5]

In this sense, his political persona overlapped with the process in which Dersim re-emerged from the shadows. What he said in the interview with *Zaman*, published on Atatürk Memorial Day, became a critical message for different political circles. In this interview, Aygün was challenging the CHP's limits:

> Dersim is a distinctive region due to its ethnic identity and religious composition, and hence it has been constantly subjected to annihilation policies for 500 years . . . The official discourse argues that there was an uprising, and the state suppressed it . . . The Dersim uprising is a made-up term; in reality there is no such thing . . . Atatürk was the head of the state during all these policies at the time. However, to separate this period from Mustafa Kemal and not to cloud his image of 'great leader', Alevis put the pictures of him next to Ali. They convinced themselves that he was not aware of this massacre.

He also added that the CHP, under Kılıçdaroğlu's leadership, was 'taking a stance towards confronting our own history and publicly discussing the policies carried out'. Due to his increasing popularity, this interview triggered a large debate.

In short, as Aygün entered parliament, he immediately crossed the lines of both the Republican establishment and his own party. His statements on the 1937–38 operations, as a Tunceli MP, 'dropped a bombshell' onto the political agenda. On one hand, he was at the centre of criticism from some CHP MPs who were uneasy with the term 'New CHP' due to his critical stance. On the other hand, his statements drew particular attention from pro-AKP circles, which challenged the CHP by instrumentalising the issue of Dersim. Finally, the Kurdish movement closely observed Aygün, as he had outperformed their candidates in Tunceli. From this perspective, it is possible to understand Aygün's parliamentary membership as a symptom indicating the complexity of this opening process through which the issue of Dersim gained unexpected and controversial visibility in Turkish politics. In this sense, I argue that the media debate following Aygün's interview with *Zaman* can be studied as a case to understand the dilemmas of the opening process, on the one hand, and how Dersim intersects with various political issues in the history of the Republic, on the other.

[5] See Aygün (n. d.a and b).

The Third Dersim Incident in the Turkish Media

As already mentioned above, from Aygün's interview on 10 November 2010 until 29 December, 535 columns were published in twenty different national newspapers. Table 5.1 shows the distribution of these columns across newspapers. Table 5.2 shows their chronological distribution. Interestingly, Aygün's interview was discussed over a period of fifty days, a very long time

Table 5.1 Distribution of columns across newspapers

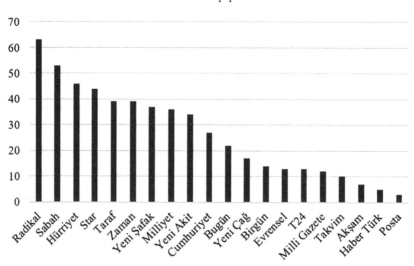

Table 5.2 Chronological distribution of columns

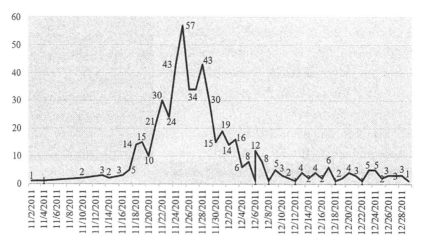

for a single issue to set the agenda in a country such as Turkey, where the political agenda changes daily.

Looking at the titles of these columns, the following words and punctuation marks were encountered more than ten times: Dersim (215), question mark '?' (111), CHP (76) and (67), the question suffix 'mi' (55), apology (52), exclamation mark '!' (52), history (23), what (22), confrontation (20), Alevi (20), Kılıçdaroğlu (16), state (15) and Prime Minister (12).

Considering this distribution, it is possible to argue the following: (1) The issue was discussed in relation to the CHP and its leader Kılıçdaroğlu (with titles such as 'The saddest story of Kılıçdaroğlu' and 'The entire burden is on Kılıçdaroğlu's shoulders'). (2) The frequent usage of the conjunction 'and' indicates that the issue of Dersim was not regarded as an individual issue of its own, but rather in conjunction with another issue (with the titles 'Dersim and 1915', 'Dersim and Atatürk', 'Dersim and Memory-cide' and 'Dersim and Revolution'). (3) Yet, we can once again emphasise the importance that the issue of Dersim gained during the opening process, as indicated by the frequent usage of concepts such as 'apology', 'history' and 'confrontation' (with the titles 'Prime Minister Rips Apart Official History with Dersim', 'Can the CHP Look at the Future without Putting Historical Events in their Proper Places?'). (4) In these 535 columns, the use of 111 question marks and 52 exclamation marks – expressing various emotions such as joy, pain, fear and astonishment – indicates the commotion in Turkish politics created by the Dersim dilemma discussed above (with the titles 'Does the CHP Think about Liberating Itself?', 'What is the CHP's Dilemma?', 'The CHP, Dersim and the Armenian Massacre!' and 'The CHP MP Who is Not a CHP MP!').

The present study analyses twenty newspapers according to five political leanings based on the way in which they handled the issue:[6]

1. Leaning 1 (Left-Liberal): *Birgün, Evrensel, Radikal, Taraf* (129)
2. Leaning 2 (Mainstream): *Sabah, Star, T24* (110)

---

[6] This classification was made according to the state of the media at that period and based on how these newspapers framed the issue of Dersim. After the handovers and seizures that took place in the Turkish media especially after the 15 July 2016 coup attempt, one cannot claim that this classification is still valid today.

3. Leaning 3 (Mainstream-Liberal): *Akşam, HaberTürk, Hürriyet, Milliyet, Posta, Takvim* (107)
4. Leaning 4 (Pro-AKP, conservative Islamist): *Milli Gazete, Yeni Akit, Yeni Şafak, Zaman* (122)
5. Leaning 5 (Anti-AKP nationalist and/or republican): *Bugün, Cumhuriyet, Yeni Çağ* (66)

The distribution of the words used in the column titles according to these leanings shows a puzzling picture. Despite varying percentages, the titles in all commonly contain 'Dersim', '?', 'CHP', 'and' and 'apology'. However, the abbreviation 'CHP' was mostly used by Leaning 3 (5.08 per cent) and Leaning 4 (5.85per cent) but used the least by Leaning 1 (1.91 per cent) and Leaning 5 (3.22 per cent). The word 'apology' was mostly used by Leaning 1 (4.4 per cent) and Leaning 5 (3.22 per cent), while used the least by Leaning 3 (1.61 per cent) and Leaning 4 (2.19 per cent) (see Table 5.3).

A chronological breakdown of the news regarding Dersim, which were published after the interview, is essential for understanding the statistical breakdown presented above. The most important detail in this table is the fact that Leaning 4, which can be regarded as the most pro-AKP, is more sensitive towards statements made by the government than other leanings.

Table 5.3 The most frequent words in the column titles according to the newspapers' leanings

■ Dersim ▨ ? ■ CHP ■ ve ▨ özür

Table 5.4   Chronological distribution of columns according to the newspapers' leanings

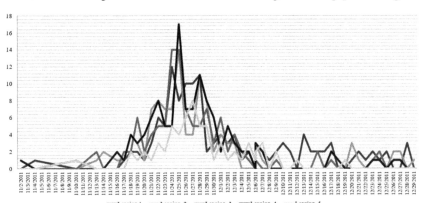

The newspapers in this leaning published more statements by government representatives, especially by the then Prime Minister Erdoğan. For example, the number of articles printed by Leaning 4 newspapers increased after 18 November 2010, when Erdoğan first expressed his opinions on the issue; in parallel with the concurrent statements by other government representatives, they printed more articles on 26 November than any other newspapers. However, there was a decline in the number in this leaning after 28 November; following the publication of public opinion polls about the issue, it declined faster than the other leanings, with just a brief peak on 3 December (see table 5.4).

Since coming to power in 2002, the AKP government has substantially re-shaped its language and the politics in Turkey. One of the most essential bases in this endeavour was its claim to resolve 'problems' that had emerged during the early years of the Republic and become chronic over time. One may argue that the AKP government presents its period of governance as a sharp dissociation from Turkish politics before the November 2002 general elections, within a discourse that can be called 'milestone-ism'. In order to support this discourse, a series of reforms was initiated under the name 'openings', which addressed several democratisation issues, especially the Kurdish problem (see Chapter 3 in this volume). For example, the amendments made to the law of associations in 2005 allowed the use of the term 'Alevi' or *cemevi* on the signboards of Alevi associations (see Chapter 13 in this volume).

However, the main aspect that raised suspicion towards and discontent about the opening efforts was the government's language. It is true that during this period the AKP government challenged and made publicly debatable republican official history, which had concealed many other issues similar to Dersim. Yet, the AKP government also attempted to write its own official history. This can be seen in the discussions in the Turkish media following Aygün's interview with the newspaper *Zaman*, which was known for its pro-AKP stance at that time. The volume of this media coverage, in fact, reveals that the satisfactory resolution of the Dersim dilemma is actually dependent on the question of how Dersim is going to be remembered. This question became highly politicised so that different political circles clashed over who would frame and how to frame historical issues such as Dersim.

Ethnographic Notes on the Dersim Revival from Little Dersim in Berlin

In this section, I present some of my notes from the fieldwork I carried out in Berlin in 2009, just before the Onur Öymen incident, in order to clarify the process through which Dersim emerged from the shadows – a process which might also be called a 'revival'. I spent nearly six months in Germany (mostly in Berlin), from January to July 2009, for my doctoral research. It is possible to list numerous characteristics that separate Berlin from other European cities. One of the most important aspects is the sense of a 'homey' familiarity incorporated into the city's fabric by immigrants from Turkey (the estimated population is around 250,000). It should also be noted that, along with London, Berlin is a city where Alevis are over-represented among immigrants from Turkey, which is not common. In an official report with the title *Muslim Life in Germany*, published by the Federal Office for Migration and Refugees (2009), Alevis were for the first time defined as a distinct category within Islam; hence, for the first time, accurate data about Alevis living in Germany were presented. Demographical data provided in this report also confirms this exceptionality.

Moreover, observations from my previous visits and six-month stay indicated that Alevis from Dersim, especially from the districts of Hınıs and Varto, were the most visible group among Alevi immigrants in Berlin. From my first day in Berlin onwards, I encountered this unique situation on various occasions. Towards the end of my visit, I realised that the city, which had hosted the 'Alevi revival' twenty-five years earlier, has also been the host of the 'Dersim revival' after 2005. While walking in Kreuzberg, one could come across a poster of an art exhibition titled *Heimat* (Motherland) by Safiye Akgündüz, consisting of paintings about Dersim, where the artist had lived in her childhood. On another poster, one could see a civic initiative call to support the attempt to establish the first German and Zaza bilingual kindergarten. On yet another poster, one could read that the '38 Dersim Oral History Project' had been initiated one month earlier, with a panel organised by the Berlin Dersim Society (*Berlin Dersim Cemaati*, BDC). The *Gağan* (New Year) Festival was also celebrated for the first time during this period. There were posters for activities organised to commemorate the Dersim *Tertelê* in several shop window displays. Zaza language courses and various social activities were organised by the BDC, which operated in the Former East German Visa Building in order to bring Dersim youth together. New book releases about Dersim and Dersim musicians' albums (see Greve 2020) occupied a large portion of the shelves in the Turkish bookstore at the Kottbuser Tor. The most popular and most expensive food item in the *World Burgers* Restaurant in Kreuzberg was the Zaza Burger (see Zırh and Akçınar 2013).

People I met also confirmed that this visibility of Dersim was a newly emerging phenomenon in Berlin. For example, I was invited to a *cem* to be held 'for the first time' in the Zazaki language rather than in Turkish. When I went to the BDC on 13 February 2009, I saw that the *dede*s who were members of the Berlin Anatolian Alevis Cultural Centre (*Berlin Anadolu Alevileri Kültür Merkezi*, BAAKM) and the Faith Council were sitting on the sheepskin (*post*) and hence realised that the *dede*s I knew from the *cemevi* were also from Dersim. The same *dede*s conducted the *cem* in Turkish in the following two days at the BAAKM and then in Zazaki at the BDC. In a conversation after the *cem*, a BDC manager told me that they usually were not interested in religious activities; however, in light of the recent discussions, they had decided that religious practices were important to keep their language alive. However, this also leads to Dersim Alevism becoming more visible within the general Alevi category. Yet, there has always been a faction (of Turkish-speaking Alevis) within the Alevi movement that has kept its distance from Dersim Alevism.

In the early 1990s, independent Dersim organisations emerged as a reaction to the military operations in Tunceli, which were called the 'Second 38'. Immigrants from Dersim who previously had gathered around regional associations or football clubs, aside from the European branches of regional organisations, felt the need to gather in order to organise campaigns against the grievous events taking place in Turkey. The BDC, established in 1993, was among the first to emerge. It received heavy criticism from the Kurdish movement during this period, during which the Alevi movement also was struggling to institutionalise its own organisational structure. The Kurdish movement in the diaspora was especially critical about the 'Zazaism' thesis, developed by a tiny political group in the 1980s, which portrayed the Dersim Alevis as an ethnic group separate from the Kurds.

Like the Alevi movement, the BDC was also attacked for being 'feudal' by their former comrades and accused of being 'infiltrators' and 'separatists' by the Kurdish movement. However, a small group managed to hold the BDC together until the 2000s. This was also the period during which the Alevi movement completed its organisational institutionalisation in Europe. Local Alevi associations were organised under the national-level umbrella federations in more than ten European countries. By the mid-2000s, the issue of Dersim had gained a new currency for Alevis in the diaspora (see Orhan 2020). For example, the first public 1938 commemoration was held under the roof of the BAAKM in 2005, which would not have been possible while the Kurdish movement was very critical of the issue. This fraternisation between the BAAKM and the BDC over the common ground of Dersim Alevism continued in the following years, with several other joint activities such as panels about Dersim Alevism and concerts in Zazaki.

In February 2006, the European Federation of Dersim Associations (ADDF) was established. Forty-five delegates from nine associations in Germany attended the inaugural meeting held in Dortmund. The First General Assembly Meeting held in Cologne in October 2006 attracted participants from other associations in Amsterdam, Basel, Paris and Vienna. Seventy-two delegates attended the meeting; the most important agenda item was the issue of how to institutionalise the European Dersim Culture Festival, first held in 2005. This was a period when debates about the contents of the Munzur Festival, held in Tunceli since the early 2000s, emerged among Dersim organisations. Accordingly, the Kurdish movement made a constant effort to present more ethno-linguistically Kurdish content during this festival through the agency of the Tunceli Municipality, over which they had control (see Sözen 2019).

With the establishment of the ADDF, the developing fraternisation between the BAAKM and the BDC, which had started locally in Berlin, was carried on to the European level. Since its establishment, the Federation of Alevi Unions in Germany (*Almanya Alevi Birlikleri Federasyonu*, AABF) has had a sympathetic attitude towards the problems in Tunceli. The AABF ensured that European committees visited the region during 1994 and 1995, when military operations were most intense, and also tried to bring the issues to the European agenda by preparing human rights reports. The first 'Add Another Brick' campaign was organised for Tunceli, and hence the foundations for the current *cemevis* were laid in 1996. Today, AABF's management attends all events of the ADDF as guests of honour. In the speeches of its directors, such as Ali Ertan Toprak, who is of Dersim origin and who served as the federation's spokesperson in the 2010s, the term 'we' is used to refer to both institutions together.

This fraternisation offers a great learning experience for both institutions. For example, participation in the singing contest 'For the Love of Folk Songs', which was first held in 2009 by Yol-TV (a satellite-based Alevi broadcasting channel from Europe) and included thirteen cities in Europe, was previously limited only to the Turkish language. At the sixth stage of the contest held in Hamburg on 22 February 2009, the fourteen-year-old contestant Baran Can wanted to sing in his mother tongue, Zazaki, while on air. With the support of local Alevi organisations, the contest was opened up to 'other languages spoken by Alevis' as well. With this opening, Berfin, who participated in the ninth stage of the contest held in Zurich on 15 March 2009, could sing her song in Kurdish. Furthermore, the AABF supports the ADDF on every occasion. The TV programme titled *Venge Dêrsimî* (Voice of Dersim) produced by the ADDF and aired on Yol-TV has long been the only independent programme broadcast on air in the Zaza language (see Emre-Çetin 2018). The AABF's long-standing institutional experiences and Europe-wide lobbying activities have contributed to the ADDF in directing their campaigns. For example, one of the most important achievements of the ADDF was UNESCO's recognition of Zaza as an endangered language in 2009. The cooperation between these two main organisations also paved the way for the specific regional organisations representing Kurdish-speaking Alevis outside Dersim, such as the Koçgiri and Pazarcık platforms.

When I boarded one of the busses full of people traveling from Berlin to Bonn in order to attend the 4th European Dersim Culture Festival on 13 June 2009 as a guest of the BDC, I still had not yet developed a clear understanding of the 'Dersim revival'. What I encountered in Berlin for the first time was exciting, but this mobilisation could have been limited to this city. However, the festival, attended by 15,000 persons from all over Europe, was an important experience in order to clearly see the extent of this revival. The most popular person at the festival was Rüstem Polat, the grandson of Seyyid Rıza, the iconic leader of the 1937–38 period. Germany-born youth were waiting in line to take a picture with him. The most interesting stand among the many on display at the festival were the 'Before the Last Witnesses Migrate' booth of the Archive and Documentation Initiative Centre, which presented the two most current essential aspects of the Dersim issue, 1938 (yesterday: ethnic massacre) and the Dam Project (today: environmental massacre); and the 'Protect Munzur' booth, which had been put up thanks to the joint efforts of environmental organisations. The 'Dersim Jugend' (Dersim Youth) stand presented hundreds of photographs from Dersim, and it sold necklaces representing Dersim Alevism, T-shirts with phrases such as 'Ez (We) © Dersim', '62' and '24' (license plate codes for Tunceli and Erzincan, respectively) and printed pictures of Seyyid Rıza and Deniz Gezmiş. Moreover, there were about twenty booths selling books.

After taking pictures of the bookstalls, I could make the following classification of the books on offer: (1) classical international left-socialist literature written by figures such as Marx, Lenin, Stalin and Mao; (2) left-socialist literature from Turkey; (3) literature about left-socialist figures such as Mahir Çayan, İbrahim Kaypakkaya, Deniz Gezmiş and Yılmaz Güney; (4) Alevi literature produced since the early 1990s; (5) research pieces on Dersim in various fields such as language, culture, faith, politics and history, mostly published after 2005; and (6) reference books such as Zazaki-Turkish dictionaries and grammar guides, as well as books translated into Zazaki, such as *The Little Prince*. All these notes from my field research in Germany in 2009 indicate that, even before Dersim re-emerged from the shadows in Turkey, the revival process had already begun in the diaspora, with various historical, cultural, linguistic, religious and political aspects of the Dersim issue brought to the fore.

Conclusion: The Recognition/Definition Question that Emerged during the Revival

The Dersim revival emerged in the early 2000s as one of the most critical developments related to Alevism. It is apparent that Dersim has become a controversial issue, gaining sharp visibility in parallel to the democratic opening process initiated by the AKP government. In this chapter, I have explored this process by focusing on three incidents: the Onur Öymen incident (2009), the 12 September Referendum period (2010) and, lastly, Hüseyin Aygün's interview with *Zaman* (2011). In light of these examples, I argue that Dersim Alevism provides a critical case for understanding the nation-building process in Turkey, by drawing fault lines between republican secularism and political Islam, and republican and Kurdish nationalisms.

The Dersim revival has also significant similarities to the development of the Alevi revival in the early 1990s. We witness very similar struggles that took place in this period, such as emerging controversies regarding the question of how to define Alevism. Alevi organisations and various political circles attempted to frame Alevism according to their political motivations. This framing contest also became an issue within the context of the Dersim revival.[7] As such, many interesting things that would have been hard to imagine during the 1990s happened in this period. Once a taboo, Dersim has now gained substantial legitimacy and controversial visibility since 2009, with all the unique aspects it represents. However, this also comes with a price to pay. Especially since the 15 July 2016 coup attempt, AKP's promises regarding the opening process have faded into political uncertainties.

During the democratic openings period, the AKP government tried to instrumentalise the Dersim issue for its political interests, and this, in turn, caused a problem of trust. Analysing the examples of these two revivals,

---

[7] For example, for the first Zazaki *cem* in Berlin, the large hall of the Berlin Dersim Community was organised as a town square, and a poster of Ali was put up on the wall. Some of the participants demanded that the poster be taken down, claiming that Dersim Alevism is not related to Islam. A *dede* from Dersim who attended the *cem* from Turkey opposed this idea with a short explanation and stated that there could be no *cem* without Ali. A similar discussion had also taken place in Europe in the late 1990s; as a result, Turkish flags and Atatürk posters were not supposed to be put up in *cemevi*s because they were considered political symbols.

Alevism in the 1990s and Dersim Alevism in the 2000s, it is possible to say that the question of how to manage the aftermath is as important as how to achieve the revival. It is noteworthy to keep in mind that, during the revival, identity is re-defined among different and often rival groups. An entire negotiation process is set in motion to weave a new historical narrative around this newly defined identity. The struggles for sub-identities such as Alevism or Dersim Alevism[8] under the category of national identity to express themselves as a distinct category are directly related to how Turkishness is defined. For this reason, the demands formalised by the Alevi movement during the revival process are persistently confounded within the context of how to define Alevism. These discussions are no doubt important for everyone. It should not be forgotten that the demands for rights (equal citizenship, as defined by the Alevi movement) that were voiced during the revival have legitimacy also beyond discussions about the definition of Alevism.

Bibliography

Albayrak, H. (2010). We Thought It was Dersim, but It Turned out to be Tunceli! *Yeni Şafak*. 15 September.

Albayrak, Ö. (2010). Dersim: Stockholm Syndrome of Alevis. *Yeni Şafak*. 17 October.

Aslan, S., ed. (2010). *Herkesin Bildiği Sır: Dersim*. Istanbul. İletişim.

Ayata, B., and Hakyemez, S. (2013). The AKP's Engagement with Turkey's Past Crimes: An Analysis of PM Erdoğan's 'Dersim Apology'. *Dialectical Anthropology*, 37, 131–43.

Aygün, H. (n. d.a). *Türkiye Büyük Millet Meclisi*, Website. [Viewed 3 February 2021]. Available from: http://www.tbmm.gov.tr/develop/owa/milletvekillerimiz_sd.bilgi?p_donem=23&p_sicil=6486

Aygün, H. (n. d.b). *Türkiye Büyük Millet Meclisi,* Website. [Viewed 3 February 2021]. Available from: http://www.tbmm.gov.tr/develop/owa/milletvekillerimiz_sd.bilgi?p_donem=24&p_sicil=6826

Aygün, H. (2006a). A Live Witness of Dersim 1938. *Birgün*. 29 December.

Aygün, H. (2006b). Dersim Lost Its 'Ancient Wise Tree'. *Birgün*. 20 July.

---

[8] See Gezik and Gültekin (2019), Goner (2017) and Goner and Rebello (2017) for analyses of Dersim Alevism.

Aygün, H. (2007a). *Eve Tarixe Ho Teri Amaene*. İstanbul: Tij.

Aygün, H. (2007b). Villagers have been Tried in Military Court. Birgün. 19 August.

Aygün, H. (2007c). Armenians and the Concept of 'Us'. Birgün. 29 August.

Aygün, H. (2007d). The Righteous Fear of Alevis. Birgün. 4 December.

Aygün, H. (2007e). Confronting a Different History. Birgün. 23 January.

Aygün, H. (2007f). Dersim: A Clean Page of 1915. Birgün. 5 March.

Aygün, H. (2007g). Mistakes Learned from the Past. Birgün. 19 November.

Aygün, H. (2009a). *Dersim 1938 ve Zorunlu İskan*. İstanbul: Arketip.

Aygün, H. (2009b). A Letter on Dersim to the Prime Minister. Birgün. 22 November.

Aygün H. (2011). *0.0.1938: Resmiyet ve Hakikat*. Ankara: Dipnot.

Bakıner, O. (2014). Can the 'Spirit of Gezi' Transform Progressive Politics in Turkey? In: Özkırımlı, U., ed., *The Making of a Protest Movement in Turkey: #occupygezi*. London: Palgrave Pivot. pp. 65–76.

Birgün (2009). Bu Söz CHP'yi Dersim'de Bitirdi. *Birgün* [online]. 11 November. [Viewed 1 March 2021]. Available from: http://www.birgun.net/haber-detay/bu-soz-chp-yi-dersim-de-bitirdi-49369.html

Cansun, S. (2013). Türkiye'de Aleviler ve Siyasi Partiler İlişkisi: Cumhuriyet Gazetesi Üzerinden bir İnceleme. *Sosyal ve Beşeri Bilimler Dergisi*. 5(2), 453–65.

Dilşa, D. (2020). Re-Assessing the Genocide of Kurdish Alevis in Dersim, 1937–38. *Genocide Studies and Prevention: An International Journal*, 14(2), 20–43.

Doğancan, O. (2019). Türkiye'de Bir Yeni-Belediyecilik Filizi: Komünist Başkan'ın Zaferi. *Kent Akademisi*, 12(4), 657–69.

Emre Cetin, K. B. (2018). Television and the Making of a Transnational Alevi Identity. *National Identities*, 20(1), 91–103.

Federal Office for Migration and Refugees in Germany (2009). *Muslim Life in Germany: A Study Conducted on Behalf of the German Conference of Islam* [online]. [Viewed 3 February 2021]. Available from: http://www.npdata.be/Data/Godsdienst/Duitsland/fb6-muslimisches-leben-englisch.pdf

Gezik, E., and Gültekin, A. K., eds (2019). *Kurdish Alevis and the Case of Dersim: Historical and Contemporary Insights*. New York: Lexington Books.

Goner, O. (2017). *Turkish National Identity and Its Outsiders: Memories of State Violence in Dersim*. London: Routledge.

Goner, O., and Rebello, J. (2017). State Violence, Nature, and Primitive Accumulation: Dispossession in Dersim, *Dialectical Anthropology*, 41(1), 33–54.

Greve, M. (2020). Miracles and Tears. Religious Music in Dersim/Tunceli. In: Greve, M., Özdemir, U., and Motika, R., eds, *Aesthetic and Performative Dimensions of Alevi Cultural Heritage*. Würzburg: Ergon Verlag. pp.103–32.

Hürriyet (2010a). Başbakan: Türkiye'yi Başkalarına Benzetmeyin. *Hürriyet* [online]. 1 June. [Viewed 1 March 2021]. Available from: http://www.hurriyet.com.tr/basbakan-turkiyeyi-baskalarina-benzetmeyin-14901622

Hürriyet (2010b). Erdoğan: Dersim'i CHP Bombaladı. *Hürriyet* [online]. 14 August. [Viewed 1 March 2021]. Available from: http://www.hurriyet.com.tr/erdogan-dersimi-chp-bombaladi-15555270

Hürriyet (2009). Kılıçdaroğlu: Öymen Gereğini Yapsın. *Hürriyet* [online]. 16 November. [Viewed 1 March 2021]. Available from: http://www.hurriyet.com.tr/kilicdaroglu-oymen-geregini-yapsin-12957003

Jenkins, C., Aydin, S., and Cetin, U., eds (2018). *Alevism as an Ethno-Religious Identity: Contested Boundaries.* London: Routledge.

Kamış, M. (2010). Falling in Love with the Executor. *Zaman.* 8 August.

Lord, C. (2017). Rethinking the Justice and Development Party's 'Alevi Openings'. *Turkish Studies,* 18(2), 278–96.

ODTÜ SFK (2014). Ovacık'ı Komünistlerin Kazandığını Duyunca Tayyip. [online]. Ankara: ODTÜ SFK. [Viewed 31 March 2021]. Available from: https://www.youtube.com/watch?v=2MpmFQoJARU

Orhan, G. (2020). Remembering a Massacre: How Did the Rise of Oral History as a Methodology Improve Dersim Studies? *Wrocławski Rocznik Historii Mówionej,* 9, 95–118.

Özkul, D. (2015). Alevi 'Openings' and Politicization of the 'Alevi Issue' During the AKP Rule. *Turkish Studies,* 16(1), 80–96.

Sözen, U. (2019). Culture, Politics and Contested Identity among the' Kurdish' Alevis of Dersim: The Case of the Munzur Culture and Nature Festival. *Journal of Ethnic and Cultural Studies,* 6(1), 63–76.

Tunç, S. (2010). Simons Who Reside in CHP! *Yeni Şafak.* 26 August.

Zırh, B. C., and Akçınar, M. (2013). Derin Bir Kuyu Dersim'e Berlin'den Bakmak. In: Aslan, Ş., Aydın, S., and Hepkon, Z., eds, *Dersim'i Parantez'den Çıkartmak.* Istanbul: İletişim. pp. 43–75.

6

ALEVISM AS A 'MAJORITY': ALEVI AND SUNNI COMMUNITIES IN DERSIM

AHMET KERİM GÜLTEKİN

Introduction: An Alternative Understanding of Alevism[1]

As elaborated in Chapter 2 in this volume, the term 'Alevism' should be considered in the context of Turkey's modernisation processes throughout the twentieth century.[2] Alevism today refers to different ethno-religious groups, located from the Balkans to the Middle East. Discourses on Alevi identity presented in the literature are mostly guided by preconceptions reflecting an understanding of Alevism as the religion or socio-cultural reality of a victimised minority. These include the idea that Alevis have always been subject to oppression and discrimination; yet, despite this, they managed to preserve their beliefs and worldviews. Therefore, the Alevis have maintained a dissident and rebellious attitude in the face of oppression,[3] which led to

[1] This chapter is a revised part of the author's MA thesis (submitted to the Department of Social Anthropology and Ethnology, Ankara University, in 2007), which focuses on ethno-political aspects of ethno-religious identities in Dersim. The thesis was published by Berfin publications; see Gültekin (2010). The data used in this chapter were obtained through fieldwork conducted in Dersim (Tunceli) and Elazığ between November 2005 and August 2006.

[2] See also Dressler (2013).

[3] For examples of this see Zelyut (1990), Köksal (2006) and Öz (2008).

an alliance with the Kemalist Revolution.[4] Furthermore, Alevism is generally considered a rural culture, with the consequence that the comparison of rural and urban forms of Alevism produces descriptions of urban or modern Alevi practices as examples of the dissolution of 'authentic rural Alevism'. Although this does reflect a determining aspect of reality, it is possible to present an alternative interpretation, based on the unique character of the Alevis in the province of Tunceli (in connection with the historical background of Dersim).

The scholarship on Alevi Kurds in Turkey has grown over the last three decades (see Gezik and Gültekin 2019, Cetin et al. 2018, 2020). The politicisation of Alevism and Kurdishness has also increased the visibility of Kurdish Alevis. In this context, Tunceli comes to the fore with a new Kurdish Alevi identity, with similarities with other Alevi communities and specific oral traditions, sacred place (*jiare*) practices, religious organisations, discourses and rituals. Nowadays, Kurdish Alevis mostly define themselves as Kurds, but their cultural heritage features many differences from other Kurdish communities (Gültekin 2019, pp. 3–6; Gezik 2014, pp. 19–45). The purpose of this chapter is to understand Alevism (as associated with Kurdish identity) in Tunceli where – in relation to the Sunni population – Alevis constitute the majority. This approach will present an alternative picture of the relations between Alevi and Sunni communities.

The Distribution of Alevi and Sunni Communities in Tunceli

Tunceli (Dersim) is a province where both identities are uniquely combined, and Kurdish Alevi (Kırmancki- and Kurmanci-speaking)[5] communities constitute the majority of the population. Tunceli is located in the Eastern Anatolia region and surrounded by high mountains, as well as big dam lakes. I assume that these mountains and lakes create a kind of psychological boundary for Alevi Kurds. The Munzur Mountains cover its western and northern borders,

---

[4] For a critical analysis of these views, see also Massicard (2013, pp. 140–50).

[5] The heated debate between those who claim that Kurmanci and Kırmancki are different dialects of Kurdish and those who hold that they are entirely different languages (Kurdish and Zazaki, respectively) continues. On one side of the debate stand those who dissociated themselves from Kurdish nationalism and described Kırmancki and its various dialects as Zazaki, whereas the other side is mainly comprised of certain foreign linguists with their own theses. For sources supporting each view, see Bulut (2002), Keskin (2010, pp. 221–45) and Gezik (2014, pp. 19–32).

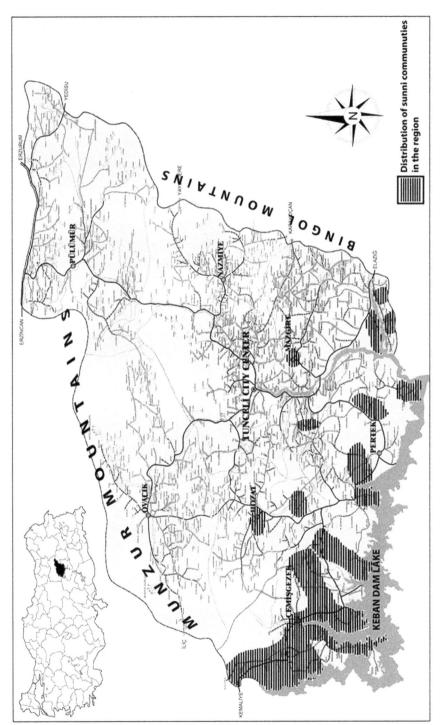

Map 6.1   Distribution of Sunni communities in Tunceli

the Bingöl Mountains delimit the east, and the Keban Dam Lake completes this circle to the south. I have named this province 'Inner Dersim' in my previous studies (Gültekin 2010, p. 35).[6] Inner Dersim has been the geographical, historical and religious centre of all Alevi Kurdish tribes. It is still important according to their cosmology and ritual practices. In particular, Inner Dersim's other names are *Jaru Diyar* (Land of Sacred Place) or *Herdu Dewres* (Land of Dervishes) in Kırmancki. These terms refer to a cultural identity that belongs to a special region, which for Alevi Kurds is inherited through both ancestral ties and secret religious knowledge.[7]

The way in which Alevi and Sunni communities are settled throughout the region is worthy of attention. The settlement pattern is connected to the province's geography, in relation to a 'highly mountainous north' and a relatively 'bottomland south', where one can find the local Sunni[8] villages.[9] This

[6] The term 'Inner Dersim' refers to those regions where Alevis who speak Kırmancki and define their religious identity as *Raa Haq* (literally, 'the way of truth') are demographically and socioculturally dominant. It is possible to regard Inner Dersim as the core of a vast region encompassing the lands inhabited by Kurdish Alevis who speak both Kurmanci and Kırmancki, and as the religious and social centre of these communities. For a substantial guide on the ethnocultural, religious, historical and social aspects of Dersim, see Gezik and Gültekin (2019), Gezik (2014) and Deniz (2012).

[7] For detailed information about the religious terms of Kurdish Alevis, see Gezik and Çakmak (2010) and Çakmak (2013).

[8] There exist no official data regarding the number of Alevis and Sunnis in the province of Tunceli. However, I was able to identify and mark some Sunni villages during my fieldwork (see Map 6.1). These data depend on my personal experience as well as my field notes. I estimate that Sunnis constitute a maximum of 7 to 10 per cent of the population of Tunceli. According to Tunceli's last census data in 2020, the current population is 84,660. See Tunceli Nüfusu (2020). However, this population also includes other Sunnis who were not born in Tunceli, such as military officials and civil officers of the state, their families and the majority of the students of Munzur University. With the term 'local Sunnis', I refer to the Sunni population who originate from the villages and district centres of the province and who speak Kurmanci or Turkish. Hereafter, I use the terms 'Sunni' or 'local Sunni' to refer to these communities exclusively. For more information about the increasing population of 'new' Sunni groups in the province and its effects on daily social life, see Gültekin and Yeşiltepe (2015, pp. 108–19).

[9] According to data obtained from fieldwork, in the past some Sunni communities attempted to settle in the northern and eastern districts of Pülümür and Nazımiye, but because Kurdish Alevis dominated these areas, they failed to do so and were forced to migrate. See also Deniz (2012, pp. 46–47). However, one can still find some Sunni families in the district centre of Hozat and even in Pülümür.

is an area ranging from the southwestern part of the province to the south-eastern part, aligned with the borderline of the dam lake of Keban, in the districts of Çemisgezek, Pertek and Mazgirt. Besides this general pattern of settlement, Sunnis can even be found in a village in Hozat, which is the old-est administrative centre of Dersim. The Sunnis of Tunceli province mostly speak Kurmanci, and a few of them have spoken Turkish for generations. However, after the *coup d'état* of 1980, under the Turkish state's immense nationalist pressure, the 'Kurdish language' lost its visibility in the public space and was replaced by Turkish. Interestingly, most of these Sunni com-munities are connected to the Kadiri sects of Islam, which base themselves on the notion of love towards the Prophet's family and especially his cousin Ali, as do Alevis. Moreover, they share sacred place practices with their Kurdish Alevi neighbours (Gültekin 2010, pp. 125–35).

The district of Çemisgezek in the southwestern part of the province is home to the largest community of Sunnis in Tunceli, who constitute three-quarters of the district's population. The way in which Sunni and Alevi settle-ments are distributed throughout the district bears a resemblance to how the settlements of these communities have spread throughout the province. The majority of the Alevi communities in the area resides in the mountain-ous territories in the northeastern part of the district. Nevertheless, it is also possible to come across Alevi communities in various rural settlements near the district centre and the southern regions. It must be mentioned that there is a crucial distinction between Alevi communities in Çemisgezek. Those residing in the mountainous villages and hamlets[10] of the northeast speak Kırmancki and therefore have stronger ties and cultural affinities to Inner Dersim, whereas the Alevis in the southwestern and southeastern parts of the district speak Kurmanci (Gültekin 2010, pp. 125–35).

The district of Pertek has the second-largest population of Sunnis. It con-stitutes a region of the southern border of Dersim, and nearly a quarter of the population is Sunni. Here, most of the Sunni communities are found in the western and southern parts of the region. There are only a few villages and hamlets in the district inhabited by Sunnis exclusively. They mostly live side by side with Alevis. However, in the district centre and the villages, the Sunni and Alevi neighbourhoods are usually separate. Through the specific

---

[10] A hamlet consists of a few houses and is administratively related to a village.

names of these neighbourhoods, these communities create a kind of spatial differentiation, and this practice of discernment can be understood as a way of strengthening their identities (Gültekin 2010, pp. 125–35).

The district of Mazgirt, on the southeastern border of Tunceli, is home to the third-largest Sunni community in the city. They reside in the township of Akpazar, in the southeastern part of the district. In Mazgirt, there are almost no townships, villages, or hamlets with an exclusively Sunni population. According to my fieldwork, it seems that the only settlement with a homogenous Sunni community is a village in the township of Akpazar. In the district centre and other settlements with Sunni residents, the population is mixed. And within Akpazar, Sunnis are mostly concentrated in the southern regions, encompassing the township centre. In other parts of the district, communities are predominantly Alevi (Gültekin 2010, pp. 125–35).

The last district in Dersim (Tunceli) with a Sunni population is Hozat. Some Sunni families live in the district centre; moreover, the village of Inciga (Altınçevre) in the southern township of Çaglarca, which borders on Çemisgezek and Pertek, is home to a Sunni community. The district centre has a mixed population, and Alevis are in the majority. While the village of Inciga also presents a mixed settlement, the majority there is Sunni. Compared to the other Sunni inhabited districts of Tunceli, Hozat has the lowest number of Sunni residents (Gültekin 2010, pp. 125–35).

A Short History of Sunni Communities in Dersim

Dersim (including present-day Tunceli) became an administrative province as late as 1880. Before that, some of the districts currently within the province (such as Çemişgezek, Çarsancak [Akpazar], Mazgirt, Pertek, Kuzuçan, Ovacık, Pah and Kızılkilise)[11] were parts of other, larger provinces in the area (Yılmazçelik and Erdem 2017, pp. 223–43).[12] Because of the region's political

---

[11] As a look at the administrative and social history of Dersim proves, these districts and townships are settlements with far-reaching historical roots. Throughout history, they have constituted important administrative and commercial centres. They had originally been located in the foothills of the Murat River Valley before the region was submerged by the Keban Dam Lake.

[12] See also Yılmazçelik (2011), Gül (2015, pp. 23–54) and Yıldırım (2012, pp. 23–37).

and military instability, these regions' administrative status was subject to constant change. With the declaration of the *Tanzimat* in 1839, the Ottoman state's policies towards the eastern territories changed. The state intensified its policy of intervention in the Dersim region. The reforms aimed to transform the administrative structure of the region. Military operations were conducted to end the autonomous structure of the Kurdish Alevi tribes. In this period, the area's economic centres, located in the southwestern, southern and southeastern regions of the province, gained importance. The spheres of influence of Çemisgezek, Pertek and Mazgirt waxed and waned as a result of the relationship that the Ottoman state formed with the tribes of Inner Dersim. It can be said that the Ottoman state, with the change of its eastern policies after the declaration of the *Tanzimat*, started to view Dersim as a constant threat to public order and state rule (Yıldırım 2018, pp. 59–69). The strained relationship, often marked by clashes between the above-mentioned district centres and the inner regions to the north of Dersim, continued for nearly a century, until 1938. Historical changes in areas with Sunni communities can be better understood in light of this relationship.

Administrative reports in the Ottoman Archives of the Prime Ministry clearly show that, during the second half of the nineteenth century and the first half of the twentieth century, districts with a high concentration of Sunnis were, in fact, the commercial and social hubs of the province. Despite the confrontations between the two communities, commercial relations continued to maintain their significance during this period. The mines in Elazığ, to the south of the province, and, to a lesser extent, those in Diyarbakır and even further south were one of the main motivations for trade. The charcoal essential for these mines' functioning came from present-day Pertek and Mazgirt. Those engaged in mining activities were exempt from various local taxes, as they were under constant threat of raids by the tribes of Inner Dersim (Yılmazçelik 1998, p. 175).

Apart from mining, artisans' production and local animal and agricultural products were other important pillars of commercial life. Almost all such productive activities took place in the southern district centres, mostly inhabited by Sunnis. In the Inner Dersim regions inhabited by Kurdish Alevi tribes, geographic conditions made the land unsuitable for agriculture. This, combined with the constant raids and skirmishes between the various tribes, made the Alevis of the north dependent on the south's commercial markets. The limited amount of arable land in the province lies mostly within Çemisgezek, Pertek and Mazgirt.[13] Also, small land ownership and 'share-cropping'[14] were general practices in these lands. This led to a perpetual increase in the number of landless peasants, and over time residents were forced to emigrate. This was one of the most important determinants of population movements in the region.[15] Similar processes continued with ever-increasing intensity throughout the twentieth century.

Another factor that determined the nature of population movements in the area consisted of armed confrontations, which lasted from the second half of the nineteenth century until 1938. After thirty years of intermission, these confrontations recommenced in the 1970s and have continued until today. Before World War I, there occurred uprisings in the area, and the state conducted campaigns of suppression. Many Alevi and Christian (Armenian) communities were displaced during this period.[16] Similarly, many Alevi (and even some Sunni) communities were forced to migrate due to the massacre of 1938.[17] Most recently in 1994, as the clashes between the PKK and the state

[13] For a brief study on this 'plunder economy' of Dersim tribes, see Deniz (2013, pp. 71–113).

[14] Share-cropping is a system of production and distribution based on landless peasants selling their labour to land or herd owners in exchange for products. For further information about the pre-republican era of the Dersim economy, see Yıldırım (2013, pp. 41–70).

[15] Yılmazçelik (1998, p. 177) cites an Ottoman document demonstrating that there was another important factor leading to peasants losing their land. Çerçis (hawkers) who came from Iran were crucial to commercial life in the region. They often sold their commodities for a payment deferred for six months, at an extremely high rate of interest. Due to the poor quality of production and the large number of share-croppers, the peasants were often unable to pay the interest rates and had to sell their land for less than what it was worth. Thus, the peasants were left landless and found themselves forced to migrate to larger settlements or other rural areas.

[16] Until 1915, the population of Dersim was dominated by Kurdish Alevi tribes and Armenians. Due to the Armenian genocide and forced migrations, the Armenian population decreased immensely. For a description of how the Ottoman bureaucracy saw the Alevis and the Armenians as collaborators, see Akpınar (2019) and Kevorkian (2011). For more information about the demographic situation in the pre-republican era of Dersim, see Sertel (2014, pp. 269–82).

[17] For more information about the 1938 massacre and forced evacuations, see Aygün (2009).

intensified, the state forcibly evacuated more than 70 per cent of the villages in Inner Dersim (Jongerden 2001, pp. 80–86). This was the most critical forced migration of the recent history of Dersim, and its consequences have been manifold.

Prior to the Republic's full consolidation in the Dersim region, Sunnis constituted an important population group in Çemisgezek, Pertek and Mazgirt. The decrease in their numbers between 1938 and the 1970s is mostly due to economic reasons. The limited amount of arable land, low level of productivity, the increasingly heavy pressure placed on livelihoods due to population growth and, after the 1950s, migration to the western cities of Turkey and Europe were the fundamental causes of population movements. Between 1938 and the beginning of the 1970s, the Sunnis gradually sold their lands and homes to Alevis from Inner Dersim. Many of them invested the earnings from these transactions in the big cities. Some of them, in contrast, preferred to settle on more fertile lands nearby. All in all, the Sunni population, over the past decades, has been continuously on the decrease (Gültekin 2010, p. 133).

The polarisation and conflicts of the 1970s, mostly based on religious identity, were another important reason behind the Sunnis' migration from Tunceli.[18] These events profoundly impacted particularly the eastern regions of Pertek. For example, the township of Pınarlar and the surrounding villages, mostly inhabited by Sunnis, became utterly deserted after the deadly attack that they had organised against their Alevi neighbours in the late 1970s (Gültekin 2010, pp. 331–36). Today there are only eleven Sunni

---

[18] During the 1960s the struggle for economic, social and political rights in Turkey gradually intensified: eventually, by the 1970s this struggle gave rise to armed revolutionary movements. The most important social basis of such movements was the rural, mostly Alevi, communities who throughout history had generally been at odds with the state. From this period onwards, Tunceli became the most important centre for many armed left-wing movements. One of the state's policies against revolutionary movements in the 1970s was to mobilise Sunni communities against Alevis, with the use of right-wing organisations. Apart from such organisations, which provided an advantage for individuals when it came to accessing political and economic resources, paramilitary organisations such as the Liberation Army of Enslaved Turks (*Esir Türklerin Kurtuluş Ordusu*, ETKO) and the Turkish Revenge Brigade (*Türk İntikam Tugayı*, TIT) were formed. The outcome was violent attacks perpetrated by both sides, and eventually the Sunni communities were forced to migrate from Tunceli *en masse*. For more information, see Gültekin (2010, pp. 306–41).

households in Pınarlar, and most of the settlements in the area are home to mixed communities.

Another factor contributing to the decrease of the Sunni population in the province, especially in the southern regions, was the evacuation of the villages on the Murat River banks due to the opening of the Keban Dam in the 1970s. The evacuation of these flooded villages also opened the floodgates for further southward migrations from Inner Dersim. This, together with the armed clashes and the large-scale Maraş and Çorum massacres of Alevis in the 1970s, strengthened the already existing conflicts between the Alevi and Sunni communities in the region and accelerated the migration process of Sunnis (Gültekin 2010, pp. 125–44).

Sunnis' migration had relatively lost its impetus in the 1980s, but it intensified once again in the 1990s, with the resurgence of armed conflict. This state of war, whose significance to the history of Dersim is comparable to the events of 1938, has shaped the current geographic distribution of Sunni communities in the region (Bruinessen 1995). It has also dramatically influenced how both Sunni and Alevi identities are perceived in Dersim. One example of the migrations of the 1990s is the high number of Sunnis. They once lived in the villages and hamlets to the east of Pertek but migrated to other areas during this period. However, with the intervention of the Turkish state, they were eventually forced to return. Quite a large number of them did, however, settle in the neighbouring provinces, mainly Elazığ. Alternatively, many Alevis from Inner Dersim settled in the Pertek district centre. While the district's Sunni residents continued to stay, the Sunni population in the rural settlements to the east decreased significantly (Gültekin 2010, pp. 336–57).

Descriptions and Self-descriptions among Alevis and Sunnis: *Barmazlı*, Turk and Kurd

A brief look into the complex subject of ethnic boundaries and the definitions that the communities in southern Tunceli produce about each other could help us understand the social relations between Alevis and Sunnis. For example, the terms that Alevis in Tunceli use to describe Sunnis living in the rural areas in the eastern parts of Pertek are worthy of consideration. Among the names they use to describe the Sunnis in the area, '*Barmazlı*' is the most common. This expression is also used by most Sunnis who live in rural settlements in the area and implies that the person is 'different from Alevis' – in other words, the person is Sunni. While the term means the same thing for Alevis, both groups have different explanations regarding the origin of this identity.

Alevi communities affiliated with the Pilvenk, the dominant tribe in the region, live side by side with the *Barmazlıs*; according to them, this identity describes Alevis who, over time, have become Sunnis. In this context, Alevis find it natural that the Sunnis of the area participate in certain Alevi rituals (although this was more common before the 1980s). They believe that one can explain these Sunnis' continuing visitation at Alevi shrines and other sacred places only in light of their Alevi heritage. Another important indicator of their Alevi origin is that these communities (at least the older generations) maintain the *kirvelik*[19] relations with Alevis.

For Alevis, the question of how the *Barmazlıs* became Sunni is an important one. *Barmazlıs* speak Kurmanci. They pursue livelihoods similar to those of the Alevis' in the region. They worship the same sacred places, love Ali and his descendants, tell their stories (that is, they read *Cenkname*s)[20] and sometimes even consult Alevi institutions and religious authorities, such as *cem* rituals and *pir*s. Hence, there should be an explanation about these communities' religious differences. Alevis usually describe this process as one where a people who are 'deep down Alevis' gradually became Sunni through external interventions. According to this narrative, Sunnis who 'came' or were 'brought' to the region from outside of Dersim made this 'subsequent Sunnification' possible because, while Dersim identity is conceptualised based on both Alevism and Kurdishness, it directly refers to

---

[19] In terms of *Raa Haqi* (Dersim Alevism), *kirvelik* is a fictional kinship, or can be considered a godfather relationship between two families. It is also a crucial institution for social solidarity in the region, based on male circumcision. This kinship brings sexual taboos, so that marriages are forbidden between *kirvelik* families. *Kirvelik* relations between Alevis and Sunnis in the region are likely to refer to political alliances or patronage relations rather than its religious aspects. See Gültekin (2010, pp. 173–200). For general information, see Kudat (2004); for a focus on social roles among Kurdish communities, see Strohmeier and Yalçın-Heckmann (2013).

[20] *Cenkname*s are epic texts on Ali and his sons' (Hasan and Hüseyin) war stories, favoured among both Alevis and Sunnis who follow the Kadiri creeds.

the Kurdish Alevi belief system (*Raa Haqi*),[21] which could only be inherited by birth. Hence, the conceptualisation of 'subsequent Sunnification' carries extremely negative connotations, as in this way of thinking it allows for only two options: either they must have broken the sacred bond (*ikrar*) of Alevism, or they must have been forcibly Sunnified. This approach is the basic justification for all negative opinions on local Sunnis.

The concept of '*Barmazlı*' is, quite interestingly, virtually unheard of in areas outside the territory of the Pilvenk tribe, and especially in Inner Dersim. During my fieldwork, most Alevis residing in Inner Dersim were quite surprised to hear of local Sunnis living in Dersim. Upon hearing of their existence, they immediately started asking questions. This stems from the fact that *Dersimli* identity is seen as synonymous with Alevism, as well as the perception of Kurdishness associated with it.[22]

Alevis and Sunnis in the region are divided across religious identity lines, and they also define each other by referring to modern national identities – that is, Turkish and Kurdish. Alevis quite commonly use the term 'Turk' when referring to 'Sunni'. Thus, they regard the Sunnis of rural and urban Pertek as Turks. At this point, *Barmazlı* identity gains a second meaning.

---

[21] *Raa Haqi* (in Kırmancki, Path of Truth) or Dersim Alevism are both relatively new terms to explain the unique properties of the belief system of Kurdish Alevis. In this belief system, the religious relationship between *ocak*s and *talip*s is organised into four major social positions. From bottom to top, first, there are the *talip*s, the objects of holy lineages. They speak mostly Kırmancki, but there are also Kurmanci- and Turkish-speaking *talip*s of *ocak*s. Second, there are the *rayber*s, members of holy lineages; these can be considered local, practical guides of religious affairs. Third, there are the *pir*s (or *seyit*s) who hold the key role in the religious system. They are the spiritual guides of their objects. Fourth, the *mürşid*s are also members of holy lineages, like the *pir*s. They hold a type of master or juridical position of other *ocak*s, who obey them. *Rayber*, *pir* and *mürşid* are positions held only by holy lineages, and these *ocak*s share similar obligatory relationships, like those between *talip*s and *pir*s. All these positions are legitimised based on paternal hereditary principles. Another central aspect of *Raa Haqi* consists of the beliefs and practices shaped around the sacred places and objects called *jiare* (in Kırmancki) or *ziyaret* (in Turkish). For more detailed information about the Kurdish Alevi belief system, see Gezik and Çakmak (2010), Deniz (2012), Çakmak (2013), Gezik (2014), Deniz (2019) and Gültekin (2019).

[22] For more information on terms such as Turk, Kurd, Zaza and Kırmanc (or *aşiret*), see Gültekin (2010, pp. 49–74), Fırat (2010, pp. 139–55) and Gezik (2014, pp. 26–32).

When Sunnis are referred to as Turks, *Barmazlı* refers to those who live in the countryside and are engaged in livelihood practices similar to those of Alevis. Hence, the expression *Barmazlı* is important to distinguish those Sunnis who have come to Pertek or Elazığ from the countryside.

As for Sunnis, the origins of the *Barmazlı* identity are quite clear. Barmaz (or Behrimaz) is the name of a plain located near the Maden district of the province of Elazığ, whence they originally hailed. Thus, they named themselves (or were named by others) after their place of origin. The *Barmazlıs* find the idea that they should be Alevis who have been Sunnified over time unacceptable. Quite the contrary, they believe that the majority of Alevis are the descendants of Turcoman (Turkish) tribes who settled in the region centuries ago and eventually became Alevicised (in other words, 'Kurdified') (Gültekin 2010, pp. 155–63).[23]

Sunnis' explanations regarding Alevis also vary from generation to generation. For instance, older Sunnis living in the rural settlements east of Pertek use the terms '*aşiret*' (tribe)[24] or 'Kurd' when referring to Alevis. Among younger generations (underage or middle-aged) living in Pertek or Elazığ, the terms used remain the same, but now they have political implications whose roots can be traced back to the 1970s. In this context, being 'Kurdish' or *aşiret* is synonymous with having 'left-wing views' and 'being against the state' – in other words, 'being the political enemy'. In a way, Sunnis view those communities

---

[23] In the years following my fieldwork, the *Barmazlıs* formed an association, located in the city centre of Elazığ. Their main arguments about *Barmazlı* identity are the following: they are descendants of the famous archaic Turkish tribe of the Oğuzlar; they settled in Tunceli (in the Çemişgezek and Pertek districts) from Erzurum; they are renowned in the region for their religiosity (in terms of Sunni Islam) and interest in education; and they are good neighbours to the Alevis. Moreover, they also used the forced evacuations, which seriously affected them after the 1980 *coup d'état* (due to armed conflicts in the region), as one of their main arguments to clarify ethnic boundaries. This comes in relation to their nationalist and religious 'loyalty', which they describe by the motto 'Motherland-Flag-Nation'. For an extremely striking manifestation of the dominant perception regarding the cultural identity of Dersim's Sunni communities, see Tunceli Nüfusu (2020).

[24] Until the late twentieth century, Kurdish Alevis mostly led a semi-nomadic life-style, and their settlements were located in rural mountainous areas. For social and religious tribal organisations, see Gezik (2014, pp. 45–55), Deniz (2012, pp. 52–82) and Gültekin (2019).

who identify themselves as Alevi or Kurdish as people who have been alienated from their true identities (Gültekin 2010, pp. 289–302).

These opposing perceptions of Turkishness and Kurdishness demonstrate that the people of the region associate themselves with political codes of identity. This could be considered a consequence of the uses of Turkishness and Kurdishness as categories of ethnicity in Turkey. They became more commonplace in the 1970s in Tunceli, Elazığ, Sivas, Maraş and Malatya, where particularly (Kurmanci- and Kırmancki-speaking) Alevis from Dersim live together with Sunnis.[25] The meaning associated with these terms has displayed a certain variety and continues to do so. Nonetheless, it can be said that there exist two general trends. The Turkish nationalist discourse, which is dominant among Sunnis residing in Tunceli, sees Turkish and Sunni identities as inseparable elements defining each other. Moreover, it claims that Alevis are Turcoman communities who have gradually become Kurdified. Interestingly, this discourse differentiates the Kurds of Dersim from the Kurds of the east and southeast because of their Alevi identity. Furthermore, the Turkish nationalist discourse, presently dominant throughout Turkey, marginalises the Kurmanci- and Kırmancki-speaking communities of Dersim, be they Sunni or Alevi. However, the Turkish nationalist discourse prevalent among local Sunnis perceives the Alevis of Dersim as leftist and secular. This discerning description emanates from the fact that they, too, 'are from Dersim'. To clarify, the Kurds are mostly Sunni, but in Tunceli this Sunni identity happens to be the only factor that determines 'Turkishness'.

However, being a Sunni plays a diametrically opposed role to the Alevi – or, in other words, Kurdish – identity in Dersim. Therefore, the differentiation between 'their own Kurds' (who are Alevi) and the other Kurds (who are Sunni) draws the borders of a cultural space dividing the Sunni community as well. The Sunnis of Tunceli identify themselves as Turkish, whereas other Sunnis in the wider region identify themselves as Kurdish. In sum, the relationship that the Sunnis of Tunceli have with the Alevis of Dersim is what

---

[25] The Alevi massacres in the 1970s may help to understand how the usage of Turkish and Kurdish ethnic definitions in relation to religious differences started. Moreover, Turkish and Kurdish nationalist interests in Alevis are important regarding their political and historical discourses. See Ağuiçenoğlu (2010, pp. 119–39), Ertan (2017, pp. 123–73) and Massicard (2007, pp. 58–67).

gives meaning to the perception of Turkishness in the province. Therefore, for the Sunnis of Tunceli, the Kurds of the east and southeast, even though they share a common religious identity, signify a far more distant identity than their Alevi neighbours whom they, nonetheless, marginalise.

At the same time, the Kurdish nationalist discourse in Tunceli claims that the Kurmanci-speaking Sunni communities of Dersim have been assimilated (in other words, Turkified) due to the state's Turco-Islamic cultural interventions. The language spoken by Sunni communities constitutes the basis of this argument. Moreover, various aspects of Sunni daily life in the region are regarded as proof of their connection to Kurdish culture. All in all, the Sunni identification with Turkish identity is based on the divide between the basic religious identities of Alevism and Sunnism. This continues to be the dominant viewpoint on the matter. The following words of a Sunni interviewee clarify my point:

> We speak Kurmanci. Our culture is Kurdish. But ever since we first came here, we have been called Turks. They forced the name on us; they never accepted us as Kurds. Yet, the generation before us cannot speak a word of Turkish.[26]

Kurdish and Turkish identities are built on this distinction. For either side, Kurdishness and Turkishness constitute an entire group, which they perceive as the 'other', depending on their group affiliation. For example, Alevis refer to *Barmazlı*s as well as Sunnis from Pertek or other regions of Dersim as 'Turks'. Likewise, Sunnis use the general identifier 'Kurd' to describe all Alevis, regardless of their tribal affiliation.

'Alevi', 'Kurd' and *aşiret* are the most popular terms used by Sunnis to describe Alevis. However, there exist important distinctions between the Kırmancki-speaking Alevis of Inner Dersim and the Kurmanci-speaking Alevis who live near Sunni communities in the south. For Sunnis, the most important term that differentiates neighbouring Alevis from the complex entirety is the term *kirve*. The expressions *kirve*[27] and 'neighbour' display

---

[26] Field notes from a conversation with a Sunni interviewee, Elazığ, dated 22 April 2006.

[27] Here, the term *kirve* refers to a specific (closer) degree of social relations between Alevi and Sunni families. Sunnis categorise the Alevis according to the social, political and economic relations they have with them.

the Sunnis' level of social relations with the Alevis by way of this definition. The vast majority that remains outside of this description is dubbed 'Kurd', 'Alevi' and *aşiret*.

When describing themselves, Sunnis emphasise that they have no tribal (*aşiret*) affiliations. This is used to underline an important cultural characteristic that distinguishes them from the Alevis surrounding them. Identifying themselves according to their place of origin (as seen with the *Barmazlı*s) serves as example of such a characteristic. For instance, while Alevis use the term *Barmazlı* to describe all Sunnis living in Pertek, some Sunnis claim that their roots are different from that of the *Barmazlı*s. The *Hasananlı* Sunnis, for instance, say that they originally came from the village of Hasanlı, in the Hınıs region of Bingöl. According to this narrative, the *Hasananlı*s had initially settled in Inner Dersim, but could not withstand the pressure from Alevi tribes and were forced to migrate to areas with *Barmazlı* settlements. Since Alevis widely use the term *Barmazlı* in the region, these differences among Sunnis bear no relevance in their daily interactions with Alevis. This situation also points to a type of relationship long accepted by Sunnis. Such intra-community differences are sub-identities which, despite their importance, can only be identified 'from the inside' and reveal themselves only in social relations within the community (Gültekin 2010, pp. 155–63).

Co-existence and Power Relations between Alevis and Sunnis: *Kirvelik* Relations and *Cem* Ceremonies

Within the borders of Tunceli, I estimate that Alevis constitute more than 90 per cent of the population. In other words, the Alevis are 'in power'. Nonetheless, this 'power' emanates from being the majority in demographic terms, not in administrative terms. The unequal demographic distribution of Alevis and Sunnis has led to relations of power that have, throughout history, varied in form and content. In my view, both Alevis and Sunnis have taken advantage of some religious institutions (such as *kirvelik* relations and *cem* ceremonies) or authorities (such as *pir*s or *baba*s)[28] for their

---

[28] Similar to the *talip-pir* relations among Kurdish Alevis, there exists a *mürit-baba* relationship among Kadiri Sunni communities. For more information concerning the *baba*s and their *mürit*s among the Tunceli Sunnis, see Gültekin (2010, pp. 144–55).

economic, political and safety-related benefits. As a matter of course, Sunnis living among the Alevi majority sought the advantages of possessing strong patronage relationships with Alevi families and the help of Alevi religious authorities, and much more. In this regard, when looking at the nature of such power relations, we can speak of two different periods: before and after the 1970s, when Alevis and Sunnis became politically polarised. Nevertheless, some Alevi institutions seemed to be presented as conflict-solving mechanisms, until the politicisation of religious identities.

In this sense, the *kirvelik* institution gains noticeable importance. For example, by forming *kirvelik* bonds with an Alevi family of high economic or social status, Sunnis could gain a strong foothold in the community. Due to the strong and diverse social ties existing among Alevi communities, the scope of these *kirvelik* ties would eventually expand. All Alevi families are connected through patrilineal bonds to larger families in terms of the *aşiret* (tribe). These extended families are in contact with a large number of other families through the ties of *kirvelik* or *musahiplik*.[29] In addition to such attachments, the multi-dimensional and complex tribal and *talip-pir* relations of Alevis were also factors determining the range of their social relationships. When we consider that all these relations existed in the close vicinity of places inhabited by Alevis, we can see that Sunnis' *kirvelik* ties greatly enriched their web of social relationships with the majority. Religious faith is both the source of the *kirvelik* and *musahiplik* relations and the basis of their enforcement. Therefore, the social processes emanating from these relations bore a certain consistency, founded on religion. Because of this, the influence that the Sunnis gained through the *kirvelik* institution was significant for them.

The Sunnis living in the villages and hamlets of Pertek have very much adopted the concepts dominant in the social and religious lives of the Alevi

---

[29] *Musahiplik* is a type of fictive kinship, much like *kirvelik*. However, a Kurdish Alevi can only be a *musahip* to another Kurdish Alevi. Accordingly, choosing a *musahip* from outside the community is impossible. It is an obligatory, institutionalised fictive kinship for all Kurdish Alevis created through a brotherhood of two young unmarried male members of the community. *Musahip* families are to have stronger alliances with each other than with their actual blood relatives. For more information, see Çakmak (2013, pp. 47–66), Deniz (2012, pp. 83–101), Munzuroğlu (2012, pp. 70–71), Gezik and Çakmak (2010, pp. 123–28) and Çem (2011, pp. 68–70).

majority. The reason for this is that they have shared this land, where production is based on agriculture and non-nomadic farming, and all its natural resources (such as forests, rivers, pastures and fields) for centuries. Mutual problems independent of human activity (such as natural disasters) affecting these sources, as well as shared difficulties experienced in the markets where the product gains its exchange value, have brought the two communities together on the mutual basis of 'being members of the peasantry'. This has resulted in the emergence of a common attitude and behaviour patterns regarding various problems. This is precisely why the concept of *Barmazlı*, in comparison to non-*Barmazlı*, carries a more positive connotation for the Alevis of Tunceli. Perhaps the unique examples of these relations are the shared beliefs and rituals related to the existence of various practices of *ziyaret*,[30] sacred to both Alevis and Sunnis. Furthermore, narratives of common religious-social activities sometimes performed under the guidance of *pirs*, and sometimes *babas*, exist among Sunnis.

Until the 1970s, mutual contact between the communities was facilitated through the *cem*, the basis of Alevi religious structure, with the *talip-pir* institution, on one hand, and the Sunni community leaders, known as 'prominent families', on the other. Of course, other religious figures were just as important as the prominent families in Sunni communities: the *babas*. The *pirs* and the *babas* preserved the legitimacy of inter-community competition and communication for centuries (Gültekin 2010, pp. 290–302). The defects in the Turkish Republic's economic and social structure also contributed to the continuation of such feudal actors and institutions.

Additionally, Sunnis did not opt to take advantage of the state institutions. This can also be understood as an indicator of their lack of trust towards the Turkish Republic. Considering the state's view of Turkishness and Sunnism as its founding elements, such an approach would have been wise for the

---

[30] *Jiare* refers to sacred places and holy objects. The integration of natural elements into the religion becomes visible in the ritual of *jiare*, which refers to visiting a holy place such as the grave of a holy *pir*, trees, mountains, rocks, caves, rivers, lakes, water sources and some holy objects (relics) that are kept by holy lineages. *Jiare* cults play an important role in Kurdish Alevis' daily life. For more information about the sacred place cults of Kurdish Alevis, see Gültekin (2004, 2010, 2020), Gezik and Çakmak (2010, pp. 97–98), Çem (2011, pp. 73–101) and Çakmak (2013, pp. 171–76).

Sunnis. However, until the confrontations organised by the state, the Sunnis displayed no such tendency. The reason may have been that Dersim constitutes a region that, despite the constant reform policies put into practice both by the Ottoman Empire and the Republic of Turkey, has maintained its Alevi majority and identity. Thus, one may claim that the general interactions of the Sunni community have been mainly with the Alevi majority. Sharing a common social, economic and religious space with the Alevis has led the Sunnis to accept the majority's authority and institutions.

Even though traditional relations have lost their relevance, due to the dissolving consequences of modernisation and politicisation[31] influencing socio-religious relations, *kirvelik* has maintained its importance. Alevi customary law still organises and sustains local daily life. Evidence shows that Alevi law has gained legitimacy in areas populated by Sunni majorities, such as the district centre of Pertek. Even today, for many Sunni families *kirvelik* constitutes the basis of their inhabitation in rural settlements in Pertek and the surrounding areas.

Apart from *kirvelik* relations, Sunni communities have developed another strategy around the socio-religious institutions (*cem* rituals)[32] of the Alevi majority, which dominated daily life and were strongly re-consolidated in the republican era (after 1938). In this way, they could pressure the problematic individuals or groups through social and religious institutions whose effectiveness far surpassed that of the state. Until this period, Alevi communities'

---

[31] The last decades have witnessed large-scale social transformations among Kurdish Alevis. Over barely a quarter of a century they have expanded worldwide, especially in Western Europe. Their lifestyles have dramatically changed, they have faced forced evacuations, their settlements have been mostly demolished, and their socio-religious organisations have been broken up. However, they are still able to maintain close contacts with their sacred and beloved land, Dersim. Dersim is a powerful symbol, as well as a lively image of this cultural identity. Then again, local Sunnis have also had to leave Tunceli. They were associated with Turkish nationalism as well as Islamist movements by state policies. They gained strong positions in public authorities, possessed economic networks and left behind the old *mürit-baba* religious relations, which they call 'traditional'. As a result, the relations between Alevis and Sunnis gradually weakened. See Gültekin (2010, pp. 135–144).

[32] *Cem* ceremonies in Dersim were practised once a year, during visits by *pirs* of their *talips*. These times were also the chance for Sunnis, if they had any problems with their neighbours, to seek help from their religious authority. See Gültekin (2010, pp. 289–395).

internal issues, especially those in rural areas, were never resolved through state institutions (Korkmaz 2003, p. 125). According to an elderly Alevi interviewee, during the Ottoman period, applying to a *şeriat* court for the resolution of an internal issue was seen as such a heinous crime by Alevis that it was punishable by *düşkünlük* (excommunication). Therefore, in an environment where most of the population refused to acknowledge the state as a tool of reference for resolving intra-community matters, the Sunni minority applied to those institutions that held power over the members of the majority.[33]

For the Sunnis of Pertek, the Alevi majority's dominance has been more limited when compared to the countryside, where the Sunni communities rely on the Alevis' social structure. The relationship between Alevis and Sunnis in the countryside reflects the social institutions of the Alevi majority. In contrast, the Sunni-dominated official institutions and the dominant traditional structure determine commercial and social life in the district centres. This spatial difference came to the fore in various forms in the 1970s.

Concluding Remarks

Until the early twentieth century, Dersim was an Ottoman principality. It was a vast area in eastern Anatolia, dominated mostly by Kurdish Alevi tribes. It covered a cluster of Turkey's present-day eastern provinces, with the province of Tunceli almost at its centre. After the Ottoman-Safavid wars, the region's borders were redrawn several times due to administrative regulations. Eventually, it gained formal status in the nineteenth century and was still renowned for its Kurdish Alevi tribes, who have always been a problem for the state. For almost one-hundred years, a period that ended with the 1937–38 large-scale massacres in Tunceli, Kurdish Alevis gradually lost their dominance in the region.

Yet, Tunceli, which could also be called Inner Dersim, has always been a historical and important religious centre for Kurdish Alevi tribes. It has always been considered a sacred land as well as a stronghold. Until 1938,

---

[33] Nonetheless, it must be stated that this 'local Alevi power' is not related to political subordination. Sunni communities maintain their own internal customary laws, while they rely on the cultural mechanisms of the dominant majority.

Kurdish Alevis held on to tribal social organisation models and maintained a kind of socio-religious caste system between 'holy families' (*ocak* tribes) and subjects (*talip* tribes). They conducted rather complex socio-religious and economic relations within *ocak* tribes and *talip* tribes separately. Tunceli (Inner Dersim) is still the homeland of these *ocak*s. Furthermore, it is the land of sacred places (*jiares*), which are also important pilgrimage sites for Kurdish Alevis today. Accordingly, Kurdish Alevis still refer to this territory as 'sacred land' (*Jaru Diyar* in Kırmancki). Today, Tunceli is the only province of Turkey where the Kurdish Alevi population holds the majority and socially dominates without dispute.

With the rising influence of identity politics, especially the politicisation processes of Alevism in Turkey over the past decades, Tunceli has come to the fore with its controversial historical past. Accordingly, as Zırh shows in Chapter 5 in this volume, the term Dersim has once again become well-known, after a long period of silence. This time, it carries the symbolic significance of Alevism and Kurdishness with a unique ethnic identity in contemporary Turkey. Regarding the ongoing political and military struggle between the Turkish state and Kurdish nationalism, as well as the Alevi movements' ongoing battle for formal recognition, discourses about Dersim have become more noticeable but also highly controversial. In fact, as Zırh highlights in Chapter 5 in this volume, Dersim has become one of the most contentious topics in contemporary Turkish politics.

Religious identities (both Alevi and Sunni) have been determinant aspects of all other ethnic definitions in Tunceli for centuries. After the Turkish Republic's foundation, this differentiation resulted in the labelling of national identities as Turk and Kurd. Nonetheless, Alevi and Sunni identities continue to form the main identity borders for all forms of ethnic belonging. Hence, the situation creates a unique social sphere to understand Alevism as a majority and dominant socio-religious identity. Local Sunnis in Tunceli are a minority, as Turks among Kurds and Sunnis among Alevis; yet they possess a national (major and formal) socio-political identity in Turkey.

Regarding the Alevis' relations with the Sunni minority living among them, some Alevi religious institutions should be examined from this perspective. As we see in the case of Sunnis who live in Pertek, the *cem* institution's social functions are not limited to Alevis only, as once thought. Sunnis are also able to seek juridical considerations regarding their problems, and they are well-received. Furthermore, in some cases, these kinds of relations have also had an assimilative function for Sunnis. On the Sunni borderline of southern Tunceli, from Çemişgezek to Mazgirt, some Alevi tribes still remember their 'Sunni past' (Gültekin 2010, pp. 282–89), and they talk about the miracles of the *pirs* who made the conversion possible.

Likewise, *kirvelik* institutions between the Alevi majority and the Sunni minority may serve to show an alternative way of looking at patronage relations and Alevis' strategies of survival in Sunni-dominated social spheres. For example, it is commonly believed that Alevis have to hide their religious identity to maintain economic relations with Sunnis and not face suppression. Otherwise, they have to find strong alliances with those superior to them in terms of political influence or economic power. However, in the case of Pertek, it appears that this common assessment is false. Alevis use the same strategy while patronising Sunnis. In this way, they can manage the Sunnis' wide networks and official institutions.

As this case study-shows, due to their status as a majority in Tunceli, Alevis have created hierarchical relations with minorities. Their religious institutions and oral traditions have supported this superiority. Their economic opportunities and security-related power relations, which they also provide to Sunnis, constituted strengthening points behind their majority. According to them, the Sunnis' existence on 'sacred lands' can only be possible due to an external factor, such as the state. According to the Kurdish Alevis of Dersim, local Sunnis could either be settled as outsiders or Turkified – or, in other words, Sunnified – Alevis. The Kadiri sect's presence among the Sunni minority explains their acceptance by Alevis in this matter. Until their dominance came to an end, they ruled over the minorities of Dersim. After the Turkish Republic's victory, Kurdish Alevis maintained patronage relations, bracing to become the majority of the local population. The politicisation of identities such as Kurdishness (in relation to leftism) and Turkishness (in relation to political Islam and Turkish nationalism) significantly changed the relations between Alevis and Sunnis in Tunceli. This unique case needs to be examined for a better understanding of Alevism.

Acknowledgements

I am grateful to Çiçek İlengiz and Markus Dressler for their comments. I would also like to thank Sinan Jabban, for his contributions to this chapter's first translation, and Ömer Akyüz, who created the image. A debt of gratitude is also due to the reviewers and editors for their contributions, which helped the chapter take its most recent form.

Bibliography

Ağuiçenoğlu, H. (2010). Alevilik Örneğinde İnanç-Etnik Kimlik İlişkisi Üzerine Yapılan Tartışmalara Kısa Bir Bakış. In: Aslan, Ş., ed., *Herkesin Bildiği Sır: Dersim*, Istanbul: İletişim. pp. 119–39.

Akpınar, A. (2019). Perceptions of Alevism under Abdülhamid II: Moves to 'Civilize' and Sunni-Ize. In: Gezik, E., and Gültekin, A. K., eds, *Kurdish Alevis and the Case of Dersim: Historical and Contemporary Insight*. New York: Lexington Books. pp. 3–14.

Aygün, H. (2009). *Dersim 1938 ve Zorunlu İskan*. Ankara: Dipnot.

Bahadır, İ., ed. (2003). *Bilgi Toplumunda Alevilik*. Ankara: Bilefeld Alevi Kültür Merkezi Yayınları.

Bozarslan, H. (2005). Araştırmanın Mitosları ya da Aleviliğin Tarihsel ve Sosyal Bir Olgu Olarak Değerlendirilmesinin Zorunluluğu Üzerine. *Kırkbudak: Anadolu Halk İnançları Araştırmaları Dergisi*, 1, 5–20.

Bruniessen, M. V. (1995). *Forced Evacuations and Destruction of Villages in Dersim (Tunceli) and Western Bingöl, Turkish Kurdistan September–November 1994*. Utrecht: Utrecht University Repository.

Bulut, F. (2013). *Dersim Raporları*. Istanbul: Evrensel Basım Yayın.

Bulut, F. (2002). *Kürt Dilinin Tarihçesi*. Istanbul: Berfin.

Cetin, U., Jenkins, C., and Aydın, S., eds (2020). Special Issue: Alevi Kurds: History, Politics and Identity, *Kurdish Studies*, 8, 1.

Çakmak, H. (2013). *Dersim Aleviliği: Raa Haqi*. Ankara: Kalan.

Çakmak, Y., and Gürtaş, İ., eds (2015). *Kızılbaşlık Alevilik Bektaşilik*. Istanbul: İletişim.

Çem, M. (2011). *Dersim Merkezli Kürt Aleviliği*. Istanbul: Vate.

Deniz, D. (2019). Kurdish Alevi Belief System, Rêya Heqî/Raa Haqi: Structure, Networking, Ritual, and Function. In: Gezik, E., and Gültekin, A. K., eds, *Kurdish Alevis and the Case of Dersim: Historical and Contemporary Insights*. New York: Lexington Books. pp. 45–73.

Deniz, D. (2018). Aleviliğin Türk İslam Sentezine Uyarlı Yeniden İnşası: Üretilen Yazılı Kaynaklar ve Bu İnşada Akademianin Rolü Üzerine. *Semah*, 41, 22–25.

Deniz, D. (2013). Dersim'in Ekonomi Politiği İçinde Talanın Yeri: Antropolojik Bir Yaklaşım. In: Tuna, Ş. G., and Orhan, G., eds, *Dört Dağa Sığmayan Kent: Dersim Üzerine Ekonomi-Politik Yazılar*. Istanbul: Patika Kitap. pp. 71–113.

Deniz, D. (2012). *Yol/Re: Dersim İnanç Sembolizmi, Antropolojik Bir Yaklaşım*. Istanbul: İletişim.

Dressler, M. (2013). *Writing Religion: The Making of Turkish Alevi Islam*. New York: Oxford University Press.

Erdemir, A., et al. (2010). *Türkiye'de Alevi Olmak*. Ankara: Dipnot.

Erdemir, A. (2005). Tradition and Modernity: Alevis' Ambiguous Terms and Turkey's Ambivalent Subjects. *Middle Eastern Studies*, 41(6), 937–51.

Ertan, M. (2017). *Aleviliğin Politikleşme Süreci – Kimlik Siyasetinin Kısıtlılıkları ve İmkanları*. Istanbul: İletişim.

Etten, J. V., et al. (2008). Environmental Destruction as a Counterinsurgency Strategy in the Kurdistan Region of Turkey. *Geoforum*, 39(5), 1786–97.

Fırat, G. (2010). Dersim'de Etnik Kimlik. In: Aslan, Ş., ed., *Herkesin Bildiği Sır: Dersim*, Istanbul: İletişim. pp. 139–55.

Gezik, E., and Çakmak, H. (2010). *Raa Haqi-Riya Haqi, Dersim Aleviliği İnanç Terimleri Sözlüğü*. Ankara: Kalan.

Gezik, E. (2014). *Dinsel, Etnik ve Politik Sorunlar Bağlamında: Alevi Kürtler*. Istanbul: İletişim.

Gezik, E., and Gültekin, A. K., eds (2019). *Kurdish Alevis and the Case of Dersim: Historical and Contemporary Insights*. New York: Lexington Books.

Gül, A. (2015). Dersim Sancağının İdari Yapısı ve İdarecileri (1846–1918). *Akademik Sosyal Araştırmalar Dergisi*, 17, 23–54.

Gültekin, A. K. (2020). *Kutsal Mekanın Yeniden Üretimi: Kemeré Dızgı'dan Düzgün Baba'ya Dersim Aleviliğinde Müzakereler ve Kültür Örüntüleri*. Istanbul: Bilim ve Gelecek Kitaplığı.

Gültekin, A. K. (2019). Kurdish Alevism: Creating New Ways of Practicing the Religion. *Working Paper Series of the HCAS 'Multiple Secularities: Beyond the West, Beyond Modernities'* 18. Leipzig: Leipzig University.

Gültekin, A. K. (2018). Alevilik Yazınına Eleştirel Bakışlar – Bitmeyen Polemik: Aleviler Kimdir? *Bilim ve Gelecek: Aylık Bilim, Kültür, Politika Dergisi*, 173, 70–75.

Gültekin, A. K., and Yeşiltepe, U. (2015). (Dersimli) Alevilerin Makûs Talihi mi? Dersim (Alevileri) için Yeni Fırsatlar mı? Kent Merkezinde Sünni Nüfusun Artışı ve Alevilerin Ötekiyle İmtihanı, *Birikim*, 109/110, 108–19.

Gültekin, A. K. (2010). *Tunceli'de Sünni Olmak: Ulusal ve Yerel Kimlik Öğelerinin Tunceli Pertek'te Etnolojik Tetkiki*. Istanbul: Berfin.

Gültekin, A. K. (2004). *Tunceli'de Kutsal Mekân Kültü*. Ankara: Kalan.

Issa, T. ed. (2017). *Alevis in Europe: Voices of Migration, Culture and Identity*. New York: Routledge.

Jenkins, C., Aydın, S., and Cetin, U., eds (2018). *Alevism as an Ethno-Religious Identity. Contested Boundaries*. London and New York: Routledge.

Jongerden, J. (2010). Village Evacuation and Reconstruction in Kurdistan (1993–2002). *Études Rurales*, 186, 77–100.

Jongerden, J. (2001). Resettlement and Reconstruction of Identity: The Case of the Kurds in Turkey. *The Global Review of Ethnopolitics*, 1(1), 80–86.

Keskin, M. (2010). Zazaca Üzerine Notlar. In: Aslan, Ş., ed., *Herkesin Bildiği Sır Dersim*. Istanbul: İletişim. pp. 221–45.

Kevorkian, R. (2011). *The Armenian Genocide: A Complete History*. London, New York: I. B. Tauris.

Korkmaz, E. (2003). *Ansiklopedik Alevilik-Bektaşilik Terimleri Sözlüğü*. Ankara: Kaynak.

Köksal, S. (2006). *Ortakçı Toplumdan Bugüne Kızılbaşlık*. Ankara: Ütopya.

Kudat, A. (2004). *Kirvelik: Sanal Akrabalığın Dünü ve Bugünü*. Ankara: Ütopya.

Massicard, E. (2013). Aleviler: Cumhuriyet Tarihyazımında Unutulmuş Özneler? In: Bilmez, B., ed., *Cumhuriyet Tarihinin Tartışmalı Konuları*. Istanbul: Tarih Vakfı. pp. 140–50.

Massicard, E. (2012). *The Alevis in Turkey and Europe: Identity and Managing Territorial Diversity*. Abingdon: Routledge.

Massicard, E. (2007). *Türkiye'den Avrupa'ya Alevi Hareketinin Siyasallaşması*. Istanbul: İletişim.

Munzuroğlu, D. (2012). *Toplumsal Yapı ve İnanç Bağlamında Dersim Aleviliği*. Istanbul: Fam.

Olsson, T., Özdalga, E., and Raudvere, C., eds (1998). *Alevi Identity: Cultural, Religious and Social Perspectives*. Istanbul: Swedish Research Institute in Istanbul.

Öz, B. (2008). *Alevilik Nedir?* Istanbul: Der.

Sertal, S. (2014). Türkiye Cumhuriyeti'nin İlk Genel Nüfus Sayımına Göre Dersim Bölgesinde Demografik Yapı. *Fırat Üniversitesi Sosyal Bilimler Dergisi*, 24(1), 269–82.

Sökefeld, M. (2015). Almanya'da Aleviler: Takiyeden Alevi Hareketine. In: Çakmak, Y., and Gürtaş, İ., eds, *Kızılbaşlık Alevilik Bektaşilik*. Istanbul: İletişim. pp. 397–423.

Tuna, Ş. G., and Gözde, O. (2013). *Dört Dağa Sığmayan Kent: Dersim Üzerine Ekonomi-Politik Yazılar*. Istanbul: Patika Kitap.

Tunceli Nüfusu (2020). *Türkiye Nüfusu* [online]. [Viewed 20 january 2021]. Available from: https://www.nufusu.com/il/tunceli-nufusu

Yıldırım, M. (2018). Arşivlere Göre 19. Yüzyılda Osmanlı Devleti'nin Dersim'e Vergi Politikaları ve Hozat'ın Havik Nahiyesindeki Uygulamaları. In: Hepkon, Z., and Aslan, Ş, eds, *Hozat*. Ankara: Ütopya. pp. 59–69.

Yıldırım, M. (2013). Dersim'in Cumhuriyet Öncesindeki Sosyo-Ekonomik Yapısı Üzerine Bir İnceleme. In: Tuna, Ş. G., and Orhan, G., eds, *Dört Dağa Sığmayan Kent – Dersim Üzerine Ekonomi-Politik Yazılar*. Istanbul: Patika Kitap. pp. 41–70.

Yıldırım, M. (2012). Desimlu Aşiretinden Dersim Sancağına. *Tunceli Üniversitesi Sosyal Bilimler Dergisi*, 1, 23–37.

Yıldırım, R. (2018). *Geleneksel Alevilik*. Istanbul: İletişim.

Yılmazçelik, İ., and Erdem, S. (2017). II. Abdülhamid Döneminde Dersim Sancağındaki İdari Yapı ve Ulaşım Ağı. *Gazi Akademik Bakış Dergisi*, 21, 223–43.

Yılmazçelik, İ. (2011). *Osmanlı Devleti Döneminde Dersim Sancağı*. Ankara: Kripto.

Yılmazçelik, İ. (1998). *XIX. Yüzyılın İkinci Yarısında Dersim Sancağı: İdari, İktisadi ve Sosyal Yapı*. Elazığ: Çağ Ofset Matbaacılık.

Zelyut, R. (1990). *Öz Kaynaklarına Göre Alevilik*. Istanbul: Anadolu Kültürü Yayınları.

Part II

ALEVIS IN THE DIASPORA: PROSPECTS FOR RECOGNITION

7

FROM CULTURE TO RELIGION: REFRAMING ALEVISM FOR RECOGNITION IN GERMANY

MARTIN SÖKEFELD

Introduction

The beginnings of scholarship on contemporary Alevism dates to the 1980s. In 1986, a large conference in Strasbourg was held, with leading scholars working in Alevi and Bektaşi studies. In the 1990s, 'Alevi identity' became a hot topic. The conference titled 'Alevi Identity', organised by the Swedish Research Institute in Istanbul in 1996, and the resultant volume (Olsson et al. 1998) was an example of this growing scholarship in Alevi studies. Since then, a substantial number of publications have been written about Alevis, most of them referring to 'identity' in one way or another. Also, Alevism itself has changed. The prominence of 'identity' in academic works about Alevism is also a reflection of the fact that identity was hotly debated among Alevis themselves; it was perhaps the most important topic of the 'Alevi revival'. Three decades on, identity is still very much discussed and contested among Alevis, but it seems that the debate has cooled down to some extent.

The scholarship on Alevism has discussed the question of identity since the late 1980s not only in Turkey, but also in the context of the diaspora. Indeed, diasporic actors were at the *centre* of those processes that actively transformed Alevism and its position within society at large. Given one highly significant result of these processes – that is, the formal recognition of Alevis as a religious community in Germany – the conventional relationship between 'centre' and 'diaspora' has even been turned upside down. In a way, diasporic (in particular German) Alevism has become a model for Alevism in Turkey, too. For the wider scholarship on Alevism it is therefore highly significant to focus on developments in Germany. If we look at the contemporary Alevi movement, which demands the public and formal recognition of Alevism, and the final termination of *takiye* (the dissimulation of religious belonging in the face of persecution) and discrimination in all places where Alevis live, diasporic – that is, especially German – Alevi actors have indeed played a central role. From its very beginning, the Alevi movement was a *transnational* movement in which actors in Turkey and Germany – and in other European countries – were closely interlinked (see Chapters 8, 9 and 10 in this volume).[1] In this chapter, I will trace an important step of this movement in Germany. This is the shift from framing Alevism as 'culture' to framing it as 'religion', which was a necessary precondition for achieving recognition in Germany.

Diaspora and Opportunity Structures

Scholarship on diaspora is useful for understanding Alevism in Germany in relation to Turkey. Diaspora is conventionally conceived as a group's dispersal from a common origin, a centre, to several other places. In most cases, diasporas are named after their presumed origins. For example, we speak about the Indian or the Armenian diaspora. According to the conventional line of thought, diaspora is thus created through a movement of migration from the origin to an 'elsewhere'. This results in a quite loose but essentialising conception of diaspora where almost any migration produces a diaspora. Diaspora is merely another term for migrants, and migrants are thought to bring some essence of culture and identity that makes them a kind of extension of 'their origin'. In his study on the Sikh diaspora, Brian K. Axel (2001) calls this the 'place of origin thesis', according to which diaspora is an almost natural outcome of migration. Turning conventional thinking on diaspora upside down, Axel argues that, in fact, the 'origin' is often imagined from

---

[1] For other recent studies of the European Alevi diaspora and the transnational aspects of Alevi mobilisation, see Jenkins and Cetin (2018), Jenkins et al. (2018), Issa (2017), Özkul (2019) and Massicard (2013).

'the diaspora'. Thus, the idea of a Sikh homeland that needs to be freed from India was promulgated particularly in the diaspora. Similarly, the 'homeland' of the Jewish diaspora, Israel, is a diasporic creation, and also the independence movement of Croatia received a considerable boost from Croatians living outside of their 'country of origin'.

Taking a cue from this argument, I suggest a more specific understanding of diaspora, which avoids essentialisation. I conceive of diaspora as *an imagined transnational community*. For a diaspora to come into being, migration is a necessary precondition, but not the only one. In addition to spatial movements of migration, people have to be mobilised for a particular (imagination of) community that often has effects on the homeland. In other words, migration and mobilisation are independent processes. People might migrate without ever being mobilised for such a community, for instance, because they assimilate into their new society of residence. Or, mobilisation might take place much later than migration. This is also the case with Alevis who started to migrate to Germany in the 1960s as labour migrants, but began to mobilise for an Alevi community in Germany – and to identify as such – only in the late 1980s. And while diasporic Alevis never imagined a separate Alevi homeland, diasporic Alevi mobilisation did have a strong impact on the Alevi struggle for recognition in Turkey.

Elsewhere I suggest a social movement approach for analysing the mobilisation of diaspora (Sökefeld 2006). This is a de-essentialising approach to diaspora, because the political and societal context of the country of residence has a strong influence on strategies for and outcomes of mobilisation. It offers particular 'opportunity structures'. Opportunity structures are a central concept of social movement theory, which refers to the specific conditions that enable or hinder the mobilisation of a social movement in any given social context (Tarrow 1998).

Mobilisation may take very different directions, depending on specific opportunities. Instances of the 'same' diaspora in different countries may be quite different (see Chapters 8, 9 and 10 in this volume for a comparison). Further, there is no 'essence' which is simply transferred from the 'home' to the 'host' country, but diaspora is constructed in a new societal context, although, in most cases, in close transnational connection with the context of origin. Germany offers very different opportunities to Alevis, compared to

Turkey. Whereas, for instance, freedom of organisation in Germany enabled the formation of explicitly *Alevi* associations in this country, legal conditions prohibited this in Turkey. While Alevi and other diasporic actors often take a rather essentialist perspective on Alevi identity, asking for their 'real' and 'true' identity, we have to take a strictly constructionist approach to analyse diasporic identities – Alevi identity included (Sökefeld 2008a, p. 16ff).

Alevi Migration to Germany

Alevi migration to Germany started as labour migration in the mid-1960s, after an agreement between the German and Turkish governments.[2] The migration of Alevis was unmarked – that is, Alevis were not recognised as a separate group. They were just 'Turks'. Data from my survey among the members of Alevi associations in Hamburg show that we can distinguish three phases of migration.[3] The first phase started with the beginning of labour migration and ended with the termination of recruitment in 1973. The second phase peaked in the late 1970s and the early 1980s and consisted of mostly politically motivated migration before and after the 1980 military *coup* in Turkey. The third phase largely paralleled the rise of the conflict between the state and the Kurdish PKK in Turkey and had its peak in 1989 (Sökefeld 2008a, p. 41).

In Germany, Alevis continued *takiye* – that is, they did not openly identify as Alevis. In many cases, fellow Alevis did not know that the other person was Alevi, too. Because they feared discrimination and stigmatisation, just like in Turkey, affiliation with Alevism was kept strictly secret, especially from fellow migrants from Turkey. *Takiye* also meant that Alevis did not organise as Alevis. While Sunni migrants often quickly established provisional mosques, Alevis desisted from any public religious activities. Many Alevis became members of political organisations instead. This was mostly a continuation of activities in

---

[2] This section largely relies on Sökefeld (2008a, p. 37ff).

[3] I conducted ethnographic fieldwork among Alevis in Hamburg and other places in Germany roughly between 1999 and 2004. In addition to qualitative methods such as participant-observation and open-ended interviews, I conducted a survey among the members of the then seven Alevi associations in Hamburg. Around one third of the membership completed my questionnaires (n=233). Research was generously funded by the Deutsche Forschungsge-meinschaft (DFG).

Turkey, as many Alevis there had already been involved in Kemalist or leftist parties. Also, within the political organisations Alevis did not identify as Alevis. Religion was somewhat anathema, as especially left-wing ideologies completely rejected any religious orientation as 'false consciousness'. For leftist Alevis in Germany, the exile organisation *Dev Yol* (Revolutionary Path) played a central role. Many relationships between activists of the later Alevi movements date back to their joint membership in *Dev Yol*.

The Maraş massacre of December 1978 brought some change in this regard.[4] Alevi members of the *Halk Devrimci Federasyonu*, the migrant organisation linked to the CHP, left in protest because they thought that the then CHP government, under then Prime Minister Bülent Ecevit, did not react appropriately to the massacre. In some cities such as Berlin and Hamburg they formed their own, exclusively Alevi organisations named *Yurtseverler Birlikleri* (Union of Patriots), which, however, once again did not outwardly identify as Alevi. Nonetheless, activists of the *Yurtseverler Birliği* in Hamburg organised the first public *cem* in the city, which took place in 1984 and drew a crowd of several hundred people.[5] But also this *cem* was not advertised as an Alevi event. Nevertheless, there was a particular shift in orientation.

Towards Alevi Identity in Germany

The shift towards Alevi identity took place within a global change of political perspectives. During the 1980s, socialist ideas and ideals lost their persuasiveness, and the goal of the recognition of difference replaced the goal of economic equality for all. Political philosophy, therefore, speaks of a shift from the paradigm of redistribution to the paradigm of recognition (Fraser and Honneth 2003). 'Identity' became a hot topic, a global catchword that in many contexts motivated people to political action.

The shift towards an Alevi identity in Germany took place within three contexts of 'identity politics', two of them related to Turkey and one to Germany. In Turkey, the 'Turkish Islamic synthesis' was emphasised as a hegemonic idea to create a new unity of the nation after the deep ideological struggles between

---

[4] See also the analysis of the importance of the Maraş massacre for the mobilisation of Alevis in Britain in Chapter 10 in this volume.

[5] On *cem* in Germany, see Sökefeld (2004) and (2005).

left and right that in the 1970s tore the country apart and led to the military *coup* of 1980 (Waxman 2000, p. 18). However, Alevis felt marginalised and excluded by the Turkish Islamic synthesis, as it was based exclusively on the Sunni version of Islam. The second context in Turkey was the escalating conflict between the Kurds and the state. This is another instance of the shift from redistribution to recognition, as the PKK was established as a socialist party, but gained much more leverage as a militant identity movement. As many Alevis (especially activist Alevis) are also Kurds, they were affected by the movement and experienced repression by the Turkish state. Finally, the contest between rising multiculturalism and a new racism in Germany was significant for Alevis. On the one hand, the right side of the political spectrum demanded that migrants assimilate into 'German culture',[6] while on the other hand multiculturalist discourses expected 'foreigners' – that is, migrants – not to assimilate but 'preserve' their culture and identity. The multicultural perspective was dominant especially in cities such as Frankfurt, Berlin and Hamburg, where multiculturalism was partly institutionalised.

In Hamburg, multiculturalist centers were established in districts with a high proportion of migrant populations. Among the leftist Alevis, revolutionary fervour waned in the mid-1980s. *Dev Yol* was disbanded because the goal of a revolution in Turkey was considered unobtainable. Some former members of *Dev Yol* became 'multiculturalist activists' and worked in multicultural centres. Discourse about equality and the recognition of cultural identities, which took place within the centres, also nourished the debate on Alevi identity. Some Alevis thought that not only Turkish or Kurdish identities needed to be made an issue, but also Alevi identity. In December 1988, twelve Alevis came together and formed the Alevi Culture Group Hamburg.[7] They quickly concluded that the dissimulation of Alevis had to be brought to an end and *takiye* broken once and for all. For this purpose, they agreed to organise a public Alevi festival. The group met regularly and grew fast. They developed relationships with Alevis in Turkey, such as singer and *saz* player Arif Sağ, who at that time was a member of the Turkish parliament and

---

[6] Note that this was the time of the first racist murders of immigrants in Germany. In 1985, skinheads killed the Turkish immigrants Mehmet Kaynakcı and Ramazan Avcı.

[7] A decade later, the Alevi Culture Centre Hamburg published the story of these veterans. See Hamburg Alevi Kültür Merkezi (1999).

took part in one of their meetings.[8] In October 1989, the group organised the Alevi Culture Week, which took place at the University of Hamburg. The Culture Week comprised panel discussions, a *cem* and concerts with Alevi musicians. Around 5,000 Alevis from all over Germany, as well as from neighbouring countries and Turkey, participated in the Culture Week. The event was a remarkable success. The Alevi Culture Group had drafted an *Alevi Declaration*, which demanded the legal and public recognition of Alevism in Germany and Turkey and which was disseminated during the event.[9] The *Declaration* from Hamburg served as model for the *Alevi Bildirgesi*, which was jointly published by Alevi and non-Alevi intellectuals in Turkey in the daily *Cumhuriyet* in 1990 (see Zelyut [n. d.], p. 414ff).

The Alevi Movement for Recognition

Because the Alevi Culture Week was the first-ever public event explicitly titled 'Alevi', I consider it as the starting point of the Alevi movement. Previously, Alevis had established associations in some German cities; however, these associations did not operate under the name of Alevism, but used the name of Hacı Bektaş Veli (*Bektaşi Dernekleri*). The activities of these associations were not meant for the general public. After the Alevi Culture Week, however, associations that publicly presented Alevism and demanded its recognition were formed. In Hamburg, the Alevi Culture Group was turned into a formal association, the Hamburg Alevi Culture Centre, and along the same lines, Alevi Culture Centres were established in many German cities. These efforts towards Alevi self-organisation reached a new peak after the Sivas massacre in July 1993. A few days after the massacre, around 60,000 Alevis joined a protest demonstration in Cologne. More Alevis became members of the existing associations or formed new ones. In the year after Sivas, about one-hundred new Alevi associations were established across Europe, including a new umbrella organisation, the European Union of Alevi Associations (*Avrupa Alevi Birlikleri Federasyonu*, AABF), which was based in Cologne.

The organisational structure has changed several times. Today, there are national federations of Alevi associations in most countries receiving Alevi

---

[8] For an account of the early Alevi movement in Turkey, see Vorhoff (1995).

[9] The *Alevi Declaration* is republished in Hamburg Alevi Kültür Merkezi (1999, p. 14).

migration. In Germany, this is the Alevi Community Germany (*Alevitische Gemeinde Deutschland*, ACG). The national federations have jointly formed a European umbrella organisation, the Confederation of Alevi Associations in Europe (*Avrupa Alevi Birlikleri Konfederasyonu*), which also has its office in Cologne. The Alevi movement in Europe is dominated by German Alevis, as Germany has the largest Alevi population outside of Turkey. Today, the membership of the ACG comprises more than 130 local associations. Not all local Alevi associations are members of the ACG. Some are sympathisers of the *Cem Vakfı* in Turkey, an organisation which has rather close links to the Turkish state and which is rejected by the ACG. There are also specific Kurdish Alevi associations, although many of the local associations of the ACG have a strong Kurdish membership, too.

Opportunity Structures and Shifting Identity

If we examine the dominant self-portrayal of Alevis in Germany, we discover an interesting shift taking place in recent years. The central actors of the early Alevi movement had been socialised within the leftist movement, either in Turkey or in exile. In the late 1980s and the 1990s, they considered Alevism as culture and, based on leftist ideology, rejected its conceptualisation as religion. For instance, they referred to Pir Sultan Abdal, the famous historical figure of Alevism, as a freedom fighter or poet, but not as a religious figure or *pir*. Similarly, Alevism's ritual dance, the *semah*, which is a very significant element of the *cem*, was practised at culture festivals as a kind of (secular) folklore. Accordingly, in the 1990s, these activists established Alevi Culture Centres and not religious communities.

Today, however, Alevi associations are considered precisely that, religious communities, and most of the erstwhile culture centres have switched their names to *Alevitische Gemeinde* – *Gemeinde* being the typical German expression for a local religious community (parish).[10] Since 2002, the ACG defines itself as a 'community of faith' (*Glaubensgemeinschaft*) in its statutes. Before, it had been defined in the typical leftist jargon as a 'democratic mass organisation' (*demokratik kitle örgütü*, in the Turkish version of the statutes). The

---

[10] The Alevi Culture Centre Hamburg accordingly became the *Alevitische Gemeinde Hamburg* in the German language, but retained the 'Culture Centre' in its Turkish designation as *Hamburg Alevi Kültür Merkezi*.

idea that Alevis are a religious community has become a matter of common sense. However, it is not the case that now 'religiously-minded' Alevis have taken over the associations. On the contrary, many of the old 'leftists' are still important activists, and they have not become essentially 'religious persons' now, either. What has happened then?

Successful politics of recognition also have to be strategic. This means that it has to take into account its counterpart from which recognition is demanded – its conditions, interests and perceptions. German Alevis have indeed done so. At this point, it is beneficial to think of the politics of recognition together with the concept of 'regimes of incorporation', as formulated by, for instance, Yasemin Soysal (2004). While the 'ability' of migrants to 'adapt to' or 'integrate in' a country of residence is conventionally considered in terms of the migrant's individual 'cultural baggage', Soysal instead focused on the political, legal and social conditions of the country of residence for the process of incorporation. Regimes of incorporation include the conditions and opportunities for self-organisation and the articulation of the interests of a group of migrants in a particular political context. Successful politics of recognition have to adjust and adapt to such regimes of incorporation.

In Germany, immigration has almost consistently been framed as a problem in public and political discourse. The dominant political position was that migration should be temporary and that Germany is not a country of immigration. The German term for immigration, *Einwanderung*, is even today largely banned from political discourse. Stereotypically, migrants have been considered problematic figures unwilling to 'integrate' and learn the German language, to mention just two common prejudices. This 'problematisation' of migration has probably been the most significant element of the conditions of incorporation in Germany. The pluralisation and heterogenisation of German society, which was thought to be culturally homogeneous, has been regarded as particularly dangerous and problematic.[11]

---

[11] Recently, a certain relaxation of the axiom that immigration in the first place constitutes a problem can be observed in media and political discourse. This has to do with demographic developments and projections that clearly point to the necessity of immigration for the purpose of countering the decrease of the 'native' population in Germany and securing 'human resources'. To a certain extent, this is reminiscent of the 'guest-workers' discourse of the 1950s and 1960s. Alevi politics of recognition, however, took place largely within the framework of immigration as a problem.

Strategies for Recognition

From this regime of incorporation by problematisation, two strategies for successful politics of recognition could be deduced almost logically. First, migrants have to represent themselves as 'non-problematic' immigrants. Second, their demand for recognition has to refer to a form of plurality, which is also considered as being non-problematic in German discourse. Alevi associations resorted to both of these strategies. They always represented themselves as non-problematic migrants, based on a supposed sharp contrast to Sunni-Muslim immigrants from Turkey. They represented themselves as being completely compatible with German society, for instance, regarding secularity, the equality of the sexes and other value-orientations. They thereby distanced themselves from Islam, which is mostly considered as being somehow problematic and potentially dangerous. Also, they have sought recognition as a religious community, and in Germany religion is a recognised, largely unproblematic form of plurality.

While groups of migrants mostly affirm their identity by demanding recognition of their cultural differences from the majority population of the host country, Alevis instead emphasise their difference from Turkish Sunni immigrants. By drawing attention to the contrast between Alevis and the 'fundamentalist' image of Sunni Islam, they affirm at the same time the similarity and compatibility of Alevi and German culture. They emphasise their complete acceptance of values that are construed as universal, such as values derived from enlightenment, human rights and the equality of the sexes. The headscarf is a significant symbol in this context, and Alevis are never tired of pointing out that, in contrast to 'Muslims', Alevi women do not cover themselves (see Mandel 2008, p. 303f). In the context of the rather sketchy categories of German discourses on migration and integration, which construes Muslims as largely anti-modern and being the most different and alien of all migrants, Alevis position themselves unequivocally on the 'modern' side of the divide – that is, on the German side. The discursive emphasis on a deep and unbridgeable difference between Sunnis and Alevis can thus be seen as an effort to represent Alevis as migrants that are not alien. German and Alevi discourses on Islam are very similar. In both discursive contexts, (Sunni) Muslims are seen as potentially dangerous. In Alevi discourse, Islam is often plainly equated with 'Islamism'.

Initially, the German public did not distinguish between Sunnis and Alevis among the migrants from Turkey. Accordingly, to stress the difference between Alevism and Sunni Islam was initially the most significant strategy for recognition that Alevis used in Germany. A second strategy is what I call 'institutional integration'. Alevis were very eager to establish relations of cooperation on different levels, between their associations and German politicians, the public administration, religious communities, or civil society organisations (see also Massicard 2013, Özkul 2019 and Chapter 8 in this volume). Alevis consider such relationships as evidence of recognition because their associations are accepted as partners. Institutional integration takes place at the local level through local Alevi associations, as well as at the federal level, where the Alevi Community Germany is the central actor. At the local level, Alevi associations commit themselves to neighbourhood initiatives or local interreligious dialogue. They invite German representatives to their events and thereby intend to foster relations with parties, parishes and the local government.

At the federal level, the strategy of institutional integration of the ACG became particularly successful after a coalition of the Social Democrats and the Green Party came to power in 1998, because this government was much more sympathetic concerning issues of immigrants than previous governments. Several projects were initiated with the support of the federal government, among them a 'campaign for naturalisation', which accompanied new citizenship legislation in 2000. Funded by the federal government, the ACG produced a bilingual brochure on the new law and conducted seminars to disseminate information about the changes among the local associations. Interestingly, the rate of naturalisation among Alevis had already been very high before this campaign started. In a survey I conducted in late 2002 among the members of the local Alevi associations of Hamburg, I found that 55.6 per cent of the membership had already been naturalised, many in the 1990s. Compared to the naturalisation of migrants of Turkish origin in general, this is a very high rate.

Alevi Classes in Schools

The most important project of institutional integration and recognition was the effort to start Alevi religious classes in public (state) schools. Because of the federal organisation of the German education system, there exist different provisions for religious education in different federal states. In Hamburg, a campaign for the introduction of Alevi classes in schools was initiated as early as 1991. However, Hamburg has an exceptional organisation of religious education. In public schools, there is 'religious education for all' – in other words, students are not separated according to their religious affiliation. This religious education is organised under the lead-management of the Protestant Church in cooperation with the education authority, but teaching and learning content is discussed at a 'Roundtable for Interreligious Religious Education', which meets regularly. Representatives of the Alevi Culture Centre Hamburg soon became active participants of this roundtable. In 1998, Alevism formally became part of the curriculum for religious instruction in primary schools in Hamburg. The Alevi associations celebrated this as the first instance of the formal recognition of Alevism by a state. In 2002, separate Alevi religious classes were introduced in primary schools in Berlin, as there was no interreligious model of religious education. This was also the case in all other federal states. In 2006, Alevi classes started in Baden-Wurttemberg. North Rhine-Westphalia, Hessen and Bavaria followed briefly thereafter.

Efforts towards the introduction of Alevi classes and the commitment to the 'Roundtable for Interreligious Religious Education' dialogue show the importance of religion in Alevi politics of recognition, although the Alevi debate of whether Alevism in the first place is a 'religion' or 'culture' (Sökefeld 2004) has by no means been finally concluded.[12] Many Alevi associations still carry 'culture' in their names, and many Alevis consider themselves 'atheists' or at least thorough secularists who personally assign little importance to religion.

However, in spite of this debate, Alevism was formally defined as a religious community – or rather, as a 'community of faith'. In September 2002, the general assembly of the ACG adopted new statutes, which formally define the umbrella association as a 'community of faith in the sense of the [German] constitution', instead of the earlier self-definition as a 'democratic mass organisation'.[13] This new self-definition is not simply based on a rediscovered religiosity among Alevis, although an increasing interest for Alevism as religion can be observed, especially among young Alevis. More

[12] See Chapter 2 in this volume for a discussion on the definition of Alevism.

[13] See section 2.1 of the statutes, adopted on 21 September 2002. Significantly, the term used is 'community of faith' (*inanç örgütü* in Turkish), and not 'religious community' (*dini örgüt* in Turkish), as the Turkish word for religion, '*din*', is considered to be too close to Islam.

significant, however, are the German institutional structure and the conditions of recognition. In contrast to religion, 'culture' is not a category of recognition in the German legal-institutional and discursive framework. There is no opportunity for formal recognition as a 'cultural community' in Germany. Religious communities, in contrast – most importantly, the major Christian churches, but also the Jewish community – are legally and politically recognised as public corporations (*Körperschaft des öffentlichen Rechts*). They enjoy a legal status that confers considerable rights and privileges. Because of the existence of several churches, religion is thought of as a plurality, while a cultural plurality (that is, heterogeneity) is still mostly considered undesirable and a potential problem for society. The almost continuous debate about the 'dangers' and 'failure' of multiculturalism speaks volumes in this respect. This also explains why there was no opportunity for Alevis to achieve recognition as 'culture', in contrast to recognition as 'religion' in Germany. With the introduction of Alevi religious classes in the Bundesländer Baden-Wurttemberg, North-Rhine Westphalia, Hesse and Bavaria, Alevis have achieved this legal recognition as a religious community.[14]

Alevism in Germany and Islam

I argue that the Alevi debate about whether Alevism is part of Islam or a separate religion in its own right has to be understood within the framework of German opportunities for recognition. The relationship of Alevism with Islam is the most disputed question in current debates on 'Alevi identity'. The primary arguments for both positions are quite simple and do not require specific theological knowledge. They are succinctly summed up in the following two antithetic statements, which I quote from interviews with members of Alevi associations in Hamburg:

> 'Islam has five pillars. We do not adhere to them. We don't pray in mosques, we don't keep the fast in Ramadan, and we do not undertake the pilgrimage to Mecca. Why then should Alevism be part of Islam?'
> 'In *cem*, we invoke Allah, Muhammed, Ali. How could we maintain then that Alevism is not a part of Islam?'

[14] The decision of the federal states was based on two expert opinions. The first was about the question of whether Alevism is a separate religion; the second was about the question of whether the ACG as an organisation is a religious community. Both expert opinions were positive toward the Alevis' case. For details, see Sökefeld (2008b, p. 287).

These statements form an aporia that is difficult to resolve. It seems that the majority of German Alevis is of the opinion that Alevism is somehow part of Islam. Given the fact that almost all Alevis in Turkey hold this view, it is somewhat surprising that a considerable number of Alevis in Germany takes the opposite position – namely, that Alevism is entirely separate and different from Islam. According to my survey taken in late 2002, more than a third of the membership of the Alevi associations in Hamburg shares this opinion (Sökefeld 2008b).

The question of the relationship between Alevism and Islam is very complicated.[15] Also, those for whom Alevism is part of Islam do not equate it with Sunni (or any other form of) Islam. On the contrary, according to their point of view, Alevism is the 'real' original Islam, while Sunni Islam is just a diluted version of authentic Islam.

The question of Alevism's relationship to Islam is mostly an issue of the Alevi diaspora. For the overwhelming majority of Turkish Alevis, there is no question that Alevism is part of Islam. Among the Alevi associations in Turkey, it is mostly the Pir Sultan Abdal associations that take a more ambivalent position, by emphasising that Alevism is a syncretistic culture and religion, which incorporated elements from many different traditions. The idea that Alevis are Muslims is also decidedly endorsed by the Turkish state. Turkish passports state the religious affiliation of their bearers and identify Alevis as Muslims. The unquestioning identification of Alevis as Muslims is also the most crucial argument for the policy of the Turkish Directorate of Religious Affairs (*Diyanet İşleri Başkanlığı*): the *Diyanet* caters to the religious needs of Muslims, Alevis are Muslims and, accordingly, there is no need for a specific policy towards Alevis, such as supporting and funding Alevi *cemevis*.[16]

This rather inclusive policy of the Turkish Republic has replaced the earlier restrictive policy of the Ottoman Empire towards Alevis. In the Ottoman Empire, Alevis were regarded as heretics, and *fatwas* of the *ulema* that denounced Alevis on behalf of the state often sanctioned the execution

---

[15] See Chapter 2 in this volume for an analysis of this complexity.

[16] See Chapter 3 in this volume for an analysis of the ruling Justice and Development Party's policies towards Alevis in Turkey, and Chapter 13 for an analysis of (the lack of) state support for *cemevis* in Turkey.

of apostates. The religiously inclusive policy of the Turkish Republic, however, subsumes Alevis under the Sunni version of Islam. Because they are regarded as Muslims, Alevi students have to take part in the (Sunni) Islamic religious classes in Turkish schools. Consequentially, Alevis in Turkey mostly consider themselves Muslims, but at the same time insist that they belong to a specific kind of Islam that radically differs from the version of Islam that is embodied and endorsed by the state.

In the German diaspora, however, the parameters of religious and national identities have fundamentally shifted. Many Alevis do not even consider themselves as members of the Turkish nation in the first place. Also, for many who identify as Turks, the close linkage of Islam and Turkish national identity has become very questionable. Beyond all religious and theological disputes, the (political) necessity for Alevis in Germany to identify as Muslims has mostly vanished. On the contrary, given the peculiarities of the discourse and politics on migration, as well as the increasingly critical discourse about Islam in Germany, it almost suggests itself to emphasise the difference between Islam and Alevism.

Also, the project of Alevi religious classes in schools almost presupposes the separation of Alevism from Islam. Regardless of whether they consider Alevism part of Islam, Alevis unanimously hold the position that Alevi students should not be taught together with Sunni students in common religious classes, but that separate Alevi classes are required. As it is quite difficult to explain to the education authorities that Alevis need different classes if Alevism is part of Islam, the project of Alevi religious instruction fosters the clear-cut separation of Alevism from Islam. German authorities demand time and again that Muslims in Germany should establish a joint institutional representation that could serve as their counterpart for all questions regarding Islamic classes. A self-identification of Alevis as Muslims would suggest that Alevis should also become part of such an institution. This, however, would be wholly unacceptable for Alevis who define themselves in contrast to (Sunni) Islam.

Conclusion

The Alevi movement for recognition started in Germany in the late 1980s, with an understanding of Alevism as 'culture'. In the course of the movement, however, the dominant self-definition of Alevism shifted from culture towards 'religion'. Also, at the beginning of the movement, there were some activists, mostly among the *dede*s,[17] who decidedly considered Alevism to be a religion and who regarded any conceptualisation of Alevism as culture as the outcome of leftist adulteration and corruption, which needed to be fought. However, the later shift towards Alevism as religion is not an indication that these activists have won their battle. I have argued, in contrast, that the shift towards religion is much more a consequence of the German opportunity structures for recognition than of any fundamental understanding or 'essence' of Alevism. In Germany, 'religion' is a category that enables legal and political recognition, while 'culture' is not. In addition to being conducive to the reframing of Alevism as religion, the political opportunities for recognition in Germany also clearly favour the separation of Alevism and Islam.

Taking a quite strategic approach, Alevi politics of recognition have been highly successful in Germany. The institutionalisation of Alevism in Germany continues to proceed quickly. In 2014, a course for the education of teachers for Alevi classes at the teacher training college in Weingarten and a junior professorship for Alevism at the University of Hamburg were established. Similar initiatives have since been launched in other cities. Finally, in late 2020, Alevism was officially recognised in North Rhine-Westphalia as a public corporation (*Körperschaft des öffentlichen Rechts*), like all other religions recognised in Germany. Referring to the conventional practice of *takiye* among Alevis, the opening speech of the Alevi Culture Week in October 1989 ended with the the following wish: 'Anyone who wants to should be able to say, "I am Alevi"'. At that time, this wish was quite utopian, even in Germany – only a minority of Alevis dared to go public. In the following three decades, however, it has become very normal for the first generation of Alevis that has grown up in the country to say 'I am Alevi'. Even though in Germany there may be a substantial number of Alevis who would still refrain from stating that they are Alevis, the role of the Alevi movement in helping (or encouraging) Alevis to come out in public is undeniable.

---

[17] Traditionally, *dede*s serve as guides for the community on spiritual and social matters. See Sökefeld (2002) on *dede*s in Germany, and Langer et al. (2013) on *dede*s in general.

Acknowledgements

I am very grateful to the *Deutsche Forschungsgemeinschaft*, which generously funded my research on this topic.

Bibliography

Axel, B. K. (2001). *The Nation's Tortured Body: Violence, Representation, and the Formation of a Sikh 'Diaspora'*. Durham, NC: Duke University Press.

Cohen, R. (1997). *Global Diasporas: An Introduction*. London: UCL Press.

Fraser, N., and Honneth, A., eds (2003). *Redistribution or Recognition? A Political-Philosophical Exchange*. London: Verso.

Hamburg Alevi Kültür Merkezi. (1999). *Onların Öyküsü*. Hamburg: HAKM.

Issa, T. ed (2017). *Alevis in Europe: Voices of Migration, Culture and Identity*. London: Routledge.

Jenkins, C., and Cetin, U. (2018). From a 'Sort of Muslim' to 'Proud to be Alevi': The Alevi Religion and Identity Project Combatting the Negative Identity among Second-generation Alevis in the UK. *National Identities* [online]. 20(1), 105–23. [Viewed 30 March 2021]. Available from: doi: 10.1080/14608944.2016.1244933

Jenkins, C., Aydın, S., and Cetin, U., eds (2018). *Alevism as an Ethno-Religious Identity: Contested Boundaries*. London: Routledge.

Langer, R., et al., eds (2013). *Ocak und Dedelik: Institutionen religiösen Spezialistentums bei den Aleviten*. Frankfurt: Peter Lang.

Mandel, R. (2008). *Cosmopolitan Anxieties: Turkish Challenges to Citizenship and Belonging in Germany*. Durham, NC: Duke University Press.

Massicard, E. (2013). *The Alevis in Turkey and Europe: Identity and Managing Territorial Diversity*. Abingdon: Routledge.

Olsson, T., Özdalga, E., and Raudvere, C., eds (1998). *Alevi Identity: Cultural, Religious and Social Perspectives*. Istanbul: Swedish Research Institute in Istanbul.

Özkul, D. (2019). The Making of a Transnational Religion: Alevi Movement in Germany and the World Alevi Union. *British Journal of Middle Eastern Studies* [online]. 46(2), 259–73. [Viewed 30 March 2021]. Available from: doi: 10.1080/13530194.2019.1569304

Sökefeld, M. (2002). Alevi Dedes in the German Diaspora: The Transformation of a Religious Institution. *Zeitschrift für Ethnologie* 127, 163–86.

Sökefeld, M. (2004). Religion or Culture? Concepts of Identity in the Alevi Diaspora. In: Kokot, W., Tölölyan, K., and Alfonso, C., eds, *Diaspora, Identity and Religion: New Directions in Theory and Research*. London: Routledge. pp. 143–65.

Sökefeld, M. (2006). Mobilising in Transnational Space: A Social Movement Approach to the Formation of Diaspora. *Global Networks* 6, 265–84.

Sökefeld, M. (2005). Cem in Deutschland: Transformationen eines Rituals im Kontext der Alevitischen Bewegung. In: Langer, R., et al., eds, *Migration und Ritualtransfer: Religiöse Praxis der Aleviten, Jesiden und Nusairier zwischen Vorderem Orient und Westeuropa*. Frankfurt: Peter Lang. pp. 203–26.

Sökefeld, M. (2008a). *Struggling for Recognition: The Alevi Movement in Germany and in Transnational Space*. Oxford: Berghahn Books.

Sökefeld, M. (2008b). Difficult Identifications: The Debate on Alevism and Islam in Germany. In: Thielmann, J., and Al-Harmaneh, A., eds, *Islam and Muslims in Germany*. Leiden: Brill. pp. 267–97.

Soysal, Y. N. (2004). *Limits of Citizenship: Migrants and Postnational Membership in Europe*. Chicago: University of Chicago Press.

Tarrow, S. (1998). *Power in Movement: Social Movements and Contentious Politics*. Cambridge: Cambridge University Press.

Vorhoff, K. (1995). *Zwischen Glaube, Nation und neuer Gemeinschaft: Alevitische Identität in der Türkei*. Berlin: Klaus Schwarz Verlag.

Waxman, D. (2000). Islam and Turkish National Identity: A Reappraisal. *The Turkish Yearbook of International Relations* 30, 1–22.

Zelyut, R. (n. d.). *Öz Kaynaklarına Göre Alevilik*. Istanbul: Karacaahmet Sultan Derneği Yayınları.

8

THE ALEVI MOVEMENT IN GERMANY AND AUSTRALIA: TOWARDS A TRANSNATIONAL MOVEMENT

DERYA ÖZKUL

Introduction[1]

In response to Germany's then President Joachim Gauck's comment 'I should confess developments in Turkey horrify me', when he talked about the lack of democracy during his visit to Ankara in 2014,[2] Turkey's then Prime Minister, Recep Tayyip Erdoğan, replied with criticism towards Germany:

> In Germany, there is a phenomenon called Alevism without 'Ali', I mean, there is a structure of an atheist understanding, [of an atheist] mentality [presenting itself] under the garment of Alevism; a structure that they [the German governments] have supported (Cumhuriyet 2014).

What was appalling in this statement was Erdoğan's attempt, as Prime Minister and Sunni individual, to define Alevism outside of Turkey based on his own beliefs and perceptions. Yet, this quote also evoked the question of whether

---

[1] This chapter is partly derived from the author's doctoral dissertation, titled 'Transformation of Diasporas from a Labour Movement towards a Transnational Religious Movement: The Alevi Diaspora in Germany and Australia', which was submitted to the University of Sydney in 2016.

[2] Today's Zaman (2014). This and all interview quotes in this chapter are the author's own translation.

(and if so how) new destinations affect migrants' (in this case, Alevis') practices of community formation, culture and faith, as well as their claims for social and political recognition.

Although there is a significant amount of research on the effects of immigration on receiving countries, there is less consideration about how migratory processes and the receiving states' approach towards migrants change their representation and practices of cultural and religious traditions. Exceptions include valuable research carried out by Martin Sökefeld (2003, 2008) on changing recognition claims and by Robert Langer (2008, 2010) on changing rituals in the context of Alevi migration to Germany. The chapters on the Alevi diaspora in Part II of this book also show how different national contexts have provided different circumstances for Alevis.

In this chapter, I compare the cases of Germany and Australia – two countries with different historical traditions concerning migrants. While Germany for a long time was unwilling to accept temporary migrants as settlers in Germany, Australia welcomed them as permanent settlers. These policies have changed over the past sixty years, with Germany becoming relatively more open to (what is called 'skilled') migrants and refugees and Australia favouring temporary migration and gradually demanding migrants to adapt to 'Australian values'. The findings are based on fieldwork carried out in Germany (Berlin, Cologne and Bielefeld) and Australia (Sydney and Melbourne) in 2012 and 2013.

Following Sökefeld (2006)'s analysis, I conceptualise migrants' movements as inconstant, like all social movements, depending on how structural conditions alter and how members of the movement respond to those changes. According to this perspective, diasporas, like any other social group, may emerge, dissolve, or continue their activities under different frameworks. Sökefeld's findings (see Chapter 7 in this volume) suggest that the political opportunity structures in Germany led Alevi institutions to define themselves as a religious organisation. I also find that Alevi organisations have gradually changed their focus, not only due to the structures in their country of residence, but also due to the changing conditions in Turkey and elsewhere. By looking at two countries with different policies, I argue that national political structures may be important in shaping migrants' social movements, while transnational forces also play a role.

In the following sections, I explain the changes between the 1960s and 2010s in three phases. The section on the 'settlement phase' explores Alevis' migration history, together with an overview of the two countries' past immigration and diversity policies. The section on the 'formation phase' explores the newly emergent Alevi movement as a 'cultural identity movement' through the 'Alevi revival' in the diaspora and consecutively in Turkey. The section on the 'transformation phase' examines the Alevi movement's self-identification predominantly as a religious movement. The implications of these changes in the Alevi movement are noted at the end of the chapter. Note that the analysis focuses on the changes at an organisational and not at an individual level.

The Settlement Phase in Germany and Australia (1960s–80s)

The history of Alevis' immigration to Germany and Australia mainly started in 1961 and 1968, respectively. Initially, most migrants had planned to stay for only a short period; yet, over time, some of them stayed longer and settled in their new countries (see Abadan-Unat 2011, İçduygu 1991 and Şenay 2012 for an extensive historical overview of both contexts). The late 1970s and the 1980s witnessed the arrival of those who escaped from political persecution in Turkey. Today, migrants from Turkey, in both Germany and Australia, include those who came to seek a better life and employment opportunities and/or refuge from the growing persecution in Turkey. Migrants also include those who arrived through family reunion and, more recently, students and so-called 'highly skilled' workers.

Turkey does not keep official demographic records for Alevis and Kurds. Neither Germany nor Australia has been interested in ethnic and religious differences (at least until the 2000s) – because they were either unaware of or disinterested in internal differences among what they perceived merely as 'Turks'. Therefore, today there exists no exact figures of how many Turkish/Kurdish Alevis immigrated to Germany and Australia, but Alevi organisations estimate the community members to be around 600,000 to 800,000 in Germany and 30,000 in Australia. Despite its apparent disregard for its emigrant population's ethnic and religious composition, the Turkish state has historically discriminated against Alevi citizens, ignoring their demands from the state or remaining silent against discriminatory practices towards Alevis.

Similarly, several of my interviewees in both countries believed that, in some instances between the 1960s and 1970s, there was a deliberate attempt to make them leave the country. For example, one interviewee in Australia argued that, in the later 1970s, one of the undersecretaries at the MİT (Turkish National Intelligence Organisation) and a newly appointed Alevi vice-president at the Employment Office's Ankara branch worked together to identify Alevi villages and to encourage emigration abroad. This issue also came up with some of the interviewees in Berlin from Varto, a district of Muş, populated predominantly by Alevis. In Varto, the 1966 earthquake killed more than 2,000 persons, and the Turkish parliament subsequently passed legislation assigning those affected priority to immigrate abroad.[3] Some suggested that the same process also happened to villages affected by earthquakes in Erzincan and Ağrı. Whether there was a deliberate attempt or not, most of the interviewees in both countries considered themselves ostracised by the Turkish state.

The fundamental difference between the two contexts is that, historically, perspectives on settlement and citizenship differed significantly. In Germany, belonging was based on 'blood' (family) ties, while in Australia the idea of belonging to a community was shaped around common territory. As a settler country, Australia was dependent on immigrants; hence, Australian citizenship was based on the *jus soli* (right of the soil) principle. By contrast, the German Confederation was formed in 1871 through the unification of thirty-nine previously independent sovereign states, which led to a common national German ideal based on the *jus sanguinis* (right of blood) principle. Germany's citizenship policies thus prioritised ancestry through symbolic 'blood' ties and ethnic-racial heritage as the primary criteria for accepting an individual into its political sphere.[4]

Therefore, although both Germany and Australia started large migration programmes around the same time in the post-World War II era, they presented different conditions for migrants' settlement and incorporation processes. Shortly after the first influx of immigrants from Turkey, Australia

---

[3] In 2011, it was estimated that approximately 20,000 persons originally from Varto lived in Germany (Gedik 2011, p. 160).

[4] Castles (1984) has suggested that one of the reasons why Germany in the 1970s did not want migrants to stay was also because they were becoming too mobilised and unruly.

acknowledged the new settlers' socio-cultural demands and, in 1973, established multiculturalism as a government policy. By contrast, Germany did not provide any such policies,[5] let alone any settlement policies for temporary migrant workers, as they were then seen. There also exist significant differences in the legal orders of the two countries. Germany locates 'freedom of religion' as one of the primary individual and group rights in its constitution and provides substantial support to recognised religious institutions. Conversely, Australia's multiculturalism policies consider religion as part of culture and do not promote it *per se*.

Nonetheless, at the time, Alevi migrants' fundamental needs in both cases were not so much about the recognition of their cultural and religious identity, but about acquiring social and economic rights. Throughout the 1970s, many Alevi migrant workers, like their counterparts in Turkey, joined left-wing organisations. Thus, the initial mobilisation began in the 1960s and 1970s, when some Alevis started to migrate to cities, a process that fundamentally impacted Alevi institutions (see Aktürk 2020). In cities, some of those who had been alienated from their elderlies' faith system (due to decades of state control and prohibition in Turkey) devoted themselves to working on issues related to social inequality within left-wing politics. Hence, the initial mobilisation emerged as a social justice-oriented, urban-based movement without a direct reference to Alevi faith and philosophy.

Almost all of the first-generation interviewees who participated in these organisations said that they devoted their efforts to social rights, social equality and improvements in workers' pay rates, health and safety conditions, and compensation arrangements. Some reflected on those years as an educational process during which they learned about the capitalist system and their rights within it. In some cases, this learning process led to a grudging admiration for the host country's conditions in comparison with Turkey. Several first-generation interviewees who worked as factory labourers stated that their new countries had been almost like a 'school' for them, while others had already been involved in similar organisations in Turkey. Some formed coalitions with workers from other nationalities to address common concerns in their immediate situation in their new countries, while continuing to work

---

[5] This was with the exception of very few cities, such as Frankfurt.

for social change in Turkey. Early on, in both countries they established associations, together with Sunni migrants, with a focus on issues of class equality and social justice.

In Germany, conflicts between migrants arose in conjunction with those in Turkey. In 1971, the then President of the Republican People's Party (*Cumhuriyet Halk Partisi*, CHP), Bülent Ecevit, requested financial aid from diaspora members. Disputes occurred over whether to support Ecevit, a mainstream social democrat. On 12 March 1973, those who supported Ecevit established the Citizens of Turkey Centre Left Association (*Türkiyeli Ortanın Solu Derneği*). The association changed its name in September 1975 to the Populist Revolutionary Union (*Halkçı Devrimci Birliği*, HDB) to emphasise the CHP's principles of populism and revolutionism. In 1977, HDBs in various European cities came together to establish the Federation of Social Democrat Populist Associations (*Sosyaldemokrat Halk Dernekleri Federasyonu*, HDF) on Turkish Republican Day (29 October), with representatives from the CHP and the Social Democratic Party of Germany. Together with the Turkish Workers Union (*Türk Ameleler Birliği*), HDBs were active on the social democratic side, while the Revolutionary Path (*Devrimci Yol*) operated on the far left-wing side.

Some organisations also came together in 1977 to establish the Federation of Labour Associations in Germany (*Federal Almanya İşçi Dernekleri Federasyonu*). This was a federation for workers only, dominated by the Turkish Communist Party (*Türkiye Komünist Partisi*, TKP). In parallel with developments in Turkey, in the emerging Kurdish movement of the 1970s some associations struggling for Kurdish rights in Turkey were also established. These officially came together in 1979, as the Union of Associations from Kurdistan (*Kürdistan Dernekleri Birliği*, KOMKAR) to work for Kurds' social rights in Germany and their cultural rights in Turkey (Başer 2015, p. 71; Østergaard-Nielsen 2003). Alevis joined these organisations according to their political views (centre left/far left; pro-Turkish/pro-Kurdish). At the time, only some expressed their Alevi identity publicly.

In Australia, major organisations founded by migrants from Turkey were involved in local activism but remained interested in their homeland politics (see Şenay 2012). The Union of Australian and Turkish Workers, the Victorian Labour Association, the Union of Turkish Workers' Committee in Melbourne, the Sydney Union of Workers from Turkey (*Sydney Türkiyeli İşçiler Birliği*) and the Turkish People's Houses in Sydney and Melbourne (*Sidney Türk Halk Evi* and *Victoria Halkevi*) were actively involved in the labour movement. In 1979, five Turkish organisations – the Sydney Turkish People's House, the Australian Contemporary Turkish Workers' Association, the Turkish Education and Cultural Organisation, the Association of Progressive Women and the Turkish Kindergarten Co-op – came together to establish the New South Wales Federation of Democratic Turkish Associations (FDTA). The Australian Turkish Cultural Association (ATCA), which had been established in Melbourne in 1971, joined the FDTA in 1980.

These organisations' primary objective was to raise awareness about social inequality among migrants from Turkey through meetings, protests and cultural performances, as well as to promote social change (and, for some, revolution) in Turkey. Although they did not have cultural and religious motivations, some of their members were Alevis. This was in parallel with developments in Turkey, where a significant number of Alevis especially in cities supported left-wing groups without putting their cultural and religious background at the forefront of their political identities. As a formerly active interviewee in Berlin explained, most of the members of these groups 'were just not interested in the traditional conceptualisation of religion and rejected the inherited leadership of *dedes*' who, as they thought, 'exploited' the villagers who followed them. In the late 1980s, in parallel with developments in Turkey, the movement gradually changed into an identity movement.

The Formation Phase as an Identity Movement (1980s–2000s)

Interestingly, the first attempts to organise around Alevism in the 1980s came also from existing left-wing organisations. How, then, did Alevis' initial concerns about workers' rights evolve into concerns about their cultural and religious rights? Several factors seem to have played an important role. These were (1) growing organisational problems (that is, the increasing discrimination within left-wing organisations and the decline of these organisations after the 1980 military *coup* in Turkey and the end of the Cold War); (2) changing welfare needs (including the ageing of the first generation of migrants and the emerging problem of where to conduct funerals); and, finally and most obviously, (3) the physical attacks against Alevis in Turkey.

Growing Organisational Problems

One of the major problems within most left-wing organisations at the time was that they disregarded the discrimination towards Alevis. For example, in 1978, several Alevi members of the Populist Revolutionary Federation (*Halkçı Devrimci Federasyonu*, HDF) wanted to react against the Maraş massacre in Turkey. Halis Tosun, an Alevi who was then the president of the supervisory board, called the general president Ertekin Özcan to discuss how the HDF should respond to this incident, but Özcan and other leaders of the federation refrained from taking any action apart from proposing to publish a condemnation note. They thought that standing against the then government party CHP would lead to even more severe consequences.

The disagreement led a group of forty Alevis to resign from their membership and to establish their own organisation, the Turkish Workers Peace Union (*Türk İşçileri Barış Birliği*) in May 1979 (Tosun 2002, p. 3). The name of the organisation later changed to the Patriots Peace Union (*Yurtseverler Barış Birliği*), also known as the Patriots' Union (*Yurtseverler Birliği*, YB). In the early 1980s, thirty YBs decided to come together under the Federation of Patriots Union (*Yurtseverler Birliği Federasyonu*, YBF) (Tosun 2002, p. 3). The YBF had close ties with the Unity Party (*Türkiye Birlik Partisi*, TBP), whose leaders often travelled to Germany to visit and organise Alevis to support the party (Şahin 2005, p. 472). In its initial process of establishment, the YBF had only around 4,000 members (Tosun 2002, p. 7; Sökefeld 2008, p. 52), but, most importantly, it was the first attempt by Alevis to establish an umbrella organisation at the national level in Germany.

The second major organisational problem was the emotional loss caused by the 1980 *coup d'état* in Turkey and the broader decay of left-wing politics after the end of the Cold War. For example, the YBF stayed active only until 1983 and gradually weakened after the *coup*. As left-wing activism slowly declined in Germany and Australia towards the late 1980s, some Alevis turned their attention to Alevi organisations, founded with a focus on Alevi culture.

Changing Welfare Needs: Funerals

The period of establishing Alevi organisations in the late 1980s and early 1990s was also when the first-generation migrants were reaching old age. Both in Germany and Australia, many members of Alevi organisations consistently gave examples of elderly members of the community dying and their families having problems when they went to mosques to ask for funeral services. When some *imams* (prayer leaders in mosques) refused to undertake Alevi bodies, on the basis that they were Alevi, Alevi families thought that they needed to have a place to live and maintain, in their words, their 'own rituals'. Thus, surprisingly, as Zırh (2012 p. 292) elaborates in his work, funerals constituted 'a key catalyst of the process through which the Alevi revival emerged and developed'. This was, for instance, one of the primary reasons for establishing the organisation in Melbourne, Australia. Between 1990 and 1992, the Alevi community in Melbourne had three funerals refused by mosque officials. The community then decided to establish its own mortuary services.[6] Many of the other interviewees in both countries emphasised the extent to which their respective organisations helped them undertake this responsibility in such difficult times, which was an important factor that attracted other community members to newly emerging Alevi organisations.

First Attempts at Institutionalisation and the Rapid Growth
following the Massacres

The first time that Alevis established an organisation under the Alevi name was in the late 1980s. In Germany, an Alevi Cultural Week (*Alevi Kültür Haftası*) was organised between 2 and 7 October 1989. In its aftermath, despite the reservation of some organisers, a group of Alevis decided to establish an Alevi Cultural Centre (*Alevi Kültür Merkezi*, AKM) in Hamburg. Soon, Alevis in other cities founded similar organisations. The violent massacres of Alevis in Sivas and in the Gazi neighbourhood of Istanbul catalysed the Alevi movement and resulted in the rapid growth of Alevi organisations. It is important to note that the process of institutionalisation did not always run smoothly. Numerous conflicts erupted between individuals over the question of who would lead the organisation and how the organisation would approach the Turkish state. In general, the Alevis who were from socialist backgrounds, were openly critical of the Turkish state. Others were more reserved and less keen to criticise the state overtly.

---

[6] See Alevi Federation of Australia (©2008).

In Germany, those who were on the political left organised around Alevi Cultural Centres (AKMs), while others organised around Hacı Bektaş associations. The latter group was relatively more closed and seemingly apolitical, working mostly to provide spiritual guidance to its members, rather than being involved in political activities to defend the Alevis' political rights. In 1990, eleven associations of this fraction came together to establish the Federation of Alevi Communities (*Alevi Cemaatleri Federasyonu*) and invited other AKMs to join them (Sökefeld 2008, p. 82). Derviş Tur, a *dede* and also one of the founders of the organisation in Mainz, was elected as the chairman of this first umbrella organisation. However, shortly thereafter, the Sivas massacre occurred in Turkey, and as a reaction those who were on the political left wanted to organise and protest against the Turkish state. In contrast, those who were relatively right-wing remained silent. This was the first significant division between the two fractions. Left-wing Alevis took the lead and called for a major protest in Germany on 7 July 1993. Approximately 60,000 persons attended this rally, and soon thereafter, many other AKMs were established. Formal gatherings also occurred in other parts of the country, and in 1998 the federation changed its name to Federation of Alevi Unions in Germany (*Almanya Alevi Birlikleri Federasyonu*, AABF).

In Australia, political views towards the Turkish state's approach towards Alevis also had an impact on the unity of community members. For instance, in Sydney some community members accused the Australia Alevi Cultural Centre (AACC) of being too close to the Turkish Consulate in Sydney and, thereby, the Turkish state. Around the time of the Sivas massacre in Turkey, in 1994, several community members wanted to buy their own property. The major clash occurred in 1995 when the Turkish Council General offered to donate 5,000 Australian dollars to the organisation to help them buy their own premises. In this incident, the Turkish state's involvement led to contentions. While some contended that the donation could help them financially, others wished to stay away from the Turkish state at all costs. Later, another group of Alevis established another organisation under the name of Sydney Alevi Bektaşi Cultural Centre (now referred to as the Union of Sydney Democratic Alevis [*Sydney Demokratik Aleviler Birliği*]).

On the contrary, in Melbourne, twelve Alevis founded the Victoria Alevi Cultural Centre on 10 May 1992. Three months before, they had formed a committee and started working to establish a new organisation. Their membership grew in number immediately after the Sivas massacre, and they changed the name of the organisation to Melbourne Alevi Cultural Centre. Later, when the group became more institutionalised by establishing several independent committees, its name once more changed, to Alevi Community Council of Australia (ACCA). After the establishment of the Confederation in Europe, the ACCA sought to bring all organisations in Australia under the same umbrella. For the first time, on 5 February 2005, several meetings took place between the existing six associations in the country. All associations – except for the AACC in Sydney – formally came together under the Alevi Federation of Australia (AFA) on 22 November 2008. As will be seen below, in line with the rise of Islamophobia in the West and Islamist politics and growing threats towards Alevis in Turkey, the issues that were important in both countries changed again throughout the 2000s and 2010s.

The Transformation Phase: Alevism as a Religious/Faith-based Movement (2000s–Present)

At a structural level, the 1990s and 2000s witnessed the transformation of diversity policies in both Germany and Australia. Following a period of clear divergence in the 1990s, Germany turned to multiculturalism policies. The new Nationality Act of 2000 lifted the requirement of having a German parent to become a German citizen. Children born after 2000 to non-German parents could acquire German citizenship at birth, if at least one parent had a permanent residency permit or had been residing in Germany for at least eight years. At the same time, cultural diversity policies in both contexts have remained limited. In Australia, multiculturalism has been criticised since the 1990s, with conservative governments accusing some migrant groups, especially asylum-seekers and refugees, of being 'un-Australian'.[7] Multiculturalism in Australia was initially a component of citizenship (during the Keating government), but since the Howard government it has become a component of 'social cohesion' and nationalism. Despite some progressive changes to the new act, similar debates about national identity being endangered by immigration also occurred in Germany. In 2000, Friedrich Merz,

---

[7] Humphrey (2010a) refers to this form of governance as 'conditional multiculturalism'.

the former chairman of the conservative Christian Democratic Union of Germany and the Christian Social Union of Bavaria parliamentary group, started a widespread controversy by claiming that migrants had to adopt a German '*Leitkultur*'.[8] Throughout the 2000s, the term 'multiculturalism' lost its place in Germany and was replaced by the term 'integration'. In the Australian context, the 2000s witnessed the definition of multiculturalism transform into one that focused on individual responsibility and 'social cohesion' rather than group rights, with a neoliberal discourse emphasising economic growth (Schwarz 2007, pp. 72–74, 83).

Furthermore, both countries have been affected by the transnational 'securitisation of immigration' and the identification of, in particular, Muslim immigrants with potential terroristic attacks. Such fears towards immigrants have also influenced the policies of multiculturalism. In the context of Germany, as Tezcan (2012) suggests, immigration and integration policies changed towards 'religious integration'.[9] Comparing Australia with Germany, Michael Humphrey (2009, 2010b) argues that similar practices of securitisation and domestication of Muslims and Islam also happened in Australia. The entire discussion on global *jihad* developed as if the two worlds (Western countries and Muslims) had been living in complete isolation from each other, ignoring some of the Western countries' direct intervention in the Middle East.

These processes of the 2000s coincided with what Cihan Tuğal (2009) calls a 'passive revolution' of Islamist politics in Turkey. The ruling AKP government in Turkey significantly grew in power. The AKP's Alevi 'openings', which initially started on a promising tone, only helped emphasise the differences between Alevis rather than meeting their long-standing demands from the state (Özkul 2015). After a series of meetings, the 'openings' were finally set aside (see Chapter 3 in this volume). In 2018, the old parliamentary system was changed into a heavily presidential one. The Alevis' demands from the state

---

[8] *Leitkultur*, which literally means 'dominant culture' or 'leading culture', was a term introduced in the late 1990s by Bassam Tibi (1998, p. 154). Following him, Friedrich Merz used the term to imply and insist that the German nation had certain values that immigrants were obliged to adopt in order to be accepted into German society. See Merz (2000).

[9] In the German context, the term 'integration' has at times been used interchangeably with 'assimilation' and 'incorporation' (see Penninx et al. 2006, in particular Chapter 6).

were not only ignored, but an atmosphere of intolerance and fear emerged. Discrimination towards Alevis in some neighbourhoods and workplaces went unpunished. The increasing threats against Alevis and the growing infringement on their rights in their homeland (see, for instance, Erdemir et al. 2010) also concerned Alevis abroad.

Parallel to these transnational changes, associations slowly but increasingly started to define themselves as unique religious/faith-based organisations. In Germany, this was made clear in the following developments: increasingly, the names of some organisations were changed from Alevi Cultural Centres to Alevi Communities, and the institutional space was re-defined as *cemevis* instead of *dernek* (meaning organisation). The Federation of Alevi Communities of Germany (AABF) started to request the official recognition of Alevism as a unique religion of its own. In Germany, this was possible under the legislation of German states. In his response to the criticism of then Prime Minister Erdoğan, the then President of the Confederation, Turgut Öker, stated: 'As an institution of faith, we do not receive a single cent from the German state. Some of the rights we have obtained are those that originate from the German constitution' (Evrensel 2014).

Indeed, the German constitution guarantees the collective freedom of religion through religious organisations' self-management (see Article 136–41). Article 137.3 notes that 'religious societies shall regulate and administer their affairs independently within the limits of the law'. Article 141 also states that 'to the extent that a need exists for religious services [. . .] in the army, in hospitals, in prisons, or other public institutions, religious societies shall be permitted to provide them, but without compulsion of any kind'. Religious organisations in Germany can be established as a corporate body or registered voluntary organization – that is, *eingetragener Verein* (e. V.). Among those, the statute of *Körperschaft des öffentlichen Rechts* (a corporate body under public law) allows organisations to collect contributions (such as church tax), to provide religious education in state schools and to be represented in media-consulting committees. The status of *Körperschaft des öffentlichen Rechts* can be obtained only if the organisation can give assurance of their permanence (through the number of their members and of the years they have been operating), which in the Alevis' case was achieved over time.

For example, Alevi organisations invested in and put their efforts towards providing education on Alevism in state schools. The first lessons started in Berlin in 2002, followed by Baden-Württemberg in 2006 and Northern Rhine-Westphalia (NRW) and Bavaria in 2008. These are optional courses that are subject to grading and taught in German. The curriculum was prepared through suggestions gathered during two conferences (organised in November 2005 and March 2007) and further consultation with local AKM board members, teachers and *dede*s. The final curriculum was approved on 29 September 2007 at the AABF General Council. For courses to be initiated, specific requirements needed to be met. As of 2015, in Hessen and Baden-Württemberg, for instance, at least eight students needed to request the course; in NRW, that number is at least twelve students. Mostly because of these requirements, students of different ages often came together to form a class. Initially, there was also the problem of finding an adequate number of teachers capable of teaching Alevism. To that end, the AABF and local AKMs have started training Alevi teachers employed in state schools (teaching various subjects) and recommending them to the Ministry of Education. The Ministry of Education then makes the necessary arrangements for either two or four hours of teaching weekly. In late 2014, 1,490 students were taking such courses, and there were sixty-five teachers employed by 120 schools in nine states (Ha-ber.com 2014). As of 2020, Alevism was taught in ten states. Following the signing of the Equality of Rights Agreement in Hamburg, in 2015 a chair in Alevi studies was also founded at Hamburg University's Academy of World Religions.

Apart from these developments, the way in which organisations were institutionalised was also changing. For instance, organisation large enough established faith councils composed of different *dede*s who chose one among them as the head of the council. Some of the organisations also started to create an Alevi calendar. Just as in the attempts to celebrate the birth of Prophet Muhammad among Sunnis in *Kutlu Doğum Haftası* activities, the Alevi calendar throughout the 2000s included Imam Ali's birthday on 21 March coinciding with celebrations of Nowruz.[10] Weekly short courses on 'Alevi religion' have been introduced in organisations. Organisations large enough

---

[10] See Alevitischer Kalender (©2020) for further information.

have started providing Alevi faith consultation services to those in need in hospitals, prisons, migrant dormitories and nursing homes. Local organisations began to be involved in interfaith initiatives, mostly with Christian groups (as a faith system different from Islam). Overall, with such changes, the organisational space has been re-built as one where discussion revolves around the Alevi faith.

The AABF's efforts to have Alevism recognised as a unique religion by the German state gradually yielded results. Alevi organisations signed the Equality of Rights Agreement in November 2012 with the Hamburg government, in 2013 with the Lower Saxony government, in 2014 with the Bremen government and in 2019 with the Rheinland-Pfalz government. The Equality of Rights Agreement grants the right to celebrate religious holidays, to educate clerics, to open childcare centres and schools, to establish chairs in Alevi studies in universities, to have the right to participate in media consultation committees and to have the same public recognition as Christians and Jews. Turgut Öker argued that they could legitimately receive these rights following their long-standing efforts to teach Alevism in schools over the past twelve years (Hürriyet 2014).

In Australia, demands directed to the state were not the same. To start with, it is not feasible for Alevis in Australia to provide Alevi education in state schools. The lower numbers and the vast landscape between suburbs and cities make it impossible to reach students studying in different schools. But in terms of structural changes, the AFA followed a path similar to the AABF by establishing the Faith Council and Alevi Community Council of Australia. Again, similar to the attempts to claim recognition through numbers in Germany, several Alevis in Australia also campaigned to introduce Alevism as a separate religion in the 2011 census, by encouraging community members to answer the question of 'What is your religion?' with 'Alevi' under the category of 'Other'. However, Alevis in Australia did not seek official recognition as a unique religion from the Australian state, either because it was not feasible due to their smaller numbers, or because there was no particular need or demand for it. Nonetheless, organisations in both Sydney and Melbourne have continued working to meet community members' faith-related needs by organising *cem* gatherings, distributing food at the end of fasting periods and conducting funerals according to Alevi customs.

Like all social groups, Alevis are not homogenous and may have different views of Alevism and politics in general. Indeed, in both contexts, there have been differences in defining Alevism (whether inside or outside of Islam), locating Kemalist symbols and Mustafa Kemal Atatürk's place within organisations, or expressing views towards the Turkish state's approach towards Kurds and Kurdish activism in Turkey. However, Alevi organisations in both Germany and Australia have successfully managed to unify community members in resisting the AKP administration's neglect (if not blatant persecution) of Alevis in Turkey. In contrast to the growing threats towards Alevis for their belief systems in Turkey, Alevis in both countries have been able to perform their beliefs and rituals, as well as to express their views free of state persecution.

Conclusion

Overall, we can see that, in both countries, Alevis who were involved in mixed organisations with other migrants and dealing with issues of class equality and workers' rights later founded their own organisations under the framework of Alevi culture. In Germany, the Alevi movement later sought and ultimately acquired public recognition as a unique religion from the German state. These achievements were followed by the acquisition of the status of *Körperschaft des öffentlichen Rechts* in North Rhine-Westphalia in December 2020. This is a significant event, as North Rhine-Westphalia is the largest German state; hence, other states will likely follow the same decision. The acquisition of this status was preceded by Alevi organisations' long-standing efforts to define and teach Alevism in state schools and organisations. In Australia, Alevi organisations did not seek such official recognition.

Comparing these two contexts, the struggle in Germany to find recognition as a unique religion can be seen within the framework of political opportunity structures. However, their demands should also be considered against the background of changes in Turkey. It is not surprising that Alevis in Germany turned to emphasising their differences from Islam, *vis-à-vis* growing Islamist movements in Western countries and the ruling AKP administration's overt neglect, denigration, if not oppression of Alevis' demands in Turkey. Therefore, the Alevi movement's changing dynamics should be examined in parallel with changes in national political structures, growing radical

Islamist movements and prejudices against Muslims in Western countries, as well as the rise in Islamist politics and discrimination towards Alevis in Turkey.

Acknowledgments

I would like to express my endless gratitude to all my interviewees who took the time to talk, opened their homes and shared their meals and many of their personal stories with me. I also thank Cemil Boyraz, Hege Markussen and Besim Can Zırh who read earlier drafts of this chapter.

Bibliography

Abadan-Unat, N. (2011). *Turks in Europe: From Guest Worker to Transnational Citizen*. New York: Berghahn Books.

Alevi Federation of Australia (©2008). Australia Alevi Toplum Konseyi [Viewed 25 February 2021]. Available from: http://www.alevi.org.au/kurum/AATK.asp

Alevitischer Kalender (©2020). *Alevitischer Kalender* [online]. [Viewed 25 February 2021]. Available from: http://www.alevitischer-kalender.de/

Aktürk, H. (2020). *Modern Alevi Ekolleri*. Istanbul: İletişim.

Bahadır, İ. (2003). *Bilgi Toplumunda Alevilik*. Bielefeld: Bielefeld Alevi Kültür Merkezi Yayınları.

Başer, B. (2015). *Diasporas and Homeland Conflicts: A Comparative Perspective*. Surrey: Ashgate.

Castles, S. (1984). *Here For Good: Western Europe's New Ethnic Minorities*. London: Pluto.

Cumhuriyet (2014). Erdoğan, Misafir Alman Cumhurbaşkanı'na Verdi Veriştirdi. *Cumhuriyet,* 29 April.

Dressler, M. (2006). The Modern *Dedelik*: The Parameters of Alevism's Religious Authority in Contemporary Turkey. *Sociologie et Societes*, 38(1), 69–92.

Erdemir, A., et al. (2010). *Türkiye'de Alevi Olmak*. Ankara: Alevi Kültür Dernekleri.

Evrensel (2014). Avrupa'daki Alevi Örgütlerinden Başbakana Tepki. *Evrensel*. 30 April.

Gedik, E. (2011). Migrant Organizations in Turkey and Germany: Local, Transnational and Global Contexts of Kurdish-Alevis from Varto, Turkey. *Urban Anthropology*, 40(1), 151–205.

Ha-ber.com (2014). Almanya'da Alevilik Dersleri Yayılıyor. *Ha-ber.com* [online]. 30 September. [Viewed 25 February 2021]. Available from: https://www.ha-ber.com/almanyada-alevilik-dersleri-yayiliyor/59473/

Humphrey, M. (2009). Securitization and Domestication of Diaspora Muslims and Islam: Turkish Immigrants in Germany and Australia. *Diversities*, 11, 136–54.

Humphrey, M. (2010a). Conditional Multiculturalism: Islam in Liberal Democratic States. In: Ivison, D., ed., *The Ashgate Research Companion to Multiculturalism*. Farnham: Ashgate. pp. 199–216.

Humphrey, M. (2010b). Securitization, Social Inclusion and Muslims in Australia. In: Yasmeen, S., ed., *Muslims in Australia: The Dynamics of Exclusion and Inclusion*. Carlton: Melbourne University Press. pp. 56–78.

Hürriyet (2014). Alevis in Germany's Bremen Win Equal Status as Other Religious Communities. *Hürriyet* [online]. 17 October. [Viewed 25 February 2021]. Available from: http://www.hurriyetdailynews.com/alevis-in-germanys-bremen-win-equal-status-as-other-religious-communities.aspx?pageID=238&nID=73141&NewsCatID=351

İçduygu, A. (1991). *Migrants as a Transnational Category: Turkish Migrants in Melbourne, Australia*. Unpubl. doctoral dissertation, Australian National University.

Langer, R. (2008). Alevitische Rituale. In: Sökefeld, M., ed., *Aleviten in Deutschland: Identitätsprozesse einer Religionsgemeinschaft in der Diaspora*. Bielefeld: Transcript. pp. 65–108.

Langer, R. (2010). Hacı Bektaş Veli'nin Almanya'ya Varışı: Göç ve Diaspora Çerçevesinde Yurtdışındaki Alevilikte Dinsel Ritüel Dönüşüm-Değişimler. In: Kılıç, F., ed., *Doğumunun 800. Yılında Hacı Bektaş-Veli Sempozyumu*. Nevşehir: Atatürk Kültür Merkezi. pp. 379–88.

Merz, F. (2000). Einwanderung und Identität. *Die Welt* [online]. 25 October. [Viewed 31 March 2021]. Available from: https://www.welt.de/print-welt/article540438/Einwanderung-und-Identitaet.html

Østergaard-Nielsen, E. (2003). *Transnational Politics: Turks and Kurds in Germany*. New York: Routledge.

Özkul, D. (2019). The Making of a Transnational Religion: Alevi Movement in Germany and the World Alevi Union. *British Journal of Middle Eastern Studies*, 46(2), 259–73.

Özkul, D. (2015). Alevi 'Openings' and Politicization of the 'Alevi Issue' during the AKP Rule. *Turkish Studies*, 16(1), 80–96.

Penninx, R., Berger, M., and Kraal, K. (2006). *The Dynamics of Migration and Settlement in Europe: A State of the Art*. Amsterdam: Amsterdam University Press.

Şahin, Ş. (2005). The Rise of Alevism as a Public Religion. *Current Sociology*, 53(3), 465–85.

Schwarz, A. (2007). Strategic Uses of Multiculturalism in Germany and in Australia. In: Schwarz, A., and West-Pavlov, R., eds, *Polyculturalism and Discourse*. Amsterdam: Rodopi. pp. 67–90.

Şenay, B. (2012). *Beyond Turkey's Borders: Long-Distance Kemalism, State Politics and the Turkish Diaspora.* London: I. B. Tauris.

Sökefeld, M. (2003). Alevis in Germany and the Politics of Recognition. *New Perspectives on Turkey*, 28, 133–61.

Sökefeld, M. (2006). Mobilizing in Transnational Space: A Social Movement Approach to the Formation of Diaspora. *Global Networks*, 6(3): 265–84.

Sökefeld, M. (2008). *Struggling for Recognition: The Alevi Movement in Germany and in Transnational Space.* New York: Berghahn Books.

Tezcan, L. (2012). Göç ve Uyum Politikalarında Din Dönüşümü. *Die Gaste*, 22.

Tibi, B. (1998). *Europa ohne Identität? Die Krise der multikulturellen Gesellschaft.* Gütersloh: C. Bertelsmann.

Today's Zaman (2014). German President 'Horrified' by Developments in Turkey. *Today's Zaman.* 28 April.

Tosun, H. (2002). *Alevi Kimliğiyle Yaşamak.* Istanbul: Can Yayınları.

Tuğal, C. (2009). *Passive Revolution: Absorbing the Islamic Challenge to Capitalism.* Redwood City: Stanford University Press.

Zırh, B. C. (2012). *Becoming Visible through Migration: Understanding the Relationships Between the Alevi Revival, Migration and Funerary Practices through Europe and Turkey.* Unpubl. Doctoral Dissertation, University College London.

9

THE ALEVI DIASPORA IN FRANCE: CHANGING RELATIONS WITH THE HOME AND HOST STATES

AYCA ARKILIC

Introduction

This chapter provides a detailed analysis of the Alevi community's changing relations with the Turkish and French governments over the past two decades. It contributes to the Alevi studies literature in two important ways. First, unlike the majority of the existing works that examine Alevis' identity and mobilisation either from a home or host state perspective, it looks at how the interaction between the two affects Alevis. Second, given that the Alevi diaspora literature has mostly focused on Alevis in Germany and, in later years, on the Kurdish Alevi community in the UK, this chapter broadens our understanding of the Alevi émigré community by offering fresh insights into Alevis in France, who remain an understudied group.[1]

More specifically, this chapter focuses on the ramifications of the changing political atmosphere in Turkey and France since the early 2000s for the Alevi diaspora in France. I examine how the leaders of the Federation of Alevi Unions in France (*Fédération Union des Alévis en France*, FUAF), the largest and most active Alevi organisation in France, have responded to critical political

---

[1] For existing research on the German Alevi diaspora, see Sökefeld (2008), Özkul (2019) and Chapters 7 and 8 in this volume. For existing research on the Alevi community in the UK, see Jenkins et al. (2018), Cetin et al. (2020), Akdemir (2017) and Chapter 10 in this volume.

developments that took place in their homeland and host state. These include the 'Alevi Opening' (*Alevi Açılımı*), the Sunnification of Turkish domestic and foreign policy, and the French government's increasing interest in the Alevis. Even though Alevis in France have long felt excluded by the Turkish state, their marginalisation by the Turkish state has intensified over the past two decades, against the backdrop of the development of a Turkish diaspora policy that promotes Sunni-Muslim nationalism in the Alevi transnational space. These developments have led FUAF officials to distance themselves from their homeland more than ever. French Alevis' deepening distrust towards Turkey has triggered many homeland-oriented Alevi political rallies and campaigns launched in France. In the meantime, the rise of Sunni extremism in France has brought Alevis to the forefront as a dialogue partner and ally for the French government. In other words, as Alevis in France have felt discriminated against by their homeland, they have aligned more with their host state in recent years. The FUAF's growing political mobilisation, visibility and recognition in France is seen as a positive development by Alevi leaders. However, the FUAF's political actions are still predominantly driven by homeland-related concerns. This orientation slows down their localisation. The analysis presented in this chapter draws from a careful examination of organisational documents and news sources in English, French and Turkish, as well as interviews conducted with Alevi representatives and Turkish and French officials between 2013 and 2019.

The History of the Alevi Diaspora in France

The size of the Turkish population in France is estimated to be 650,000 persons (Turkish Ministry of Foreign Affairs 2021). The majority of Alevis emigrated to France between the 1970s and 1980s. There are approximately 150,000 Alevis in France (Gorzewski 2012). Alevi expatriates established their first organisations in Strasbourg and Metz in the early 1980s. These organisations were mainly concerned with social, cultural and religious activities, such as gatherings with socio-religious leaders (*dede*) and spiritual meetings (*cem* or *muhabbet*) (Koşulu 2013, p. 266).

The influx of Turkish political dissidents and asylum-seekers into Europe in the aftermath of the 1980 Turkish military *coup* led Alevi organisations in France to shift their focus from cultural and religious services to ideological and political activities. In this period, similar to developments in the

Alevi diaspora in the UK (see Chapter 10 in this volume), Alevi organisations tended to merge with secular, left-wing and Kurdish organisations. The leaders of these organisations remained embroiled in domestic Turkish politics and showed little interest in the economic, social and political life of France (Ögelman 2003, pp. 178–80).

From the late 1980s onwards, Alevi officials in France have begun to emphasise their distinct religious identity by pointing to significant differences between Alevism and Sunni Islam. Over time, they have also devoted themselves to Alevis' integration into French society and diversified the scope of their organisational activities. Yet, the Alevi community's small size, geographical dispersion and relatively short history in France did not allow Alevi mobilisation to flourish until the 1990s (Akgönül 2009).

The first Alevi Cultural Centre (*Alevi Kültür Merkezi*) was established in Paris in 1992, with 600 members. The second Alevi Cultural Centre came into existence in Strasbourg a year later. In 1998, the FUAF was founded in Strasbourg as an umbrella organisation.[2] Today, the FUAF serves as the largest Alevi organisation in France, with forty-one Alevi Cultural Centres under its roof. The FUAF is a founding member of the Confederation of European Alevi Unions (*Avrupa Alevi Birlikleri Konfederasyonu*, AABK). According to its website, the FUAF prioritises the preservation and recognition of Alevi culture and faith, while working for the empowerment and integration of the Alevi community in France. In addition, it strives to improve Alevis' and other immigrant groups' living conditions by promoting an 'equal rights' rhetoric. It upholds pluralistic, progressive and multiculturalist values and emphasises the equality of women and men as a fundamental principle, so the website notes.[3] In January 2016, the FUAF moved its headquarters from Strasbourg to Paris.[4] In September 2016, the organisation founded the Union of Young Alevis of France (*Union des Jeunes Alévis de France*), the first youth organisation established by Alevis in France.[5] The FUAF's women's unit, the Union of Alevi Women in France (*Union des Femmes Alévis de France*), opened its doors in April 2017.[6]

---

[2] Personal interview with a FUAF official, 21 January 2019, Paris.
[3] For more information, see FUAF (©2021).
[4] For more information, see Fransa24.com (2016).
[5] For more information, see FUAF (2016a).
[6] For more information, see FUAF (2017a).

Although the FUAF has gradually become more interested in local problems, Alevis are not immune to tensions emanating from the homeland (Massicard 2013). As an Alevi official pointed out during an interview, 'it does not matter if we [Alevis] are dual citizens. Our body is here [in France], but our mind is there [in Turkey]'.[7] FUAF representatives lobby for a variety of causes aimed at the homeland. As explained by the FUAF's chairperson, Erdal Kılıçkaya, French Alevis' main demand is the constitutional recognition of Alevis as a distinct religious group in Turkey (Kılıçkaya 2012). Some of their other demands emanate from the Alevis' quest for official recognition in Turkey, such as equal citizenship, recognition of *cemevi*s,[8] the elimination of discrimination against Alevis, the abolishment of compulsory religious courses taught in Turkish public schools and the safeguarding of Turkish *laïcité*. These requests still remain unmet by the Turkish government.

The Transformation of French Alevis' Relations with their Homeland

Alevis followed the AKP's rise to power in 2002 with wariness. However, with the inclusion of 'pluralism' into the state discourse in the mid-2000s, the AKP government began to address Alevi demands (Tambar 2014). In 2007, the Alevi Opening became the first official state policy to address Alevis' requests (see Chapter 3 in this volume). This initiative marked the beginning of an optimistic period for Alevis in Turkey and abroad. A more promising development took place between June 2009 and January 2010, when the Turkish government organised seven Alevi workshops (*Alevi Çalıştayları*). These workshops were aimed at building a bridge between the Turkish government and Alevi representatives (Subaşı 2010, p. 165). Despite their differences, Alevi representatives attending the workshops reached a consensus on their major demands (Arkilic and Gurcan 2020).

While the Alevi Opening was a crucial step for enhancing communication between Turkish officials and Alevis, the process quickly stalled when the AKP began to present Alevism as a form of Turkish Islam and systematically downplayed the differences among Alevis (Massicard 2013, Özkul 2015).

---

[7] Personal interview with an official from the Paris Alevi Cultural Centre, 9 December 2013, Paris.

[8] While the number of *cemevi*s built in Turkey increased from 106 in 2002 to 937 in 2013, they are still not officially recognised as places of worship. See Akşam (2013).

Despite the initial euphoria, the chairpersons of the leading Alevi organisations, including the Alevi Bektaşi Federation (*Alevi Bektaşi Federasyonu*, ABF) interpreted the Alevi Opening as an assimilatory move (Köse 2010; see also Chapter 3 in this volume). The Alevi community representatives in Europe also expressed discontent with the Alevi Opening, criticising it as a fake initiative. For example, the leaders of the FUAF and the Federation of Alevi Unions in Germany (*Alevitische Gemeinde Deutschland*, AABF) complained that the majority of the participants in the workshops were non-Alevis. Moreover, these workshops restricted the platform mostly to the national arena by not inviting an adequate number of diaspora representatives, therefore ignoring the transnational dimensions of Alevism. According to the representatives of the FUAF and the AABF, the main motivation behind the Alevi Opening was not to meet Alevis' demands but to assimilate them. These officials believed that the Alevi Opening was a redundant platform given that Turkish officials already knew what Alevi demands were (Arkilic 2016). An Alevi organisation member even argued that 'the Alevi Opening should take place only after *cemevi*s are recognized'.[9] The AABK's response to the Alevi Opening was even fiercer. The organisation's chairperson, Hüseyin Mat, defined the Alevi Opening as 'a new political trap' jeopardising Alevis. European Alevis' disapproval of the Alevi Opening precipitated the formation of an Alevi Forum and a roadmap for the future of Alevi mobilisation in Europe.

A 2012 announcement by a Turkish court that the Sivas trials had lapsed due to time statute limitations[10] and President Recep Tayyip Erdoğan's comment that these time statute limitations were an auspicious development for Turkey[11] antagonised Alevis even further. Four days after the court decision, on 16 March 2012, 50,000 Alevis took to the streets of Bochum to protest the oppression of Alevis by the AKP government.[12] As the editor-in-chief of the magazine *Alevilerin Sesi* (Voice of Alevis) noted, this was an unprecedented Alevi collective political action (Alevilerin Sesi 2012). The magazine's columnist concluded that, while in the past Alevis in Europe had

---

[9] Personal interview with an official from the Paris Alevi Cultural Centre, 9 December 2013, Paris.

[10] Sabah (2012).

[11] Hürriyet (2012).

[12] For more information, see Demokrathaber (2012).

organised rallies to raise generic identity-based demands, for the first time in their history they had come together to protest a specific government and political leader (Ateş 2012).

The Alevi diaspora's grievances toward Turkish officials have escalated with the AKP's sectarian Syria policy that presents Turkey as a homogenously Sunni state and subdues expressions of Alevi religious identity (Tank 2015). This policy is a projection of Turkey's broader neo-Ottoman foreign policy agenda that constructs Turkey's involvement in Syria as a revival of its glorious Ottoman legacy. Alevis are not part of this neo-Ottomanist ideal, 'because they would have been included within the Muslim Ottoman *millet*, which categorically assimilated their difference to the Sunni-Hanafi norm' (Walton 2017, p. 98). More specifically, the AKP government's focus on bringing down Bashar al-Assad's regime by supporting the Islamist opposition groups, such as Jabhat al-Nusra and Ahrar al-Sham, and its partnership with Saudi Arabia in an attempt to form regional alliances with Sunni actors in the region have increased the polarisation within Turkish society along the Sunni-Alevi cleavage (Tank 2015). According to Alevi leaders, the attempt to connect Alevis to Syrian Alawites, the sect-kin of al-Assad and his regime, has contributed to the demonisation of Alevis in Turkey.[13] On 31 October 2012, the AABK organised a mass protest in Berlin to oppose the AKP's Syria policy.[14]

Even though the rift between Sunnis and Alevis had long existed under previous Turkish governments, the members of the Alevi diaspora in Europe perceive the AKP government as more aggressive and threatening when compared to other Turkish governments (Arkilic 2016, 2020). The FUAF's chairperson confirmed that the Sunni–Alevi divide has intensified under AKP rule:

> Alevis feel even more suppressed under the AKP government than they did in the past [. . .] We are worried about the AKP government's and Erdoğan's assimilation and 'othering' policy and their goal of raising a vindictive and pious generation [*kindar ve dindar bir nesil*].[15]

---

[13] Personal interview with a FUAF official, 21 January 2019, Paris.

[14] For more information, see SOL (2012).

[15] Interview with the chairperson of the FUAF. See ABF (2012).

French Alevis also believe that Turkey's post-2003 diaspora institutions and strategies (Arkilic 2021a, 2021b) discriminate against them because they favour conservative-nationalist organisations, such as the *Diyanet*-linked Turkish-Islamic Union for Religious Affairs (*Diyanet İşleri Türk İslam Birliği*, DİTİB), the *Millî Görüş* and the Union of Islamic Cultural Centres (*İslam Kültür Merkezleri Birliği*). A representative from the Paris Alevi Cultural Centre argued that the FUAF does not receive financial support from the YTB for its projects and activities and that no Alevi representative from France serves on the YTB's advisory board. For this official, the lack of Alevi representation in the committee points to Alevis generally being ostracised in Turkey's diaspora policy. Representatives of the Alevi diaspora in France have also refused to participate in meetings and workshops set up by the UID and the YTB, because Turkish officials allegedly show no effort to include Alevi representatives in these meetings.[16] AABF leaders in Germany shared similar concerns.[17]

The establishment of the Strasbourg Theology Institute in 2011 with full funding from the *Diyanet* was another development that frustrated Alevis in France. In the past, only religious personnel sent by the *Diyanet* could serve the Turkish community in Europe. Over time, some European countries, notably Germany, expressed their discontent with the *Diyanet*-affiliated religious personnel's symbiotic ties to the Turkish state and requested that religious personnel serving in European mosques learn the language of their host country and receive training in Europe. While Germany has restricted and strictly monitored the *Diyanet*-linked DİTİB's involvement in the Islamic theology institutes established in various German cities, the DİTİB in France has maintained discretion in the design of the curriculum and the appointment of teachers at the Strasbourg Theology Institute (Arkilic 2016). Students who complete this program receive a bachelor's degree from Istanbul University's Faculty of Theology and become eligible to work in DİTİB mosques in France, which number around 253.[18] This project trains clerical staff who can speak French and Turkish and are familiar with both cultures. Therefore, it allows Turkish religious authorities to reach out to second- and

---

[16] Personal interview with an official from the Paris Alevi Cultural Centre, 9 December 2013, Paris; and an official from the FUAF, 21 January 2019, Paris.

[17] Personal interview with an AABF official, 25 February 2019, Berlin.

[18] Interview with a DİTİB official. See Dünyabizim (2012).

third-generation Muslims more easily.[19] However, since the Strasbourg Theology Institute mostly attracts Sunni Muslim students and provides employment opportunities for them, it is likely to estrange the Alevi youth in France.

According to some Alevi leaders, Turkey's new diaspora policy has also vested more power and legitimacy in Alevi expatriate organisations linked to the Cem Foundation (*Cem Vakfı*) and the World Ahlal Bayt Foundation (*Dünya Ehl-i Beyt Federasyonu*).[20] These organisations do not define Alevism as a religion in its own right and seek integration with the Turkish state. Since the 1990s, Islamist parties in Turkey have tried to establish close ties with these Alevi actors. Before the 1994 local elections, the Welfare Party (*Refah Partisi*, RP) even nominated a few Alevi candidates that had links to these organisations. However, the AKP has formed a closer relationship with these Alevi organisations (Massicard 2013).

Similar to the process in Turkey, these organisations' overseas branches, such as the *Cem Vakfı*-affiliated organisations in Europe and the Ahlal Bayt Alevi Federation of Europe (*Avrupa Ehl-i Beyt Alevi Federasyonu*), have forged good relations with the Turkish government in recent years. For example, the *Cem Vakfı*-linked organisations have engaged in a joint project with the *Diyanet*, which sends Alevi *dede*s to Europe to deliver talks on Islam, the Alevi faith and the Prophet Mohammed's life (Hürriyet 2014a). In a similar vein, an official from the Ahlal Bayt Alevi Federation of Europe sits on the advisory board of the YTB.[21] This official's take on the Alevi Opening highlights his organisation's ideological differences from that of the AABK, the AABF and the FUAF:

> If Alevism means love for Ali, then I am an Alevi. Islam does not differentiate between Alevis and Sunnis. Alevism should not be recognized as a faith outside of Islam. Unfortunately, some Alevis interpret Alevism very differently [. . .]. The AKP government is the only government in the Turkish Republic's history

---

[19] Personal interview a DİTİB official, 28 May 2013, Strasbourg.

[20] Personal interview with an official from the Paris Alevi Cultural Centre, 9 December 2013, Paris; and a FUAF official, 21 January 2019, Paris.

[21] Local Alevi associations that are linked to the *Cem Vakfı* have been headquartered in Essen (Germany) since 1997. The Ahlal Bayt Alevi Federation of Europe has been operating in Europe since 2001 with its sixty-three branches (personal interview with an official from the Ahlal Bayt Alevi Federation of Europe, 29 November 2013, Cologne).

that approaches Alevis with good intentions. This government organised seven Alevi workshops. This means that Turkish officials accept Alevis as a unique group and that they are ready to listen to Alevis' problems. This is a historical development. It would be too naïve to expect [them] to resolve complicated problems overnight. We will support every step our government takes.[22]

The Ahlal Bayt Alevi Federation of Europe is also supportive of the Turkish government's diaspora outreach policies in Europe. The organisation sees Turkey's growing patronage over its émigré community as an outcome of Turkey's expanding economic and political power. According to one of its representatives, the organisation has not yet received any financial assistance from the YTB. However, this official is confident that funding will be provided once his organisation submits appropriate project proposals to the YTB.[23]

Similar to the Alevi Bektaşi Federation supporters in Turkey, Alevis affiliated with the AABK, the AABF and the FUAF view these Alevi actors as pawns of the AKP government. For them, such pro-government organisations have no legitimacy in the eyes of the majority of the Alevi community, due to their limited representation and problematic definition of Alevism. As an Alevi representative in Paris pointed out, Alevis in France see the proliferation of Alevi organisations that are ideologically closer to the incumbent government as a threat to Alevis' unity in France.[24]

The empowerment of the *Cem Vakfı*-affiliated organisations and the Ahlal Bayt Alevi Federation of Europe is a reverberation of the reframing of Alevism within a Turkish-Islamic framework under the AKP government (Lord 2017). As can be seen in Chapter 8 of this volume, a telling example of the incumbent government's intervention in Alevi actors' framing process is President Erdoğan's defamatory remark that 'Alevism in Germany does not include Ali [*Ali'siz Alevilik*]. This is an atheist mentality' (Hürriyet 2014b). According

---

[22] Personal interview with an official from the Ahlal Bayt Alevi Federation of Europe, 29 November 2013, Cologne.

[23] Personal interview with an official from the Ahlal Bayt Alevi Federation of Europe, 29 November 2013, Cologne.

[24] Personal interview with an official from the Paris Alevi Cultural Centre, 9 December 2013, Paris.

to Erdoğan, Alevis who agree to go to the mosque are 'Alevis with Ali' – in other words, 'good' Alevis (Taştekin 2014). Echoing Erdoğan's words, the then Deputy Prime Minister asserted: 'We cannot recognize *cemevi*s as houses of worship because we consider Alevism inside Islam. Since the majority of Alevis consider themselves to be Muslims, Islam's house of worship is the *masjid*, the mosque' (Akşam 2014). This statement follows from a definition of Alevism that bolsters the official nationalist-religious identity narrative.

Another ground-breaking development that galvanised Alevi political activism in France was the Turkish government's reaction to the Gezi Park protests. The initial demonstrations that erupted in Istanbul in May 2013 criticised the AKP's neoliberal urban transformation project targeting the Gezi Park in Taksim. Environmental and urban agendas took a backseat when a full wave of demonstrations and civil unrest engulfed Turkey over the following months. Thousands of protestors came together to raise their voices against the AKP's increasing authoritarianism and encroachment on Turkey's secularism (Tuğal 2013). The spiralling clashes between police and civilians resulted in the deaths of twenty-two persons, many of them Alevis. Moreover, 85 per cent of the protestors taken under custody were Alevis. The Alevis' high rate of involvement in the Gezi Park protests reflect the violent victimisation that Alevis have faced under the AKP government (Karakaya-Stump 2014). The increasing number of Alevis who fell victim to state violence fuelled resentment among Alevis and led to cascading large-scale anti-government demonstrations in Turkey and abroad. The AABK alone organised several anti-government protests in Germany. The sit-in held in Cologne on 31 May 2013 attracted a crowd of 10,000 from all over Europe. A month later, on 22 June 2013, 100,000 gathered in another demonstration in Cologne.[25] Approximately 50,000 persons convened in Cologne on 24 May 2014, under the leadership of the AABK (Topçu 2014).

Alevis in France had engaged in political activism well before 2013 to stand against the Turkish government's pervasive discrimination against Alevis. For example, in 2011, the FUAF introduced the 'New Alevi Establishment' (*Yeni Alevi Yapılanması*, YAY) and the 'Global Alevi Union' (*Küresel Alevi Birliği*, KALB) projects to homogenise and systematise the Alevi mobilisation in

---

[25] Personal interview with an AABK official, 26 November 2013, Cologne.

France and around the globe.[26] What is more, on 20 October 2012, 10,000 French Alevis gathered in Strasbourg to attend the 'Say No to Discrimination, Assimilation and Militarism in Turkey' demonstration staged by the AABK and the FUAF. This rally denounced the rise of political Islam in Turkey and called for equal citizenship (Alevilerin Sesi 2012).

However, similar to the situation in Germany, the Gezi Park revolt increased the frequency of Alevi political rallies and campaigns launched in France. A series of demonstrations took place in Paris and Strasbourg throughout June 2013 (Habertürk 2013). The Gezi Park protests became a turning point for Alevis in France, reminding them once again, as in 1993 and 1995, that their homeland was 'lost'.

Other political events also prompted Alevi rallies in the following years. On 23 February 2014, the FUAF staged a rally to draw attention to the attacks against Alawites in Syria.[27] On 4 October 2015, the FUAF amassed 2,000 persons in another rally to protest Erdoğan's visit to Strasbourg.[28] On 25 June 2016, a third large-scale protest took place. Approximately 10,000 gathered in front of the European Parliament under the leadership of the AABK and the FUAF to attend an anti-bigotry demonstration condemning the AKP's sectarian and authoritarian policies.[29] On 3 February 2017, the FUAF organised a press conference in Paris to urge everyone to vote 'no' in the Turkish constitutional referendum held on 16 April 2017, which would pave the way for Turkey's transition from a long-standing parliamentary system to presidentialism (Arkilic 2018a).[30] The FUAF praised these protests as examples of trailblazing political events that invigorated the Alevi movement and instilled hope and courage in the members of the Alevi community in Turkey and Europe.

The Transformation of French Alevis' Relations with their Host State

The 1905 Law on the Separation between Church and State forms the legal basis of French *laïcité*. Article II of the Law stipulates that the state should not recognise or support any *culte* (religion). Scholars have noted that the

---

[26] For more information on these projects, see Arslan (2011).

[27] See, for example, Avegkon (2014).

[28] See, for example, Alevi Kültür Dernekleri (2015).

[29] For more information on this demonstration, see FUAF (2016b).

[30] For more information on this meeting, see FUAF (2017b).

strict separation of church and state in France provides a less accommodating setting for Muslims' religious needs when compared to that of other European countries, such as Britain and Germany (Fetzer and Soper 2005). A 2004 law on secularism and conspicuous religious symbols in schools, which banned wearing the headscarf, and a 2011 law, which banned the wearing of full-face veils (*voile intégral*), entrenched France's position as a *laïc* country and called into question France's tolerance toward Muslims.

Yet, recent research found that Turkish Muslims overall have a positive experience in France, despite the rigidity of the French regime. Representatives of Turkish Islamic organisations praise France's equal distance from all religious groups as an assurance of their religious freedom (Arkilic 2015). Other studies have shown that diaspora members from Turkey do not believe that they are subject to severe discrimination in France. Their perceived level of discrimination is, in fact, lower than that of other immigrant groups in France, such as Maghrebis and Sub-Saharan Africans (Brouard and Tiberj 2011). This is a striking finding given that, in reality, emigrants from Turkey experience discrimination at rates similar to Maghrebi and Sub-Saharan African immigrant groups (Beauchemin et al. 2010).

There are several reasons why Turks feel at ease in France. Mainly before the 2000s, the Turkish community in France enjoyed privileged invisibility in the eyes of French policy-makers. France's larger size and turbulent colonial history with Maghrebi and Sub-Saharan African communities put these communities under the spotlight whenever integration-related debates emerged. In contrast, Turks drew attention to the lack of colonial legacy in Turkey and promoted themselves as a group superior to Maghrebis and Sub-Saharan Africans. According to Turkish Muslim leaders, the immigrant integration issue has never been a Turkish problem in France. Turks' disinterest in the *sans-papiers*, headscarf and *banlieue* protests of other immigrant groups in the 1990s and 2000s contributed to the French and Turkish perception that Arabs and Africans are the real troublemakers in France (Yalaz 2014, Arkilic 2016).

However, as officials from the French Ministry of the Interior (*Ministère de l'Intérieur*) and the French Ministry of Europe and Foreign Affairs (*Ministère de l'Europe et des Affaires étrangères*) made clear in an interview, Turks in France may lose their privileges in the future. For example, these officials see the establishment of the Strasbourg Theology Institute with full funding from Turkey as an intervention in France's domestic affairs.[31] Other European policy-makers have also become increasingly cautious about conservative-nationalist Turks' convergence with the Turkish government (Arkilic 2018b).

Officials from the French High Council for Integration (*Haut Conseil à l'Integration*, HCI) have expressed similar concerns. According to them, Turks in France retain solid financial and emotional ties to their homeland and prioritise the preservation of Turkish and Muslim identity over French identity. These bureaucrats find it alarming that even second- and third-generation Turks born and raised in France identify themselves as Turkish first and French second. These experts also hinted that they no longer approached Turks much differently from other Muslim groups:

> Our communication with Muslims has become more complicated in recent years [. . .] Some Muslim groups want to build a Moroccan mosque. Others want a Turkish mosque. Different Muslim groups have different demands and religious practices, and this complicates our relationship with Muslims.[32]

Another HCI expert complained about Turkish Muslims' reluctance to interact with French society. She indicated that, unlike Maghrebi organisations that seek financial support from French municipalities for their organisational activities, Turkish Islamic organisations rely mostly on Turkey's funding or their internal resources. For her, Turkish Islamic organisations hinder French Turks' integration, by perpetuating their association with Turkish-Muslim identity and by championing closed community networks and allegiance to Turkey.[33] These anecdotes reveal that the positive perception of Turks in France is, in fact, changing and that Turkish Muslims are now purportedly turning into 'bad immigrants'. President Emmanuel Macron's October 2020 announcement of a draft bill that seeks to defend *laïc* values

---

[31] Personal interview with an official from the French Ministry of the Interior, 11 March 2013, Paris; an official from the French Ministry of the Interior, 14 January 2019, Paris; and an official from the French Ministry of Europe and Foreign Affairs, 10 January 2019, Paris.

[32] Personal interview with officials from the French High Council for Integration, 22 May 2013, Paris.

[33] Personal interview with an official from the French High Council for Integration, 22 May 2013, Paris.

and to halt the export of foreign-trained *imams* also reflects French authorities' growing suspicion of Turks in the country.[34]

The rise of Islamist extremism in France is another factor that endangers Turkish Islamic organisations' advantaged status in France. The findings of a 2013 survey on Islamic fundamentalism[35] conducted in Germany, France, the Netherlands, Austria, Belgium and Sweden found that 45 per cent of Sunni Muslims with a Turkish background support Islamic fundamentalism, as opposed to 15 per cent of Turkish Alevis, 4 per cent of Protestants and 3 per cent of Catholics. In other words, while fundamentalist attitudes are widespread among Sunni Muslim communities in Europe, according to scholars, only a small percentage of Alevis have fundamentalist tendencies (Koopmans 2014, p. 11). In a similar vein, a 2017 study carried out by the French National Centre for Scientific Research (*Centre National de la Recherche Scientifique*, CNRS) on the prevalence of radical ideology among high school students found that Sunni Muslim students are much more likely to hold fundamentalist views than other religious groups.[36]

As my interviews with officials from the HCI revealed, French bureaucrats believe that there is a gap between Islamic and French values and that the rise of fundamentalism among French Muslims poses a serious challenge to French *laïcité*. These officials emphasised that a new form of 'sentimental aggression' has been unfolding in France: the native population feels emotionally threatened by the increasing public visibility of Muslim women in veils, *burqas* and *niqabs*, as well as men in Salafist garments. French society is also placed in peril due to the mushrooming of various mosques, so they suggested.[37] A poll conducted by the French Institute of Public Opinion (*Institut Français d'Opinion Publique*) in 2016 showed that anti-Muslim sentiments are indeed gaining popularity. According to this study, almost two-thirds of

---

[34] Duvar English (2020).

[35] The study's definition of religious fundamentalism captures three elements of a fundamentalist belief system: (1) 'Christians [Muslims] should return to the roots of Christianity [Islam]', (2) 'There is only one interpretation of the Bible [Qur'an] and every Christian [Muslim] should stick to that', and (3) 'The rules of the Bible [Qur'an] are more important to me than the laws of [survey country]' (Koopmans 2014, p. 8).

[36] For more information on this study, see Trécourt (2017).

[37] Personal interview with officials from the French Ministry of the Interior, 5 June 2013, Paris.

the French respondents argued that Islam has become too 'influential and visible', and 47 per cent suggested that the Muslim community posed a 'threat' to their national identity.[38] In other words, Islam has become an increasing concern in France.

The surge of intolerance towards Sunni Muslims has rendered the Alevi community a more compatible interlocutor for the French government. Alevis in France have generally enjoyed favourable relations with the French government. Since the 1980s, Alevi representatives have been present in immigration forums and councils organised by the French state. Alevi leaders' position as a key dialogue and project partner *vis-à-vis* Islamic organisation representatives has become even more palpable in recent years. French policy-makers view Alevis positively due to the Alevi community's stronger commitment to core French values. Also appealing to French policy-makers has been the FUAF's emphasis on gender equality, as evidenced by the large number of Alevi women serving in French councils and Alevi organisations, as well as Alevi politician Mine Günbay's recent rise to vice presidency in the Strasbourg Municipality (Gürsoy 2014). Alevi officials welcome the attention that they are receiving from French policy-makers. As one Alevi representative put it, . . .

> [French authorities] know that we are a transparent and legal organisation [. . .]. Our organisation [the FUAF] meets with French bureaucrats from the Ministry of the Interior and the Ministry of Europe and Foreign Affairs. They are assuring us that Alevism will be taught in public schools in the future [. . .]. We get along very well with the mayor of Boulogne-Billancort (a suburb of Paris). She offered us funding to support our projects [. . .]. While anti-immigrant acts take place in France from time to time, this can happen in any country. Muslims want to build mosques with minarets. They are loud in the metro. They do not give their seat to women. Every country has its own rules, and citizens must abide by these rules [. . .]. I disagree with the argument that France assimilates its immigrants.[39]

Alevis are regarded as 'good immigrants' in France, also because 90 per cent of French Alevis hold French citizenship. Moreover, the number of Alevi

---

[38] To access this poll, see Institut Français d'Opinion Publique (2016).

[39] Personal interview with an official from the Paris Alevi Cultural Centre, 9 December 2013, Paris.

politicians serving on French municipal councils has increased since the mid-2000s (Gürsoy 2014). This is a remarkable achievement given that Turks have the lowest naturalisation, electoral registration and voter turnout rates among all immigrant groups in France, including Maghrebis, Sub-Saharan Africans, Cambodians and Vietnamese (Yalaz 2014, Arkilic 2016).[40] In addition, Alevi students have a high success rate in public schools (Gürsoy 2014). Alevis' academic success stands out particularly in light of a 2013 report published by the HCI illustrating that Turkish students have the worst school attendance and success record after Maghrebis in France.[41] The rise of young and educated Alevis in the FUAF organisational ranks has facilitated Alevis' communication with French bureaucrats.[42]

A noteworthy example of Alevis' thriving relations with France is FUAF leaders' one-on-one meetings with French officials from the Ministry of the Interior and the Ministry of Europe and Foreign Affairs since July 2012.[43] More importantly, on 12 November 2014, France's former President François Hollande invited FUAF leaders to the Élysée Palace for a special meeting. The FUAF's chairperson Erdal Kılıçkaya and head of the Diplomacy Council Ali Karababa explained that a recurrent theme in this meeting consisted of the common values shared by France and Alevis, such as *laïcité* and gender equality. FUAF officials also informed Hollande about human rights violations committed against women and minorities in Turkey. Following the meeting, Hollande vowed to include Alevis in other meetings and working groups to be held at the palace.[44] This was a critical development for the institutionalisation and recognition of the FUAF. The inauguration of the first *cemevi* in Paris in March 2015 was another indicator of the French government's renewed interest in the Alevi community. Prominent policy-makers, such as the president of the French National Assembly, Claude Bartalone, and

[40] The 1999 and 2008 censuses reveal different immigrant groups' naturalisation, electoral registration and voter turnout rates. To access these censuses, see INSEE: http://www.insee.fr/en/bases-de-donnees/

[41] For a full list of HCI reports, see Haut Conseil à L'intégration: http://archives.hci.gouv.fr/-Rapports-.html

[42] Interview with FUAF chairperson Erdal Kılıçkaya; see Kılıçkaya (2014).

[43] For more information, see Alevi Kültür Dernekleri (2020).

[44] For more information, see Alevi Kültür Dernekleri (2015).

various French parliamentarians and mayors attended the inauguration.[45] Moreover, the FUAF's relations with the Paris Municipality have solidified over the past few years.[46]

The FUAF's rapprochement with French bureaucrats resulted in another historical event. On 16 December 2016, the FUAF organised a first-of-its-kind symposium on Alevism at the French National Assembly, following the Socialist parliamentarian Jean-Pierre Blazy's invitation.[47] During the meeting, FUAF representatives delivered a presentation on the Alevi community and Alevism in France. According to the FUAF's chairperson, this meeting marked the beginning of a new era between Alevis and France:

> [A] dialogue process between Alevis and French politicians has begun, and the closed door has finally become wide open [. . .]. [French politicians] accept us with our real [. . .] identity. They recognize us as Alevis. They do not place us under wrong categories. This is very important for us.[48]

In January 2017, an Alevi Council (*Alevi Meclisi*) gathering coordinated by the FUAF attracted top public officials, such as the Green Party deputy and former minister Cecile Duflot, the European Parliament deputy Marie-Christine Vergiat and the Arnouville Mayor Pascal Doll. In this meeting, French officials criticised the AKP's authoritarian policies and extended their support and solidarity to Alevis. Throughout 2017, the FUAF's Diplomacy Council has also worked closely with Benoît Hamon, a member of the Socialist Party in France. The FUAF's cooperation with Hamon is significant because he became the Socialist Party's candidate for the 2017 French presidential election after defeating Manuel Valls, the Prime Minister of France between 2014 and 2016, in the second round of the party primary.[49]

FUAF officials have boosted their relations with Eurocrats as well. On 19 January 2016, the FUAF handed a dossier to the European Court of Human Rights to inform European policy-makers about crimes committed against

---

[45] The inauguration ceremony is available on YouTube. See Sarıtaylı (2015).

[46] For more information, see Haberler (2014).

[47] For more information, see Alevinet (2014).

[48] To watch FUAF chairperson Erdal Kılıçkaya's assessment of the symposium, see Kılıçkaya (2014).

[49] For more information, see FUAF (2017c).

Alevis in Turkey. On the same day, FUAF officials held a press conference and demonstration in front of the European Parliament in Strasbourg. On 27 January 2016, they met with party group presidents at the Council of Europe.[50] Finally, the Union of Alevi Women in France visited the European Parliament on 8 March 2017. In this meeting, Alevi women reiterated the FUAF's demands and discussed potential avenues for collaboration with parliamentarians.[51]

Conclusion

Even though France has attracted a large number of Alevi emigrants since the 1970s and the Alevi diaspora's organisational life has been active over the past two decades, Alevi political mobilisation in France remains an understudied topic. This chapter examined French Alevis' political activities within the broader context of political developments taking place in Turkey and France since the early 2000s. More specifically, it shed light on how the FUAF has responded to the rise of political Islam in Turkey and French policy-makers' growing interest in Alevis.

An examination of organisational documents, media sources and interviews with Alevi representatives as well as Turkish and French officials demonstrates that French Alevis' discontent with their homeland has increased greatly since the AKP's rise to power in 2002. While Alevi exclusion is not a new phenomenon, the failure of the Alevi Opening, the AKP's sectarian Syria policy and the repression of the Gezi Park protests that resulted in the deaths of many Alevi citizens have intensified the Sunni-Alevi divide under the AKP rule. The development of a new diaspora agenda which has ignored the FUAF's demands and empowered Turkish immigrant organisations that frame Alevism within the margins of Sunni Islam has aggravated the 'us' versus 'them' dichotomy between Alevis and Sunnis. While the FUAF had engaged in homeland-oriented political activism before, the organisation's politicisation has gained momentum in recent years, in response to the AKP government's biased diaspora outreach policy that strives to impose a definition of Alevism in line with the official nationalist-religious identity narrative.

---

[50] For more information, see Birgün (2016).
[51] For more information, see FUAF (2017d).

In the meantime, French policy-makers have formed stronger diplomatic relations with Alevis. For example, FUAF officials were invited to a private meeting at the Élysée Palace in 2014. The inauguration of the first *cemevi* in Paris in 2015 and the organisation of a first-of-its-kind Alevism symposium at the French National Assembly in 2016 were other key signs of the FUAF's increasing recognition and respect in the eyes of French bureaucrats. French policy-makers' renewed interest in Alevis is linked to the rise of Sunni extremism and anti-Muslim attitudes in France. Even though Turkish Islamic organisations in France enjoyed a privileged invisibility *vis-à-vis* Maghrebi and Sub-Saharan African organisations in the past, their growing rapprochement with the Turkish state has begun to attract criticism. As French bureaucrats have become increasingly cautious about Turkish Islamic organisations and begun to lump them under the 'bad immigrant' category, Alevis have come to the forefront as a secular and progressive immigrant group. While the Alevis' projection as a key dialogue and political partner stands as an emblematic manifestation of the beginning of a positive era between Alevis and France, the Alevi diaspora's localisation would have been more robust, had their politicisation been directed more at their host country rather than at their home country.

Acknowledgements

I thank (in alphabetical order) Alex Kreger, Hege Markussen, Derya Özkul and Besim Can Zırh for their valuable comments and suggestions.

Bibliography

ABF (2012). Alevi Bektaşi Federasyonu [online]. [Viewed 2 February 2020]. Available from: http://www.alevifederasyonu.org.tr/index.php?option=com_content &view=article&id=1085:klckaya-biz-aleviler-cesur-olmak-zorundayz&catid=1: son-haberler

Akdemir, A. (2017). Boundary-Making and the Alevi Community in Britain. In: Issa, T., ed., *Alevis in Europe: Voices of Migration, Culture and Identity*. London: Routledge.

Akgönül, S. (2009). Turks in France: Religion, Identity, and Europeanness. In: Küçükcan, T., and Güngör, V., eds, *Turks in Europe: Culture, Identity, Integration*. Amsterdam: Türkevi Research Center. pp. 35–65.

Akşam (2014). Alevi Açılımı Genişliyor. *Akşam* [online]. 28 May. [Viewed 3 December 2020]. Available from: http://www.aksam.com.tr/siyaset/emrullah-isler-alevi-acilimi-genisliyor/haber-311527

Akşam (2013). Semah Açılımı. *Akşam* [online]. September 18. [Viewed 9 December 2020]. Available from: http://www.aksam.com.tr/guncel/semah-acilimi/haber-245596

Alevi Kültür Dernekleri (2020). Fransa Cumhurbaşkanı Alevi Birlikleri Federasyonunu Kabul Etti. *Alevi Kültür Dernekleri* [online]. [Viewed 1 december 2020]. Available from: http://www.alevikulturdernekleri.com/fransa-cumhurbaskani-alevi-birlikleri-federasyonunu-kabul-etti/

Alevi Kültür Dernekleri (2015). Fransa'daki Alevilerden Dev Protesto. *Alevi Kültür Dernekleri* [online]. 4 October. [Viewed 3 December 2020]. Available from: http://www.alevikulturdernekleri.com/fransadaki-alevilerden-dev-protestorte-hos-gelmedin/

Alevilerin Sesi (2012). Avrupalı Alevilerden Strasburg Mitingi. *Alevilerin Sesi*, 165.

Alevinet (2014). Fransa Parlamentosunda Alevi Sempozyumu. *Alevinet* [online]. 18 December. [Viewed 1 December 2020]. Available from: http://www.alevinet.com/2014/12/18/fransa-parlamentosunda-alevi-sempozyumu/

Arkilic, A. (2021a). Explaining the Evolution of Turkey's Diaspora Engagement Policy: A Holistic Approach. *Diaspora Studies* [online]. 14(1), 1–21. [Viewed 31 March 2021]. Available from: doi: 10.1080/09739572.2020.1839688

Arkilic, A. (2021b). Turkish Populist Nationalism in Transnational Space: Explaining Diaspora Voting Behavior in Homeland Elections. *Journal of Balkan and Near Eastern Studies* [online]. 16 February 2021. [Viewed 31 March 2021]. Available from: doi: 10.1080/19448953.2021.1888599

Arkilic, A. (2020). Empowering a Fragmented Diaspora: Turkish Immigrant Organizations' Perceptions of and Responses to Turkey's Diaspora Engagement Policy. *Mediterranean Politics* [online]. 16 November. [Viewed 31 March 2021]. Available from: doi: 10.1080/13629395.2020.1822058

Arkilic, A. (2018a). The 2017 Turkish Constitutional Referendum: Domestic and Transnational Implications. *New Zealand Journal of Research on Europe* 12(1), 55–72.

Arkilic, A. (2018b). How Turkey's Outreach to Its Diaspora Is Inflaming Tensions with Europe. *Washington Post Monkey Cage* [online]. [Viewed 9 December 2020]. Available from: https://www.washingtonpost.com/news/monkey-cage/wp/2018/03/26/how-turkeys-outreach-to-its-diaspora-is-inflaming-tensions-with-europe/

Arkilic, A. (2016). Between the Homeland and Host States: Turkey's Diaspora Policies and Immigrant Political Participation in France and Germany. Unpubl. doctoral dissertation, University of Texas at Austin.

Arkilic, A. (2015). The Limits of European Islam: Turkish Islamic Umbrella Organizations and their Relations with Host Countries – France and Germany. *Journal of Muslim and Minority Affairs*, 35(1), 17–41.

Arkilic, A., and Gurcan, A. E. (2020). The Political Participation of Alevis: A Comparative Analysis of the Turkish Alevi Opening and the German Islam Conference. *Nationalities Papers: The Journal of Nationalism and Ethnicity* [online]. [Viewed 31 March 2021]. Available from: doi: 10.1017/nps.2020.49

Arslan, D. (2011). Yeni Alevi Yapılanması. *Küresel Alevi Birliği* [online]. [Viewed 3 December 2020]. Available from: http://www.dailymotion.com/video/xkprqj_yeni-alevi-yapilanmasi-yay-kuresel-alevi-birligi-kalb_people

Ateş, F. (2012). Bochum'daki Tepki Yılların Birikimidir. *Alevilerin Sesi*, 158.

Avegkon (2014). Suriye'deki Alevi Katliami Protesto Edildi. *Avegkon* [online]. [Viewed 3 December 2020]. Available from: http://avegkon.org/suriyedeki-alevi-katliamai-pariste-protesto-edildi/

Beauchemin, C., Hamel C., and Simon, P. (2010). Trajectoires et origines: Enquête sur la diversité des populations en France. *INED Documents de Travail* [online]. 168. [Viewed 9 December 2020]. Available from: https://www.ined.fr/fichier/s_rubrique/19558/dt168_teo.fr.pdf

Birgün (2016). Fransa'daki Alevilerden Barış Çığlığı. *Birgün* [online]. 15 January. [Viewed 1 December 2020]. Available from: http://www.birgun.net/haber-detay/fransa-daki-alevilerden-baris-cigligi-100795.html

Brouard, S., and Tiberj, V. (2011). *As French as Everyone? A Survey of French Citizens of Maghrebin, African, and Turkish Origin*. Philadelphia: Temple University Press.

Cetin, U., Jenkins, C., and Aydın, S., eds (2020). Special Issue: Alevi Kurds: History, Politics and identity, *Kurdish Studies*, 8(1).

Demokrathaber (2012). Alevilerden Başbakana Almanya'da Görkemli Protesto. *Demokrathaber.org* [online]. 17 March. [Viewed 2 December 2020]. Available from: http://www.demokrathaber.org/guncel/alevilerden-basbakana-almanyada-gorkemli-protesto-h7682.html

Duvar. English (2020). Turkey Accuses Macron of Supporting Hate Crimes with His New Plan Against 'Islamist Separatism'. *Duvar. English* [online]. 5 October. [Viewed 3 December 2020]. Available from: https://www.duvarenglish.com/diplomacy/2020/10/05/turkey-accuses-macron-of-supporting-hate-crimes-with-his-new-plan-against-islamist-separatism/

Dünyabizim (2012). Fransa'da Müslümanlar Neler Yaşıyor? *Dünyabizim* [online]. 20 March. [Viewed 2 December 2020]. Available from: http://www.dunyabizim.com/soylesi/9283/fransada-muslumanlar-neler-yasiyor

Fetzer, J. S., and Soper, C. J. (2005). *Muslims and the State in Britain, France, and Germany.* New York: Cambridge University Press.

Fransa24.com (2016). Fransa Alevi Birlikleri Federasyonu Genel Merkezi Strasbourg'tan Paris'e Taşıdı. *Fransa24.com* [online]. 11 January. [Viewed 20 November 2020]. Available from: http://www.fransa24.com/fransa-alevi-birlikleri-federasyonu-genel-merkezini-strasbourtan-parise-tasidi/

FUAF (©2021). Qui sommes-nous? *Fédération Union des Alévis en France* (FUAF) [online]. [Viewed 20 November 2020]. Available from: https://alevi-fuaf.com/tr/qui-sommes-nous/

FUAF (2017a). Fransa Alevi Kadınlar Birliği Kuruldu. *Fédération Union des Alévis en France* (FUAF) [online]. 3 April. [Viewed 30 November 2020]. Available from: http://alevi-fuaf.com/tr/2017/04/03/fransa-alevi-kadinlar-birligi-kuruldu/

FUAF (2017b). Basına ve Kamuoyuna. *Fédération Union des Alévis en France* (FUAF) [online]. 3 February. [Viewed 3 December 2020]. Available from: https://alevi-fuaf.com/tr/2017/02/03/basina-ve-kamuoyuna/

FUAF (2017c). 'HAYIR'ımız Hayırlı, Uğurlu Olsun! *Fédération Union des Alévis en France* (FUAF) [online]. 3 February. [Viewed 1 December 2020]. Available from: http://alevi-fuaf.com/tr/2017/01/29/fransa-cumhurbaskanligi-secimleri/

FUAF (2017d). FAKB Avrupa Parlementosunda Ağırlandı. *Fédération Union des Alévis en France* (FUAF) [online]. 11 March. [Viewed 18 February 2021]. Available from: http://alevi-fuaf.com/tr/2017/03/11/fakb-avrupa-parlemento-sunda-agirlandi/

FUAF (2016a). Fransa Alevi Gençler Birliği Kuruldu. *Fédération Union des Alévis en France* (FUAF) [online]. 6 September. [Viewed 30 November 2020]. Available from: http://alevi-fuaf.com/tr/2016/09/06/fransa-alevi-gencler-birligi-fagb-kuruldu/

FUAF (2016b). Alevilerin Strasbourg'dan Gericiliğe Dur Mesajı. *Fédération Union des Alévis en France* (FUAF) [online]. 6 September. [Viewed 3 December 2020]. Available from: http://alevi-fuaf.com/tr/2016/09/06/alevilerin-strasburgdan-gericilige-dur-mesaji-turan-eser/

Gorzewski, A. (2008). Alevis in France: Striking a Balance Between Old and New. *Qantara* [online]. 11 July. [Viewed 9 December 2020]. Available from: https://en.qantara.de/content/alevis-in-france-striking-a-balance-between-old-and-new

Gürsoy, D. (2014a). Fransa Alevilerinden Tarihi Buluşma. *BirGün* [online]. 17 December. [Viewed 3 December 2020]. Available from: http://www.birgun. net/haber-detay/fransa-alevilerinden-tarihi-bulusma-72734.html

Haberler (2014). Fransa Parlamentosu'nda 'Alevi Semposyumu' Düzenlendi. *Haberler* [online]. 18 December. [Viewed 1 December 2020]. Available from: http://www. haberler.com/fransa-parlamentosu-nda-alevi-sempozyumu-6785062-haberi/

Habertürk (2013). İstanbul Yanındayız: Gezi Parkı Protestolarına Yurt Dışından Destek Yağıyor. *Habertürk* [online]. 2 June. [Viewed 3 December 2020]. Available from: http://www.haberturk.com/dunya/haber/849480-istanbul-yanindayiz

Haut Conseil à l'Intégration [online]. [Viewed 2 February 2021]. Available from: http://archives.hci.gouv.fr/-Rapports-.html

Hürriyet (2014a). Diyanet Alevi Dedeleri Almanya'ya Gönderdi. *Hürriyet* [online]. 4 February. [Viewed 3 December 2020]. Available from: http://www.hurriyet. com.tr/diyanet-alevi-dedeleri-almanyaya-gonderdi-5890952. Last accessed on 03.12.2020

Hürriyet (2014b). Almanya'daki Alevilerden Yanıt: Erdoğan Nezdinde Terfi Ettik. *Hürriyet* [online]. 24 April. [Viewed 3 December 2020]. Available from: http:// www.hurriyet.com.tr/almanya-daki-alevilerden-yanit-erdogan-nezdinde-terfi-ettik-26318618

Hürriyet (2012). Başbakan Erdoğan'dan Sivas Davası Yorumu. *Hürriyet* [online]. 13 March. [Viewed 2 December 2020]. Available from: http://www.hurriyet.com. tr/basbakan-erdogandan-sivas-davasi-yorumu-20115497

Institut Français d'Opinion Publique (2016). [online]. [Viewed 2 December 2018]. Available from: http://www.ifop.com/media/poll/3373-1-study_file.pdf

INSEE, *Institut National de la Statistique et des Études Économique* [online]. [Viewed 1 December 2020]. Available from: http://www.insee.fr/en/bases-de-donnees/

Jenkins, C., Aydın, S., and Cetin, U., eds (2018). *Alevism as an Ethno-Religious Identity: Contested Boundaries.* London: Routledge.

Karakaya-Stump, A. (2014). Alevizing Gezi. *Jadaliyya* [online]. 26 March. [Viewed 9 December 2020]. Available from: http://www.jadaliyya.com/pages/index/17087/ alevizing-gezi

Kılıçkaya, E. (2014). Fransa Ulusal Meclisi Alevileri Ağıladı. *Youtube* [online]. 28 December. [Viewed 1 December 2020]. Available from: https://www.youtube. com/watch?v=diG-o_KcikE.

Kılıçkaya, E. (2012). Turquie: Les Alévis tirent la sonnette d'alarme. *Le Monde* [online]. 30 July. [Viewed 9 December 2020]. Available from: https://www. lemonde.fr/idees/article/2012/07/30/turquie-les-alevis-tirent-la-sonnette-d-alarme_1739037_3232.html

Koşulu, D. (2013). The Alevi Quest in Europe through the Redefinition of the Alevi Movement: Recognition and Participation, a Case Study of the FUAF in France. In: Nielsen, J., ed., *Muslim Political Participation in Europe*. Edinburgh: Edinburgh University Press. pp. 255–76.

Koopmans, R. (2014). Religious Fundamentalism and Out-Group Hostility among Muslims and Christians in Western Europe. *WZB Discussion Paper*. No. SP VI 2014-101.

Köse, T. (2010). The AKP and the Alevi Opening: Understanding the Dynamics of the Rapprochement. *Insight Turkey* 12(2), 143–65.

Lord, C. (2017). Rethinking the Justice and Development Party's Alevi 'Openings'. *Turkish Studies*, 18, 278–96.

Massicard, E. (2013). *The Alevis in Turkey and Europe: Identity and Managing Territorial Diversity*. London: Routledge.

Ögelman, N. (2003). Documenting and Explaining the Persistence of Homeland Politics among Germany's Turks. *International Migration Review* 37(1), 163–93.

Özkul, D. (2015). Alevi 'Openings' and Politicization of the 'Alevi Issue' during the AKP Rule. *Turkish Studies* 16(1), 80–96.

Özkul, D. (2019). The Making of a Transnational Religion: Alevi Movement in Germany and the World Alevi Union. *British Journal of Middle Eastern Studies*, 46(2), 259–73.

Sabah (2012). Sivas Davası'nda Karar! *Sabah* [online]. 13 March. [Viewed 2 December 2020]. Available from: http://www.sabah.com.tr/gundem/2012/03/13/sivas-icin-karar-gunu

Sarıtaylı, T. (2015). Paris Alevi Kültür Merkezi'nin Cem Evi'ni Fransa Meclis Başkanı Açtı. *Youtube* [online]. 10 March. [Viewed 1 December 2020]. Available from: https://www.youtube.com/watch?v=lyHuD1KG4ME

SOL (2012). Alevi Örgütlerinden Erdoğan Protestosu: 'Ortadoğu Diktatörünü Almanya'da İstemiyoruz'. *SOL* [online]. 31 October. [Viewed 2 December 2020]. Available from: http://haber.sol.org.tr/soldakiler/alevi-orgutlerinden-erdogan-protestosu-ortadogu-diktatorunu-almanyada-istemiyoruz-haberi

Sökefeld, M. (2008). *Struggling for Recognition: The Alevi Movement in Germany and in Transnational Space*. Oxford: Berghahn Books.

Subaşı, N. (2010). The Alevi Opening: Concept, Strategy and Process. *Insight Turkey* 12(2), 165–78.

Tambar, K. (2014). *The Reckonings of Pluralism: Political Belonging and The Demands of History in Turkey*. Stanford: Stanford University Press.

Tank, P. (2015). The 'Sunnification' of Turkey's Foreign Policy. *The New Middle East Blog* [online]. 13 August. [Viewed 6 January 2021]. Available from: https://

newmeast.wordpress.com/2015/08/13/the-sunnification-of-turkeys-foreign-policy/

Taştekin, F. (2014). Alevileri Ali'siz Birakmak. *Al-Monitor* [online]. 2 June. [Viewed 6 January 2021]. Available from: https://www.al-monitor.com/pulse/tr/originals/2014/06/turkey-erdogan-alevi-sunni-sectarian-cemevi-sabahat-akkiraz.html

Trécourt, F. (2017). Une vaste enquête sur la radicalité chez les lycéens. *Centre National de la Recherche Scientifique*, CNRS [online]. [Viewed 3 December 2020]. Available from: https://lejournal.cnrs.fr/nos-blogs/face-au-terrorisme-la-recherche-en-action/une-vaste-enquete-sur-la-radicalite-chez-les

Tuğal, C. (2013). Occupy Gezi: The Limits of Turkey's Neoliberal Success. *Jadaliyya* [online]. 4 June. [Viewed 6 January 2021]. Available from: http://www.jadaliyya.com/pages/index/12009/occupy-gezi_the-limits-of-turkey's-neoliberal-success

Turkish Ministry of Foreign Affairs. (2021). Relations between Turkey and France. [Viewed 18 February 2021]. Available from: www.mfa.gov.tr/relations-between-turkey-and-france.en.mfa

Walton, J. (2017). *Muslim Civil Society and the Politics of Religious Freedom in Turkey*. New York: Oxford University Press.

Yalaz, E. (2014). Immigrant Political Incorporation: Institutions, Groups, and Inter-Ethnic Context. Unpubl. doctoral dissertation, Rutgers University.

10

FROM PARTICULARISTIC ORGANISATION TO FEDERATION: MOBILISATION FOR ALEVI IDENTITY IN BRITAIN

AYŞEGÜL AKDEMİR

Introduction

Most Alevis in Britain migrated from the central and central-eastern parts of Turkey – such as Maraş, Sivas and Kayseri – and arrived in the country in the late 1980s as asylum-seekers.[1] Although they mainly come from Kurdish ethnic origins and have had the experience of being refugees, their identification and social mobilisation around these identities vary significantly. Using the political opportunities of living in a 'liberal' state and framing a common Alevi identity were crucial factors that enabled mobilisation and ultimately transformed the community's organisational structure. Alevis in Britain have organised mainly around the England Alevi Culture Centre and Cemevi (*İngiltere Alevi Kültür Merkezi ve Cemevi*, İAKM) (hereafter EACC) since 1993 and have been expanding their activities and broadening their networks in their struggle for recognition.

In this chapter, I discuss the history of Alevi mobilisation, particularly in London. First, I will provide a brief history of emigration from Turkey to Britain. Then I will explain the organised activism and history of the EACC

---

[1] The European Community Association Agreement, which is known as the Ankara Agreement, allows entrepreneurs from Turkey establish businesses in the UK. This migration route has recently replaced the search for asylum as a way to migrate to Britain.

and discuss the transformation since 2008, when the administrative board and chairperson changed through a lengthy judicial process. Over time, the EACC was able to mobilise more people than ever before, by creating consensus among the community members and expanding their interests and activities. It has transformed from a small-scale community centre into a national-level federation that cooperates at a transnational level with local organisations in Turkey, the European Alevi Unions Confederation (*Avrupa Alevi Birlikleri Konfederasyon*, AABK) and supranational institutions. I will demonstrate that a combination of opportunities for mobilisation and framing a more comprehensive Alevi identity made it possible for the EACC to generate consensus among the community on defining Alevi identity and mobilising for recognition of their cultural rights. Here I analyse Alevi mobilisation in Britain on national, supranational and transnational levels to outline their demands and struggle for recognition on multiple levels: the national level comprises the activities that focus on recognizing Alevi identity and consolidating the community through cultural activities in Britain. The supranational level consists of the links to supranational institutions to which Alevis can apply so as to their cultural rights and 'equal citizenship' in Turkey, using Turkey's EU membership goal as leverage. Finally, the transnational level includes sustained border-crossing links with Alevi communities elsewhere.[2]

The findings are based on an ethnographic study conducted between July 2012 and August 2013 in London, which explored the Alevi communities' transnational attachments with Turkey and elsewhere in their struggle for recognition and 'equal citizenship'. Forty-one semi-structured interviews were conducted with the EACC's leaders and Alevi migrants who come from different parts of Turkey and who identify with Alevism to varying degrees.

Alevis in Britain differ from other Euro-Alevis because of their reasons for migrating and their ethno-linguistic background. The majority of Alevis in Turkey define themselves as Turkish, and a relatively smaller number is Kurdish. While other European countries that received economic migrants from several regions of Turkey reflect Turkey's demographic composition and have more diverse Alevi communities, Alevis in Britain are mainly asylum-seekers from the Kurdish-speaking regions of Central and Eastern

---

[2] See Özkul (2019b) for a comprehensive review of the scholarship on transnational migration.

Anatolia. This makes them a doubly discriminated group on religious and ethnic grounds; thus, framing a unifying Alevi identity that surpasses ethnic and linguistic differences becomes even more important. This study shows that mobilisation occurs due to both the internal dynamics of the group and the opportunity structures, as well as the available public discourses in the host country and transnational social links; it complements previous research on Alevi communities in Europe (Cetin et al. 2020, Coşan-Eke 2017, Issa 2017, Jenkins et al. 2018, Kaya 1998, Massicard 2013, Özkul 2019a, Sökefeld 2008).

Alevi Migration to Britain

Migration from Turkey to Britain dates back to the 1940s, mostly identified with Cypriots (Düvell 2010, p. 1). A significant number of migrants from Turkey started to arrive in the UK in the 1980s. Düvell estimates that 'there are at least a quarter of a million Turks residing in Britain' (2010, p. 1). İsrafil Erbil, the former chairperson of the EACC and the British Alevi Federation (*Britanya Alevi Federasyonu*, BAF), estimates that at least 300,000 persons migrated from Turkey to Britain. Nearly 80 per cent of this population live in London (AleviNet 2021). The exact proportion of Alevis among immigrants from Turkey is unknown, as there are no official statistics.

Some immigrants from Turkey arrived in Britain through the help of relatives and fellow townsmen, particularly from Turkey's Kurdish-speaking regions. For example, some of my interviewees estimated that in London there were nearly 3,000 persons from one village, Tilkiler (in Maraş, southeastern Turkey), and around 750 families from Kırkısrak village (in Kayseri, central Turkey). These immigrants have extensive kinship relations, and the concept of 'chain migration' explains the high number of immigrants from a small number of regions.

While migration from Turkey to Britain had several reasons, the legal basis was political, and most Alevi immigrants were asylum-seekers. A relatively small number in the first wave of immigrants arrived in Britain to study or work as professionals. To obtain refugee status, asylum-seekers reported the human rights violations in Turkey against Kurds and/or Alevis. The late 1980s and 1990s were a peak time in the armed conflicts between the Turkish army and the Kurdistan Workers' Party (PKK). Therefore, in the asylum-seeking process being Kurdish was a characteristic more prevalent than being Alevi. Also, membership in radical leftist organisations[3] and living under the threat of detention and torture constituted other reasons to obtain refugee status, especially for Turkish Alevis. Smuggling has had a significant role in this migration wave: around 100,000 persons were smuggled from Turkey to Britain (Düvell 2010).

Although the legal basis of immigration was political, other factors also motivated migration to Britain. Most of my interviewees expressed that they had economic concerns and wanted to live a more prosperous life in a liberal country.[4] The UK was the only possible destination, as the conventional routes of migration to continental Europe were either less desirable or unattainable by the 1980s. Following the military *coup* in 1980 and the state pressure against Kurds and Alevis, the political and economic hardships motivated people to look for better chances elsewhere. Bauböck (2003, p. 709) argues that the sending countries may have specific motivations for encouraging emigration, such as human capital upgrading, remittances and the political lobbying of the receiving countries' governments. While the Turkish state had previously expected remittances and improved technical skills from economic migrants (Martin et al. 2001), Kurdish and Alevi immigrants' political lobbying was viewed with suspicion. Moreover, some of my interviewees believed that the Turkish state wished to dismiss the Kurds and the Alevis, ignoring human trafficking and irregular migration.

Therefore, a complex web of factors determined the destination. The host country's opportunities and the first immigrants' accounts of life in the new country influenced these decisions. The asylum policies of the receiving countries and the availability of social benefits for asylum-seekers also had an impact on their choices. For instance, most of my interviewees had connections in Germany, the most popular destination for immigrants from Turkey. However, after comparing advantages and disadvantages, they either did not

---

[3] Some powerful leftist organisations in London include *Dev-Sol* (*Devrimci Sol*, Revolutionary Left), TKP/ML (*Türkiye Komünist Partisi/Marksist Leninist*, Turkish Communist Party/Marxist Leninist) and MLKP (*Marksist Leninist Komünist Parti*, Marxist Leninist Communist Party).

[4] Freedom associated with living in a liberal country was discussed particularly in interviews with female interviewees.

prefer Germany or decided to immigrate to Britain after having stayed in Germany for some time. For instance, one interviewee compared Britain and Germany regarding asylum-seekers' conditions as follows:

> In the first years here [in Britain], there were more rights. I stayed in Germany for six months; they put you in a *Heim*, like a massive hotel with a bath and toilet in the same place. They put you in a room with four to five other people. The dirty ones and good ones, pardon my language, but people from all walks of life are there. They serve sausages in the morning, noon and evening. They give you food but no bread with it. Eat it or not; nobody cares. When you go out, you show your ID. They don't provide houses. Here it wasn't like that. This country had more advantages (female, 39, London).

Most immigrants from Turkey concentrated in London due to access to the job market. Those who lacked a work permit and the necessary skills, such as English and occupational training, had to take up informal jobs in the textile sector, under poor working conditions. When the textile sector collapsed due to competition from cheaper markets in Eastern Europe and South Asia in the 1980s, these job opportunities gradually decreased and eventually ceased to exist. However, by that time, migrants had already settled, sending their children to schools. Some managed to buy houses, obtain refugee status and eventually acquire British citizenship. Instead of returning to Turkey, they adapted to these changes and found alternative employment opportunities.

Some late-comer migrants also looked for jobs, but eventually had to either change their preferred industry or be open to new business options. One of the interviewees, who arrived in Britain in 1999, for instance, explained the impact of the sectoral change as follows: 'We came here in the hope of finding jobs in the textile factories. The year we arrived all factories began to shut down one by one' (male, 43, London). This interviewee had previously been working in the construction sector in Turkey; therefore, he could find a job in this sector. Many immigrants tried to adapt in similar ways, by either finding jobs in the service sector, or opening up their own businesses.

Following the initial stages of migration, during which they worked in textile factories from the late 1980s to mid-1990s, the Alevis' living standards gradually improved because they could accumulate their savings and invest in real estate in London. İsrafil Erbil, who had arrived in London in 1986 as a teenager, explained this process:

> Towards the 2000s, those who invested in real estate, at least those who bought their own houses because the market was booming in England, found themselves well off economically in the 2000s. It was never in the history of England. Exactly when people from Turkey migrated here, real estate prices increased five times more in that historical period. The people who noticed that with an entrepreneurial mind and with feelings of solidarity, they either bought their own house or bought another for investment. Because the English economy went through a crisis in '89, the real estate prices went down. Therefore, our people bought those houses for the lowest prices. Naturally, when prices went up again, those investments gained value (male, 45, London).

Despite the capital accumulation and the successful adaptation to the changing job market through the establishment of small businesses, generally immigrants from Turkey still live in the most deprived boroughs of London and suffer from 'high levels of deprivation, housing needs, high levels of unemployment (up to 40 percent) and educational failure' (Düvell 2010, p. 4). Moreover, Kurds are more disadvantaged than ethnic Turks and Turkish Cypriots, because they are the relatively most recent immigrants from Turkey (Enneli et al. 2005, p. 48).[5]

The Rise of Alevi Identity in Britain

Identity politics and mobilisation around Alevism began only after certain factors emerged sometime after the Alevis had migrated to Britain. Firstly, the global context has transformed social movements, and from the 1960s and 1970s onwards new social movements have become sensitive to human rights and identity issues (Habermas 1981, Melucci 1985, Polletta and Jasper 2001). Gradually, identity began to be considered a right, which influenced immigrant groups' and minorities' demands for their cultural rights (Soysal 2000). The mobilisation of Alevi identity in Britain only began in the 1990s. The community members had already considered Alevism a persecuted identity, but Alevism became publicly visible only in the 1990s because of the particular

---

[5] For studies on education and identity perspectives on British Alevi Kurds, see Jenkins and Cetin (2018) and Jenkins (2020).

context in which the community wanted to open up a space for Alevi identity. This process took place in Turkey and in European countries, especially in Germany (see Özkul 2019a, and Chapters 7 and 8 in this volume).

Secondly, Alevis witnessed significant changes in their traditional social networks and solidarity mechanisms, mainly due to migration and urbanisation in Turkey and abroad, and ultimately the emergence of modern institutions such as Alevi organisations and *cemevi*s in urban centres (on the implications of these processes, see Aktürk 2020, Şahin 2005). In addition to providing faith-based services, *cemevi*s provide solidarity networks for Alevis in cities. Alevi mobilisation gained momentum in the mid-1980s in Turkey's big cities and towns and in European capitals due to the Turkish state's policies during the post-1980 *coup* period. These policies included the Turkish-Islamic Synthesis (*Türk-İslam Sentezi*). This state policy aimed to eliminate identity claims, especially those of Kurds, to create unity around Turkish and Sunni identities. The promotion of this view led to strict policies and targeted social control at a time of tremendous social and economic change (Akın and Karasapan 1988). The Turkish-Islamic Synthesis policy and the threat of assimilation concerned Alevis in both Turkey and in Europe; hence, there emerged a strong need for unity.

Thirdly, the broader mobilisation around Kurdish identity was also significant for the later growth of interest in Alevi identity.[6] Since many Alevis in Britain are also of Kurdish origin and claimed asylum mainly through their Kurdish identity,[7] the homeland politics of new migrants initially focused on Kurdish, rather than Alevi identity (Wahlbeck 1999, p. 158). According to my interviewees, some people joined PKK-affiliated organisations after their migration to Britain because the active Kurdish movement in London influenced them. Being political immigrants, some of the Kurdish Alevis already exhibited sympathy or economic or social support for Kurdish identity politics and the armed struggle against the Turkish army.

---

[6] This mobilisation has also resulted in a growing interest in Dersim and the Kurdish Alevi communities in Turkey. See Chapters 5 and 6 in this volume. See also Gezik and Gültekin (2019).

[7] Some interviewees stated that they did include their Alevi background in their asylum application and argued that they were persecuted because of being Alevi. However, the majority reported fear of detention/persecution due to being Kurdish and/or a member of illegal political organisations as their justification for seeking asylum.

These changes can be seen in the transformation of relevant organisations. For example, one of London's earliest community centres was the *Halkevi* (People's House), which initially had a pluralistic membership. Later it was dominated by the Kurdish movement and the Kurdish Community Centre (*Kürt Toplum Merkezi*, KCC), and it promoted Kurdish identity, in addition to providing 'advice on welfare, housing and asylum issues, language and training courses as well as various social and cultural activities' to immigrants from Turkey (Wahlbeck 1999, p. 156). This strong presence of Kurdish identity in London was a concern for the first-generation Alevi migrants who wished to keep a distance between faith and politics and to mobilise solely around Alevi faith and culture. This perspective dominated the initial years of Alevi organisations in London and created an apolitical organisational attitude. The two pillars of this apolitical attitude were maintaining a distance from Kurdish identity politics and framing Alevism as the heart of Islam. The concern to keep the younger generation safe from Kurdish influence (and prevent them from joining PKK-affiliated organisations) made the EACC apolitical and cut off its communication with other community centres in London.

Lastly, most Alevis in Britain lived in North London; apart from meeting at community centres, they socialised at picnics and weddings, but lacked a social space where they could get together and receive faith-based services, such as funeral ceremonies. At the time, the political organisations that were established in London competed to recruit members. The large number of Alevis in Britain and their political background as asylum-seekers mainly from Kurdish-speaking regions made them an important recruitment source for leftist organisations. Two competing organisations at the time, the Turkish Communist Party (*Türkiye Komünist Partisi*, TKP) and the *Halkevi*, later dominated by the PKK, raced for the recruitment of Alevis. One Alevi association, the *Canlar Birliği* (Union of Souls), was founded in 1992 in such a context, by the leftist organisation *İşçi Birliği* (Workers' Union). Therefore, the foundation of the EACC was a reaction to the politicisation of Alevis and aimed to 'prevent Alevism from being misused by political organisations' and 'to provide a safe community environment for Alevi youngsters without the extortionate membership fees charged by the political organisations' (Zırh 2012). Similar to the situation in Turkey and abroad, the Sivas massacre facilitated further mobilisation and increased membership in the *cemevi*.

Finally, in 1993, the EACC was established in London, and various other *cemevi*s in different parts of Britain followed.

The EACC's apolitical attitude towards ethnic conflicts in the 1990s did not satisfy the younger and more educated Alevis who challenged the organisation in the 2000s. Kurdish-speaking Alevis, who valued their ethnic and religious identities equally, were not content with the EACC's apolitical attitude either (Akdemir 2017). The interviewees in this study, for instance, often expressed that they did not go to the EACC at the time of the previous administration and regarded mobilising for Alevi identity as 'backward' (*geri kalmış*) and 'reactionary' (*gerici*), because it excluded their ethnic identity. The younger generation of Alevis felt conflicted and wished to initiate a new mobilisation model, by framing the Alevi belief as an overarching identity beyond ethnic, linguistic and other cultural differences in this context.

Alevi Mobilisation at the National Level

The Alevi community's practical needs and struggle for visibility and cultural recognition were the primary motivations behind mobilising at the national level in Britain – and mainly in London, due to Alevis' concentration in that city. Alevi identity was already present in the early stages of Alevi mobilisation; however, the framing of this identity as an overarching belief that surpasses ethnic, linguistic, or cultural differences was the critical factor that transformed the EACC's organisational attitude from being an apolitical organisation into one that is nationally linked as a significant actor that represents Alevis.

This transformation did not occur without conflict. Alevi individuals' and leaders' understanding of their belief, their relationship to Islam, the Turkish state and Kurdishness have been the main contention points within the community. The new EACC administration framed Alevi identity in such a way as to create consensus and unity among Alevis regarding the pillars of their collective identity. The core of this identity was framed as being non-violent, maintaining distance from armed conflict and illegal organisations, yet welcoming members of other organisations. At the same time, they also actively rejected the doctrine of a Turkish-Islamic Synthesis, which they argued the former administration had adopted.

An elderly interviewee who had lived in London since 2008 explained to me how his opinion on *cemevi*s changed for the better, and how he started visiting the *cemevi*, although he was still critical of it:

> I am also a member of the *cemevi*, but I go there once a month, and that is only recently. I did not want to go there before. They still have the previous administration's point of view. If you were a member of another community centre, the previous administration would not allow you to become a member, even if you are Alevi. They would accuse you of being Kurdish, being Communist, Marxist. In my political view, this was against democratic institutions. [. . .] I became a member to fix this. When they make mistakes, I intervene. I also say it when socialists make a mistake; I say this is the right thing. I also tell these people (male, 67, London).

As Poletta and Jasper (2001) suggest, prior social ties encourage individuals' participation in social movements through norms of obligation and reciprocity. The organisation's leaders also used existing social ties and framed a comprehensive Alevi identity so that people would willingly take part in the community centre's activities.

The earlier apolitical attitude also had not satisfied younger generations who regarded Alevism as an identity beyond ethno-linguistic differences. This new attitude was incorporated in İsrafil Erbil's leadership and became dominant after 2008, with the change of the EACC's administration. The new administration framed Alevi identity mobilisation as a struggle for democratic rights and had a more inclusive approach towards Kurdish-speaking Alevis, but it was also careful to separate it from Kurdish armed conflict and illegal activities. They believed that Alevism was fundamentally different from mainstream religions in its incorporation of a belief in worldly matters such as justice and equality. This approach was quickly accepted by a large segment of Alevis in Britain and allowed the leaders of the organisation to cooperate with other groups to work on democratisation and equal citizenship in Turkey.

Also, there have existed constraints that prevented Alevis' involvement in contentious politics. Historically, the Turkish state has not welcomed any challenges to the notion of a monolithic and centralist state through identity politics. In the 1990s, during the rise of identity politics (especially that of Kurdish and Islamist identities), the state instrumentalised its relationship with the Alevis: on the one hand, as a safeguard against a rising Islamist threat; on the other hand, detaching them from the Kurdish movement (van Bruinessen 1996). At this point, there was even support for the construction of *cemevi*s (Şahin 2005), although it was the state-friendly right-wing section of Alevi organisations with which the state cooperated.[8] Overall, the Turkish state regarded Alevis' involvement in any broader protest movement that could bring them together with other subaltern groups as a threat and approached the left-wing Alevi organisations with suspicion. Instead, it cooperated with those Alevi organisations which frame Alevism mainly as a belief-culture without strong political references, such as the *Cem Vakfı*.[9] The absence of such constraints in the UK enabled the EACC's new managerial committee to frame Alevism in political rather than only in belief-culture terms.

The social and political opportunities in the UK, resources that are external to the group dynamics, have significantly affected this process. As Tarrow (1994, pp. 28–29) argues, 'people engage in contentious politics when patterns of political opportunities and constraints change, and then by strategically employing a repertoire of collective action, creating new opportunities, which are used by others in widening cycles of contention'. The liberal context provided a safe space to discuss issues and even promoted Alevis' public manifestations of culture and identity as a right. British Alevis' activities aim to gain recognition in the host country at local, national and EU levels, and to transfer this recognition to Turkey as much as possible. First-generation Alevi migrants in Britain regard British culture as a culture of rights and mainly associate it with civic-political identity rights, like many other immigrant groups in Britain (Sales 2012). For that reason, they cooperated and maintained positive relations with British authorities, which

---

[8] For a study of the distribution and development of *cemevi*s in Istanbul, see Chapter 13 in this volume.

[9] The *Cem Vakfı* is the second-largest Alevi organisation in Turkey and attempts to influence the Alevi communities in Europe. It mainly represents Turkish-speaking Alevis, has an apolitical stance, locates Alevi faith within Islam and aims to ensure the integration of the Alevi community with the Turkish state (Okan 2004). The previous EACC administration cooperated with the *Cem Vakfı* but this support ceased after Erbil's takeover. See Chapter 2 in this volume for the *Cem* Vakfı's stance in relation to the Turkish state and other perspectives on Alevism.

have been instrumental for gaining recognition. The values associated with multiculturalism and freedom of expression provided opportunities for the Alevis' public visibility.

In addition to national political opportunity structures, local institutions and networks were utilised for recognition. Neighbourhoods in East and North London have a significant population of migrants from Turkey, including Alevis. A local Labour Party politician in Enfield, Yusuf Çiçek, explained how they represented Alevi belief and culture in the town council's annual opening. As part of the opening ceremony, prayers from different faith groups are said each year, and in 2012 they included the *gülbeng* (Alevi prayers) in the ceremony. Çiçek explains the significance of this event as follows:

> We opened the official town council on 29 February 2012 with the *gülbeng* with the EACC and their *dede*. It was very nice. As opposed to the power that rejects and ignores us in the country we were born in, the state here gave us such a chance, and it was very good. All the media was there, the English media. There were many people from different cultures, from different ethnicities (male, 54, London).

This example demonstrates that, in contrast to the Turkish state, British authorities support the manifestation of minority cultures. Their belief systems can be recognised in local government, such as in town councils. This support is an opportunity for presenting Alevism in public as a legitimate belief system compatible with the norms of the host society.

The EACC has benefitted from this liberal context and maintained positive relations with the local politicians of the districts where they live. Inviting politicians to their events is one form of such cooperation. For example, the annual Hacı Bektaş Veli[10] Youth Festival, which the new administration established in 2009, offers Alevis visibility at the local level. Meg Hillier, the then Labour Party MP for the London Borough of Hackney, was invited by the EEAC to one of these annual festivals in October 2012 to give a speech. In her speech, Hillier addressed the Alevis' problems in Turkey, stressing that the Turkish government urgently has to deal with the discrimination against

---

[10] Hacı Bektaş Veli is a thirteenth-century Sufi saint very much respected by Alevis. See Melikoff (2009) for a comprehensive study.

Alevis if it wishes to become an EU member. Also, the annual Alevi summer festival in Hackney is inaugurated with a reception at Parliament, and in 2013 the then MPs Meg Hillier and Diane Abbott hosted the EACC representatives. In their speeches, they emphasised their support for the Alevis' cultural rights. A similar case is a statement made by London Borough of Enfield MP, Joan Ryan, about the *coup* attempt in Turkey on 15 July 2016. Ryan expressed her concern for the Alevis and Kurds' situation in Turkey and asked President Erdoğan to protect the democratic process and the rule of law (Ryan 2016). Such recognition results from this new organisational attitude and constitutes an important leverage for the Alevis' broader mobilisation to demand recognition and protection of their rights.[11]

This organisational transformation also led to the growth of Alevi mobilisation all over Britain.[12] In the 2010s, new branches of Alevi Culture Centres were established in London, Coventry, Croydon, Sheffield, Doncaster, Nottingham, Glasgow, the East Midlands and Hull. The British Alevi Federation (*Britanya Alevi Federasyonu*, BAF) was founded in 2014 to connect all the members and to strengthen their cooperation. Later in the same year, the BAF also joined the European Alevi Unions Confederation (*Avrupa Alevi Birlikleri Konfederasyonu*, AABK). Currently, the BAF has fifteen members and is an active member of the confederation. Active engagement can be observed in the organisation leaders' efforts to maintain close relations with community members and offer solutions to their social problems. This helps to consolidate the group and increase solidarity among its members. For example, the number of suicides among young second-generation Kurdish Alevi men in London was a pressing issue that compelled the community leaders to find solutions. While first-generation Kurdish Alevis tried to make the best of their new lives through hard work, the second generation neither wanted their parents' lives, nor was able to integrate into Britain successfully. This situation left them in a state of anomaly and at higher risk of suicide (Cetin 2015). The community centres aimed to prevent further deaths and cooperated to create safe spaces

---

[11] For a study of Alevi festivals as means of gaining recognition, visibility and networking, see Salman (2020).

[12] It is important to note that the rapid growth in the number of Alevi organisations within a few years did not result from an increase in their population, but more so from a growing awareness of and activism for Alevism.

where Alevi youth could socialise. İsrafil Erbil and many EACC volunteers repeatedly stated the importance of cultural belonging for young immigrants to integrate into Britain more easily.

Since multiculturalism and identity rights are the available public discourses for migrants in many Western European countries, social problems may be blurred with or reduced to identity issues. As Kaya (1998) argues in his research on Alevis in Germany, the multiculturalist discourse and policies in the 1990s reduced social problems and inequality to the culturalisation of differences. A similar pattern is observed in Britain, where the unequal distribution of material goods and life chances is conflated with the struggle for symbolic resources.

Community centres' leaders and volunteers focused on identity and solidarity to solve the growing problem of suicides. A young interviewee who represents the youth branch of the Turkish and Kurdish Community Solidarity Centre (*Türk ve Kürt Toplum Dayanışma Merkezi*, DAY-MER) explained the role of the *cemevi* in connecting different community centres:

> Here, within a year, there were many cases of suicide among the youth from Turkey. Sometimes we received news [of suicide] once a week. Here the young people in community centres had a responsibility. Therefore, we cooperated with the community centres in the leadership of the *cemevi* (female, 27, London).

When the EACC organised a protest in London on 16 February 2013, the leaders addressed a wide range of issues. The protest raised concerns regarding the situation in both Turkey and Britain. These included immigrant youth's problems, gang involvement and drug abuse (Cetin 2020), as well as the violation of Alevis' rights in Turkey (Alevinet ©2021). For the sake of visibility, the demonstration took place in Trafalgar Square in central London. Their main demands included the recognition of Alevism in Turkey, opposition to the Turkish state's involvement in the conflict in Syria and protecting younger generation from drugs and gangs. These demands reveal that Alevis in Britain struggle with a broad range of issues. This protest was significant for demonstrating creative ways of protest, using a 'repertoire of contention' from Turkish and British political cultures. Although shouting slogans is a common way of protest in Turkey, marching or standing quietly with banners is more prevalent in Britain. Alevis used this latter form and also added cultural and folkloric elements in their protests. For instance, during the demonstration in London, they performed the *semah* and set pigeons free as a symbol of freedom and peace.[13] Hence, the *semah* as a cultural element and pigeons as a universal symbol were used to emphasise their demands' non-violent nature.

Beside the street protests, the EACC's organisational leaders promote ways of manifesting Alevi identity that can survive in the long term. İsrafil Erbil, for instance, often stated that writing about Alevi culture and archiving documents are as important as street protests. He argued that street protests were forgotten over time, but academic works such as books and papers remained. My interviewees also perceived academic studies as a contribution to giving a voice to Alevis and, therefore, were willing to share their experiences. One of the administrators of the EACC explained this when I asked for permission to use a voice recorder:

> We have to deal with these, because [they] were not previously recorded. [. . .] Putting forward the Alevi belief seems to me as one of the most challenging tasks, as a historical identity. Because it is so much under pressure, so much troubled in a history full of blood. They carried that identity to this day without yielding. I do appreciate that (male, 33, London).

Particularly the younger and educated members of the community state how important it is to contribute to the Alevis' visibility through research on Alevism that adheres to research ethics.

Similarly, the teaching of Alevism in schools was an essential step in framing Alevi identity and gaining visibility in the wider broader society. Promoting education and providing a curriculum for its teaching in schools has been an integral part of community-making. By including Alevism in the religious education and ethics curriculum in some schools in North London neighbourhoods with a large Alevi population, the community increased their public visibility in Britain and ensured that future generations would be informed about their belief system. The lesson content was prepared with great care to prevent internal conflicts and to ensure that Alevism was presented as a peaceful and egalitarian belief system. İsrafil Erbil argued that,

---

[13] A photograph of this performance can be found on the front cover of Issa (2017).

before Alevism was incorporated into religious education in schools, Alevi children could not identify themselves as Alevi, while other children in the same age group could identify with their family's religion. The *cemevi* administration took these lessons very seriously since they consolidate children's awareness about their homeland identity. In all these activities, it was crucial to frame Alevism in a way acceptable to the majority of community members and to use the opportunity structures of the host country. As the community became more organised and gained visibility, they also managed to form an All-Party Parliamentary Group (APPG) for Alevis on 3 December 2015 (AleviNet 2016). The APPG is an unofficial platform run by the members of Commons and Lords, providing Alevis with a chance to express their socio-political aspirations and to ensure their religious and cultural rights in Britain and overseas.

Alevi Mobilisation at the Supranational Level

Alevis who had migrated and settled in Western Europe gained visibility and sought recognition for Alevis in Turkey by using the power of supranational organisations, such as that of the European Union. The civil rights associated with ethnic, religious and cultural differences were more established in Europe than in Turkey, where a legal and political framework for minority rights is almost non-existent. As Turkey's quest for EU membership gained force in the 1990s, minority rights (as one of the most important criteria for membership) became leverage for these groups in Turkey. For instance, the European Commission progress reports on Turkey, published since 1998, have frequently mentioned discrimination against Alevis. The 2013 report reveals that Alevis have difficulty opening places of worship despite the so-called 'Alevi Opening' in 2009. They are systematically discriminated against in the education system and civil service. These concerns continued in the European Commission's reports until the time of writing. In 2020, the European Commission (2020, p. 32) reported:

> A comprehensive legal framework in line with European standards still needs to be put in place, and appropriate attention must be paid to implementing the ECtHR judgments on compulsory religion and ethics classes, indication of religious affiliation on identity cards and Alevi worship places. Alevis continue to face hate crimes but investigations have proved to be ineffective so far.

The universal human rights discourse and the institutions they embodied provided Alevis with a framework for demanding their cultural rights. My interviewees constantly compared the attitudes of the UK and Turkey and were well aware that supranational institutions monitor human rights issues in Turkey. The EACC leaders raise awareness about Alevis' and other persecuted groups' problems in the European Parliament (EP). The BAF represented Britain's Alevis in a meeting with EP officials in Brussels, and other Alevi federations from Europe were also present. Erbil stated that Alevi identity should be recognized and that they should be represented in the host societies' administrations (Mete 2014).

As Mau et al. (2008) have argued, cross-border relations foster global interrelations and a sense of political responsibility beyond the state. The experience of moving from the periphery to the centre through international migration helps Alevis raise issues beyond their own group. For instance, regarding the massacres against Alawis and Yezidis in the Middle East, the BAF on 17 February 2014 sent an open letter to the United Nations Security Council. In this letter, they expressed their concerns about security in the region, due to the frequent attacks on civilians and the Turkish government's responsibility in the matter ('AleviNet İngiltere Alevi Kültür Merkezi ve Cemevi' n. d.).

The UN framework affords opportunities for oppressed groups to raise their demands when states are not responding adequately to their problems. The BAF referred to the specific laws that were binding for Turkey and claimed that the UN must take action against the Turkish government; the Security Council should investigate the accounts regarding the Turkish government's support for the Syrian opposition. Furthermore, in September 2014, the EACC initiated an anti-war protest, including sixteen other political and hometown associations in London, which had been established by immigrants from Turkey. They all condemned the massacres against the Alawi, Kurdish, Turcoman and Yezidi populations in Rojava and Shengal with a press release in the *cemevi* and initiated a campaign to raise donations to help the victims. The opportunity structures and engagement with other ethnic and religious groups motivated the EACC to embrace a political position beyond the Alevis' religious and cultural demands. In 2018, as a result of the supranational-level engagements of the EACC, the BAF and other

European Alevi organisations, the Alevi Friendship Group was founded in the European Parliament. This group emerged upon the initiatives of Socialists and Democrats Group and aims to give voice and visibility to 1.5 million Alevis across Europe (Euroactive 2018).

Alevi Mobilisation at the Transnational Level

The transnational activities in this section refer to Alevis' simultaneous relations with Alevi organisations in Turkey and European countries. As the organisational attitude changed and became more open to outside institutions, transnational involvement in other organisations also intensified. One of the most critical steps in mobilising the Alevi community in Britain on transnational issues was addressing their collective memory about the Maraş massacre, which took place in 1978 and resulted in the killing of over one-hundred persons (see Sinclair-Webb 2003). The massacre escalated from the killing of two Alevi teachers and the explosion of a sound bomb in a movie theatre to the raiding of Alevi people's homes and shops. This massacre is extremely important for Alevis in Britain since most of them come from Maraş, a southeastern province in Turkey. Those who migrated from Maraş either experienced the massacre or witnessed it through others who had experienced it first-hand. As one of my interviewees explained, the memory of Maraş is still vivid and powerful among the community members:

> I remember the Maraş incident. One of our neighbours was in Maraş, right in the middle of the incidents. He came back; he could not sleep in his home for maybe about one or two months. He used to tell how everyone died. We were young at that time, and we were so shocked that such things could happen. At that time, I was not aware of being Alevi or Sunni, but what he told us haunted me. There were many who lost their loved ones in the villages (female, 54, London).

İsrafil Erbil explained that, previously, only the Sivas and Çorum massacres had been commemorated in the *cemevi*, but not the Maraş massacre, although a significant population from this region lived in Britain. According to my interviewees, the previous administration had regarded the Maraş massacre as a right-left clash rather than an attack explicitly targeting Alevis. Therefore, they did not organise any commemorative events for it. As this historical event is so significant for the community, the new administrators began to organise commemorative events in London. They cooperated with local Alevi organisations in Turkey to initiate protests and ceremonies in Maraş. Since 2010, upon the initiatives of Erbil and the local Alevi activists in Maraş, commemorations have been held in Maraş's town centre, where the massacre took place. The EACC also built a *cemevi* and a cultural centre in the Yörükselim neighbourhood, on the site of a house that had been burnt down in 1978. This centre has now become one of the symbols of violence against Alevis in Turkey.

Moreover, commemorations are held in various locations every year, with panels and the screening of movies and documentaries in community centres. In the 2012 commemoration event in London, the *cemevi* administrator, *Dede* Mehmet Turan, and a witness to the events shared their sentiments and experiences of the incident as well as the meaning of remembering Maraş. The *dede* stated: 'We will continue to commemorate so that new Maraş incidents, Çorum incidents, Gazi, Dersim, Roboski[14] incidents will not happen. We will continue to commemorate so that people will not be killed. We will continue to commemorate so that they [the victims] will always be in the light' (field notes, 28 November 2012). He connected the various moments of victimisation in Alevi history to the incident of Maraş and showed his empathy with other persecuted groups by including an atrocity that did not target Alevis. The *dede*'s speech received applause when he mentioned Roboski, which had received little media coverage at the time. The way in which Alevi identity was presented in these commemorations recognised state violence against social groups beyond the Alevis. The commemoration of Alevi massacres has also spread to UK institutions due to the Alevis' organisational expansion. For instance, the fortieth anniversary of the Maraş massacre, co-hosted by the APPG and the BAF, was commemorated in Westminster. The same narrative of a series of massacres that link Alevi history was repeated here as well (AleviNet 2018).

---

[14] On 28 December 2011, the Turkish army bombed civilians due to faulty intelligence, and thirty-five smugglers lost their lives in the southeast of Turkey. The original Kurdish name of the town (Roboski) was changed to Uludere long before the incident; therefore, the *dede*'s choice of the Kurdish name over the official Turkish name indicates his political position.

In addition to organising local events to show solidarity with Alevis elsewhere, the EACC supported the protests of Alevis in Turkey and other European countries. These were large-scale demonstrations on Alevis' major demands, which were often referred to as 'equal citizenship' (*eşit yurttaşlık*), as well as other protest marches and demonstrations that directly targeted the AKP's policies concerning Alevis. As the then Turkish Prime Minister Erdoğan targeted Euro-Alevis as 'outside-related inside threats', the protests against him intensified (Zırh 2015). Numerous demonstrations were organised in various cities in Turkey and Europe: Istanbul (2012), Berlin (2013, 2018 and 2020), Strasbourg (2013 and 2016), Paris (2020), London (2013 and 2020), Vienna (2020), Cologne (2014, 2016 and 2018), Hamburg (2019) and Copenhagen (2020), among others. The EACC, well networked with the European federation, also arranged a bus trip from London to the demonstrations in Strasbourg and Cologne to show their support for the protests. Their participation in such events is important for gaining visibility in Britain and in the transnational space. These protests were also able to incorporate many different aspects of the violation of Alevis' rights in continuity with contemporary problems.

Finally, Alevis in Britain also organised a number of protests in solidarity with the Gezi protestors in Turkey. As the Turkish government did not appease the public and as police violence against the demonstrators increased in Turkey, many Alevis in Britain joined the protests, marches and forums in London, either with the EACC or individually, along with non-Alevi students, intellectuals and artists who supported the aims of the Gezi protests. The EACC initiated most of these activities in Britain but worked in cooperation with other political groups. The banners in these protests reflected the variety of concerns and demands regarding the protests. In addition to general anti-AKP slogans, Alevis' demands for recognition and equality were also present. During these protests, I noticed a banner held by a man, which read: 'I found out I was Alevi when I was 14'. Although the focus of the protests was solidarity with the Gezi protests in Turkey, protesters also expressed their claims regarding their Alevi identity.

Alevi activism in Britain has intensified following the years of my fieldwork. The organisational structure enabled Alevis to link their activism at different levels; thus, they were able to benefit from the host country's opportunity structures. Hence, the Alevi movement in Britain could evolve from a small-scale community centre to a supranationally linked organisation in dialogue with several political entities in Europe.

Conclusion

Alevis in Britain have transformed within a very short period from an invisible community to a visible one with established networks at local, national, supranational and transnational levels. This specific group, who arrived in Britain mainly as refugees in the late 1980s and 1990s, was primarily composed of Kurds and Alevis. The first organisation around Alevi identity was apolitical, serving as strategy of protection from over-politicisation. This approach resulted in remaining invisible, within the local context of London as well as the transnational Alevi movement. However, this approach could not satisfy the identity-based demands of the younger community members in particular. The transformation began as second-generation Alevis, represented by İsrafil Erbil, initiated a new organisational attitude to make Alevism visible and recognised. The most crucial factor that facilitated this mobilisation was to frame Alevism as an overarching identity beyond ethnic, linguistic and cultural differences. The new administration also used social and political opportunities at national and supranational levels to gain visibility in wider society and recognition for their cultural rights. Hence, the transformation enabled Alevis in Britain to become active and visible actors, not only in Britain but also in Turkey and other countries in Europe.

Bibliography

Akdemir, A. (2017). Boundary-Making and the Alevi Community. *Journal of Alevism-Bektashism Studies*, 11, 173–88.

Akın, E., and Karasapan, Ö. (1988). The 'Turkish-Islamic Synthesis'. *Middle East Report*, 153, 18.

Aktürk, H. (2020). *Modern Alevi Ekolleri*. Istanbul: İletişim.

AleviNet (2016). All Party Parliamentary Groups for Alevis. *İngiltere Alevi Kültür Merkezi ve Cemevi* [online]. 21 March. [Viewed 23 February 2021]. Available from: http://www.alevinet.org/MAP.aspx?pid=AleviNewsEventsArticles_en-GB&aid=nn_164734679_92832609

AleviNet (2018). Maraş Katliamı 40 Yıl Anması İngiltere Parlamentosunda. *İngiltere Alevi Kültür Merkezi ve Cemevi*. [online]. 13 December. [Viewed 23 February

2021]. Available from: http://www.alevinet.org/MAP.aspx?pid=Haberler_en-GB&aid=nn_250859631_109173189

AleviNet (2021). About Us, Who Are We? *İngiltere Alevi Kültür Merkezi ve Cemevi* [online]. [Viewed 6 February 2021]. Available from: http://www.alevinet.org/SAP.aspx?pid=About_en-GB

AleviNet (©2021). *İngiltere Alevi Kültür Merkezi ve Cemevi* [online]. [Viewed 6 February 2021]. Available from: http://www.alevinet.org/Default.aspx

Bauböck, R. (2003). Towards a Political Theory of Migrant Transnationalism. *International Migration Review*, 37(3), 700–23.

Cetin, U. (2020). Unregulated Desires: Anomie, the 'Rainbow Underclass' and Second-Generation Alevi Kurdish Gangs. *Kurdish Studies*, 8(1), 185–208.

Cetin, U. (2016). Durkheim, Ethnography and Suicide: Researching Young Male Suicide in the Transnational London Alevi-Kurdish Community. *Ethnography*, 17(2), 250–77.

Cetin, U., Jenkins, C., and Aydın, S., eds (2020). Special Issue: Alevi Kurds: History, Politics and Identity, *Kurdish Studies*, 8(1).

Coşan-Eke, D. (2017). The Resurgence of Alevism in a Transnational Context. In: Issa, T., ed., *Alevis in Europe: Voices of Migration, Culture and Identity*. London: Routledge. pp. 145–156.

Düvell, F. (2010). *Turkish Migration to the UK*. Oxford: Centre on Migration, Policy and Society (COMPAS).

Enneli, P., Modood, T., and Bradley, H. (2005). *Young Turks and Kurds: A Set of 'Invisible' Disadvantaged Groups*. York: Joseph Rowntree Foundation.

Euroactive (2018). Press Release: S&D Members Launch the Alevi Friendship Group of the European Parliament. *Socialists and Democrats in the European Parliament* [online]. 27 June. [Viewed 23 March 2021]. Available from: http://pr.euractiv.com/pr/sd-members-launch-alevi-friendship-group-european-parliament-170247

Commission of the European Communities (2007). *Turkey 2007 Progress Report* [online]. Brussels 6 November 2007. [Viewed 20 January 2021]. Available from: https://www.refworld.org/docid/47382d392.html

Gezik, E., and Gültekin, A. K., eds (2019). *Kurdish Alevis and the Case of Dersim: Historical and Contemporary Insights*. New York: Lexington Books.

Habermas, J. (1981). New Social Movements. *Telos*, 49, 33–37.

Issa, T., ed. (2017). *Alevis in Europe: Voices of Migration, Culture and Identity*. London: Routledge.

Jenkins, C. (2020). 'Aspirational Capital' and Transformations in First-Generation Alevi-Kurdish Parents' Involvement with Their Children's Education in the UK. *Kurdish Studies*, 8(1), 113–34.

Jenkins, C., and Cetin, U. (2018). From a 'Sort of Muslim' to 'Proud to be Alevi': The Alevi Religion and Identity Project Combatting the Negative Identity among Second-Generation Alevis in the UK. *National Identities*, 20(1), 105–23.

Jenkins, C., Aydın, S., and Cetin, U., eds (2018). *Alevism as an Ethno-Religious Identity: Contested Boundaries*. London: Routledge.

Kaya, A. (1998). Multicultural Clientelism and Alevi Resurgence in the Turkish Diaspora: Berlin Alevis. *New Perspectives on Turkey*, 18, 23–49.

Martin, P., Midgley, E., and Teitelbaum, M. (2001). Migration and Development: Focus on Turkey. *International Migration Review*, 35(2), 596–605.

Massicard, E. (2013). *The Alevis in Turkey and Europe: Identity and Managing Territorial Diversity*. Abingdon: Routledge.

Mau, S., Mewes, J., and Zimmermann, A. (2008). Cosmopolitan Attitudes through Transnational Social Practices? *Global Networks*, 8(1), 1–24.

Melikoff, I. (2009). *Hacı Bektaş: Efsaneden Gerçeğe*. Istanbul: Cumhuriyet Kitapları.

Mete, S. (2014). Avrupa Parlementosu'nda Alevilik Rüzgarı. *OdaTv* [online]. 24 February. [Viewed 6 February 2021]. Available from: https://odatv.com/avrupa-parlementosunda-alevilik-ruzgari--2402141200.html

Okan, M. (2004). *Türkiye'de Alevilik: Antropolojik bir Yaklaşım*. Ankara: İmge Kitabevi.

Özkul, D. (2019a). The Making of a Transnational Religion: Alevi Movement in Germany and the World Alevi Union. *British Journal of Middle Eastern Studies*, 46(2), 259–73.

Özkul, D. (2019b). Transnationalism. In: Inglis, C., Li, W., and Khadria, B., eds, *Sage Handbook of International Migration*. New York: Sage. pp. 433–50.

Polletta, F., and Jasper, J. M. (2001). Collective Identity and Social Movements. *Annual Review of Sociology*, 27(1), 283–305.

Ryan, J. [@joanryanEnfield]. (2016). [My letter to @theresa_may expressing concern for safety of #Alevis & #Kurds in #Turkey, following the attempted coup] [Twitter]. 1 August. [Accessed 7 February 2021]. Available from: https://twitter.com/joanryanEnfield/status/760058655576383488?s=20

Sales, R. (2012). Britain and Britishness: Place, Belonging and Exclusion. In: Ahmad, W., and Sardar, Z., eds, *Muslims in Britain: Making Social and Political Space*. London: Routledge. pp. 42–61.

Salman, C. (2020). Diasporic Homeland, Rise of Identity and New Traditionalism: The Case of the British Alevi Festival. *Kurdish Studies*, 8(1), 113–32.

Sinclair-Webb, E. (2003). Sectarian Violence, the Alevi Minority and the Left: Kahramanmaras 1978. In: Jongerden, J., and White, P. J., eds, *Turkey's Alevi Enigma: A Comprehensive Overview*. Leiden: Brill. pp. 215–35.

Soysal, Y. N. (2000). Citizenship and Identity: Living in Diasporas in Post-War Europe? *Ethnic and Racial Studies*, 23(1), 1–15.

Sökefeld, M. (2008). *Struggling for Recognition: The Alevi Movement in Germany and in Transnational Space*. Oxford: Berghahn Books.

Şahin, Ş. (2005). The Rise of Alevism as a Public Religion. *Current Sociology*, 53(3), 465–85.

van Bruinessen, M. (1996). Kurds, Turks and the Alevi Revival in Turkey. *Middle East Report*, 200, 7–10.

Wahlbeck, Ö. (1999). *Kurdish Diasporas: A Comparative Study of Kurdish Refugee Communities*. New York: St Martin's Press.

Zırh, B. C. (2012). Becoming Visible Through Migration: Understanding the Relationships Between the Alevi Revival, Migration and Funerary Practices Through Europe and Turkey. Unpubl. doctoral dissertation, University of London.

Zırh, B. C. (2015) Alevi Diasporası: Yeniden Haricileşen Dahili Bir Mahrem Olarak Alevilik. *Birikim*, 309/10, 80–92.

Part III

BEYOND RECOGNITION: CHANGES IN ALEVI RITUALS, REPRESENTATION AND AUTHORITY

11

THE TRANSFORMATION OF THE SACRED AUTHORITY OF THE ÇELEBIS: THE ULUSOY FAMILY IN CONTEMPORARY TURKEY

MERAL SALMAN YIKMIŞ

Introduction[1]

This article is about the Çelebi branch of the Bektaşi order and, more specifically, about the persistence of the Ulusoy family as the leading sacred patrilineage of the Alevi-Bektaşi community[2] in the Turkish republican period. Studies on holy lineages in Turkey include Caroline Tee's (2010) ethnographic study on the Derviş Kemal Ocağı, focusing on the transformation of the organisation of the holy lineage through geographical distribution and urbanisation. Further, Peter Andrews and Hıdır Temel

---

[1] This article is based on my doctoral dissertation titled 'The Persistence of a Sacred Patrilineage in Contemporary Turkey: An Ethnographic Account on the Ulusoy Family, the Descendants of Hacı Bektaş Veli', submitted to the Middle East Technical University in 2012; it has been published by İletişim Press as book titled *Hacı Bektaş Veli'nin Evlatları 'Yol'un Mürşitleri: Ulusoy Ailesi* in 2014.

[2] The Ulusoy (Çelebi) family members generally call their disciples Alevi-Bektaşi. In this chapter, hereafter, the term Alevi-Bektaşi is used to refer to the community affiliated with the Ulusoy family through *babas* or *ocaks* or personally. The Bektaşi order has two branches. Both the Babagan branch (the Bektaşis) and the Çelebi branch stem from the same order; however, they are organised in two different ways. The Babagan branch of the Bektaşis claims that Hacı Bektaş Veli was celibate and that succession is only possible by discipleship based on learning. Their way of organisation is closer to other Sufi traditions in terms of receiving

(2010)'s descriptive study gives some information on the sacred lineage of the Hubyar, its geographical distribution, organisation and rituals. Regarding the Ulusoy family, the oral history book *Cumhuriyet'in Aile Albümleri* (1998) uses photographs from the family album. Ayşe Berktay Hacımirzaoğlu presents snapshots from family life and gives a short history of the family during the republican period. Another study, an article on the Ulusoy family, written by Benoît Fliche and Elise Massicard (2006) and titled '*L'oncle et le député: Circuits de ressources et usages de la parenté dans un lignage sacré en Turquie*', investigates how the family dealt with the collective religious and economic sources that remained from the time of the Ottoman Empire, in the period after the foundation of the Republic. This chapter aims to contribute to this literature on sacred genealogies in the field of Alevi studies. This article's data were gathered during fieldwork conducted in Hacıbektaş and Ankara from December 2008 to September 2010.[3]

To understand the characteristics of the sacred authority of the Ulusoy family, we need to comprehend the concept of *velayet*, which literally means 'to be close (to God)' or 'to be a friend (of God)', in its Shi'ite and Sufi forms. After Muhammad, the revealed law (*şeriat*) was accepted as guiding principle and protected by guardians and interpreters – namely, the *ulema* (Trimingham 1998, p. 33). However, those who think that the exoteric law does not suffice hold that the divine revelation also has hidden and spiritual meaning. They

---

esoteric knowledge and spirituality through spiritual progression. The Çelebi branch, however, claims to be progeny of Hacı Bektaş Veli. The hereditary succession is the basic principle of the legitimacy of their sacred authority. As a sacred patrilineage, the Çelebi lineage is closer to the organisation of the Alevi-Kızılbaş. The Alevi-Kızılbaş community is organised based on *ocak*s – namely, the sacred patrilineages of sacred guides, *dedes,* many of whom claim an Alid genealogy. Some of these *ocak*s are affiliated with the Ulusoy (Çelebi) family. However, independent *ocak*s assert that they have priority in the Alid genealogy, and they do not feel obliged to receive permission from the children of Hacı Bektaş Veli (Yaman 2006). In this chapter, Alevi, as a comprehensive term, is also used in reference to the community that includes both the Alevi-Kızılbaş and the Alevi-Bektaşi community. For a detailed discussion of the genealogy of the term Alevi and Alevilik, see Dressler (2013); for the debate on the ambiguity of the terms of Alevi and Bektaşi, see Yıldırım (2010).

[3] The Çelebi family adopted the surname Ulusoy (meaning sublime lineage) after the enactment of the Surname Law in 1934.

claim that the prophetic revelation is twofold: it includes both the exoteric (*zahir*) and the esoteric (*batın*) – namely, both *şeriat* and *hakikat*. Furthermore, the spiritual reality, *hakikat*, cannot be derived from *şeriat* by logic. The Shi'ite tradition claims that the interpretation of *hakikat* requires inherited knowledge and spiritual guidance. Following the closure of the cycle of prophecy, therefore, the guidance of the *batın* on the way of God has to be provided by the cycle of *velayet* – the cycle of *Imam*s (Corbin 1993, p. 27).

The *batın* and the *velayet* are part of Sufism's structure; however, the way in which Sufi guides receive the knowledge of the *batın* is different from the Shi'te understanding. Unlike the *Imam*s, they receive esoteric knowledge not genealogically, but through their spiritual progression. The knowledge of *batın* comes to them via a spiritual chain, which begins with Muhammad and continues with elected masters, as well as direct inspiration from God (Trimingham 1998, p. 135).

Regarding the sacred authority of the Ulusoy family, the *velayet* of Hacı Bektaş Veli is closer to the term of *velayet* in Shi'ite belief than in Sufi belief. According to the Alevi-Bektaşi tradition, Hacı Bektaş Veli inherited *velayet* genealogically, through his ancestral links to the seventh *Imam* of the Twelver Shi'ites, Musa al-Kazım. In this respect, with the inherited knowledge of *batın* and its spiritual form of *velayet*, Hacı Bektaş Veli became the carrier of the role of *Imam*s in terms of spiritual guidance, through which he could initiate and supervise his *talip*s. Furthermore, based on the belief in the incarnation of divinity in the human body and the transmigration of the soul, Hacı Bektaş Veli was the incarnation of Ali ibn Abu Talip, because death is only the end of the physical form in cyclical time and because *velayet* never ends with death (Babayan 2002, pp. xlv, xv–xvi; Ulusoy 2009, p. 49).

As the possessor of the *velayet* and as the incarnate of Ali ibn Abu Talip, Hacı Bektaş Veli established the Bektaşi order –that is, the Alevi-Bektaşi 'path'. He became a spiritual guide and was called *pir*. Consequently, the Çelebis or the Ulusoy family, as the progeny of Hacı Bektaş Veli, became heirs to his sacred authority, which was inherited by their descendants through blood ties and transmigration. As *mürşit*s, the Ulusoy family has undertaken the role of the spiritual guide, as well as the leadership of some other sacred *dede* (guide) lineages, called *ocak*s, and of their *talip*s, to regulate and supervise their life by means of *batın*, divine knowledge.

The Transformation of the Ulusoy Family's Sacred Authority

For centuries, the Çelebis (the Ulusoy family) have supervised the communities related to them and appointed the sacred guides (*dede*s) of the *ocak*s on the grounds of being the hereditary successors of Hacı Bektaş Veli. As *postnişins*[4]/*mürşit*s of the *dergah* of Hacı Bektaş Veli, throughout the Ottoman period, they also supervised all the Bektaşi dervish convents associated with the main *dergah*. As part of the system of charitable endowments in the empire, the Çelebis were officially recognised as descendants of Hacı Bektaş Veli by the central administration and received privileges due to their position as trustees and administrators of the charitable endowment supporting the main *dergah*. The formal recognition accorded to the Çelebis also provided them with opportunities to exercise religious authority, which was inseparable from economic and judicial power at the official level. However, the privileges granted to the Çelebis were not stable and heavily depended on the changing policies of the endowment system. The system itself depended on processes of the centralisation and decentralisation within the empire.

Following the establishment of the republican regime, the Grand National Assembly in 1925 passed Law No. 677, disbanding all dervish convents and tombs, and in 1928 decreed that the title of endowment trustee given to the *sheik*s and tomb-keepers had already been abolished with the Public Law No. 677. Thereby, sacred authority became incompatible with the new regime's secularisation attempts, and the Ulusoy family lost its formal recognition. Furthermore, the sacred authority of the Ulusoy family that covered all aspects of life, without any separation of the temporal and spiritual spheres, was being challenged and oppressed by new forms of authority established and exercised in both of these spheres.[5] Simultaneously, the structure of the rural Alevi communities substantially changed in the mid-1950s due to the spread of mass education, industrialisation, urbanisation and migration to the cities.

On the one hand, the new regime's secularisation and modernisation attempts disrupted Alevi-Bektaşi society as a whole and changed the relationship between the *mürşit*, *dede*s, *baba*s (who mediate between the *mürşit* and

---

[4] The *postnişin* is a person entitled to represent the sacred authority of Hacı Bektaş Veli.

[5] The Presidency of Religious Affairs (*Diyanet İşleri Başkanlığı*, in short *Diyanet*), which was established to control and administer religion, has not recognised the Alevi belief and has forced the Sunni form of Islam on Alevis.

Alevi-Bektaşi communities) and the *talip*s, who are either affiliated with the Ulusoy family directly and/or through the mediation of *dede*s. For the Ulusoy family, this meant the dispersion of the sacred authority from the *mürşit* to all male members of the family, as well as a decline in social differentiation between the Ulusoys and their *talip*s. On the other hand, the dissolution of the old, closed and hierarchical relations led to the emergence of new forms of authority.[6]

Efendi, an Ambiguous Position within the Alevi-Bektaşi 'Path'

The term *efendi*, meaning master or lord, is Greek in origin and was already used in Anatolia in the thirteenth and fourteenth centuries. As a designation reserved for members of the scribal and religious classes, this title was widespread in Ottoman usage. In the nineteenth century, however, the usage of *efendi* was regulated by law. The title was given only to certain people, including princes of the ruling house, the sultan's wives, the *ulema* and non-Muslim religious leaders. In the republican period, the title of *efendi*, which was also used for Hacı Bektaş Veli's descendants, was banned, together with other Ottoman titles, due to its religious connotations (Lewis 1991, p. 687).

Although the title of *efendi* is not officially used anymore, all male members of the family are designated as *efendi*s by *talip*s, regardless of whether the family members exercise their inherited sacred authority. Besides, in its contemporary usage, this title has acquired new characteristics. In addition to its old denotation, the term *efendi* now designates the position that male members of the Ulusoy family occupy within the hierarchy of the 'path' – a position that emerged after the abolition of the order.

The dispersion of sacred authority among the male family members and the emergence of new forms of authority among *efendi*s first occurred when some of them, many of whom were descendants of Cemalettin Çelebi, moved to Tokat in 1928.[7] Since privileges and formal recognitions were lost, they

---

[6] For the changing role of the *dede*s, see Yaman (2006), Shankland (1999, 2003) and Dressler (2006).

[7] Cemalettin Çelebi and Veliyettin Çelebi (Ulusoy) were brothers, and Veliyettin Çelebi became *mürşit* when his elder brother Cemalettin Çelebi died in 1921. Their families lived together in Hacıbektaş until 1928. Due to economic and familial issues, all of Cemalettin Çelebi's children, except for his youngest son, moved to Tokat. Veliyettin Çelebi's eldest son also moved with them.

needed people's support. It was the first time that the Ulusoy family, whose sanctity necessitated being secluded from the public, left the Hacıbektaş district for a more extended period and mingled with *talip*s. Despite the rules of the 'path' necessitating social differentiation, this process enabled the family members to create more personal and closer relationships with the *talip*s. According to a family member, . . .

> [a]fter migrating to Tokat, some of the family members began to visit *talip*s [to perform the task of a *dede*]. Before that, none of the male members of the family visited *talip*s because we were [we still are] at the top of the hierarchy in the organisation of the Alevi community. Our position is a kind of inspectorship. The role of teachers is given to *dede*s, and we inspect *dede*s. Until the period of Cemalettin Çelebi, the family's income came from the share that *dede*s collected from the community and the share allocated to the trustees of the charitable endowment. After the establishment of the Republic, the family tried to find different ways to make their living.[8]

Although it is the *mürşit* who is accepted as representative of Hacı Bektaş Veli, in the wake of the migration to Tokat, other male members, *efendi*s, also served as representatives of the post of Hacı Bektaş Veli and established a new form of authority over the *talip*s. This new form of authority exercised by *efendi*s put the Ulusoy family's sacred authority in a vulnerable position when they openly shared temporal concerns with *talip*s.

In addition to its vulnerability, the position of *efendi*s is subject to great ambiguity because, in the hierarchy of the 'path', they occupied a position between *mürşit* and *dede*. Shankland (2003, p. 100), who conducted research in the Alevi village of Susesi, notes three ranks within the community: *efendi*, *dede* and *talip*. *Efendi*s came to the village once or twice a year, answered villagers' questions regarding the 'path' and collected dues. However, *efendi* is a 'new' category within the 'path' in terms of exercising authority over *talip*s, and their duty is not clearly defined. A male member of the Ulusoy family explained his connection with the *talip*s as follows:

> If you cultivate the land, it will fertilise. You should always be in a close relationship with the community. If there is logic in your explanations of things,

---

[8] Interview with a male member of the Ulusoy family, 11 July 2009, Hacıbektaş.

and if you give your love to the *talip*s, it will be a genuine relationship and it will never end. [. . .] Generally, after October, *dede*s visit villages. Our task is different from the *dede*s' task. *Dede*s go to villages and solve the problems, and after that, an animal is sacrificed. This ceremony is called union sacrifice (*birlik kurbanı*). Our position is superior to *dede*s; we inspect them. We generally pay a visit to our communities in November or December after the harvest.[9]

*Efendi*s, however, cannot undertake the role of the *mürşit*. The *mürşit* appoints the *dede*s and *baba*s and executes divine justice as the successor of Hacı Bektaş Veli. Dealing with a community's serious problems that *dede*s cannot resolve is the responsibility of the *mürşit*. As an *efendi* explained, it is not *efendi*s but the *dede*s and the *mürşit* who are responsible for executing divine justice:

> If the problem of the community is not so severe, *dede*s resolve it. However, if the problem is severe, we explain it to the *mürşit*. He listens to both sides and decides like a judge. If it is necessary to give punishment to someone, he does it, and the guilty person can be excommunicated. However, that is practiced in places where people are still adherents to the 'path'.[10]

Hence, *efendi*s do not attempt to take the role of the *mürşit* or violate his position; yet, they do not act under his control either. They establish their relationship with *talip*s individually, without any consensus among the family members. When it became difficult for me to grasp the position of *efendi*s, who behave without any control mechanism for regulating their relationship with *talip*s and without any cooperation from the *mürşit* or other family members, one person from the Ulusoy family explained:

> The family members visit *talip*s on their own initiative and without any control of the *mürşit* over them. There are lots of male members of the Ulusoy family, but some of them do not visit *talip*s. I mean, some of them have a relationship with *talip*s, but some of them do not. The Ulusoys who pay a visit to *talip*s are also visited by them in Hacıbektaş during the times of the ceremony. Each house of the Ulusoys has its own *talip*s, but, in reality, all of them are the *talip*s of Hacı Bektaş Veli. Namely, the *talip* who pays a visit to an Ulusoy house can pay visits to all of the Ulusoy houses. No one has the

[9] Interview with a male member of the Ulusoy family, 14 August 2010, Hacıbektaş.
[10] Interview with a male member of the Ulusoy family, 14 August 2010, Hacıbektaş.

right to control or hinder *talip*s. To whom *talip*s pay a visit depends on their own wishes and decisions.[11]

The interviewee explained the current situation of *efendi*s without referring to competition within the family. In the past, however, the dispersion of sacred authority among the males and the *mürşit*'s lack of control over them created problems. All of the family members who moved to Tokat and grew up among *talip*s preserved their close relationship with them, even after returning to Hacıbektaş in the 1930s. In the 1950s, the *mürşit* Feyzullah Ulusoy reacted against the *efendi*s' relationship with the *talip*s in order to maintain the traditional position of the Ulusoy family. Hence, he tried to keep the *efendi*s under control, and, according to a family member, he offered to share all of the income that the family received.[12] Ultimately, he failed to control the economic relationship between *efendi*s and *talip*s. All family members, including the *mürşit,* had to establish a close relationship with *talip*s. Thus, one of the current *mürşit*s explained his relationship with the *talip*s as follows:

> Personally, I have a relationship with the *talip*s through the mediation of the *dede*s. Namely, *dede*s visit me and explain to me the problems of the community. If necessary, I go to the place where the problem has occurred. If there is an important event, such as the opening of a *cemevi*, I go to the places where the *talip*s live. Of course, it is impossible to participate in every event. I sometimes give a speech or listen to the *talip*s' problems in these places, but *dede*s and *talip*s always visit me.[13]

Currently, although *efendi*s have adapted to the changing relationships within the 'path', family members who have no ties or relationships with *talip*s but have their own professions and income, still do not approve of the issue of economic dependence on *talip*s. Those family members who are critical of *efendi*s describe the *efendi*s' activities as earning a living by performing the role of a *dede* (*dedelik yapmak*) or as visiting *talip*s and establishing an economic relationship with them (*talip üzerine gitmek*). According to one

---

[11] Interview with a male member of the Ulusoy family, 21 July 2009, Hacıbektaş.
[12] Interview with a male member of the Ulusoy family, 25 December 2009, Ankara.
[13] Interview with a male member of the Ulusoy family, 1 December 2008, Ankara.

member, neither certain family members, nor *talip*s appreciate *efendi*s who visit them often:

> My maternal uncles were visiting *talip*s. Actually, my uncle did not visit them, and my father also did not, but their children are visiting. Now, no matter whether they are young or old, ignoring their age, all of them are visiting *talip*s. Although Cemalettin and Veliyettin Çelebi were brothers, their descendants are different from each other. The descendants of Veliyettin Çelebi are educated, and they prefer not to visit *talip*s. Many of the descendants of Cemalettin Çelebi are not educated, and they generally do visit talips. [. . .] Those family members who visit *talip*s often are not very much respected. If you have a close relationship with people, that makes you unworthy in their eyes.[14]

In line with this evaluation, a couple of *talip*s sent a letter to the *mürşit* in 1991. They were critical of the internal distribution of authority within the 'path' and presented suggestions for improvement. According to them, . . .

> [t]he community is increasingly becoming more aware; it is becoming increasingly against 'taking without giving'. Efendis' visits must be organized carefully, and people should not be irritated by them. Such visits and meetings must not take place under the influence of alcohol (cited in Shankland 2003, p. 149).

While the *mürşit* agreed with the *talip*s' concerns, in his response, he explained that he had never been in favour of *efendi*s making visits to collect dues but had also not been able to prevent it. He stressed the mutual responsibility of dealing with this, as well as with the problem of meetings taking place under the influence of alcohol.

Related to this conversation, a family member complained about the corruption of the relationship between some *efendi*s and their adherents. He stressed that *talip*s had begun to choose *efendi*s according to their own interests. In other words, to be selected by *talip*s, *efendi*s turned into competitive individuals who protected their own interests without any cooperation with other family members.[15] This individualised and profaned sanctity makes

[14] Interview with a female member of the Ulusoy family, 21 August 2009, Hacıbektaş.
[15] Interview with a male member of the Ulusoy family, 25 December 2009, Ankara.

*efendi*s compete against each other and become dependent on *talip*s. In other words, the *efendis'* growing authority had changed the *dedes'* and the *mürşits'* vital role in the hierarchy. It had weakened the mediatory role of *dede*s, the communities' spokesmen, and undermined the power of the *mürşit*, who previously had only been the head of the family. Nevertheless, the *efendis'* position was also fragile due to their individualised and profaned sanctity which heavily depended on the *talip*s.

The Debate over Succession

In the republican period, the *mürşit* began to lose his power to exercise authority over *dede*s, due to the blurred relationship among the *mürşit, dede*s and *talip*s. Furthermore, the *efendis'* competing claims to sacred authority led to struggles over succession. Therefore, the identification of the *mürşit* became a sensitive issue for the family because the contest to become a *mürşit* is still disputed between the two circles around Cemalettin Çelebi and Veliyettin Çelebi, respectively.

Considering the succession rules in Twelver Shi'ism and Ismailism, *nass*, which means 'explicit designation of a successor by his predecessor', is a valid rule of succession (Daftari 2007, p. 520). For the succession of Hacı Bektaş Veli's descendants, however, *nass* does not seem to be valid. In their case, the principal requirement is that the candidate has to be virtuous and learned (*erşed ve eslah*). Moreover, for identifying the *mürşit*, there exist additional rules, such as primogeniture – that is, succession is handed down from father to eldest son. The absence of a consensus on these rules has for centuries resulted in debates over succession and paved the way for dividing the lineage into different branches.

Despite the centuries-old disagreements on succession as being maintained by one family member, the Ottoman central administration always acted as an adjudicator and decided who would become the *mürşit*. Since the Republic did not officially recognise the *mürşit*, the absence of an adjudicator rendered the disagreement even more complicated.[16] The death of Veliyettin (Çelebi) Ulusoy – the last official *mürşit* – in 1940 gave rise to a new debate between the descendants of Cemalettin Çelebi and those of Veliyettin Çelebi

---

[16] Interview with a male member of the Ulusoy family, 21 July 2009, Hacıbektaş.

over who would be his successor – a similar issue to what had happened in the sixteenth century.[17] Veliyettin (Çelebi) Ulusoy succeeded to the post after his elder brother Cemalettin Çelebi. Except for his youngest son Mustafa, all of Cemalettin Çelebi's sons died before their uncle Veliyettin (Çelebi) Ulusoy. Therefore, in the wake of the death of Veliyettin (Çelebi) Ulusoy, there were two candidates for the *mürşit* post. Cemalettin Çelebi's youngest son was eligible because he was both the eldest member of the family and the son of the *mürşit*. However, he was eliminated from the candidacy due to his ill health, which made him ineligible. The other candidate was Feyzullah Çelebi – the eldest son of the last *mürşit* Veliyettin (Çelebi) Ulusoy. The community widely accepted him as *mürşit*. However, even though his father had died without becoming a successor, Hasan Hulgü Rıza Ulusoy – the eldest grandson of Cemalettin Çelebi – claimed that primogeniture was a valid rule for succession and that, as the oldest member of the family, he was supposed to fill the post. He also received support from certain *dede*s, and this led to a division within the family and the community. According to one *talip*, the community felt disturbed by this contest and demanded reconciliation between the two *mürşit*s. Consequently, these two family members together carried out the tasks of the *mürşit*, until Hasan Hulgü Rıza Ulusoy withdrew from the *mürşit* post after being elected as CHP deputy in 1957.[18]

A second contestation occurred in 1994, when the last *mürşit*, Feyzullah Ulusoy, died. While the post was handed down from Feyzullah Ulusoy to

[17] Succession within the lineage had been contested even earlier. In the sixteenth century, before the period of Balım Sultan, the family separated into two branches: the Mürselli branch and the Hüdadadlı branch. Although both of these branches (as the progeny of Hacı Bektaş Veli) received a share from the charitable endowment of the order, only the Mürselli branch had the right to successorship and to the position of endowment trustee. According to Celalettin Ulusoy, only the *mürşit*'s sons could be the successor, provided they were virtuous and learned. If conditions required, the succession could also pass from older to younger brother. The Hüdadadlı branch was removed from the post of *mürşit* on account of this succession rule. Although the father of Hüdadad Çelebi, Rasul Bali, was *mürşit* when Rasul Bali died, the post did not pass to Hüdadad Çelebi but to his uncle, Mürsel Bali. Because Hüdadad Çelebi had died before Mürsel Bali, the son of Mürsel Bali, Balım Sultan, became the successor. Thus, the children of Hüdadad Çelebi lost their right to succession since their father had died without becoming *mürşit*. See Ulusoy (1986, pp. 70–71).

[18] Interview with a *talip*, 18 August 2009, Hacıbektaş.

his son Veliyettin Hürrem Ulusoy, the Cemalettin Çelebi branch reacted by claiming once again that this was an invalid way of succession. According to the primogeniture rule, the new *mürşit* should have been the brother of Feyzullah Ulusoy, as the oldest family member. However, the brother declined the offer, so that one of the grandsons of Cemalettin Çelebi, Yusuf İzzettin Ulusoy, claimed to be the rightful successor. Veliyettin Ulusoy has since then held the post of *mürşit* and has been widely accepted by the community, while Yusuf İzzettin Ulusoy persisted in his claim until his death in 2005. Thereafter, his half-brother Haydar Ulusoy claimed the right to successorship. He died a year later, and the Cemalettin Çelebi branch put forward his cousin Safa Ulusoy as the new successor since he was the oldest family member. Safa Ulusoy and Veliyettin Hürrem Ulusoy are currently carrying out this task together, while the tension between the two branches continues without open confrontation.

Channelling Sacred Authority into the Political Sphere

The first family member to become involved in the political sphere was Cemalettin Çelebi, when he assumed the first Grand National Assembly's second vice presidency in 1920. As Fliche and Massicard (2006, p. 33) note, Mustafa Kemal appointed him to this position because of his leading role in mobilising the Alevi-Bektaşi communities during the War of Independence. His position had symbolic power over the adherents of the Çelebis with respect to gaining the new regime's support. In this regard, he is the first family member to become a deputy; however, in becoming a non-elected deputy, he differs from other family members who since the 1950s have channelled their sacred authority into a political one.

In the early republican period, the secular politics of the single-party regime kept religion under strict control. However, with the transition to a multi-party system in 1946, both the Republican People's Party (*Cumhuriyet Halk Partisi*, CHP) and the Democratic Party (*Demokratik Parti*, DP) considered religion as a source of political support and for that reason integrated religion into politics. This allowed some Sunni orders, which were not officially recognised, to gain public visibility. The Alevi community was also recognised as a significant source of votes (Massicard 2007, p. 54), and during this period some members of the Ulusoy family entered the political sphere, too.

In 1954, Yusuf İzzettin Ulusoy, one of the *efendi*s, was elected for the first time as a DP deputy from Tokat. As descendant of Cemalettin Çelebi, who had moved to Tokat in 1928, Yusuf İzzettin Ulusoy maintained an organic relationship with the *talip*s in this city, allowing him to easily convert his sacred authority into a political one. The fact that he was elected as DP deputy is particularly noteworthy. As Massicard (2007, p. 54) indicates, contrary to the opinion that the Alevis supported the CHP, the first multi-party elections show that a sizeable Alevi electorate sided with the DP. The argument is further sustained by the fact that the Ulusoys had also supported the DP against the CHP, with a few exceptions. A family member explains his family's inclination towards the DP as such:

> Not just the Ulusoys but also the other Çelebis were right-wing. I think the underlying reason of that is the inability of our family members to evaluate and understand the period of the Second World War, during which İsmet Paşa was the national chief and people were suffering from famine and poverty. Moreover, when the dervish convents were abolished in the early years of the Republic, our family was oppressed; and it might have also affected their political opinion. They had been oppressed, and then they experienced the difficult conditions of the independence war. After the establishment of the Republic, they were again oppressed by the ban on the 'path' and the visits of *dede*s and *talip*s. The period of İsmet Paşa and the Second World War followed these hard times. Our family members could not analyse this case, and they saw İsmet Paşa as the one responsible for all the things they had experienced. They were angry with him, they even hated him, but they could not see what happened in the world at that period. [. . .] They related to the relief that the country experienced after the single-party regime with Menderes and his policies. However, that was the result of the changing conjuncture happening all around the world. I think that those generations, which did not grasp the period analytically, became right-wing.[19]

The elder half-brother of Yusuf İzzettin Ulusoy, Hasan Hulgü Rıza Ulusoy, was an exception due to his support for the CHP, while others were supporting the DP. In the 1957 elections, Hasan Hulgü Rıza Ulusoy and İzzettin Ulusoy became rivals as deputy candidates from Tokat; finally, Hasan

[19] Interview with a male member of the Ulusoy family, 3 August 2009, Hacıbektaş.

Hulgü Rıza Ulusoy was elected as CHP deputy. Their candidacy from the same constituency but for different political parties led to a conflict between the brothers. Other family members who supported the DP were also offended by Hasan Hulgü Rıza Ulusoy's involvement with the CHP.[20] Despite some family members' negative attitudes, he ran for parliament once again in the 1961 elections, as CHP candidate from Tokat. Following these two *efendi*s who were able to convert their sacred into political authority, Kazım Ulusoy, also a descendant of Cemalettin Çelebi, in 1965 became deputy of the Nation Party (*Millet Partisi*, MP). In his hometown of Amasya, he had close relationships with the Alevi-Bektaşi population.

The integration of religion into the party politics of the DP and the CHP supported and empowered Sunni Islam and the Sunni orders. The Alevi-Bektaşi belief also became a public issue after the military intervention in 1960. In 1961, General Cemal Gürsel proposed that mosques be available to Alevis to keep the peace between the Sunni and Alevi populations. Moreover, in 1963, CHP chairman İsmet İnönü proposed to establish a Department of Denominations (*Mezhepler Müdürlüğü*) within the Presidency of Religious Affairs (*Diyanet İşleri Başkanlığı*, in short *Diyanet*) in an assembly session concerning the *Diyanet*'s reorganisation. The officials contacted Feyzullah Ulusoy and offered him the role of the representative in the Department of Denominations. Feyzullah Ulusoy, however, rejected this offer because he was not eligible for the position (Sezgin 2012).

The right-wing and Islamist media reacted against the government's efforts to harmonise the Sunni and Alevi populations and refused to accept the Alevi faith as a denomination. The right-wing media's attack on the Alevi faith led to the mobilisation of Alevis. Using the term 'Alevi' for the first time, some university students issued a declaration protesting against right-wing and Islamic reactions and demanded recognition under the constitutional principle of secularism. Moreover, the establishment of the first Alevi organisations and the reopening as a museum of the *dergah* in Hacıbektaş, which had been under restoration since the mid-1950s, as well as the annual celebration of Hacı Bektaş Veli, followed the developments outlined below (Ata 2007, p. 48; Massicard 2007, p. 55).

---

[20] Interview with a female member of the Ulusoy family, 25 August 2009, Hacıbektaş.

The deputies Yusuf İzzettin Ulusoy and Hasan Hülgü Rıza Ulusoy played an essential role in the opening of the *dergah* as a museum, but there also existed another family member, Ali Celalettin Ulusoy, who took an active part in this process. He was also one of the founders and the president of the first Alevi-Bektaşi organisation, the Hacı Bektaş Tourism and Propagation Association (*Hacı Bektaş Turizm ve Tanıtma Derneği*), established in 1963. In the words of his son, . . .

> [i]f I am not wrong, the association was founded in 1963. For a long time, my father had been the president of the association. They organised a night at Büyük Cinema and some conferences on Hacı Bektaş Veli. [. . .] During the opening ceremony of the *dergah* as a museum, my father gave a speech. He said that he was happy with the dervish convent's opening as a museum, which was closed by the law regulating the status of tombs and dervish convents. A general who was eager to show his adherence to the principles of Kemalism interfered in my father's speech by saying something like 'No one is able to open a place that was closed down by Atatürk'. People started panicking because of the commander's speech. Alevis were still backward at that time, and due to the concern that the state officials would interfere in the ceremonies, many of them left the district. Then, the opening of the museum was reported in the *Ulus* newspaper. I cannot remember it word by word, but it was written that the Kemalist general put the presumptuous person into his place. However, my father was a CHP member. On the following day, my father sent a refutation, and it came out in the newspaper. He explained the opening ceremony scene and stressed that he was a CHP member and reminded them about the Ulusoy family's support for Atatürk.[21]

The first Alevi political party, the Turkish Unity Party (*Türkiye Birlik Partisi*, TBP), was founded in 1966. The authority of the Ulusoy family, especially the authority of the *mürşit*, was vital for gaining the support of the Alevi-Bektaşi community, and Feyzullah Ulusoy became one of the founders of the TBP (Massicard 2013). Like the *mürşit*, Feyzullah Ulusoy and three other Ulusoys were elected as TBP deputies in the 1969 elections. Four family members were nominated as candidates: Yusuf İzzettin Ulusoy from Tokat, Kazım Ulusoy from Amasya, who had transferred from the Republican

---

[21] Interview with a male member of the Ulusoy family, 3 August 2009, Hacıbektaş.

Reliance Party (*Cumhuriyetçi Güven Partisi*, CGP), Ali Naki Ulusoy from Çorum (he had close relationships with the *talip*s in Çorum because the city was his mother's birthplace) and Ahmet Cemalettin Ulusoy from Yozgat. Except for Ahmet Cemalettin Ulusoy, all the candidates from the Ulusoy family were elected as deputies. After the elections, Demirel needed affirmative votes from the deputies of other parties to form a government. To that end, the Justice Party (*Adalet Partisi*, AP) deputies lobbied other party deputies for their support. Five TBP deputies, including the Ulusoys, who were all in disagreement with the TBP's central executive committee, supported the Demirel government.

After that, the party members and the Alevi communities accused the Ulusoys of following their own interests. In response, the family members defended themselves by arguing that they had tried to prevent any political crisis in order to protect democracy and serve their electorate more efficiently.[22] Efforts to expel the Ulusoys from the party resulted in the excommunication of these five deputies from the 'path' by a committee constituted by the party staff. A book called *Beş Yol Düşkünü* (Five Excommunicated Persons) was published and handed out to the Alevi-Bektaşi people (Ata 2007, p. 216). According to Feyzullah Ulusoy's daughter, . . .

> [m]y father was one of the founders of the party. At that time, I was young; they insisted that my father should found the party. They visited my father many times, persuading him to establish the party. They were Alevi people, well-educated people, and my father founded the party. My uncles became deputies of the party, but they were misunderstood because of the affirmative vote. Among those who cast affirmative votes was my paternal uncle. My father told them: 'Do not cast an affirmative vote; you are right, but people can easily misunderstand you'. And that was what happened. After a while, the party was also closed. [. . .] My father did not become a deputy of the party.[23]

Thus, a political party claimed the sacred authority through which its members could excommunicate the *efendi*s. For the Ulusoy family, the TBP

---

[22] Interview with a female member of the Ulusoy family, 25 August 2009, Hacıbektaş and, with another female member of the Ulusoy family, 8 August 2009, Hacıbektaş.

[23] Interview with a female member of the Ulusoy family, 25 August 2009, Hacıbektaş.

experience had profoundly negative effects regarding its relationships both within the family and with the *talip*s. According to a family member, . . .

> [t]he Unity Party issue caused resentment among the family members. The Alevi community reviled our family for the affirmative vote of the three Ulusoys. Many rumours came out in the press; they claimed that the Ulusoys did this in return for money. No matter whether it was true or not, it destroyed our relationship with the *talip*s. My father wrote a letter in which he criticised the Ulusoys' affirmative vote. This also led to resentment among the family members, and this continued for a very long time. There is still an arms-length relationship between their children and us and even their grandchildren. The political issues damaged our family. [. . .] The relationship with *talip*s from some regions was broken. The loyalty of the *talip*s from Tokat remained. Some of our family members continued to be elected as deputies from Tokat, and the *talip*s supported Şahin Ulusoy, for example. The *talip*s from Amasya partially preserved their relationship with our family. Many of the *talip*s from the Black Sea region keep their loyalty to us, but the issue of the affirmative vote destroyed the relationship with the *talip*s, especially in Çorum. In the east, some people took advantage of this issue. Many of the sacred lineages are independent in the east, and those who claimed that Hacı Bektaş Veli had no children[24] made use of this issue.[25]

The negative experience of the TBP did not put an end to the Ulusoys' political life. In the 1973 elections, Yusuf İzzettin Ulusoy competed as an independent candidate for the deputy position for Tokat, while Kazım Ulusoy

[24] The Bektaşi order separated into two branches (Babagan and Çelebi) in the sixteenth century. Having claimed that Hacı Bektaş Veli was celibate, the Bektaşi branch challenged the sacred authority of the Çelebi lineage inherited from Hacı Bektaş Veli through blood kin or consanguinity. The separation into two branches became visible in the nineteenth century, after the abolition of the Bektaşi order by Mahmud II in 1826. In the mid-nineteenth century, the Babagan branch gained power in the administration of the main *dergah*, and the rivalry between the Babagan and the Çelebi branches became apparent. When the attacks made by the Babagan branch on the legitimacy of the Çelebis occurred in the early twentieth century, the consanguinity between Hacı Bektaş Veli and the Çelebis was in dispute. Later, some of the independent Alevi-Kızılbaş *ocak*s who did not affiliate with the Çelebi (Ulusoy) lineage and challenged their sacred authority agreed with the claim that Hacı Bektaş Veli had no children.

[25] Interview with a male member of the Ulusoy family, 3 August 2009, Hacıbektaş.

and Ali Naki Ulusoy became candidates for the CGP from Amasya and Tokat; yet, none of them were elected. In the 1973 elections, however, Haydar Ulusoy, half-brother of Yusuf İzzettin Ulusoy and Kazım Ulusoy, became CHP deputy for Tokat. Also, in the 1987 elections, Kazım Ulusoy was elected as CHP deputy from Amasya. Yusuf İzzettin Ulusoy could no longer be elected as deputy, but he became one of the founders of the True Path Party (*Doğru Yol Partisi*, DYP). The last family member to become a deputy was Şahin Ulusoy.[26] He became deputy of the Social Democratic Populist Party (*Sosyal Demokrat Halkçı Parti,* SHP) from Tokat in the 1991 elections, and he served as Minister of Tourism from 1994 to 1995. Finally, in the 1995 elections, he was elected as CHP deputy from Tokat. Despite this, some family members still see the deputy elections as a way of converting their sacred authority into a political one (Fliche and Massicard 2006, p. 66).

The fact that the *efendi*s cannot channel their sacred authority into political power may be related to the inadequacy of the traditional relations to accommodate the changing political sphere in which the Alevi movement and alternative forms of authorities emerged. By the end of the 1980s, a new Alevi movement arose after a decade of right-wing Sunni state ideology, Islamist attacks on Alevi communities, growing influence of the *Diyanet* and compulsory Sunni religious education, as well as neo-liberal economic policies increasing inequality in income distribution.

The oppression of the left-wing in Turkey after the military intervention and the rising ethnic and nationalist movements following the collapse of socialist regimes worldwide also impacted the Alevi-Bektaşi associations, which had been established on the grounds of identity politics (Vorhoff 2003, p. 96). The 1993 massacre in Sivas and the 1995 massacre in the Gazi neighbourhood in Istanbul provided additional incentives to mobilise.

Unlike the Alevi revival in the 1960s, which was characterised by the active participation of *dede*s and people adherent to the traditional way of the 'path', the second Alevi revival was driven mostly by urbanised, educated and non-*dede* Alevis (many of whom came from the left-wing political tradition). By

---

[26] Şahin Ulusoy is the son of Hasan Hulgü Rıza Ulusoy, elected as CHP deputy from Tokat in the 1957 and once again in the 1961 elections. Thus, he followed in his father's footsteps in his political career.

integrating Alevism with their political ideology, they reinterpreted the Alevi tradition. During this period, the Alevis' traditional leaders, the *dede*s, stood out as community leaders, but their influence was restricted to the religious sphere. Moreover, their existence in the Alevi movement led to contradictions between inherited sacred authority and some of the concepts defended by the Alevi-Bektaşi organisations, such as democracy and enlightenment.

In 2006, the *mürşit* Veliyettin Ulusoy organised a 'Unity Meeting' (*Birlik Toplantısı*) and a 'Unity Cem' (*Birlik Cemi*) in Hacıbektaş, together with several Alevi-Bektaşi organisations.[27] In these meetings, the Alevi-Bektaşi organisations declared that they accepted Veliyettin Ulusoy as *mürşit*. Thus, these meetings opened a new page in the history of the Alevi movement, allowing a convergence of identity politics with the 'path', without restricting the sacred leader to the religious sphere. In 2007, the Justice and Development Party (*Adalet ve Kalkınma Partisi*, AKP) government's 'Alevi Opening' (*Alevi Açılımı*) policy received strong protests by the Alevi-Bektaşi organisations, and Veliyettin Ulusoy became a visible public figure as spokesman of his community. Ulusoy demanded the secularisation of the state with the abolition of the *Diyanet* and of compulsory religious courses in schools. He also urged the state to act neutrally towards all religious communities and to ensure the freedom of all religious communities from state interference. In the course of the 'Alevi Opening' process (see Özkul 2015 and Chapter 3 in this volume), the Alevi-Bektaşi associations on 9 November 2008 organised a demonstration for equal citizenship rights, during which Veliyettin Ulusoy also gave a speech. Since the 1950s, the Ulusoys have participated in political life as elected deputies, as founders of political parties, or as the founder and president of the first Alevi-Bektaşi organisation (as in the case of Ali Celalettin Ulusoy). Veliyettin Ulusoy was the first *mürşit* to appear in the political sphere as the spokesman of his community without being connected to any party or organisation.

From 2010 to 2011, under the leadership of two *mürşit*s from the Ulusoy family – Veliyettin Ulusoy and Safa Ulusoy – meetings were organised with

---

[27] The Alevi Bektaşi Federation (*Alevi Bektaşi Federasyonu*, ABF), the European Confederation of Alevi Associations (*Avrupa Alevi Birlikleri Federasyonu*, AABF) and the Hacı Bektaş Veli Cultural Association (*Hacı Bektaş Veli Kültür Derneği*, HBVKD) were the organisers of the meeting.

*dede*s, *zakir*s, *talip*s, Alevi intellectuals and researchers all over Turkey and abroad to establish unity under the Ulusoys' sacred authority. The *mürşits'* reclaiming of the leading authority and call for unity postulates the reverence shown toward their inherited sacred authority, which has been challenged since the early nineteenth century and which has even been deemed illegitimate after the establishment of the Republic. Veliyettin Ulusoy gave a speech at the so-called 'Unity in the *Dergah* Meetings' (*Dergah'ta Birlik Toplantıları*) held on 10–11 September 2011. In this talk, he pointed to the state's oppression and discriminatory policies, elements of modernisation (such as industrialisation, urbanisation and migration), the dissolution of traditional structures and the current problems of the Alevi-Bektaşi community, including the lack of unity, the lack of institutionalisation, assimilation and the deformation of rituals.

At the 'Unity in the *Dergah* Meetings', decisions were made regarding the institutionalisation of the 'path' in correspondence with the contemporary world. In line with these decisions, the Hünkar Hacı Bektaş Veli foundation was established in December 2012, continuing the heritage of the old Hacı Bektaş Veli foundation, which in 1925 had been abolished with the Public Law No. 677. All these efforts aimed at unity and the institutionalisation of the 'path', the standardisation of rituals against their deformation and the struggle against assimilation by providing solidarity, thus indicating a new phase for the Ulusoy family's sacred authority. Under the leadership of the *postnişin*s, the charitable endowment still makes an effort to standardise the rituals of the 'path' and grants scholarship to Alevi-Bektaşi students to strengthen cohesion in the community.

Conclusion

In the Ottoman period, the Ulusoy family (the Çelebi branch) was formally recognised as Hacı Bektaş Veli's hereditary successors. After the establishment of the Republic, however, the family was no longer recognised as such and lost all of its granted privileges. Moreover, the new regime's secularisation policies, which separated and differentiated between the temporal and spiritual spheres, as well as the establishment of new institutions in these spheres no longer allowed the family to exercise their sacred authority. Mass education, urbanisation and industrialisation – in other words, the modernisation of society – transformed the rural Alevi-Bektaşi community's traditional and hierarchical structure. As a result, the Ulusoy family was displaced and put in an ambiguous position. This displacement did not end the sacred authority of the Ulusoys. On the contrary, the lack of scriptural rules and institutions made the structure of the 'path' flexible, allowing for modifications and the emergence of new forms of authority.

In this regard, the displacement might be interpreted in two different ways: either as destructive for the old and hierarchical structure of the 'path', or as constructive for newly emerging forms of authority in the 'path'. On the one hand, it was destructive because the hierarchical order within the 'path' – in other words, the old social differentiation among *mürşit*s, *dede*s and *talip*s – became blurred. In line with this development, the authority of the *mürşit* was dispersed among all male members of the family. The competing claims of the *efendi*s over the sacred authority led to further struggles over succession. On the other hand, this process was constructive because family members took on newly emerging forms of authority. One example of this is the title of *efendi*, which gained new meanings with the modification of the structure of the 'path'. This process was also constructive because the sacred authority was converted into a political one when the family members became founders of political parties, served as elected deputies in those areas where Alevi-Bektaşi communities lived, or functioned as spokesmen for the community at public events. Thus, the transformation of the sacred authority of the Ulusoy family is an ongoing process, and the establishment of the Hacı Bektaş Veli foundation might also bring about new possibilities for the family's sacred authority.

Bibliography

Andrews, P., and Temel, H. (2010). Hubyar. *British Journal of Middle Eastern Studies*, 37(3), 287–334.

Ata, K. (2007). *Alevilerin İlk Siyasal Denemesi (Türkiye) Birlik Partisi (1966–1980)*. Ankara: Kelime Press.

Babayan, K. (2002). *Mystics, Monarchs, and Messiahs: Cultural Landscape of Early Modern Iran*. Unpubl. MA thesis, Harvard University.

Berktay Hacımirzaoğlu, A. (1998). Ulusoy Ailesi. In: Baydar, O., and Çiçekoğlu, F., eds, *Cumhuriyet'in Aile Albümleri*. Istanbul: Tarih Vakfı Yayınları. pp. 256–75.

Corbin, H. (1993). *History of Islamic Philosophy*. New York: Kegan Paul International.

Dressler, M. (2006). The Modern Dede: Changing Parameters for Religious Authority in Contemporary Turkish Alevism. In: Kramer G., and Schmidtke, S., eds, *Speaking for Islam: Religious Authorities in Muslim Societies*. Leiden: Brill. pp. 269–94.

Dressler, M. (2013). *Writing Religion: The Making of Turkish Alevi Islam*. New York: Oxford University Press.

Fliche, B., and Massicard, E. (2006). L'oncle et le député: Circuits de ressources et usages de la parenté dans un lignage sacré en Turquie. *European Journal of Turkish Studies*, [online]. 4. [Viewed 31 March 2021]. Available from: doi: 10.4000/ejts.627

Lewis, B. (1991). Efendi. In: Lewis, B., et al., eds, *Encyclopedia of Islam, Vol. III*. Leiden: Brill.

Massicard, E. (2013). *The Alevis in Turkey and Europe. Identity and Managing Territorial Diversity*. London and New York: Routledge.

Massicard, I. (2007). *Türkiye'den Avrupa'ya Alevi Hareketinin Siyasallaşması*. Istanbul: İletişim.

Özkul, D. (2015). Alevi 'Openings' and Politicization of the 'Alevi Issue' During the AKP Rule. *Turkish Studies* 16(1), 80–96.

Sezgin, A. (2012). Çelebi Feyzullah Ulusoy'la Sohbet. *Haberiniz* [online] 7 March 2012. [Viewed 1 February 2021]. Available from: https://millidusunce.com/celebi-feyzullah-ulusoyla-sohbet/

Shankland, D. (1999). *Islam and Society in Turkey*. Huntington: The Eothen Press.

Shankland, D. (2003). *The Alevis in Turkey: Emergence of Secular Islamic Tradition*. New York: Routledge.

Tee, C. (2010). Holy Lineages, Migration and Reformulation of Alevi Tradition: A Study of the Derviş Cemal Ocak from Erzincan. *British Journal of Middle Eastern Studies*, 37(3), 335–92.

Trimingham, J. S. (1998). *The Sufi Orders in Islam*. New York: Oxford University Press.

Ulusoy, C. A. (1986). *Hünkar Hacı Bektaş Veli ve Alevi-Bektaşi Yolu*. Ankara: Akademi Matbaası.

Ulusoy, V. (2009). *Serçeşme Yazıları: Konuşmalar Söyleşiler*. Istanbul: Alev.

Vorhoff, K. (2003). The Past in the Future: Discourses on the Alevis in Contemporary Turkey. In: White, P. J., and Jongerden, J., eds, *Turkey's Alevi Enigma: A Comprehensive Overview*. Leiden: Brill. pp. 93–110.

Yaman, A. (2006). *Kızılbaş Alevi Ocakları*. Ankara: Elips Kitap.

Yıkmış Salman, M. (2014). *Hacı Bektaş Veli'nin Evlatları 'Yol'un Mürşitleri: Ulusoy Ailesi*. Istanbul: İletişim.

Yıldırım, R. (2010). 'Bektaşi Kime Derler?': Bektaşi Kavramının Kapsamı ve Sınırları Üzerine Tarihsel Bir Analiz Denemesi. *Türk Kültürü ve Hacı Bektaş Veli Araştırma Dergisi* 55, 23–58.

12

RITUAL, MUSICAL PERFORMANCE AND IDENTITY: THE TRANSFORMATION OF THE ALEVI *ZAKIR*

ULAŞ ÖZDEMİR

Introduction

The growing organisation of Alevis since the late 1980s has brought with it what is often referred to as the 'Alevi revival'.[1] Since the 2000s, this process has resulted in significant changes. This article examines the changes and transformation of one of the twelve *hizmet*s (services) of the Alevi *cem* ritual, that of the *zakir*, in the context of ritual, musical performance and identity. Similar to the *dede* and other services, the *zakir* holds an important role, not only in ritual, but also in non-ritual expressions of Alevi faith and society. With their music performances within and outside of the ritual, *zakir*s have become a more visible and important vehicle to shape Alevi collective identity. Exploring the changes in the institution of the *zakir* provides important clues for understanding the changes in Alevism over the past twenty years.[2] This article recommends further research to understand the transformation of the twelve 'services' carried out in Alevi *cem*s. These studies can show the changing dynamics of both Alevi *cem*s and Alevi collective identity.

---

[1] See Kehl-Bodrogi (1996), Çamuroğlu (1998), Varhoff (2003) and Şahin (2002) for more information about the 'Alevi revival'.

[2] See Özdemir (2016) for more information about the dynamics of the *zakir* institution, which is based on ethnographic research about *zakir*s in the *cemevi*s of Istanbul.

Perspectives on Alevi Music in the Modern History of Turkey

Nearly all researchers studying Alevi music use the concept of 'Alevi music', but what this concept includes changes according to the context of the study.[3] Early debates about whether to approach it as religious music changed, so that later studies adopted a folk-music-based approach. Recently, the emphasis has changed once again, and studies on Alevi music have concentrated on its relationship to Alevi identity.

Beginning in the early republican period, researchers such as Vahit Lütfi Salcı, Sadeddin Nüzhet Ergun, Rauf Yekta and Halil Bedi Yönetken, who participated in the efforts to create a national music,[4] published various research findings concerning Alevi and Bektaşi music (Salcı 1940, Ergun 1942, Yönetken 1966). During the republican era, until the 1990s, the debates on music – identified by the terms Alevi, Bektaşi and, occasionally, Kızılbaş – generally concentrated on the question of whether this music was 'religious' or 'secular'. Salcı was one of the researchers who considered Alevi literature, music and dance to be religious, based on their Islamic origins (Yaprak 2003, pp. 43–46). The 1990s witnessed a resurgence of interest in Alevi music, especially during the period known as the 'Alevi revival'. Research conducted during this period generally approached Alevi music as 'folk music'. These studies explored it in the context of the relationship between the *saz* and the lyrics, and classified the lyrics into genres such as *deyiş*, *semah*, *miraçlama* and *mersiye* according to their themes (Birdoğan 1990, Duygulu 1997, Yaltırık 2003, Onatça 2007).

Research on the topic conducted from the 1990s onwards has focused on the relationship between Alevi music and Alevi identity. Some researchers have presented Alevi music as one of the most potent carriers of Alevi identity, especially during the 'Alevi revival'. Ethnomusicologist Jean During (1995, p. 85) argues that the partial relaxation of the code of secrecy within which Alevi rituals had been practised for centuries might in fact be due to music. Another ethnomusicologist, Irene Markoff, focuses on the role of music in Alevi-Bektaşi collective memory. Rather than presenting Alevi music as a particular category,

[3] See Özdemir (2019) for a detailed discussion on the concept of 'Alevi music'.
[4] See Balkılıç (2015) for a discussion about the efforts to create a national music in the early republican period.

Markoff (1986, 1993, 2002, 2009) looks at its fundamental characteristics – such as the *bağlama*, poetry and performance – within Alevi culture. Media and communications scholar Bedriye Poyraz (2007) considers Alevi music as an area of struggle in which the emerging Alevi identity is expressed, as well as an area of consumption where Alevi music has been transformed into a commercial commodity.

Ethnomusicologist Ayhan Erol (2009, p. 100), who has made significant contributions to theoretical discussions on the topic at hand, uses the concepts of 'unity' and 'difference' to describe the Alevi community. He emphasises that the Alevi community's unique character of 'oneness' derives from the reference points on which it relies in defining itself (for example, Ali, or the 'path'). However, when it comes to belief, the unity in the 'path' differs according to social, cultural and ethnic factors. These differences lead to variations in the instruments, performance style and repertoire that make up the characteristics of Alevi music. Yet, the *cem* ceremony, which ensures the unity of faith, can still be approached as a fundamental reference point. Erol (2009, p. 102) argues that the discussion should not be about 'Alevi music' in general, but rather about the 'types of Alevi music' and, similar to studies on Alevism, not about 'what' it is, but rather 'how' Alevis have turned it into Alevi music (see also Greve et al. 2020 for recent research on Alevi music).

The Performance of Alevi Music

Conceptually, we can divide the performance of Alevi music into two main subgroups (Erol 2009, p. 135). The first is 'ritual music', which is performed during the *cem* and which emphasises the religious aspect of Alevism. This concept identifies Alevi music in the context of ritual and musical performances deriving from the unity of Alevi belief. The principal symbol of this unity – that is, the *cem* ceremony – is the reference point from which to approach Alevi music. As an integrated form, all the musical elements performed during the *cem* are carried out as necessary references over the greater geographical Alevi region.

The second is 'non-ritual music', which includes performances outside of worship. Caner Işık (2011, p. 149) characterises 'non-ritual' gatherings as an environment for the creation and transmission of knowledge in the mostly oral Alevi-Bektaşi tradition. Performances in 'non-ritual' environments generally include *deyiş* and *nefes*, while some more recent Alevi events have also featured *semah* performances (Soileau 2005). Erol (2009, pp. 135–37) finds that 'non-ritual' performances include commercial music as well as those performed at various gatherings. Indeed, Alevi music can be performed in many different places: at *muhabbet*s and other events such as weddings, in *türkü bar*s and concerts, among others.

*Muhabbet*s are meetings that serve essential functions in Alevi cultural life, as well as activities carried out in the *cemevi*. The word *muhabbet*, which refers to the opening part of the *cem* in which *deyiş* and *nefes* are performed, is also used as a general term for meetings and gatherings outside of the *cem*. In some regions, these meetings are called *Balım Sultan Muhabbeti*.[5] Although they are outside of formal worship, *muhabbet*s have their own rules of decorum. *Muhabbet*s include performances in both ritual and non-ritual environments (in other words, outside the *cem*). In *muhabbet*s, the rules of the *cem* apply only partially. On the one hand, they include a ritual component; on the other hand, they emphasise gathering for the common goal of education and knowledge. In a *muhabbet*, the performance of the *zakir* carries a central role, with new *zakir*s participating to develop their knowledge and skills.[6]

The *Zakir* Service in the Alevi *Cem* Ritual

The services in the Alevi *cem*, called *oniki hizmet* (twelve services), are believed to have been performed at the 'Cem of the Forty' (*Kırklar Cemi*); they occur at every *cem*. The twelve services can be summarised as follows:

1. The *dede* directs the *cem* (also called the *Sercem*).
2. The *rehber* assists the participants and the *dede*.
3. The *gözcü* maintains order and silence during the *cem*.
4. The *çerağcı-delilci* is in charge of the lighting of the *çerağ* (candles/lights).
5. The *zakir* plays and sings all the music in the *cem*.
6. The *ferraş* uses the *çar* (broom) to sweep and assists the *rehber*, if necessary.
7. The *sakka-ibriktar* distributes water.
8. The *sofracı/kurbancı/lokmacı* is in charge of the sacrifices and food.

[5] For infomation on Balım Sultan, see Chapters 2 and 11 in this volume.
[6] See Özdemir (2016, pp. 85–119) for more discussion about the ritual and non-ritual 'Alevi music' performances.

9. The *pervane/semahçı* dances the *semah*.
10. The *peyk/haberci* is in charge of notifying people in the village (or in the region) that a *cem* will be held.
11. The *iznikçi* is in charge of the cleanliness and the order of the *cemevi*.
12. The *bekçi* ensures the security of the *cem* and the participants' houses.

The above-listed *zakir* – derived from the Arabic word *zikr*, meaning 'to remember, to hold in mind' (Uludağ 2005, p. 393) – is the person who plays and sings the music at Alevi *cem*s. In some regions, he or she is known by other names as well, such as *sazende, sazdar, sazandar, sazcı, güyende, âşık baba* and *kamber*. Some of the *zakir*s (performers) are also local *âşık*s (poets) in their region. In some *ocak*s (genealogical lines) and regions, *dede*s perform the music as well, with no separation from the *zakir*. Some *dede*s are also *âşık*s. Therefore, *zakir* defines the performer in *cem* rituals, but *âşık* defines those who write poetry and play and sing under their pseudonyms.[7]

Whether performed by a recognised *âşık* or only a *dede*, Alevis consider the service of the *zakir* to be a sacred duty and see *zakir*s as 'sacred *âşık*s'. They believe that *âşık*s reflect all the aspects of life, including the religious aspect, in their poetry and constitute the most important transmitters of oral tradition. For Alevi-Bektaşis, *âşık*s who play the *bağlama* and write lyrics are considered to be the 'wise men' and the 'true dervishes' who leave a mark on their times. Erol (2009, p. 107) explains the role of *âşık*s and *zakir*s in Alevi society as such:

> The Alevi minstrel (*âşık, zakir*) is not a person who arranges the chain of events that he remembers in a particular style, but rather the one who expresses traditional knowledge remembered by his society, and in particular forms of expression familiar to the society. He does not transmit his own legacy, but rather the traditional legacy, which the society is accustomed to and expects, and which he is a part of. He tries to remember the patterns, which have come down to him from the Alevi minstrels before him, or by precursors nourished by the idea of 'unity'.

Nejat Birdoğan (1990) defines *zakir*s as 'Alevi folk minstrels' and divides their duties into two categories – those in the *cem* and those outside of it.

---

[7] See Dönmez (2010) for a discussion about the role of the *âşık* tradition in *cem* rituals.

According to him (1990, p. 403), the most important task within the *cem* is to work with the *dede* and to ensure the proper flow of the ritual. Noting that *zakir*s use *deyiş* to explain the rules of the 'path' in the *cem*, Birdoğan (1990, pp. 409–11) stresses that they rescue the history and attributes of the 'paths' outside of the *cem* from disappearance. *Zakir*s develop themselves in order to perform this duty; as minstrels, they verbalise the rules of the 'path' through the *deyiş* (Birdoğan 1990, pp. 409–11).

The *zakir*s' duty has been identified with different holy figures in different periods. The most critical Alevi written sources – the *Buyruk* writings – contain sections on the functioning of the *cem* and the services, including that of the *zakir*, and frequently emphasise that this duty is the legacy of the archangel Cebrail (Gabriel). Several other sources list the names of Ali's sons, Abdu's-Samed and Hasan, as well as Bilal Habeşi and İmam Cafer, as the holders of the services in the '*Cem* of the Forty' (Doğan 1998, p. 144; Ersal 2009, p. 193; Kaplan 2010, p. 264).

The sacred character of the *zakir* position derives from its status as a carrier and transmitter of the holy words that symbolise the power of God. Because the *zakir* performs this duty with his *bağlama*, this instrument is considered equally sacred. However, *Zakir* Gürani Doğan stresses that it is not enough for *zakir*s to play the *bağlama* and sing *deyiş*; their demeanour and their entire way of life must also serve as example for others to follow (Doğan 1998, p. 145). Thus, the duties of the *zakir*, much like those of the *dede* and the *rehber*, are vital services in the Alevi faith, both within the ritual and outside of it.

The Transformation of the Zakir's Identity within and outside of Ritual

From the late 1980s onwards, the 'Alevi revival' brought with it an 'Alevi music revival'.[8] During this period, Alevi musicians such as Arif Sağ, Musa Eroğlu, Yavuz Top, Sabahat Akkiraz and countless others assumed a critical function. By taking part in the ever-increasing number of Alevi events, which served as the most potent expression of Alevi collective identity, these musicians showed that there could also be an Alevi identity in the area of music.

---

[8] See Erol (2009) and Dönmez (2014) for more discussion of the 'Alevi music revival' in Turkey and Aksoy (2019) in Germany.

Since the 2000s, efforts to perform Alevi music have grown, and numerous albums, concerts and other events have been produced.[9] Also, non-Alevi artists have embraced this culture in their work. Simultaneously, the Alevi *âşık*s, who had steadily grown in popularity since the 1960s in both the music market and within Alevi society, have been replaced by popular Alevi music performers. As time moves on, these remaining *âşık*s pass away, and *dede*s or *zakir*s in *cem*s are increasingly being replaced by professional Alevi musicians or young *zakir*s who have studied music formally. Existing fieldwork studies reveal that most of the *zakir*s serving in *cem*s today are young (under thirty years old) and have been educated at a training centre, music school, or conservatory. The ever-frequent performances of these professional Alevi musicians in *cem*s in cities and the countryside can be considered a new change in the history of Alevi music. Along with the liveliness in the area of music, an increasing number of *cemevi*s are now also acquiring an educational function by offering *bağlama*, *semah* and other courses, in addition to carrying out their traditional services. All these changes point to the fact that music is taking an increasingly prominent role in *cem*s.

At the same time, the function of the *zakir* has taken on new features in musical performance, which is an indication of the ongoing renewal and change within this service. Traditionally, *zakir*s serve as a vital bridge between the functions of folk minstrels and *dede*s and ensure the smooth musical functioning of the *cem*s. Nowadays, their preference for *saz* with a microphone fitted under the bridge (*eşikaltı*) and attached to the sound equipment, their use of sheet music in a repertoire book on a music stand, their clothing (sometimes a formal suit) during their performances and other similar practices demonstrate how the performance itself has come to the forefront, especially in *cem*s open to the public.[10] This is true not only for the function of the *zakir*, but also for the performance of the *cem* as a whole. However, within the *cem* ritual, the emergence of the *zakir* on the centre stage is based more on the increasing importance of music than is the case for the other

---

[9] There has also been a steady increase of musical performances in Alevi festivals in Europe. See, for example, Salman (2020) and Chapter 10 in this volume on British Alevi festivals.

[10] See Langer (2010) for a discussion of ritual transfer and the changing dynamics of Alevi rituals.

services of the *cem*s. The *zakir*s' interactive relationship with participants is also instrumental in the creation of this dynamic.

Some associations, organisations and foundations also carry out special projects about the changing functions of the *zakir*. The fundamental goal of these projects is to present various views concerning the way in which new *zakir*s should be trained. Researchers and Alevi musicians have also expressed diverse opinions on this subject.[11] Particularly in recent years, the posters announcing special *cem*s held by organisations and foundations include the names of the *zakir*s alongside those of the *dede*s. This emphasis on the *zakir*s' role in *cem*s is another indicator of *zakir*s becoming more visible.

Existing fieldwork studies conducted in the *cemevi*s of Istanbul show that *zakir*s see their function as a service in the *cem* ritual and as a component of their identity, which they claim outside of the ritual as well. Thus, it is safe to argue that the function of the *zakir*, an essential service within the ritual, has become a fundamental point of reference for the performance of Alevi music outside of the ritual, and today it is one of the most important characteristics of the *zakir*'s identity. Overall, these findings also suggest that, from the 1990s to the present, *zakir*s have become more visible than *dede*s, both within and outside of the ritual environment. Along with these changes regarding *zakir*s, another new phenomenon is appearing: the concept of the *muhabbet* within and outside of the ritual.[12]

The Transition to the *Muhabbet*: Dertli Divani and *Mekteb-i İrfan*

In 2010, the Turkish Ministry of Culture and Tourism (Kültür ve Turizm Bakanlığı), the official partner of the United Nations Educational, Scientific and Cultural Organisation (UNESCO) in Turkey, added the Alevi-Bektaşi *semah* ritual to the 'Representatives of Intangible Human Cultural Heritage' list, and shortly thereafter recognised Dertli Divani as a 'Living Human Treasure' in the area of '*zakir*'. The fact that *zakir*s acquired formal recognition

---

[11] See Er (2013, pp. 63–67) and Erzincan (2013) for a comparison of their views on contemporary *zakir*s.

[12] See Özdemir (2016, pp. 192–95) for more information about the *muhabbet* meetings of the *zakir*s.

represents a significant development in the name of Alevi music.[13] Currently, the General Administration of the Turkish Ministry of Culture and Tourism lists 844 folk minstrels, folk poets and *zakir*s as carriers of intangible cultural heritage; each of them is given an official identification card.[14] The folklore scholar Piri Er states that, at the end of 2014, there were a total of thirty-seven *zakir*s on this list (Özdemir 2016, p. 138).[15] Among these is Dertli Divani (given name Veli Aykut), born and raised in Kısas (near Urfa), a folk minstrel who, like his father and grandfather, is linked to the Hacı Bektaş Veli Dergah. He serves as *dede*, as well as *âşık* and *zakir*. Divani initially gained recognition in 1989, with his first album *Divane Gönül*, produced by Arif Sağ, and has since released several solo albums of his own and collected numerous *deyiş*. Countless other artists have performed his songs.

An example of Dertli Divani's famous work was the group he set up in 2005, called Hasbıhâl Ensemble, when his album of the same name was released. Various Alevi musicians – such as Mustafa Kılçık, Hüseyin-Ali Rıza Albayrak, Emre Gültekin and Feyzullah Ürer – played in the ensemble with Dertli Divani. Their work marked the beginning of *muhabbet* gatherings, which fell somewhere between a *cem* ritual and an Alevi concert, as well as other events organised in this format. During the same period, Dertli Divani took part in conferences, panels, international festivals and other events around the world.

Dertli Divani's 'Youth *Muhabbet* Meetings', which began in Ankara in 2012, with around twenty-five young people, carried the Hasbıhâl *muhabbet*s to the next level and formed the basis for the so-called '*Mekteb-i İrfan*' educational efforts now being conducted in Istanbul and various cities in France, Belgium, Germany and the Netherlands. These gatherings teach young *zakir*s the twelve services, the content of *cem deyiş* and the requirements of

---

[13] According to Directive No 1.231892, dated 15 March 2020, the list of 'intangible cultural heritage carriers' still includes *zakir*s. See the latest list of cultural heritage carriers (Kültür ve Turizm Bakanlığı 2020a).

[14] For more information about the identification cards and the recorded list, see Kültür ve Turizm Bakanlığı (2020b).

[15] For more information about the selection of *zakir*s and their ID cards, see Özdemir (2016, pp. 138–41).

the service of the *zakir*, within the formal conduct of the *muhabbet*. In his work, Dertli Divani emphasises the need to institutionalise the position of *zakir*s within the Alevi faith, in order to re-establish the connection between Alevi musical performance and Alevi faith. This connection – containing the elements of manner and decorum both within the ritual (and especially within the *muhabbet* gatherings), as well as outside of it – plays a fundamental role in the modern-day expression of Alevi identity. Equally important is the fact that, since 2000, Dertli Divani has included young people in his concerts, *cem* and *muhabbet* performances, thus perpetuating the master-apprentice relationship within which he was trained. Both the responsibility accorded to him by the Hacı Bektaş Veli Dergah and his certificate as a 'Living Human Treasure' from the UNESCO have served to solidify his determination to continue helping youth through these *muhabbet* gatherings until the end of his life.[16]

The *zakir*s' training with Dertli Divani has acquired new practices. Rather than serving in one particular *cemevi*, they prefer to offer their services to different *cemevi*s; they prefer *muhabbet*s to institutionally organised *cem*s; they represent 'Alevi music' on the commercial scene through various events such as concerts and recitals; and they participate in programmes on Alevi TV channels (see Chapter 14 in this volume). Some of these *zakir*s hold the above-mentioned official identification cards provided by the Turkish Ministry of Culture and Tourism. At the same time, they continue as minstrels – that is, as *âşık*s producing their own lyrics and music.

Conclusion

Alevi musical performance has entered a new process of identity construction based on the changing status of the *zakir*. The *muhabbet* gatherings play an essential role in this transformation: Here, the *zakir*s have a fundamental function – to ensure the connection between faith and life within and outside of ritual through music. In this process, it can be said that the concept of the 'Alevi revival' is being replaced by 'Alevi maintenance' or 'Alevi survival strategies'. These survival strategies develop within the social, cultural, religious and even political dynamics of the Alevi organisation, and they include

[16] Interview, dated 29 September 2013.

muhabbet gatherings, religious courses and other institutionalisation and standardisation efforts.

For centuries, *zakir*s, together with *dede*s and *âşık*s, have been the most important carriers of Alevi cultural memory, both within and outside of ritual. In addition, they carry out one of the fundamental roles in the functioning of the *cem* ritual. Today, holding a unique position within Alevi social as well as religious life, they perform an important function in the transition between the realm within ritual and that outside of it.

Dertli Divani's work, which aims to transform the status of the *zakir* into an institution, is also part of the transformation of the Alevi institutional structure and the *cem* services. Here, the emphasis on the Alevi faith is an important point. With this emphasis, the status of the *zakir* in particular, along with all the faith-related references used outside the ritual, is being reconstructed. The *zakir*'s identity has attained a prominent position within Alevi musical performances, based on his service in the *cem*. The approval of the *zakir*'s position by the Ministry of Culture and the recognition of Dertli Divani by the UNESCO have given the *zakir* a vital role in opening Alevism to the outside world.

Bibliography

Aksoy, O. (2019). Music and Migration among the Alevi Immigrants from Turkey in Germany. *Ethnic and Racial Studies*, 42(6), 919–36.

Balkılıç, Ö. (2015). *Temiz ve Soylu Türküler Söyleyelim: Türkiye'de Milli Kimlik İnşasında Halk Müziği*. Istanbul: Tarih Vakfı Yurt Yayınları.

Birdoğan, N. (1990). *Anadolu'nun Gizli Kültürü Alevilik*. Hamburg: Hamburg Alevi Kültür Merkezi Yayınları.

Çamuroğlu, R. (1998). Alevi Revivalism in Turkey. In: Olsson, T., Özdalga, E., and Raudvere, C., eds, *Alevi Identity: Cultural, Religious and Social Perspectives*. Istanbul: Swedish Research Institute. pp. 79–84.

Doğan, G. (1998). *Alevilik'te Ön Bilgiler ve Cem, Zakirlik*. Istanbul: Can Yayınları.

Dönmez, B. M. (2010). Törensel (Cem) ve Dünyasal Türk Halk Müziği Performansı İçinde Âşıklık Geleneğinin Konumu. *C. Ü. Sosyal Bilimler Dergisi*, 1, 33–37.

Dönmez, B. M. (2014). *Alevi Müziği Uyanışı*. Ankara: Gece Kitaplığı.

During, J. (1995). Notes sur la Musique des Alevis-Bektachis et des Groupes Apparentés. In: Popovic, A., and Veinstein, G., eds, *Bektachiyya: Études sur L'ordre Mystique des Bektachis et les Groupes Relevant de Hadji Bektach*. Istanbul: The Isis Press. pp. 85–89.

Duygulu, M. (1997). *Alevi-Bektaşi Müziğinde Deyişler*. Istanbul: Sistem Ofset.

Er, P. (2013). *Yaşayan Alevilik*. Ankara: Barış Yayınları.

Erzincan, E. (2013). Alevi-Bektaşi Geleneğindeki Zâkirlik Kurumunun Sorunları ve Yeni Zâkirlerin Yetiştirilmesi. *Serçeşme Dergisi*, 1, 38–39.

Ergun, S. N. (1942). *Türk Musikisi Antolojisi, Vol 1*. Istanbul: İstanbul Üniversitesi Edebiyat Fakültesi Yayınları.

Erol, A. (2009). *Müzik Üzerine Düşünmek*. Istanbul: Bağlam Yayıncılık.

Ersal, M. (2009). Alevi Cem Zâkirliği: Battal Dalkılıç Örneği. *Alevilik Bektaşilik Araştırmaları Dergisi*, 1, 188–208.

Greve, M., Özdemir, U., and Motika, R., eds (2020). *Aesthetic and Performative Dimensions of Alevi Cultural Heritage*. Baden-Baden: Ergon Verlag.

Işık, C. (2011). Alevi-Bektaşi Geleneğinde Muhabbet: Ruhsal Bir Bilgi Ortamı. *Milli Folklor*, 89, 147–58.

Kaplan, D. (2010). *Yazılı Kaynaklarına Göre Alevîlik*. 2nd ed. Ankara: Türkiye Diyanet Vakfı Yayınları.

Kehl-Bodrogi, K. (1996). Tarih Mitosu ve Kollektif Kimlik. *Birikim*, 88, 52–63.

Kültür ve Turizm Bakanlığı (2020a). Sanat Dalları Listesi. *Kültür ve Turizm Bakanlığı* [online]. [Viewed 2 February 2021]. Available from: https://aregem.ktb.gov.tr/Eklenti/73875,degerlendirmeye-tabi-tutulacak-sanat-dallari-listesipdf.pdf?0

Kültür ve Turizm Bakanlığı (2020b). Âşık-Ozan, Halk/Kalem Şairi, Zakir 'Değerlendirme Kurulu Başvuru Belgeleri ve Değerlendirme Şartları'. *Kültür ve Turizm Bakanlığı* [online]. [Viewed 2 February 2021]. Available from: http://aregem.kulturturizm.gov.tr/TR,93486/asik-ozan-halkkalem-sairi-zakir-degerlendirme-kurulu-ba-.html

Langer, R. (2010). Marginalised Islam: The Transfer of Rural Rituals into Urban and Pluralist Contexts and the Emergence of Transnational 'Communities of Practice'. In: Brosius, C., and Hüsken, U., eds, *Ritual Matters: Dynamic Dimensions in Practice*. New Delhi: Routledge. pp. 88–123.

Markoff, I. (1986). The Role of Expressive Culture in the Demystification of a Secret Sect of Islam: The Case of the Alevis of Turkey. *The World of Music*, 28, 42–56.

Markoff, I. (1993). Music, Saints and Ritual: Sama and the Alevis of Turkey. In: Smith, G. M., and Ernst, C. W., eds, *Manifestations of Sainthood in Islam*. Istanbul: The ISIS Press. pp. 95–110.

Markoff, I. (2002). Alevi Identity and Expressive Culture. In: Danielson, V., Marcus, S., and Reynolds, D., eds, *The Garland Encyclopedia of World Music, Vol. 6: The Middle East*. New York: Routledge. pp. 793–800.

Markoff, I. (2009). Gelin Canlar Bir Olalım: Türkiye'de Alevî-Bektaşî Ortak Bilincinde Bağlayıcı Güç Olarak Müzik ve Şiir. In: Ocak, A. Y., ed., *Geçmişten*

Günümüze Alevî-Bektaşî Kültürü. Ankara: T. C. Kültür ve Turizm Bakanlığı Yayınları. pp. 416–29.

Onatça, N. A. (2007). *Alevi-Bektaşi Kültüründe Kırklar Semahı Müzikal Analiz Çalışması.* Istanbul: Bağlam Yayıncılık.

Özdemir, U. (2016). *Kimlik, Ritüel, Müzik İcrası: İstanbul Cemevlerinde Zakirlik Hizmeti.* Istanbul: Kolektif Kitap.

Özdemir, U. (2017). Rethinking the Institutionalization of Alevism: Itinerant Zakirs in the Cemevis of Istanbul. In: Papadopoulos, A. G., and Duru, A., eds, *Landscapes of Music in Istanbul: A Cultural Politics of Place and Exclusion.* Bielefeld: Transcript Verlag. pp. 141–66.

Özdemir, U. (2019). Between Debate and Sources: Defining Alevi Music. In: Weineck, B., and Zimmermann, J., eds, *Text and Cultural Heritage: Sources on Alevism Between Philological Research and Theological Canonization.* Frankfurt: Peter Lang Verlag. pp. 165–93.

Poyraz, B. (2007). *Direnişle Piyasa Arasında: Alevilik ve Alevi Müziği.* Ankara: Ütopya Yayınevi.

Salcı, V. L. (1940). *Gizli Türk Halk Musikisi ve Türk Musikisinde (Armoni) Meseleleri.* Istanbul: Numune Matbaası.

Salman, C. (2020). Diasporic Homeland, Rise of Identity and New Traditionalism: The Case of the British Alevi Festival. *Kurdish Studies,* 8(1), 113–32.

Soileau, M. (2005). Festivals and the Formation of Alevi Identity. In: Markussen, H. I., ed., *Alevis and Alevism: Transformed Identities.* Istanbul: The ISIS Press. pp. 91–99.

Şahin, Ş. (2002). Bir Kamusal Din Olarak Türkiye'de ve Ulus Ötesi Sosyal Alanlarda İnşa Edilen Alevilik. *Folklor/Edebiyat,* 29, 123–62.

Uludağ, S. (2005). *Tasavvuf Terimleri Sözlüğü.* 2nd ed. Istanbul: Kabalcı Yayınevi.

Vorhoff, K. (2003). The Past in the Future: Discourses on the Alevis in Contemporary Turkey. In: White, P. J., and Jongerden, J., eds, *Turkey's Alevi Enigma: A Comprehensive Overview.* Leiden: Brill. pp. 93–109.

Yaltırık, H. (2003). *Tasavvufî Halk Müziği.* Ankara: TRT Kurumu Müzik Dairesi Başkanlığı.

Yaprak, M. (2003). *Vahit Lütfi Salcı'nın İzinde.* Edirne: Ulusal Bellek Yayınları.

Yönetken, H. B. (1966). *Derleme Notları 1.* Istanbul: Orkestra Yayınları.

13

THE SOCIO-SPATIAL MEANING OF *CEMEVIS* IN ISTANBUL'S PUBLIC SPACE

ERHAN KURTARIR

Introduction

This chapter presents the findings of the first-ever cultural geography study on *cemevi*s in Istanbul, Turkey.[1] When I started the fieldwork, neither the Presidency of Religious Affairs (*Diyanet İşleri Başkanlığı*, DİB, in short *Diyanet*), nor the Alevi federations could give me the exact number of *cemevi*s in Istanbul or Turkey. In a preliminary online search for the number of *cemevi*s in Istanbul, I found eighty-two different Alevi organisations with names resembling *cemevi*. I aimed to contact all places of worship that provide at least *cem* ceremonies or funeral services. Seventy-three of the eighty-two *cemevi*s on the list were, in fact, *cemevi*s or *dergah*s,[2] and sixty

---

[1] Note that there exist several other studies on *cemevi*s in Turkey, but these often focus on one single district. See, for example, Karaömerlioğlu and Kourou (2020) on three different *cemevi*s in Istanbul's Gazi neighbourhood. Other studies examine the establishment of *cemevi*s in relation to the broader transformations that Alevi communities have experienced. See, for example, Andersen (2015).

[2] The *cemevi* is a special place of worship and a community centre for Alevi communities, at the same time providing religious and secular services. The main differences between *cemevi*s and *dergah*s are the following: *cemevi*s are at neighbourhood level and on a smaller scale, have a smaller catchment area, shorter history and a non-traditional architectural character. The main functions are the same, but most of the *dergah*s are historical/cultural heritage and

of these organisations were active in organising *cem* rituals and/or funeral ceremonies. Thirteen of these seventy-three *cemevi*s were in the process of establishment. The remaining nine of these eighty-two were functioning as cultural associations that did not provide *cem* or funeral rituals. During the fieldwork, I conducted interviews with founders, managers, board members and *dede*s of fifty-eight out of the sixty active *cemevi*s. The main criteria for selecting the informants were that the person should be well informed about the history of the *cemevi*, as well as the actual facilities and the challenges facing the institution.

The Lack of Recognition of *Cemevi*s as Places of Worship in Turkey

The legal definition of 'minority' in Turkey is limited to some religious groups only. The Treaty of Lausanne entrusted non-Muslim communities to the Turkish government's protection, to prevent discrimination of their cultural needs. Turkish governments have limited the application of this rule only to Christian (Greek and Armenian) and Jewish communities.[3] Apart from excluding other non-Muslim minorities – such as the Syriac Christians, Baha'is, or Yezidis – this interpretation also excludes groups considered by the state to be Muslim, but who believe and practise their faith differently from the Sunni majority. As a result, the legislation concerning construction in

---

sacred pilgrimage/visitation sites for Alevis. The *dergah*s' visitors are more diverse than those of *cemevi*s. *Cemevi*s are functional community centres that provide daily secular services to its hinterland, such as school support facilities for students. *Dergah*s are accepted as common Alevi heritage, while *cemevi*s belong to specific Alevi sub-groups. One respondent from the Şahkulu Dergah, the Cultural Heritage Complex in the Kadıköy district, described the difference between *cemevi* and *dergah* with the following analogy: '*Dergah* means a university for the Alevi community, and *cemevi*s are a high school for them'.

[3] The statute of minorities in Turkey was set in 1923 in the Treaty of Lausanne, Section III, Articles 37–44, basically meaning 'non-Muslim'. The rights granted to minority groups applied to the three largest minority groups only: Greeks (Rum), Armenians and Jews. Other smaller non-Muslim and even Christian groups have been left out of the treaty. For example, the Syriacs' right to receive education in their own language in their schools has not been applied in Article 40 (Oran 2008). The Development Plan Law, the Law of Foundations, the Municipal Revenues Act, the Conservation Law and other related laws list minorities' places of worship as church and synagogue and refer only to the above-mentioned Greek (Rum), Armenian and Jewish communities.

Turkey only accepts mosques, churches and synagogues as places of worship. The Municipal Revenues Act (No 2464) exempts only mosques, churches and synagogues from electricity and natural gas bills since by law these are accepted as places of worship. The Directorate of Religious Affairs rejects[4] the definition of *cemevis* as 'places of worship'. Further, state institutions do not have knowledge of the role (let alone the total number) of *cemevis* in Turkey, an attitude that could be regarded as turning a blind eye to cultural and religious differences (Kurtarır and Ökten 2014, 2018). Inexplicable definitions of *cemevi* by state institutions can be gathered from several court decisions, DİB announcements, the government's Alevi Workshops meetings reports (see Lord 2017, Özkul 2015 and Chapter 3 in this volume) and public speeches by government representatives.

As a local instrument for the allocation of public services, spatial plans provide the major legal framework for places of worship. With the changes introduced by the EU Harmonisation Process Package 6 in 2003, the definition of places of worship in the Law on Land Development Planning and Control (*İmar Kanunu*) was changed from 'mosque' to 'place of worship' (*dini tesis*), providing a more neutral and egalitarian wording.[5] The regulation on the Preparation of Spatial Plans was put into force on 14 June 2014; however, this regulation restricted the meaning of 'place of worship'.[6] In Article 12 and in the section on public service standards, the new regulation defines three scales of places of worship: small mosque, mid-scale neighbourhood mosque and Ottoman-style Islamic social complex (*külliye*).[7]

---

[4] In Decision No 7, the Legal Department of the Supreme Court decided in 2012 that *cemevis* cannot be accepted as places of worship and cannot be a religious service place alternative to mosques or *mescids*. This decision was based on the DİB's expert opinion (Kurtarır and Ökten 2018).

[5] In Article 9 of Law 4928, dated 15 July 2003, the expression 'mosque' in the article of the 'Law on Land Development Planning and Control' was amended to 'place of worship'.

[6] See the regulations on the preparation of spatial plans (*Mekansal Planlar Yapım Yönetmeliği* 2014).

[7] In 2017, for the first time in Turkey's legislative history, the definition of 'place of worship' became possible with the renewal of the Planned Areas Zoning Regulation (formerly Zoning Regulation). However, the Article Construction Conditions according to Parcel Usage Functions of this regulation only refers to mosques and masjids.

At the time of the fieldwork for this study, two cases relevant to Alevis were pending at the European Court of Human Rights (ECHR); in both cases, the court decided that there was discrimination against and violation of Alevis' rights in Turkey. In the case of *Cem Vakfı* (Cem Foundation) v. *Turkey* (application no. 32093/10), the ECHR's decision, dated 12 February 2014, determined a violation of Article 14 (prohibition of discrimination), together with Article 9 (freedom of thought, conscience and religion) by the Turkish government. The case was first submitted to the District Court of Beyoğlu in August 2006. Stating that the Yenibosna Centre of the *Cem Vakfı* was a place of worship for the Alevi community, its director requested an exemption from paying electricity bills, since the legislation stated that electricity bills for places of worship should be paid from a fund administered by the *Diyanet*. In a judgment on 27 May 2008, the District Court of Beyoğlu dismissed the foundation's claims, basing its decision on the *Diyanet*'s opinion that Alevism was not a religion and *cemevi*s not places of worship. The *Cem Vakfı* finally took the case to the ECHR, leading to the 2014 judgment. In this case, the ECHR found in favour of the claimant.

A more recent case was *İzzettin Doğan*[8] *and Others* v. *Turkey* (application no. 62649/10), about the refusal to provide public services and the right to freedom of religion. The applicants claimed that Alevis were subjected to discrimination in Turkey in comparison to citizens following Sunni Islam. On 26 April 2016, the Grand Chamber declared the judgment that there had been a violation of Article 9 (the right to freedom of religion) of the European Convention on Human Rights, and that there had been a violation of Article 14 (prohibition of discrimination) in conjunction with Article 9 of the European Convention. The ECHR ruled that *cemevi*s were places of worship for Alevis and that they should benefit from all the rights and privileges granted by the legal system to other recognised places of worship. These rights include the right to have operational costs for *cemevi*s be met by government agencies and the allocation of space to *cemevi*s in municipalities' development plans. The court gave the parties six months to reach an agreement to solve the case after the decision, but to date the *cemevi*s' status still has not been changed.

---

[8] Prof. Dr. İzzettin Doğan is the founder and honorary chairman of Turkey's *Cem Vakfı*.

However, the ECHR's ruling was followed by some progressive developments. For instance, the municipalities governed by the two opposition parties, the Republican People's Party (*Cumhuriyet Halk Partisi*, CHP) and the Peoples' Democratic Party (*Halkların Demokratik Partisi*, HDP) declared that they recognised *cemevi*s as places of worship. Also, the Supreme Court ruled that *cemevi*s were places of worship and that their electricity bills should be met by the state, as with other places of worship. The Court of Cassation reiterated that *cemevi*s were places of worship, referring to the ECHR judgment.

The History of *Cemevis* in Istanbul

During the fieldwork, I encountered *cemevi*s in the process of being established, as well as *cemevi*s undergoing construction, some of which are established and active today. Several other *cemevi*s I visited had moved to new places or were newly erected buildings. These rapid and continuous changes in socio-spatial data require constant updates; it is, therefore, important to note that the picture given here is based on the situation in 2014.

In legal terms, *cemevi*s are founded either as associations or as charitable endowments and, in some cases, as both. As mentioned above, I found that seventy-three organisations provided *cemevi* functions, including active and inactive ones. Twenty-eight of these seventy-three *cemevi*s had the status of a charitable endowment[9] (or branch of an endowment), while forty-five were associations (or branches of an association). There are different reasons for choosing under which type of entity a *cemevi* is to be established. Some associations' spokesmen stated that associations had more democratic decision-making mechanisms and participatory management structures, when compared to endowments. Yet, as non-profit organisations, associations are subject to certain limitations. Some interviewees, associated with endowments, emphasised that endowments had a better capacity to protect and improve their assets.

The sixty active *cemevi*s are part of different umbrella organisations. The Federation of Alevi Foundations (*Alevi Vakıfları Federasyonu*, AVF), with twenty branches in Istanbul, is the largest one. The Alevi Bektaşi Federation

---

[9] The General Secretary of the Karaca Ahmet Sultan Dergah declared that they have both legal entities at the same time. The founders first established an association and then a *vakıf* (charitable endowment) for one and the same organisation.

(*Alevi Bektaşi Federasyonu*, ABF) has twelve branches and the Federation of Alevi Associations (*Alevi Dernekleri Federasyonu*, ADF) eleven. There are also seventeen independent *cemevi*s. In 2014, there were likewise thirteen inactive Alevi organisations that were under construction, not yet fully established or providing only non-religious cultural facilities. Only two of the inactive organisations were endowments, and the rest associations. The Karaağaç Bektaşi Dergahı and the Güneş Cemevi were also among the inactive thirteen *cemevi*s, because they were under construction during the period of field-work. In 2018, there existed more than seventy-three *cemevi*s that were active and provided *cem* and funeral services. New *cemevi*s were also being estab-lished. Some *cemevi*s changed their institutional structure, for example, by becoming independent, or their physical structure by establishing new and larger complexes.

According to the respondents in the study, *cemevi* establishment stories did not start with the building of public *cemevi*s. Following the wave of migration to cities, which began in the 1950s, Alevis continued their rituals and *cem* practices in their homes or other suitable locations. Funerals, however, could not be conducted at home. They were in need of public funeral services and burial preparations. According to the Municipality Law, these services have to be available to residents in all of the greater municipalities. The munici-palities provided these services according to the rules of the Sunni Islamic tradition established by the *Diyanet*. When requesting funerals, some *cemevi* founders experienced maltreatment or rejection in the mosques, which moti-vated them to establish *cemevi*s. This motivation was the main justification for the establishment of a place of worship among Alevis and other faith groups. Funeral services are particularly effective in bringing Alevis together in the *cemevi*s, regardless of whether they are religious.

The year 1969 – when the Karaca Ahmet Sultan Dergahı and Cemevi were revitalised as a well-known gathering place in Alevi heritage – can be seen as starting point for the establishment of Istanbul *cemevi* facilities in public space. The Karaca Ahmet Sultan Dergahı was re-constructed around the tomb of the saint Karaca Ahmet, and the first members of the associa-tion started conducting the *cem* there in 1969. Until 1994, the premises were limited to the small-scale building of the cemetery and the surrounding area. However, they were at the same time the location of the first institutional

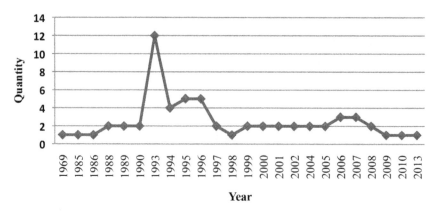

Figure 13.1   *Cemevi* establishment dates in Istanbul

attempt in Istanbul, paving the way for the establishment of contemporary *cemevis*. An even earlier precursor of this attempt to bring about the public awakening of Alevi identity and rituals was the foundation of the Hacı Bektaş Tourism and Promotion Association in Turkey. This association was first established in Ankara in 1963, with a big *cem* ceremony held at the Ankara Büyük Sinema Hall (Öz 2004). Thus, people used a cinema as *cem* ceremony place in this initial period. The *cem* ceremony was accepted as one of the earliest publicly held religious activities of the Alevi community. As shown in Figure 13.1, the number of *cemevis* in Istanbul reached its peak in 1993 and proliferated until 1997.

The *cemevis* in this study can be grouped according to their history of establishment in three chronological periods: pre-1994, between 1994 and 2000, and post-2000. As such, the first group contains twenty organisations. These were established before the Sivas massacre in 1993 and contain the biggest *cemevis* and *dergahs* in Istanbul. Their service area and the scale of the buildings are much larger than that of the *cemevis* established later. Among them, there are *dergahs* with national and international connections, which also help to meet the high number of demands for international funeral services. Following the *dergahs*, the largest *cemevis* in Istanbul include the Kartal, İkitelli, Sarıgazi, Kağıthane, Okmeydanı, Bağcılar, Gazi and Ihlamurkuyu Cemevi. Table 13.1 shows the twenty *cemevis* first established in Istanbul.

Table 13.1 Establishment dates of the first *cemevi*s in Istanbul

	Name of the *Cemevi*	Establishment Date
1	Promotion of Karaca Ahmet Sultan Culture, Solidarity and Repair of Tomb Association / Karaca Ahmet Sultan Convent	1969
2	Foundation of Şahkulu Sultan Convent	1985
3	Seyit Seyfi Association and Cemevi	1986
4	Pir Sultan Abdal Cultural Associates and Cemevi Gazi Osman Paşa Branch	1988
5	Foundation of Republican Education and Culture / Adalar Cemevi	1988
6	Kağıthane Hacı Bektaşı Veli Education and Culture Association / Nurtepe Cemevi	1989
7	Hacı Bektaşı Veli Culture and Promotion Association / Bağcılar Cemevi	1989
8	Hacı Bektaşı Veli Anatolian Cultural Foundation İstanbul Branch / Okmeydanı Cemevi	1990
9	İkitelli Cem and Culture House	1990
10	Kartal Cemevi Culture Education and Social Solidarity Foundation	1993
11	Pir Sultan Abdal Cultural Associates and Cemevi Pendik Branch	1993
12	Tokat Erbağ Keçeci Village Social Assistance and Solidarity Association / Ahi Mahmut Veli Çekmeköy Cemevi	1993
13	Sarıgazi Survival Promotion Solidarity of Cemevi Culture and Repair of the Tomb Association	1993
14	Kazım Karabekir Cemevi	1993
15	Pir Sultan Abdal Cultural Associates and Cemevi Ataşehir Branch	1993
16	Gazi Education and Culture Foundation / Gazi Cemevi	1993
17	Culture of Hacı Bektaşı Veli Survival and Promotion Association / Arnavutköy Cemevi	1993
18	Cem Vakfı Haramidere Cemevi	1993
19	Erikli Baba Cultural Association and Cemevi	1993
20	Anatolia Science Culture and Cem Foundation / Ümraniye Ihlamurkuyu Cemevi	1993

Among these, the İkitelli Cemevi has the biggest *cem* hall. The maximum capacity of this *cemevi* is recorded as 4,500 persons. Thirteen *cemevi*s have *cem* halls ranging from 500 to 1,200 square meters in size. Their capacity is at least 1,000 persons. Interviewees from small-scale *cemevi*s stated that they used all the available parts of their buildings to conduct the *cem* during celebrations and religious days. The managers of the Sarıgazi, Okmeydanı, Kartal, Garip Dede, Bağcılar, Yenibosna and Gazi Cemevi also declared that their *cemevi*s were overcrowded especially during funeral services. On average, they conduct at least forty funeral services per month. One respondent stated that the busiest funeral services provider, the Sarıgazi Cemevi, organises more than sixty funerals per month, with five funeral servants at the same time. Because of the *cemevi*'s central position in the community, these funerals are provided not only for Istanbul residents, but also for those from abroad or other parts of Turkey.

The Distribution of *Cemevis* in the City

In the master plans, most *cemevi*s are located in designated socio-cultural service areas. During my fieldwork, only the Şişli and Esenyurt Municipalities had allowed the construction of *cemevi*s in places designated as worship areas. Since then, more *cemevi*s have been built, thanks to the new mayor of Istanbul. After the fieldwork carried out for this article, several district municipalities of Istanbul (Beylikdüzü, Beşiktaş, Sarıyer, Çatalca, Pendik and Maltepe) directly built or supported the construction of *cemevi*s. Additionally, two of these municipalities, Maltepe and Beylikdüzü, organised a design competition for the construction of new *cemevi*s in their districts.[10] As of 2019, the former Mayor of Beylikdüzü, Ekrem İmamoğlu, has become Mayor of Istanbul. His inclusive policies have been influential. For example, since he has come to power, the Municipality of Istanbul has been providing public funeral services for different religious groups, allowing them to perform their own rituals. The municipality under his mayorship has also employed staff from different religious groups for the management of these services. However, even such support by some municipalities was not

---

[10] The completion of the Beylikdüzü Fatma Ana Cemevi and Cultural Centre, which features an award-winning architectural design, is planned for 2021. See İBB Kurumsal (2020a).

enough to push for the legal recognition of these *cemevis* to be designated as places of worship in the districts' implementation plans.

These municipalities' permits are not acts of formal recognition and, therefore, do not guarantee a secure status for *cemevis* (see Borovalı and Boyraz 2016). The uncertain status of these *cemevis* can be seen in the example of Sultangazi and Sancaktepe, where the *cemevi* founders were sued due to the use of unlicensed buildings. In this case, the municipalities do not seem to have allowed any space for these two *cemevis*, but the interviewees from these *cemevi* associations insisted that the former mayors had promised these building plots and that the new authorities had overturned the permissions. Therefore, with the change in local government, they were faced with judicial persecution and punishment for illegal or improper use of *cemevi* buildings.

The location and distribution of *cemevis*, as depicted in Map 13.1, demonstrate high- and low-density districts for the Alevi population of Istanbul. In a few districts, the municipalities permitted the construction of *cemevis* or directly provided a place for *cemevis*. In 2014, nine districts had no *cemevi*,[11] indicating that the authorities did not allocate a place for them, or that there was not enough demand for one in those districts.

As a result of voter pressure, some municipalities (in some cases including those run by the ruling Justice and Development Party, AKP) have supported Alevis in building or renovating *cemevis*. On 30 January 2014, the main opposition party, CHP, officially announced that '230 municipalities run by the CHP across Turkey, would start officially recognizing the *cemevis* as places of worship' (Radikal 2015). Consecutively, municipalities run by the CHP started to recognise *cemevis* as places of worship in their borough councils, with the majority of their council members voting against the governing party council members' votes. This political decision was announced after the ECHR judgment in 2014, on the existence of discrimination against *cemevis*. The ECHR issued the decision with the title 'Denying the Alevi

---

[11] There are several reasons for the lack of *cemevis* in some districts. It is known that some municipalities – such as Güngören, Beyoğlu, or Üsküdar – did not accept applications for the construction of *cemevis*, nor did they provide places for them. My interviewees also explained to me that in some cases the municipalities are willing to provide a place for a new *cemevi*, as happened in Kadıköy, but that there is no demand from the community.

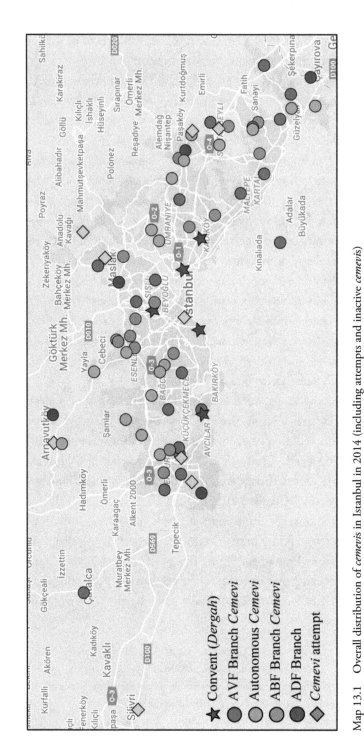

Map 13.1 Overall distribution of *cemevis* in Istanbul in 2014 (including attempts and inactive *cemevis*)

Convent (*Dergah*)
AVF Branch *Cemevi*
Autonomous *Cemevi*
ABF Branch *Cemevi*
ADF Branch
Cemevi attempt

Community Exemption from Electricity Bills Granted to Places of Worship was Discriminatory' (ECHR 2014). The ECHR defined the *cemevi* categorically as a place of worship and determined that the European Convention on Human Rights had been violated.[12]

In 2015, CHP members proposed the recognition of *cemevi*s as places of worship at the Istanbul Metropolitan Municipality Council (see Şimşek 2015), but the AKP council members rejected the proposal. The CHP and the Good Party (İYİ Party) councillors insisted on the same proposal on 16 January 2020, but the result was the same, and the councillors of the AKP and its ally, the Nationalist Movement Party (*Milliyetçi Hareket Partisi*, MHP), rejected the proposal (see İBB Kurumsal 2020b). These rejections are significant, because all public service areas are allocated by 1/5,000-scale master plans of the city.[13] These master plans are under the authority of the metropolitan municipality. I asked the interviewees whether Alevi institutions were aware of the master plan decisions regarding the *cemevi*s' plots of land. Only a few of them were aware of the master plan functions in their building plots. Map 13.2 denotes the *cemevi* spokesmen's awareness of the designation plan for *cemevi* building plots. The categories they mentioned include *cemevi*, 2B-type forest area, cultural and social amenity, religious amenity, residential, cemetery, *dergah*, commercial zone, urban transformation site and places without a planning designation.

The majority of the *cemevi*s are located on the European side of Istanbul. On the European side, there are thirty-four active and nine inactive *cemevi*s. On the Anatolian side, there exist twenty-five active *cemevi*s, while five are inactive or under construction. Table 13.2 shows the overall distribution of *cemevi*s at the district level. Pendik, Esenyurt, Küçükçekmece and Sancaktepe are districts with a higher Alevi population density, local-level democratic instruments and mechanisms, and availability of *cemevi*s. Even the municipalities run by the AKP could not remain indifferent to the Alevis' demands in these districts, although the central government policies display a strict

[12] The Court concluded that 'the *cemevi*s were, like the other places of worship, premises used for religious worship and that the situation of the applicant foundation was similar to that of other religious communities'. ECHR (2014).

[13] Land Development Plans comprise the 1/5,000-scale Master Plan and the 1/1,000-scale Implementation Plan.

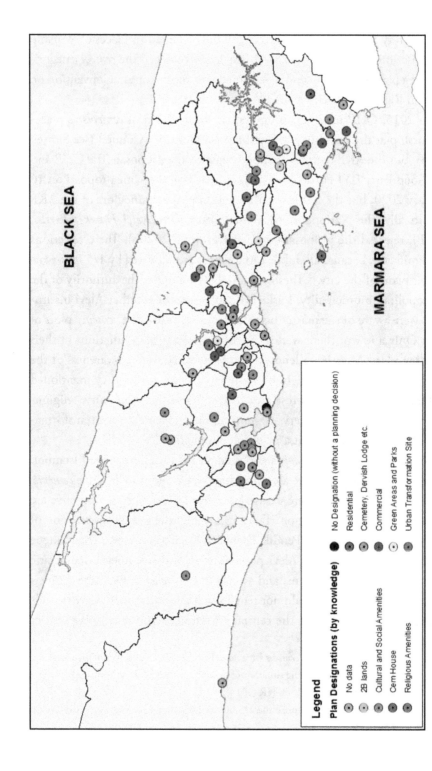

Map 13.2 Plan designation of *cemevis* by knowledge

Table 13.2   Overall distribution of *cemevi*s at the district level (2014)

	Name of the District	Number of Active and (Inactive) *Cemevi*s	Total Population
1	Pendik	5	646,375
2	Esenyurt	4 + (1)	624,733
3	Küçükçekmece	4	740,090
4	Sancaktepe	4	304,406
5	Avcılar	3	407,240
6	Sultangazi	3 + (1)	505,190
7	Tuzla	3	208,807
8	Arnavutköy	2 + (1)	215,531
9	Ataşehir	2	405,974
10	Bağcılar	2	752,250
11	Başakşehir	2 + (1)	333,047
12	Çekmeköy	2	207,476
13	Gaziosmanpaşa	2	495,006
14	Kağıthane	2	428,755
15	Sarıyer	2 + (1)	335,598
16	Sultanbeyli	2 + (2)	309,347
17	Ümraniye	2	660,125
18	Adalar	1	16,166
19	Bahçelievler	1	602,931
20	Beşiktaş	1	186,570
21	Beylikdüzü	1 + (1)	244,760
22	Beyoğlu	1	245,219
23	Çatalca	1	65,811
24	Eyüp	1	361,531
25	Kadıköy	1	506,293
26	Kartal	1 + (1)	447,110
27	Maltepe	1	471,059
28	Şişli	1	274,420
29	Üsküdar	1 + (1)	534,636
30	Zeytinburnu	1	292,313
31	Bakırköy	0	220,974
32	Bayrampaşa	0	269,677
33	Beykoz	0 + (1)	248,056
34	Büyükçekmece	0	211,000
35	Esenler	0	461,621
36	Fatih	0 + (1)	425,875
37	Güngören	0 + (1)	306,854
38	Şile	0	31,718
39	Silivri	0 + (1)	155,923

and negative attitude towards establishing *cemevi*s at the metropolitan and state level.

Having said that, local-level solutions do not guarantee ideal conditions for the establishment and continuation of *cemevi*s. Sustaining these organisations requires a legally defined status, as well as continuous financial and professional support. All these *cemevi*s are facing problems of discrimination at the national level; as mentioned above, rent, electricity, heating and water expenses are the best example of this situation. The total costs are usually said to be prohibitively high: the first three of these *cemevi*s (Yeni Bosna, Ihlamurkuyu, Şahkulu Cemevi) stated that their monthly expenses amounted to more than 50,000 TL. The Yeni Bosna Cemevi's monthly expenses were reported to be approximately 100,000 TL. These three large *cemevi*s have more than twenty staff members whose salaries are financed by the Alevi community's donations and income generated from projects undertaken by the *cemevi* staff. Also, volunteers take on some functions, such as organising and conducting religious ceremonies, education, cooking, cleaning, security, administrative tasks and the like. The small and mid-scale *cemevi*s continue their activities solely with the help of volunteers. Due to financial difficulties, some small-scale *cemevi*s stop their operations in winter in order to avoid heating expenses.

The distribution of *cemevi*s reveals another interesting fact about Alevis in Istanbul: symbolically and culturally, the old city centre of Istanbul has excluded Alevi places of worship (see Map 13.3). Istanbul's cultural and historical centre consists of Fatih, Beyoğlu, Beşiktaş, Üsküdar and Kadıköy. The symbolic atmosphere of this city centre is filled only with 'approved' and 'acceptable' cultural symbols of major recognised faith groups. The Okmeydanı Cemevi is the only one located within these historical and central districts. It is also exceptional because it was established in a well-known Alevi neighbourhood.

Table 13.2 presents the distribution of *cemevi*s in 2013–14. Among the *cemevi*s in Istanbul, there were four new ones and six newly renovated ones. For instance, the Ali Baba Cemevi in Pendik and the *Cem Vakfi*'s Sarıyer branch had recently acquired new buildings. There existed new *cemevi*s in Büyükçekmece and Sultanbeyli as well. Design competitions were held for new *cemevi* buildings in the districts of Maltepe and Beylikdüzü. Except for

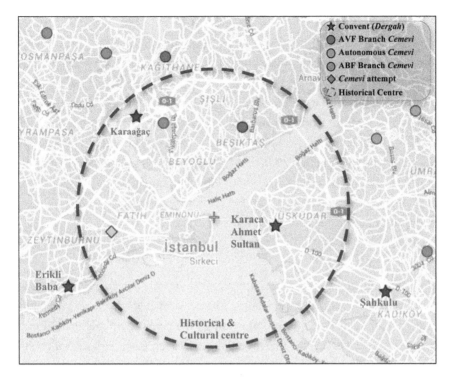

Map 13.3   *Cemevi*s and convents in Istanbul's historical and cultural centre

Sultanbeyli, all of the above-mentioned municipalities of these districts built or aimed to construct new *cemevi*s for their Alevi residents.

There are also some attempts to develop new *cemevi*s. For example, a branch of the *Cem Vakfı* was established in Beşiktaş in 2006. Furthermore, in 2013 the Beşiktaş Cemevi organisation started organising *cem* ceremonies at a temporary site not suitable for funerals. Another Cemevi Establishment Association was set up in the Fatih District in 2013. They do not have any place for *cem* ceremonies or funerals. Other initiatives shown on the map are *dergah*s that are understood as places of cultural heritage. One example consists of the Karaca Ahmet Sultan Cemevi and Association at the Tomb of Karaca Ahmet Sultan. Another is the Karaağaç Bektaşi Dergah in Sütlüce, one of the *dergah*s demolished in 1826 with the abolition of the Janissaries.

In 2004, the Alevi Bektaşi Education and Culture Foundation went to court to stop the privatisation and renewal processes of the land of the *dergah* (see Milliyet 2004). The *dergah*'s parcel was divided into two parts during the renewal process. A hotel was built on the first half of the parcel, while another building was established and rented out to the Istanbul Branch of the AKP on the second half. After a lengthy judicial process involving the Alevi foundation, building owners and municipalities, the complex today contains a two-story building and the tombs of dervishes. The Alevi foundation holds its Tuesday meetings in this building, and according to the foundation's representative, approximately 20,000 visitors visit the *dergah* during the month of *Muharrem* and on other sacred days. However, not all problems are solved: because of security measures necessary to protect the ruling party's buildings, Alevis still have problems visiting the *dergah*.

Concluding Remarks

Place-making stories and places are useful indicators for analysing the tension between state and faith groups. These places help the faith groups to protect their identity, while also protecting their rituals, symbols and cultural codes. These places also facilitate the transfer of their culture to the following generations with their multi-functional character. The *cemevis*' semi-public meeting places help the community members socialise in large numbers. It can be claimed that this type of poly-semantic place is the precondition of identity. Without a place, the cultural identity of any group may not be sustained. Therefore, in this chapter, I have examined the distribution and establishment process of *cemevis*, as well as the inherent hardships. At the end of the research period, I had identified six distinct phases of the *cemevi* establishment process:

Phase 1: Preparation phase; demand for a *cemevi* and claim to a place
Phase 2: Construction phase; spatialisation of assets
Phase 3: Socialisation of the *cemevi*; publicity, functioning and gaining a role and meaning for the society
Phase 4: Legalisation and expression of cultural and religious identity in the public space open to the broader society
Phase 5: Beautification, standardisation, improvement and rehabilitation of place
Phase 6: Universalisation of collective and symbolic value

The *cemevis* in Istanbul seem to have completed the third phase and are moving towards the fourth phase – that is, the legalisation of their identity. With the help of the ECHR's decisions and the reflection of these decisions in local courts, *cemevis* have started to be declared as places of worship in Turkey. Therefore, the municipalities of the main opposition party have agreed that *cemevis* are places of worship, and all municipalities will provide municipal services to them. Other ruling party municipalities have also started to support the construction or renovation process of *cemevis*. These conditions have helped Alevis to move forward when it comes to the above-mentioned phases of *cemevis*.

The Law on Development Planning and Control is the fundamental law for spatial plans and urban development in Turkey. Accordingly, the construction and maintenance of places of worships are defined as public service. Areas of public services are provided by master plans, and local authorities regulate these plans. As mentioned above, the new Regulation on Preparation of Spatial Plans has changed the objectivity of spatial plans regarding places of worship.[14] According to the legislative framework of Spatial Plans, only mosques, churches and synagogues are recognised places of worship in Turkey. Promoting balanced and equitable accessibility to all kinds of public services is one of the important targets of all types of spatial plans. Nevertheless, with the last regulation changes of spatial plans, access to mosques and Sunni places of worship has increased, but access to other places of worship is not included in these changes.

Looking at past and recent attempts at establishing *cemevis*, despite all the legal and political restraints, it can be argued that Alevis have succeeded in changing the public space in line with their needs, at least in some districts of Istanbul, without any governmental support. Today, *cemevis* constitute the main common places for Alevis. *Cemevis* represent Alevi identity, belief and existence in the urban areas. In some districts, Alevis built their places of worship on their own private land, but in many cases they constructed them on public land. Municipalities have allocated only a few *cemevis*. In some cases, the founders of *cemevis* were sued for unauthorised *cemevi* construction on public lands, such as in the Sultangazi, Ümraniye and Üsküdar districts.

---

[14] In 2014, the Chamber of Urban Planners went to court in order to cancel principal mistakes and discriminatory articles of regulation. See TMMOB, Şehir Plancıları Odası (2014). The higher court rejected the request to stop the implementation of the regulation, but the ministry adopted some minor changes in the text in subsequent years.

*Cemevi*s as places of worship and cultural centres constitute a continuation of traditional rituals and rural functions in their new urbanised forms. These buildings and establishments fulfil the religious and social needs of communities. *Cemevi*s and *dergah*s, in this sense, are symbols expressing Alevi cultural heritage and identity in different urban forms. These establishments help reproduce their identity in different localities, with a multi-functional character. Alevi rural communities come together in these urban settings and encounter a variety of Alevi traditions and representations. According to most interviewees, these new experiences of social interaction cause the positive acculturation of different Alevi traditions. As a result, while fulfilling the needs of Alevis, *cemevi*s also fill the gap of inequitable and insufficient public services provision in urban areas. In a fair society, all of these services would have to be provided to Alevis by the state.

The identification and recognition of this unjust urban development experience of *cemevi*s demonstrate that the planning profession must adopt universal human rights criteria in its legislation. For example, the European Convention on Human Rights can serve as a guide to what needs to be adapted in Turkey's urban planning legislation. Urban planning implementations need to find a way to adopt an inclusive planning approach. In other words, rather than short-term solutions, the Turkish planning system needs to incorporate the ideals of a just and inclusive planning system: equality, diversity and democracy.

Bibliography

Andersen, A. L. (2015). Cem Evleri: An Examination of the Historical Roots and Contemporary Meanings of Alevi Architecture and Iconography. Unpubl. doctoral dissertation, The Ohio State University.

Borovalı, M., and Boyraz, C. (2016). Türkiye'de Cemevleri Sorunu: Haklar ve Özgürlükler Bağlamında Eleştirel Bir Yaklaşım. *Mülkiye Dergisi*, 40(3), 55–86.

ECHR (2014). Press Release, 355, Cumhuriyetçi Eğitim ve Kültür Merkezi Vakfı v. Turkey. 2 December.

İBB Kurumsal (2020a). İmamoğlu: 'Fatma Ana Cemevi 2021'de Bitecek, Tüm Yönetimi Kadınlardan Uluşacak'. *İbb Kurumsal* [online]. 11 November. [Viewed 18 February 2021]. Available from: https://www.ibb.istanbul/News/Detail/37410

İBB Kurumsal (2020b). İbb Meclis Çoğunluğu Cemevine İbadethane Statüsü Vermedi. *İbb Kurumsal* [online]. 16 January. [Viewed 18 February 2021]. Available from: https://www.ibb.istanbul/News/Detail/36340

İmar Kanunu no. 3194 (1985). In: *Official Gazette* Issue 18749, e.5, vol. 24, p.378. [online]. 9 May. [Viewed 18 February 2021]. Available from: https://www.mevzuat.gov.tr/MevzuatMetin/1.5.3194.pdf

Karaömerlioğlu, M. A., and Kourou, N. S. (2020). Where Faith Meets Modernity: Cemevi and Local Alevi Politics. *Middle Eastern Studies*, 56(6), 839–53.

Kurtarır, E., and Ökten, A. N. (2014). Çeşitlenen Kentlerde Körleşen Planlama. *KBAM 5. Kentsel ve Bölgesel Araştırmalar Sempozyumu, Toplumsal Çeşitlilik: Yeni Söylem, Politikalar, Mekânsal Planlama ve Uygulamalar.* 16–18 August. Ankara.

Kurtarır, E., and Ökten, A. N. (2018). Planlama Kurumunun Görmediği Kimlik Mekânlarina Bir Örnek: Cemevleri. *METU Journal of Faculty of Architecture*, 35(1), 157–82.

Lord, C. (2017). Rethinking the Justice and Development Party's 'Alevi Openings'. *Turkish Studies*, 18(2), 278–96.

Mekansal Planlar Yapım Yönetmeliği (2014). [online]. 14 June. [Viewed 12 February 2021]. Available from: http://www.resmigazete.gov.tr/eskiler/2014/06/20140614-2.htm.

Milliyet (2004). Alevilerin 'Dergâhıma Dokunma' Gösterisi. *Millyet* [online]. [Viewed 18 February 2021]. Available from: https://www.milliyet.com.tr/pembenar/alevilerin-derg-hima-dokunma-gosterisi-187204

Oran, B. (2008). *Türkiye'de Azınlıklar Kavramlar, Teori, Lozan, İç Mevzuat, İçtihat, Uygulama*. 4th ed. Istanbul: İletişim.

Öz, B. (2004). *Çağdaşlaşma Açısından Tarikat ve Tekkelerin Kapatılma Olayı*. Istanbul: Can Yayınları.

Özkul, D. (2015). Alevi 'Openings' and Politicization of the 'Alevi Issue' During the AKP Rule. *Turkish Studies*, 16(1), 80–96.

Radikal (2015). CHP'den Cemevi Kararı: Belediyeler Cemevlerini İbadethane Olarak Tanıyacak. *Radikal* [online]. 12 February. [Viewed 30 January 2021]. Available from: http://www.radikal.com.tr/turkiye/chpden-cemevi-karari-belediyeler-cemevlerini-ibadethane-olarak-taniyacak-1283278/.

Şimşek, T. (2015). CHP'nin Cemevi Teklifine AKP'den Ret. *Çorum Haber* [online]. 7 March. [Viewed 14 February 2021]. Available from: http://www.corumhaber.net/guncel/chpnin-cemevi-teklifine-akpden-ret-h38195.html

TMMOB, Şehir Plancıları Odası (2014). Mekansal Planlar Yapim Yönetmeliği, Planlama Esaslari, Kamu Yarari ve Eşitlik İlkeleri Doğrultusunda Mahkemeye Taşınmıştır. *TMMOB, Şehir Plancıları Odası* [online]. 3 September. [Viewed 14 February 2021]. Available from: http://www.spo.org.tr/genel/bizden_detay.php?kod=5939#.V6yIjZN95E4

Tekdemir, Ö. (2018). Constructing a Social Space for Alevi Political Identity: Religion, Antagonism and Collective Passion. *National Identities*, 20(1), 31–51.

14

THE MEDIATISED REPRODUCTION
OF ALEVISM: ALEVI TELEVISION
NETWORKS AND THEIR AUDIENCES

NAZLI ÖZKAN

Introduction

The 1990s were an important turning point for Alevis in Turkey. Burgeoning Alevi associations and foundations coupled with mainstream media coverage of the community's problems created a sense of visibility among Alevis, after long-time secrecy. The era also represented some significant changes in the Alevis' media presence. The publication of a substantial number of books and periodicals on Alevism in the early 1990s and onwards (Vorhoff 1998) was followed by the founding of Alevi radio stations in the mid-1990s. For a religious community who had conducted their rituals in secret and hid their Alevi identities from the public to avoid discrimination, having a presence in newspapers and on the radio was quite a novelty. In the early 2000s, the media presence of Alevism gained more momentum with the opening of Alevi television networks. After the establishment of *cemevi*s in the city centres (see Chapter 13 in this volume) and the organisation of well-attended festivals, Alevi television networks played a significant role in rendering Alevi practices, such as the *cem*, more publicly available.

Such an unprecedented public presence of Alevism was in part the result of shifting parameters of state governance after the 1980 military *coup*. The period that culminated in the *coup d'état* was an era of intensifying pressure on leftist-socialist groups in Turkey. Since Alevis were mostly supporters of this leftist movement, after the *coup*, the state 'sought to transform [such] widespread association of Alevis with the left' (Tambar 2014, p. 91). Such an agenda involved integrating the community into the nation as representatives of a 'rich' Turkish culture (Tambar 2014, p. 91). Coupled with the neoliberal turn in Turkey, which dismantled the state monopoly over the means of media production, the post-*coup* government opened a space for the public circulation of Alevism, as long as the community portrayed itself as the bearers of Turkish culture in ways that 'validate official rubrics of national belonging' (Tambar 2014, p. 78). Kabir Tambar calls this emerging mode of governance 'disciplined liberalisation' since, beginning in the 1990s, it provided some public footing for the circulation of Alevis' practices as well as their problems (Tambar 2014, p. 91).

In this chapter, I explore the consequences of this disciplined liberalisation, by focusing on two arenas: the objectification of Alevism on Alevi television networks and the circulation of such objectification within the Alevi community. In the first part, I focus on the representations of Alevism on Alevi television networks. Here, I argue that, despite the state agenda of integrating Alevis into the nation as Turks, Alevis' use of privatised media did more than legitimise the terms of official ideology. Alevis' televised responses to this emerging mode of governance in the post-1990 era objectified Alevism in ways that simultaneously affirmed and challenged hegemonic frameworks. Major Alevi television networks – such as Cem TV, Yol TV and TV 10 – diverged in their broadcast politics in dramatic ways. Whereas Cem TV openly contributed to the official agenda of associating Alevism with Turkish nationalism, Yol TV and TV 10 reproduced Alevis' relation to leftist ideology to confront the state agenda of transforming Alevis' links with the left. In this sense, the field of televised Alevism was a contentious one where various alignments with and interrogations of Turkey's hegemonic frameworks could be located.

In the second part, I turn to the circulation of these televised renditions of Alevism within the community. Here, I reveal that the shift in the mode of governing Alevis in the 1990s operated by altering how Alevis perceive their marginalisation. Many Alevis experienced the visibility they acquired on television as an improvement, thinking that it became more comfortable for them to reveal their previously hidden identities in public. I argue that such feelings of improvement had their roots in the gradual transformation that the community had been experiencing, especially with urbanisation. With the massive wave of migration in the 1960s, modes of articulating Alevism have also changed drastically. In particular, Alevis who migrated to the city at a young age suggested Alevi television as a legitimate mode of representing their faith in the city, even when they did not endorse how Alevism was portrayed on television. Alevi television networks, therefore, emerged as mediums that reproduced Alevism in publicly intelligible terms in the mixed urban context. In doing so, they contributed to the impression among the community of a more secure public visibility, informing narratives of improvement.

This chapter contributes to a relatively less explored dimension in Alevi studies, by analysing both production and circulation of Alevi media works. Although mass media played a central role in the reproduction of Alevism in Turkey, especially in the post-1980 era, only few scholars have examined this reproduction (Çaha 2004, Vorhoff 1998, Emre Cetin 2018a, Özkan 2019). This chapter expands these works in that it questions the Alevis' experiences of the visibility brought about by Alevi television between 2009 and 2015. Examining this period has become even more critical especially after 2016, when Turkey's emergency rule stopped both TV 10's and Yol TV's broadcasts.[1] My analysis here shows the vitality of television as a platform for Alevis to reorganise their community in the 1990s and 2000s, giving insight into how the restrictions on Alevism's media visibility in the late 2010s has added another layer to the community's ongoing marginalisation.

My observations in this paper are based on research among Alevis located mostly in Istanbul. The research was conducted in different periods between 2009 and 2015. Part of the data presented here was collected through semi-structured, in-depth interviews conducted in 2009, with approximately thirty Alevi residents of two different neighbourhoods in Turkey – those of Gazi and Ünalan. These findings were then complemented by long-term

---

[1] After 2016, the field of Alevi television changed drastically. The declaration of the state of emergency after the failed *coup* attempt in the summer of 2016 culminated in executive orders that shut down TV 10, along with many oppositional and critical television networks. In the same year, the Radio Television Supreme Council (RTÜK) cancelled Yol TV's access to the TÜRKSAT satellite, ending its broadcasts in Turkey. Yol TV relaunched its broadcasts in Turkey in 2018, through an alternative satellite connection. In this period, Cem TV continued its broadcasts without interruption.

ethnographic fieldwork between 2012 and 2015 among the founders and producers of major Alevi television networks. Additional in-depth interviews conducted during the same years with audiences of these networks, living in different parts of Turkey, supported the analysis.

Historicising Televised Alevism and Media Objectification

The state's disciplined liberalisation that partially encouraged the public circulation of Alevism was also a result of the neoliberal turn in Turkey in both the economic and political realms (Öniş 2004). Beginning in the 1990s, the Turkish media scene witnessed the dismantling of the state monopoly over the means of media production, as a consequence of the International Monetary Fund's sanctioned economic liberalisation and privatisation (Öncü 2004). Deregulation policies of the era paved the way for the *de facto* establishment of private television channels beaming in from Western Europe[2] as powerful rivals to state media. In the absence of laws and official institutions to regulate this newly emerging sector of private mediation,[3] there emerged some opportunity for various groups in the country to enter the commercial media market (Öncü 2004). This relative freedom from direct state control, therefore, set the conditions to 'bring "hidden" or "distant others" into the household' (Yavuz 2003, p. 181). In this political context, Alevis joined other political groups in the country, such as the Islamists[4] and the Kurds,[5] in more actively using the tools of privatised mass media.[6]

[2] In fact, Prime Minister Turgut Özal's own son was among the owners of Turkey's first private television channel Magic Box, which started broadcasting in 1990 from Germany via satellite. This ownership signifies a planned move and is 'consistent with Özal's overall strategy for implementing deregulation in various sectors of the economy', including the media (Öncü 2004, p. 14).

[3] When commercial broadcasting started in Turkey in 1990, it took four years for the state to issue a new broadcasting law that took the newly emerging conditions of private media into account. For a detailed discussion on the making of the 1994 broadcasting law, see Kejanlıoğlu (2004).

[4] For an earlier account on the Islamist movement's uses of media, see Öncü (1995).

[5] For a recent account on Kurdish media activism, see Koçer (2013).

[6] While explaining such complex historical connections is beyond the scope of this essay, it should be noted that the rise of Alevi activism in this period must also be seen in continuation with the Alevi political activism of the 1970s in the Marxist-socialist organisations, as well as the global rise of identity politics in the 1980s. See also Şentürk (2017).

The publication of the Manifesto of Alevism (*Alevilik Bildirgesi*) in May 1990 in the newspaper *Cumhuriyet* was one of the first organised attempts among Alevis to publicly put forward their demands.[7] The manifesto was written in reaction to the state policies that promoted a Turkish-Islamic synthesis, as part of the post-*coup* agenda of countering the political conflicts of the 1970s. While opening a space for the circulation of Alevis, official strategies of the post-*coup* era, therefore, simultaneously maintained the conditions that marginalised Alevis. Policies such as 'the proliferation of state-run Qur'anic schools for children, the expansion of schools for training preachers, and the introduction of new courses on religion and morals in primary and secondary schools' further alienated Alevis in this period (Tambar 2014, p. 90). Several Alevi and non-Alevi intellectuals, journalists and artists published a declaration to criticise such policies and to publicly acknowledge their solidarity with Alevis by listing the community's political demands (Aslan 2008, Çaha 2004).[8] In this section, I will reveal how Alevi media production encapsulates these processes of cultural activism that aim to counter dominant frameworks (Marcus 1993, Ginsburg 1994, Turner, 1991). In addition, I will show how Alevis' uses of media also included practices of cultural objectification that are strategically in line with hegemonic understandings (Miller 1995, Goodman 2005). I will do so by historically discussing the emergence of Alevi television networks in Turkey.[9]

---

[7] In 1963, Alevi students in Ankara published a similar statement that was followed by a brief period of Alevi activism. The establishment of some Alevi associations and the foundation of Turkey's first party representing Alevis, the Turkish Unity Party (*Türkiye Birlik Partisi*, TBP) – although not openly defining itself as an Alevi political party – coincided with the same period of the 1960s. However, unlike the assertions in the 1960s, the 1990 *Alevilik Bildirgesi* was the first attempt to openly list the political demands of Alevis as a religious community (Aslan 2008).

[8] This statement was based on an earlier declaration made by the founders of the 'Alevi Culture Group' in Hamburg, Germany, 'that had been published in Spring 1989 and promulgated especially during the event of the "Alevi Culture Week"' (Sökefeld 2008, p. 16). This declaration in Hamburg is noteworthy to underline the transnational ties in the making of the Alevi movement in Turkey. See Chapter 7 in this volume.

[9] It should be stated that this chapter gives only a partial glimpse of the history of Alevi visibility on television by limiting its scope to Turkey. The beginnings of such a history could go back to early-1990s Germany where Alevi migrant Halit Büyükgöl aired the very first

The *Alevilik Bildirgesi* was followed by the publication of Alevi periodicals such as *Nefes, Cem, Serçeşme* and *Pir Sultan Abdal Kültür ve Sanat Dergisi*,[10] as well as the emergence of Alevi radio stations such as Cem Radyo, Radyo Barış and Mozaik Radyo in the 1990s. At the beginning of the 2000s, Alevis began to actively use televised media. One of the first major projects of representing Alevism on television came into existence in 2004 on the mainstream news channel Kanaltürk during the Alevis' holy month, *Muharrem*. With the lead of the Confederation of European Alevi Unions (*Avrupa Alevi Birlikleri Konfederasyonu*, AABK) and the collaboration of the Alevi associations in Turkey, Kanaltürk aired the first series of programmes named *Muharrem Sohbetleri* (*Muharrem* Conversations) in 2004 during the twelve-day period of mourning in commemoration of the Karbala massacre. The programme hosted several Alevi *dedes*, intellectuals, activists and *zakirs* who discussed issues ranging from widespread prejudices against the community to the basics of Alevi faith.

While the programme received great audience ratings from Alevis, 'who sent 42,000 text messages on the first day',[11] Kanaltürk also received serious threatening calls during the programme. Necdet Saraç, a former member of the AABK and one of the organisers of the programme, explained the Alevis' great interest in the broadcast by suggesting that *Muharrem Sohbetleri* had enormous symbolic value for the community: 'Think about Ramadan, for instance, every single television network airs special programmes for Sunnis, but the holy month of Alevis is not even noticed. *Muharrem Sohbetleri* broke this silence and achieved a first'.[12] One of the hosts of the programme, in contrast, underlined that they received threatening calls especially after they discussed 'some taboo issues' on a national television network such as

---

representations of Alevi faith and culture on Berlin's Open Channel (Özkan 2016). Moreover, television networks such as TV Avrupa, founded in Cologne in 2004, and Düzgün TV, founded in Dortmund in 2005, are also parts of this history.

[10] Especially in Germany, there were other periodicals being published by Alevi migrants, such as *Dem, Zülfikar, Gerçek İlim, Alevilerin Sesi, Mürşit* and *Kerbela*. Among them, *Alevilerin Sesi*, published by the Confederation of European Alevi Unions (AABK), is one of longest-standing periodicals, focusing on Alevi issues, surviving to this day.

[11] Interview with one of the organisers of the programme, September 2015.

[12] Interview with the author, 2015.

Kanaltürk, which reached a mixed audience. 'For instance', the host continued, 'during the programmes we would question if *cemevi*s could also be considered places of worship for Muslims, and then we received threatening calls because of this'.[13]

After *Muharrem Sohbetleri* aired in 2004, Cem TV launched its test broadcasts in September 2005, as the first Turkey-based Alevi television network that was on the national satellite of TÜRKSAT. Cem TV garnered great audience interest, especially in its early years. Owned by İzzettin Doğan's *Cem Vakfı*, the television channel became one of the longest-standing Alevi presences in Turkey's televisual media scene. Starting by mostly airing Alevi music video clips, network in its content became more diverse with the production of daily newscasts, news and discussion programmes that paid special attention to Alevis' problems, live music programmes and religious programmes on Alevism. It also attracted an Alevi audience with its broadcasts of the *cem* every Thursday after the newscast. Televising *cem* surely was a novel way of reproducing the ritual, given the previously hidden and intimate conditions of its conduct.

In its broadcasts, however, Cem TV put forward a very exclusionary portrayal of Alevism that defined the faith as the Turkish version of Islam. In this sense, since its inception, the network has been one of the major Alevi-owned television stations to serve the state's interests in integrating Alevism into the nation by portraying the faith as exclusively Turkish. More critical and oppositional Alevi activists highly criticised Cem TV on these grounds, stating that it excluded, for example, Kurdish Alevi communities. Despite the wide attention that Cem TV received from an important portion of Alevis, such an exclusionary framework further alienated Alevis who did not conform to such norms.

Cem TV did not remain the only outlet for Alevi audiences in Turkey for long. Another Alevi television network, Su TV from Cologne in Germany, challenged its monopoly in representing Alevism on Turkey's media scene in 2005. In so doing, it also provided an alternative rendition of Alevism, especially by promoting the faith as having an organic link with leftist ideology. The majority of the founders and the initial producers of the network

---

[13] Interview with the author, October 2015.

consisted of migrants to Germany who had left Turkey for political reasons after their activism in leftist-socialist organisations of the 1970s. In this sense, their backgrounds in leftist ideology were reflected in the Su TV broadcasts. Besides broadcasting discussion programmes centring on Alevis' problems, *cem* and special episodes commemorating Alevi massacres, the network also aired programmes focusing on important figures of the leftist movement in Turkey.

As a result of the split in the cadre of Su TV staff due to political and economic disagreements, two more Alevi television networks emerged and pursued the political agenda of Su TV. The AABK founded Yol TV in 2006 in Cologne. Some former members of Su TV founded Dem TV in 2007 in Istanbul. Su TV also continued its broadcasts by moving the network's headquarters to Turkey. Among these television channels, Yol TV became another long-standing Alevi television network. With its broadcast policy, which avoided putting forward a single definition of Alevism, Yol TV attracted especially Alevi groups excluded by Cem TV, as the words of an Alevi Yol TV audience nicely illustrated: 'You cannot find a single person from Tunceli[14] who does not watch Yol TV'.[15] Besides reproducing Alevism as leftist ideology, Yol TV also played a major role in organising commemoration ceremonies of the major Alevi massacres in Turkey, such as the 1993 Sivas massacre. Dem TV continued to expand the viewership of Alevi television with its open agenda of publicising Kurdish Alevis' problems. After Dem TV's closure, TV 10, founded in Istanbul in 2010, advanced Dem TV's and Su TV's agenda in prioritising the problems of Alevis, socialists and Kurds. TV 10 attracted the attention of a broad audience, especially with its broadcasts of the *cem* in Zazaki.

In the contentious field of televised Alevism, therefore, one can locate the articulations of the faith that confirm the state agenda of representing the community as having Turkish origins, as the case of Cem TV has revealed.

---

[14] Tunceli is the new name that the newly established nation-state in the 1930s gave to one of the four regions of the Ottoman Empire's Dersim province. Zazaki-speaking Kurdish Alevi groups dominate the city of Tunceli in eastern Turkey. For a detailed analysis of the politics of dividing and renaming the region and the ensuing Dersim massacre in 1937–38, see Ayata and Hakyemez (2013).

[15] Personal conversation, May 2015.

These articulations contribute to the reproduction of exclusionary frameworks promoted by the post-1980 state rule. There are, however, other networks such as Yol TV and TV 10 that challenge such exclusionary articulations, by forging Alevis' relation, not only to the leftist stance, but also to Kurdish politics. In this sense, such great variety of political positioning in the realm of Alevi television, ranging from Cem TV over Yol TV to TV 10, underlines that Alevis' media visibility does not always align with official portrayals of the faith as representing the richness of Turkish culture; it also interrogates such exclusionary framings by putting forward alternative depictions of Alevism.[16]

The Circulation of Televised Alevism among Alevi Audiences

> We were, let's say, attending a social gathering, [and] they would ask where we were from. I am from Sivas. 'Are you Sunni or Alevi?' I was afraid to answer. Now that we have these *cemevi*s, these things were *explained*, *Alevilik* is on television, and we learned everything. We feel very peaceful.[17]

These words were told by a woman in her early fifties, Fatma, living in Istanbul's Gazi neighbourhood, which is predominantly populated by Alevis, leftist-socialists and Kurds. Fatma was born in the city of Sivas, to a family who migrated to Istanbul in the 1970s. She was one among many other Alevis who considered Alevism's presence on television, along with other developments of the 1990s, such as the opening of *cemevi*s, as an 'improvement' for the community. Similar to many others who migrated to Istanbul as a result of the rapid urbanisation and industrialisation of the 1960s, in her words, it was in Istanbul that she first experienced and realised the distinction between Alevis and Sunnis in such stark ways.

With the state in the leading role, a shift from agrarian economy to massive industrialisation took place in Turkey from the 1960s onwards. As a result, an

---

[16] See also Emre Cetin (2018b) for an analysis of differences in the transnational presentation of Alevi identity between Cem TV and Yol TV. Emre Cetin (2020)'s scholarship also shows how the media and in particular satellite television has enabled the 'mediatised culturalisation' of second-generation Alevis in the UK. These studies show that the media holds an important role in constructing and constesting transnational social imaginaries of Alevis in the diaspora.

[17] Interview with the author, November 2009.

urban wave of migration took Alevis to the industrialised cities. Even though Alevis over time created a new form of sociality around *cemevis* and Alevi associations in the urban centres, the community initially had difficulties in finding places to conduct their rituals. Whereas some solved such problems by reserving the uppermost floors of their apartments for the performance of the ceremony, gathering in the city proved to be difficult for other reasons as well. Finding jobs primarily as wage laborers, the close-knit Alevi communities in villages became scattered in cities, making it harder to come together to conduct the ritual.

After Fatma moved from her Alevi village to Istanbul, she began to grasp Alevism from a different perspective; in the mixed urban context, she acquired a new approach to Alevism that was neither available nor required in a predominantly Alevi environment. This perspective adopted in the city was expectedly marked by discrimination and fear. Prejudiced renditions of Alevism among Sunni Muslims, such as the notion of *mum söndü*, which accuses the community of engaging in incest during the *cem*, played a great role in creating such fears. Moreover, the memories of the 1970s' horrific massacres against the community were still fresh. The Alevis' identification with the left in the 1970s had bloody consequences for the community, as rightist mobs attacked them on the grounds that the minority was 'embodying the communistic threat' (Sinclair-Webb 2003, p. 216). During the attacks in the city of Maraş in 1978, ultra-nationalist rightists, who were mostly backed by the Nationalist Action Party (*Milliyetçi Hareket Partisi*, MHP), targeted Alevi households in their fight against 'the communistic threat', 'leaving over one-hundred people dead – the majority including women and children, murdered in cold blood in their homes, about forty-three of the dead drawn from fourteen families – many hundreds injured, thousands displaced and sheltering in the local governor's building' (Sinclair-Webb 2003, p. 222). Carrying the weight of this history, as Fatma said, Alevis 'were hiding in Istanbul; our parents would warn us not to say that we were Alevis'.[18]

Fatma described, however, how in the late 1990s and early 2000s, she felt more comfortable about revealing her Alevi identity given that, in her

[18] See Chapter 10 in this volume for accounts on Alevi remembrance of the Maraş massacre among Alevis in Great Britain.

words, Alevism was 'explained' on television and through *cemevis*. Fatma was not the only one who pointed to such feelings of improvement. Many of my interviewees who had migrated to Istanbul around the same time as Fatma also underlined that revealing their Alevi identities to their neighbours became much easier compared to the past. Another Alevi woman, Sevcan, for instance, highlighted the negative portrayals of the *cem* ceremony she encountered:

> Now I feel more empowered. When we heard about the *mum söndü* accusations back in the day, we could not say much, so we often remained silent. If I hear anyone making that accusation now, I know that I can bring them to a *cemevi* or show them a *cem* ceremony on television.[19]

I consider such descriptions as pointing to a shift in the community's understandings of their marginalisation. Such descriptions revealed that it became easier for Alevis to publicly embrace their Alevi identities with their visibility on television and with the *cemevis*. These stories underlined an urge to confront negative renditions of Alevism as circulated by Sunni Muslims and referred to television and *cemevis* as the most important mediums enabling such confrontation.

Although the difficulties that newly migrated Alevis experienced in the city were in part informed by the memories of past persecutions, I argue that they also resulted from shifts in the modes of articulating Alevism. With urbanisation, the ways in which Alevis reproduced their rituals, ways of life and philosophy had also altered to a great extent. It is in such a shifting and new context that Alevis faced the urge to explain their difference to outsiders. Alevi television, therefore, responded to this need and provided Alevis with a new tool or way to explain Alevism in publicly intelligible terms.

While figuring out new ways of organising themselves around their faith in the cities, confronting negative portrayals of Alevi practices proved to be difficult. Aysel described this difficulty she experienced as a new urban migrant with the feeling of emptiness: 'When they [Sunni Muslims] pressed us so heavily, we felt empty (*Onlar o kadar yüklendiğine göre biz kendimizi boş hissettik*)'.[20] Here, Aysel pointed to the negative portrayals of Alevism that she

---

[19] Interview with the author, November 2009.
[20] Interview with the author, November 2009.

encountered when she came to Istanbul and her inability to come up with any response to counter them. Her feeling of emptiness coincided with her own struggle of making sense of and relating to her Alevi background in a new context. Lacking the very means for such articulation, Alevis initially felt at a loss when explaining Alevism to outsiders – in their words, 'to prove the prejudiced renditions of their faith wrong'.

As the primary party responsible for teaching Alevism to the next generations, one *dede* pointed to such challenges more elaborately:

> It was easier in the past when we were in the villages. You would teach Alevism to the youth by being around them, by eating with them and by interacting with them. Now you have to explain everything; you have to instruct them. It is hard to convey Alevism in this manner. In fact, even now things are easier in the villages. I spent two months with my ten-year-old grandsons in our village this summer. They got so interested in Alevism; they were all singing *deyiş* [Alevi hymns] in the car on our way back to Istanbul. They spent two weeks here, all of that is gone now.[21]

As the means to reproduce Alevism were transformed with urbanisation, producing a publicly clear explanation about the Alevi faith also became harder. The *dede*'s words underlined the need for a new mode of articulating Alevism in the city context in order to make the faith intelligible, not only to outsiders, but also to the next generation of Alevis. This mode of articulation required more 'instruction' about the characteristics of the faith, in his words. Exemplary behaviours were not enough to communicate the specifics of being an Alevi, as the *dede* underlined that he needed to rely more on descriptive articulations to 'explain' Alevism. Fatma, Aysel and others had to face prejudiced renditions of Alevism amid similar struggles of making sense of and relating to Alevism in a new context; hence, they found it challenging to give counter-explanations.

Televised Alevism partly fulfilled this emerging need that Alevis increasingly felt in this context: the urge to explain what Alevism is in ways that are intelligible to outsiders. In doing so, such visibility on television altered how Alevis conceived their marginalisation. With Alevism on television, some Alevis thought that they were provided with a secure and legitimate

---

[21] Interview with the author, October 2015.

public footing to counter the daily forms of discrimination they quite often encountered. Considering the context of Fatma's shifting experiences in the city, I argue that the visibility of Alevism on television, for many Alevis, was an assurance in the sense that Alevis had nothing to hide. Everything was out in the open on the screen. It was a means to counter the feeling of emptiness. When they encountered negative portrayals of the *cem*, for instance, there were television programmes they could advise others to watch in order to prove these prejudices wrong. Hence, some Alevis thought that their position had improved with the developments of the 1990s, which brought public visibility to the community through television and *cemevi*s.

Such feelings of improvement, however, neither remained unchallenged nor resulted from a straightforward appreciation of Alevism's televised representations. A dialogue I witnessed between Hüseyin Amca, in his seventies, and his son, Merdan Abi, was an instance that pointed to both the complexity of these feelings of improvement and the absence of such a sense of advancement among some Alevis. As part of my fieldwork, I was invited to some of my interlocutors' homes every once in a while. During one such visit, my interlocutor Merdan Abi, who was in his fifties, was complaining about how he had difficulties explaining his Alevi background to outsiders. Working for a state institution, Merdan Abi said that he preferred to hide his identity since he had no idea how to clarify how Alevis differed from Sunnis. In fact, he went even further to suggest that he was questioning if they really were from an Alevi background, given the lack of any practice of Alevism in their family. Hüseyin Amca responded by pointing to his inability to teach Alevism to his children, with an openly regretful tone: 'Back then we came to the city, and here we could not teach you Alevism. But if they ask you what kind of Alevi you are, just say that we are Alevis like the ones on Cem TV'.

Merdan Abi's complaints revealed that especially Alevis who were born and grew up in the cities had difficulties in relating to their Alevi backgrounds, mostly because they felt that they were deprived of the very means that would enable them to make sense of Alevism. In Merdan Abi's case, working for a state institution made it even more of a challenge for him to relate to his faith. His feeling of loss, however, triggered questions about the efficiency of the newly invented ways of reproducing Alevism in the cities, such as *cemevi*s and Alevi associations, as well as Alevi television networks. His account paralleled those of others who did not think that things had improved and in fact blamed Alevi television networks for assimilating Alevism into the hegemonic understandings of religion. These critiques went so far as to state that there were no truly Alevi television networks, hence the phrase 'Alevi television' was an oxymoron. The accounts of improvement, therefore, were accompanied by narratives of assimilation, pointing to the fact that neither the understanding of discrimination had come to an end, nor did the community have better means for comprehending and reproducing their faith with the media visibility of the last decades.

Hüseyin Amca's suggestion to his son about an Alevi television network as the most appropriate way of articulating his Aleviness showed that, for some Alevis, these networks still had a central place for publicly embracing Alevi identity. For Hüseyin Amca, Alevi television networks were a solution to his incapability to teach Alevism to his son. A later interview with Hüseyin Amca revealed that he, in fact, did not necessarily agree with the representation of Alevism on Cem TV. What led him to suggest the network to his son, however, was his inability to articulate Alevism in the way in which Cem TV did. During the interview, I asked Hüseyin Amca whether what he had known about Alevism was similar to the information presented on Cem TV. Rather than elaborating on similarities, he laid out many differences, especially about the way in which the *cem* was conducted. He said that even the name *cem* was new to him. Back in the village, they would not call the gathering *cem* but *muhabbet*, which means a deep conversation among close companions.

Despite these differences, however, Hüseyin Amca still considered Alevi television a viable source for Alevis, mostly because it fulfilled the need to articulate Alevism in ways which he was not capable of doing. His understanding of Alevism was based on a different mode of articulation that emerged in a predominantly Alevi context where there was no immediate need to explain what Alevism was and, more importantly, how it differed from the dominant Sunni Islam. Televised Alevism presented an objectification of the faith by addressing the questions that emerged in the urban context; in doing so, it provided, for Hüseyin Amca and others, a more intelligible mode of articulation. The availability of such a new way of representation has partly informed the accounts of improvement among Alevis, altering how they conceived of their marginalisation.

Conclusion

The televised visibility and the improvement stories that it generated reveals that the shift in the mode of governing Alevis in the 1990s ended up transforming how some Alevis perceived their marginalisation. It created among some community members the feeling that, compared to the past, it was now easier for Alevis to embrace their Alevi identity publicly. While this does not mean that Alevis stopped hiding their identities, as the ethnographic examples here also reveal, it shows how Alevis incorporated the mediatised objectification of their faith as grounds for confronting some forms of discrimination that they encountered in their daily lives, such as the negative renditions of the *cem*. How such an incorporation enabled newer forms of governance is the next question to ask and the subject of another discussion and analysis. Here, suffice it to say that official attempts to represent Alevism as part of Turkish culture ended up creating new forms of visibility for Alevis. The circulation of such visibility then changed how some Alevis conceived of their marginalisation by creating a sense that the community now has a more secure public footing.

Even though this government strategy had the purpose of incorporating Alevis into the nation by portraying them as members of Turkic culture, the public space it opened for this purpose was filled with renditions of Alevism that both confirmed and challenged such an official portrayal. As mentioned, even though Cem TV serves the state's interests in defining Alevism as inherently Turkish, other Alevi television networks such as Yol TV and TV 10 contest this portrayal, by forging the Alevis' relation to not only leftist socialism but also Kurdish political activism. When considered together with Alevis' daily engagements with this televised visibility, such political heterogeneity in the field of Alevi television exposes the diverging consequences of disciplined liberalisation within the Alevi community in Turkey.

Finally, despite the agendas of Alevi television networks in either supporting or questioning the official agenda, Alevis viewed these networks as legitimate reference points that allowed them to explain their identities in public, without necessarily paying attention to the networks' political responses to the state agendas. In her study on the reception of televised melodramas in Egypt, Lila Abu-Lughod (2004, p. 237) argues that Egyptian women accepted the moral and national messages attached to the television series 'only when these resonated with their worlds'. In this sense, how women in Egypt responded to the various portrayals of the Egyptian nation on television depended on their everyday experiences on the ground (Abu-Lughod 2004, p. 14). Similarly, Alevi audiences' responses to televised Alevism were informed by their everyday experiences of discrimination and fear. Even though Alevi television networks circulated various and conflicting renditions of Alevism that both challenged and confirmed the state's rendition of the faith, Alevi audiences did not always pay attention to such media content when watching these television networks. Instead, since most Alevis felt at a loss in the mixed context of the cities when experiencing and explaining Alevism to others, they engaged with these networks by incorporating the legitimate and secure visibility they provided.

Acknowledgements

I wish to thank Jessica Winegar and Elizabeth Derderian for their critical feedback on earlier drafts of this chapter. I am also deeply grateful to the Alevis who shared their valuable experiences with me. This chapter is a product of their generosity.

Bibliography

Abu-Lughod, L. (2005). *Dramas of Nationhood: The Politics of Television in Egypt.* Chicago: University of Chicago Press.

Aslan, S. (2008). *The Ambivalence of Alevi Politic(s): A Comparative Analysis of Cem Vakfi and Pir Sultan Abdal Kultur Dernegi.* Unpublished MA thesis, Bosphorus University.

Ayata, B., and Hakyemez, S. (2013). The AKP's Engagement with Turkey's Past Crimes: An Analysis of PM Erdoğan's 'Dersim Apology'. *Dialectical Anthropology*, 37(1), 131–43.

Çaha, Ö. (2004). The Role of the Media in the Revival of Alevi Identity in Turkey. *Social Identities*, 10, 325–38.

Emre Cetin, K. B. (2020). Mediatised Culturalisation Through Television: Second-Generation Alevi Kurds in London. In: Kaptan Y., and Algan, E., eds, *Television in Turkey.* Cham: Palgrave Macmillan. pp. 207–22.

Emre Cetin, K. B. (2018a). Communicative Ethnocide and Alevi Television in the Turkish Context. *Media, Culture and Society*, 40(7), 1008–23.

Emre Cetin, K. B. (2018b). Television and the Making of a Transnational Alevi Identity. *National Identities*, 20(1), 91–103.

Ginsburg, F. (1994). Embedded Aesthetics: Creating a Discursive Space for Indigenous Media. *Cultural Anthropology*, 9(2), 365–82.

Kejanlıoğlu, B. (2004). Broadcasting Policy in Turkey since 1980. *Boğaziçi Journal*, 18, 77–91.

Koçer, S. (2013). Making Transnational Publics: Circuits of Censorship and Technologies of Publicity in Kurdish Media Circulation. *American Ethnologist*, 40(4), 721–33.

Marcus, G. (1998). Ethnography in/of the World System: The Emergence of Multi-Sited Ethnography. *Annual Review of Anthropology*, 24, 95–117.

Miller, D. (1995). Introduction: Anthropology, Modernity, Consumption. In: Miller, D., ed., *Worlds Apart: Modernity through the Prism of the Local*. London: Routledge. pp. 1–23.

Öncü, A. (1995). Packaging Islam: Cultural Politics on the Landscape of Turkish Television. *Public Culture*, 8, 51–71.

Öncü, A. (2004). The Interaction of Media and Politics: The Remaking of the Turkish Media Industry in the 1990s. *Boğaziçi Journal*, 18(1–2), 11–26.

Öniş, Z. (2004). Turgut Özal and His Economic Legacy: Turkish Neoliberalism in Critical Perspective. *Journal of Middle Eastern Studies*, 40(4), 113–34.

Özkan, N. (2016). The Emergence of Alevi Televisual Activism: From Secrecy to Visibility. *MERIP: Middle East Research Project* 281 (Winter 2016).

Özkan, N. (2019). Representing Religious Discrimination at the Margins: Temporalities and 'Appropriate' Identities of the State in Turkey. *PoLAR: Political and Legal Anthropology Review* 42(2), 317–31.

Sinclair-Webb, E (2003). Sectarian Violence, the Alevi Minority, and the Left: Kahramanmaraş 1978. In: White, P. J., and Jongerden, J., eds, *Turkey's Alevi Enigma: A Comprehensive Overview*. Leiden: Brill. pp. 215–36.

Sökefeld, M. (2008). *Struggling for Recognition: The Alevi Movement in Germany and in Transnational Space*. New York: Berghahn Books.

Şentürk, B. (2017). Urbanization, Socialist Movements and the Emergence of Alevi Identity. In: Issa, T., ed., *Alevis in Europe: Voices of Migration, Culture and Identity*. London and New York: Routledge.

Tambar, K. (2014). *The Reckoning of Pluralism: Political Belonging and the Demands of History in Turkey*. Stanford: Stanford University.

Turner, T. (1991). Representing, Resisting, Rethinking: Historical Transformations of Kayapo Culture and Anthropological Consciousness. In: Stocking, G., ed., *Colonial Situations*. Madison: University of Wisconsin Press. pp. 285–313.

Vorhoff, K. (1998). Academic and Journalistic Publications on the Alevi and Bektashi of Turkey. In: Olsson, T., Özdalga, E., and Raudvere, C., eds, *Alevi Identity: Cultural, Religious, and Social Perspectives.* Istanbul: Swedish Research Institute in Istanbul. pp. 23–50.

Yavuz, H. (2003). Media Identities for Kurds and Alevis, In: Eickelman, D. F., and Anderson, J. W., eds, *New Media in the Muslim World: The Emerging Public Sphere.* Bloomington: Indiana University Press. pp. 180–89.

EPILOGUE

15

BACK TO ANATOLIA: REFLECTIONS ON TWENTY-FIVE YEARS OF ALEVI RESEARCH

DAVID SHANKLAND

Introduction

In the early days of the so-called Alevi revival, a large number of publications concerning various aspects of Alevi religious thought, history, culture and ritual place in the Republic appeared. Unlike the somewhat sporadic publications of the previous decades, they were nearly all written by Alevis themselves. As a good proportion of the authors were also active within civil society organisations, this, in turn, marked the emergence of Alevi associations as important players in public debates concerning the Alevi community, and above all the growing influence of the diaspora, especially, but not only, in Germany (see Part II on Alevis in the Diaspora in this volume).

The question which mostly preoccupied me during this period was how, as researchers coming from outside, we were to relate to the emerging debate in the public sphere that would inevitably ensue, both in Turkey and in Europe more widely (Shankland 1998). Although the question remains as relevant as ever, as it turned out, this has not been – or at least appears not to have been – as problematic as I feared. It is true that the number of researchers working on Alevis has expanded. It now encompasses a great range of committed contributors, including distinguished academics drawn from Alevis who have taken up university positions in Turkey and overseas and who occupy a simultaneous position as outsiders and insiders within the ever more complex debates. However, even though there are occasional differences of opinion and indeed of approach, the insider/outsider problematic has not become a cornerstone of controversy.

Instead, the field has been dominated by issues which preoccupy the Alevis themselves – issues which, as far as I can tell, are not an artifact of those external researchers who have worked with them. Among these problems one may include the relationship between the Turkish state and the Alevi community;[1] belief and the relationship between the Alevis and Islam;[2] the transmission of *Alevilik* to the next generation; the role and changing place of Alevi organisations and associated *cemevis* within the life of the community;[3] the future role of the *dede* lineages; and the place of Alevis in the international arena, including their links with the states where they are found and with the European Union.[4]

If my fears in regard to these problems have not been borne out, then so much the better. However, there is another assumption that I made, which was also not correct, but I only wish it had been: after the initial and very substantial interest in the Alevis had become evident throughout the last years of the twentieth century, it seemed a reasonable conclusion that there would follow a large number of studies which would illuminate with some accuracy the range of forms that *Alevilik* has taken in Anatolia. For this reason, earlier rural studies would become superseded as these newer studies established their authority. During later years, invaluable rural studies of the Kurdish Alevi population in the Dersim area have been published,[5] but for a long period of time, my research was the only one based on empirical research carried out among the Alevi villages. Contemporary urban and diasporic aspects of the situation of the Alevis nationally and internationally can hardly tell us anything directly about *Alevilik* as it

---

[1] See, for example, Chapter 3 in this volume for these relations under the AKP administration, and Chapter 4 in this volume for the ways in which the Turkish state has handled the politics of memory around the Sivas massacre. See also Karakaya-Stump (2018) and Göner (2017).

[2] See Chapter 2 in this volume for a discussion of various positions in this debate.

[3] See Chapter 13 in this volume on the history and mapping of *cemevis* in Istanbul.

[4] See Özkul (2019) and Chapters 7, 8, 9 and 10 in this volume.

[5] See Gezik and Gültekin (2019), as well as Chapter 6 in this volume.

developed and had been practised for centuries before its opening to the world, with its accompanying plethora of publications, mass migration and transnational doctrines.

A moment's pause for reflection will serve to tell us why this is the case. The Alevis have traditionally been a rural community, one that has taken shape in Anatolia. The influences on them have been manifest and manifold, ranging from Hurufism, Bektaşism, Shamanism, Caferism, Christianity, Manichaeism, as well as the mostly unwritten but profound mix of folkloric belief that accompanies Turkish Islam, one that is now giving way to a more scriptural form encouraged by the global resurgence in Wahabbism and its related belief currents.[6] However, there is no specifically centralised doctrine among Alevis. Although, on occasion, texts can be very significant for the Alevis, there are no standard rules from which they have drawn codification of their form of Islam.

To clarify this point, we should say that it is necessary to distinguish between the intention to guide and doctrinal regulations. The accounts of the life and teachings of Hacı Bektaş are known to nearly all Alevi communities and have been profoundly influential. Likewise, the texts of instruction variously known under the heading *Buyruk* (Decree) constitute another source of inspiration. However, these have not resulted historically in a close reading of the text, which concatenates policing conduct with its tenets. Instead, textual passages are drawn upon selectively, and the way in which the ritual cycle is celebrated and the specific regulations governing the practice of the Alevi form of Islam within the community are diverse. In sum, in custom and practice, the oral contract – which is made between the local *dede*s and their immediate community – is dominant.

I would not wish to suggest for a moment that there are not some core elements that appear to be constant to all Alevi communities. All concur that some hierarchy between Alevis is a legitimate assumption – that is, some lineages are favoured by God, either today or at some time in their past, which means that they accordingly are given the right to teach Alevi tenets and to lead within the rituals favoured by the community. They all, provided that they are practising, hold *cem* ceremonies at which a sacrifice is offered, and

[6] On the influences on *Alevilik*, see the writings of Melikoff (1998).

the 'twelve duties' are undertaken.[7] Typically, they insist that both women and men are present at these ceremonies. Equally, the possibility of a religious bond between Alevis, as far as I know, extends to all communities through the notion of *musahiblik*.

However, within this general outline, there are immensely varied possibilities. The age at which participants are permitted to take part varies. Some villages may have a form of initiation ritual; others may not. Some may celebrate the most important annual *cem*, the *görgü cem*, in the autumn, others in the spring. Some may regard the links between the followers (*talip*) and *dede*s as unchanging, decided by Hacı Bektaş, while others may consider the structural relationship between follower and *dede* as taking place at the level of the village or a number of villages as a whole. That is, a cluster of villages may all regard their *dede*s as hailing from a specific village, but to which individual *dede* a person may have recourse is not decided by descent but by choice, giving rise to a pattern close to that described by Gellner (1969) in his *Saints of the Atlas*. We can see the way in which *Alevilik* has emerged and developed only by examining the great diversity in these patterns of belief and custom.

Another way of stating this point is as follows: Although text is essential in various ways, it has throughout the centuries been subordinate to the preferred method that the community and their *dede* lineages desire to celebrate their religion. The only way that we can learn about this is to return to Anatolia.

This call is very much more than mere nostalgia for the past. It is, on the contrary, absolutely vital for us to be able to navigate the changing geopolitical arguments surrounding the Alevis, which feature in precisely those developments in the diaspora that are attracting so much attention. This is because so much of the necessary articulation of the debates involves truth claims: statements that are categorical about what *Alevilik* is or is not. These, in turn, entail inevitable questions such as the population of the Alevis, their geographic distribution, their similarity with other Islamic currents, their religious beliefs, their status as a distinct community and the appropriate way to teach *Alevilik* in the future. Within all these debates, either explicitly or implicitly, are assumptions about the traditional practice of *Alevilik* in

---

[7] See Chapter 12 in this volume for an in-depth analysis of changes in one of these twelve duties, the *zakir*.

Anatolia. However, unless we undertake the appropriate research, how can we be sure that these claims have any validity? In the next section of this chapter, I shall give three examples of the sort of research that I believe would help to illustrate these points.

Population, Maps and the Alevis

As any reader of the literature will be aware, the question of the size of the Alevi community frequently forms part of the preliminary discourse of discussions of their predicaments, whether in Turkey or as part of the transnational debates concerning their place in Turkish society. The question equally plays a role in conversations and speeches. Sometimes these estimates are high, perhaps suggesting 30 per cent or more. Others are low, proposing that 10 per cent or even less of the population of Turkey are Alevi. More than likely, the truth lies somewhere in between. However, one indirect way to gain a better appreciation of the extent of the traditional Alevi community is to study their distribution within Anatolia.

To this end, Dr Peter Andrews very kindly joined a small research team, which I headed at the University of Bristol, enabling us to gain the benefit of his long experience in mapping. Together, we re-examined his *Ethnic Groups in Turkey* and isolated the material concerning the Alevis. Also, we took into account a series of corrections that he had noted since the publication of the first edition in 1989 (see Andrews 1989). The resulting maps, which were published in the *British Journal of Middle Eastern Studies*, show the fruit of our labours (see Shankland 2010, 2012; Figures 15.1–4 below). One may notice certain limitations: when Dr Andrews conducted this research, he made particular distinctions as to whether a community regarded itself as being Tahtacı, Alevi Kurd (Zaza), Alevi Kurd (Kurmancı), or Turkish Alevi. It is indeed possible to make distinctions finer than this, as is clear from his tables of ethnic classifications, but these finer sub-categories do not appear on the maps from which our re-analysis was conducted.

We should note that we do not for a moment consider these maps as being complete or conclusive in any way. It may be recalled that Dr Andrews conducted this research originally as part of a much larger project devoted to mapping ethnic groups in the Middle East and Turkey. It was not practicable to put into the field the enormous number of researchers that would have

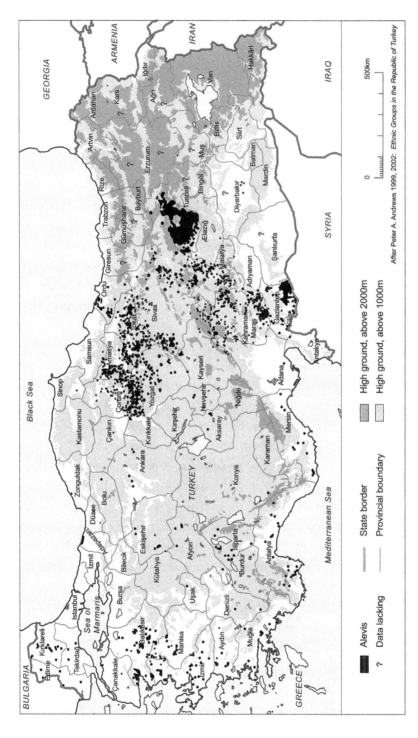

Map 15.1   Provisional general map showing the distribution of Alevis in Turkey

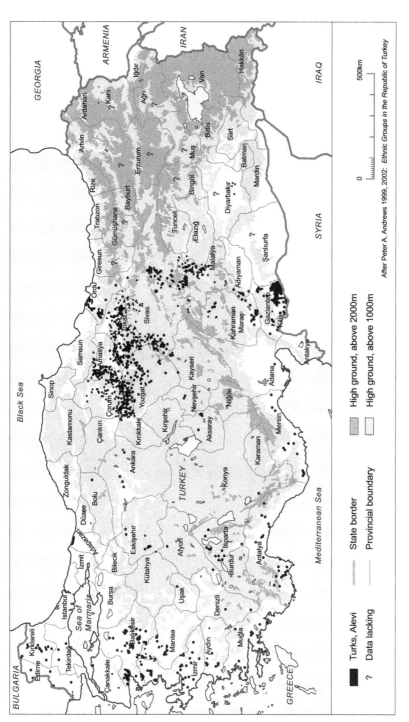

Map 15.2   Provisional map showing the distribution of Alevi Turks

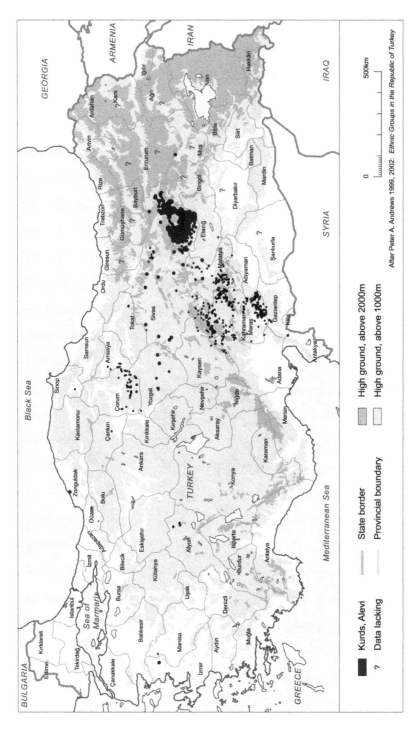

Map 15.3   Provisional map showing the distribution of Kurdish-speaking Alevis

Kurds, Alevi

? Data lacking

State border

Provincial boundary

High ground, above 2000m

High ground, above 1000m

0   500km

After Peter A. Andrews 1999, 2002: *Ethnic Groups in the Republic of Turkey*

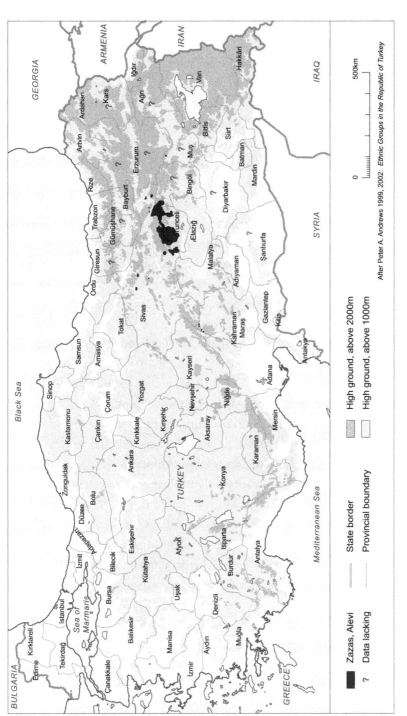

Map 15.4 Provisional map showing the distribution of Zaza-speaking Alevis

After Peter A. Andrews 1999, 2002: *Ethnic Groups in the Republic of Turkey*

Zazas, Alevi

? Data lacking

State border

Provincial boundary

High ground, above 2000m

High ground, above 1000m

0   500km

been necessary to work out these ethnic distinctions first-hand. Therefore, he relied on systematic interviews with migrants in the diaspora setting, cross-checking their results as he moved from community to community. Even though I was skeptical at first as to the accuracy of this method, it has the great advantage that results can be corrected as further interviews take place, and the overall picture that it presents is convincing. That is, although they will need refining, these maps present a picture that is not altogether wrong, or misleading, as long as they are treated as preliminary, even if fairly full, results understood as work in the making.

What can we tell from these maps? First and foremost, they tell us conclusively where the preponderance of the Alevi population lies, not considering the mass migration to the cities that began in the last decades of the twentieth century. Broadly speaking, they inhabit the central eastern and lower Black Sea regions, where the Turkish Alevis gradually give way to the Kurmancı- and Zaza-speaking Alevis as one moves further east. There is then a sharp cut-off, almost a line extending from north to south. To the east of this point, there appear to be very few Alevis, if any at all. Likewise, on the Black Sea Coast itself, there are fewer Alevis than in Central Anatolia. To the west, there are Tahtacı villages, famously relocated there by the Ottoman Empire when they needed their expertise in wood-cutting for warships.

It should be reiterated that I do not consider these maps exhaustive. It is a consequence of the way in which the material was collected that the Alevis who did not speak with Dr Andrews as he was compiling the maps, or about which he did not hear, will not appear. For this reason, there are almost certainly villages that will need to be added to his catalogue. Nevertheless, I am sure that the general shape is reasonable enough. What does it tell us? There immediately emerges one confirmation of a general point made by the Alevis themselves: they often inhabit areas higher in terms of elevation. The band of Anatolia occupied by them is well above the average elevation, and where they are densest of all, Tunceli, is a high natural plateau. While it is dangerous to extrapolate population size from a distribution map, I certainly think that rough and ready estimates could be made which at least have the benefit of being based on some empirical evidence. This would suggest, indeed, that the estimate of 30 per cent of Anatolia's population being Alevi is rather too high, because they do not inhabit that proportion of the land mass. However, in saying so, it should be recalled that the map does not measure population directly, but village settlements. Thus, more precisely put, we should say that the proportion of Alevi to Sunni village settlements in the late twentieth century, when the information underlying this map was gathered, is certainly less than 30 per cent.

There are further, admittedly speculative, points that could be made; however, when looking at the information, I have been struck by the way in which the Alevi population appears to be equidistant between the great powers of Istanbul and the Sublime Porte, on the one hand, and Iran, on the other. It is also striking that the Alevis are mostly settled or semi-settled populations rather than purely nomadic. Looking at this purely from the point of view of an anthropologist and not a historian, it is tempting to suggest that two influences might be at work here. Purely as a speculation, one might suggest that, during the defeat of the Safavids and the growing establishment of central state power over Anatolia, the tribal formations in the east were encouraged to convert *en masse* to Sunni Islam. However, in the more fragmented highlands, which lay in between the tribal east and the centralised west, there was some space, allowing the Alevis to settle, as long as they kept to themselves and did not rebel. Not all tribes obeyed this blandishment – hence, the Dersim revolt of the 1920s. However, the broad mass of Turkish Alevis adopted a form of religion that operated at the village level; infused with Bektaşism, they were able – often also through the *ocak*s reaching a modus operandi with the sultan – to get by. I hope to outline my thinking behind this argument in a more detailed fashion in the future. I cannot claim to be an expert on the emergence of Sunni Islam among the Kurdish tribes, and I concur that it is not enough for the model to be possible sociologically; it also must be supported by historical evidence. However, it is a train of thought that was stimulated by the maps, and there surely are other possibilities. Clearly, however, the essential point is made: potentially we can learn a very great deal by studying the distribution of the Alevis in their rural hinterland.

The Place of the *Dede* Ocaks

To offer my second example, I need to draw briefly on a later research project that I conducted in Germany as a Humboldt Fellow at the outset of the 2000s (see Shankland and Çetin 2005). This again was an extremely interesting time.

Just at that point, Alevis had become recognised as a distinct religious community by the German authorities in several German provinces.[8] This meant that, should a sufficient number of students be present in any one school, they would have the right to receive tuition on the Alevi religion from a qualified teacher. The teachers, in turn, would be provided by the German state, having received the necessary education in Alevi tenets. Responsibility for delivering teacher training and otherwise providing accompanying material was vested in the Alevi Federation in Cologne.[9]

As was evident at the time, recognition of the Alevis as a distinct religious community immediately raises fundamental issues, because it implies that the Alevis potentially were attempting to separate from Islam. Yet, the traditional way in which this relationship has been negotiated in Anatolia is the opposite. The Alevis in Anatolia are quite clear that they are Muslim. However, they utilise a device common within all Sufi movements in order to explain their difference, saying that the orthodox tenets of Islam – known for short as *şeriat* – are not illegitimate but superficial, that they fail to capture the depths of meaning under the surface (Shankland 2003). Instead, the Alevi way is the *tarikat* way, the one that captures the reality of existence and transcends the *şeriat*. This means that, throughout Anatolia, it can be regarded as acceptable from the Alevi point of view if one of their number goes to a mosque, or prays, but their creed does not give precedence to these activities, regarding them as optional. The dominant position taken through the Alevi Federation in Cologne at that time, however, was that Islam has influenced the Alevi form of religious thought, but that this influence concealed the true depths of the religion and could now be dispensed with. In other words, true *Alevilik* has nothing to do with Islam at all.

This is quite at odds with the dominant sentiment in Anatolia and has consequences that are not yet completely clear. In practice, one would expect there to be some reconciliation that enables the federation to draw back from this rather stark position. However, it also impacts and emerges from another debate, which is the place of the *dede* lineages. The *ocak*s, the traditional

---

[8] This period is captured well in the work of Sökefeld (2008a, 2008b).

[9] See Chapter 7 and 8 in this volume for later developments. See also Jenkins and Cetin (2018) for an analysis of the introduction of *Alevilik* into the curriculum in schools in the UK.

leaders of the Alevi form of Islam, who frequently trace their descent from the family of the Prophet, certainly oppose any separation from Islam, but they also may find themselves in opposition to the federation in that their expectation of being leaders of the community lies in their being born into an *ocak* lineage. However, those who work in the federation and are now charged with providing materials for the Alevi religion are themselves not necessarily from a *dede* lineage – in fact, usually they are not.

The picture is further complicated by the fact that, in any case, social change has rendered the position of the *dede* lineages weak. *Alevilik* works most effectively when the community is comparatively closed, or at least when the members of the community know each other. The face-to-face rituals, which culminate in the *cem*, are an extremely useful form of social control, one that is in effect a localised court where the faults and activities of most of the participants are known to each other. As migration has become significant, the *dede*s can hardly be expected to be able to conduct affairs with their previous authority. This is especially the case if the questions which they may be asked to consider have arisen outside the community – for example, at work. Nor is the threat of excommunication effective if a community is attempting to restrict population loss – all the more so, if the means of economic survival have moved from subsistence farming to remittances coming into the community from outside.

The *dede*s themselves are aware of this difficulty, and I think they would not find it a realistic presumption that they can ever go back entirely to their past status. However, what is to be their role? It is a characteristic of the federation (or at least one dominant mood within the federation) to regard the idea of inherited sanctity as *passé* – that within one or two generations it will simply fade away, as one of the officials there remarked to me. However, this has turned out to be over-sanguine. There has been a remarkable tenacity of support for the idea of inherited sanctity from the general Alevi community, which has meant that it has not been possible for any quick or easy removal of the *dede*s from the current reformulation of the place of Alevi religion. This has meant that, even if younger *dede*s may be invited to go on a course (rather than their previous in-house apprenticeship being regarded as sufficient), they have been unable to dispense with inherited sanctity entirely. It is quite normal, not just in the federation, but also across the many Alevi associations throughout the diaspora communities, that there is a *dede* committee within the association, and that the *dede* community has an essential voice in the way in which the association's activities are founded, as well as over the conduct of *cem* ceremonies.

Over and above this, even as the movement to create a standardised Alevi curriculum goes forward, there is a reaction from several of the migrant groups which are forming, instead of a firm and indissoluble link with the federation, movements that reflect the particular local form of *Alevilik* with which they are comfortable. They may say, for example, that their form of *Alevilik* is the 'sweetest' and in turn desire to bring their own *dede*s to their ceremonies. This persistence of the local will, I believe, be an important factor in the future.

It is possible to point out several reasons why this may be the case. One possibility is that the variety is so high, in terms of music, *semah*, ritual conduct and so on, that a congregation feels uncomfortable unless it is held in their accustomed way. More than this, however, we can think about the situation structurally. The replacement of the *dede*s by inheritance is, from one point of view, at least a move toward democracy. During the 1970s, there were movements from within the Alevis themselves, where the left-wing-influenced younger Alevis, many of whom later became part of the associational activity that eventually flourished greatly in Germany, regarded the *dede*s as a regression to a feudal way of life. They resisted their power and their tendency toward conservatism in the sense of wishing to keep the community intact, and they also could find the insistence on conformity, which is imposed by village life, irksome. All this meant that individualism could be seen as an attractive alternative.

However, for the mass of the village population, the argument can be put in a rather different way. It is quite true that the *dede* lineages are decided by birth, and that it is very unusual for a new *dede* lineage to emerge. However, *which* person from the *dede* lineage will eventually be an active and practising *dede* is not at all foretold. The person has to have the personal characteristics necessary to be a *dede*, in that he is honest, married with a family, able to lead Alevi rituals and to get on well with his peers. He has to have the approval of his lineage, who will suggest that he is the right person to take over responsibility for the following lineages that the *dede* lineage has traditionally supported.

Over and above this, the follower lineages have to accept him as their *dede*. It is only by their offering him a sacrifice that the *cem* can be triggered. It is only when the *dede* is invited that he can resolve a dispute within the community, and although the *dede* may maintain ties with his followers by annual visits, if he is not received hospitably, he is hardly likely to visit again.[10]

The implication of this is that the *ocak*s and their situation look different depending on the way in which one approaches the problem. From a liberal point of view, it may appear that they should gracefully give way to a more contemporary form of religious practice, all the more so as it is hardly possible for them to achieve and retain their old authority. However, from the point of view of Anatolian villagers who over the centuries have reached an accommodation with regard to the way in which they prefer their own form of worship to take place, it may appear to be a less flexible option to be forced to lead their ceremonies according to a centralised bureaucracy, with a *dede* with whom they are not familiar and over whom they have little control.

It is hardly likely that this question will go away soon. My impression is that it is possible, at least to some extent, for new forms of *Alevilik* based on the associations and centralised texts to exist alongside the established community forms of *Alevilik*, perhaps even attracting different constituencies. We may see, then, a flourishing of both kinds of religious activity from the organisational point of view, with the associations and the *ocak*s working together. If this is the case, we will need to research the variety, history and locations of the *ocak*s in Anatolia, as much as the associations and the work that they are doing to perpetuate *Alevilik*.

Change and Simplification

A third reason as to why it is important to conduct research in the villages is because it becomes only possible through understanding the way in which Alevi life is lived within them that we can comprehend the way in which *Alevilik* is changing. To illustrate this point, we should consider once more the Alevi revival, which perhaps could equally be called a transformation. The 1980s marked the point at which the Alevis began to build for themselves a

---

[10] See Chapter 11 in this volume for a discussion on the authority of *dede* and *efendi*, as well as their relations to their villages within the Çelebi lineage.

public religious discourse out of what was previously a closed, often some-what secretive set of ideas that were highly localised. Since that point, we have seen not just the emergence of associational activity of the sort manifested by the federation in Cologne, but also from within Turkey: the movement led by the *Cem Vakfı* and Professor İzzettin Doğan. This has gradually grown, becoming an increasingly structured organisation seeking to provide the doc-trinal framework for a form of Alevi worship that suits the migrant villagers in their new setting. Additionally, because such worship is held in public and often recorded, it aims to illustrate that there is nothing within Alevi religion that is incompatible with being part of contemporary Turkey and with Islam (see Chapter 14 in this volume). Among the publications of the *Cem Vakfı* are a series of instructions as to how the *cem* should be held, which provide the necessary framework for ritual in all of Turkey's *cemevis* that regard them-selves as being under the aegis of the *Cem Vakfı*. Thus, just as in Germany, in Turkey too there is a movement that seeks to create a form of textual exegesis suitable for the Alevi community, even though the two versions are hardly compatible with one another: one seeks to distance the Alevis from Islam, the other seeks to show that *Alevilik* is compatible with it.

In contrasting these reformulations of Alevi tradition – whether in the version preferred by the federation, or that of the *Cem Vakfı* – with traditional Alevi village life, we should recall that this is not just a question of a private religion being made public. Rather, it is a way of life previously occluded, from which is being extracted the overtly religious parts that are then pressed into service as part of the new texts. This process of ritual transfer results in a drastic simplification of the complexity of ritual, as it is known in village life. Not just this, in ring-fencing part of Alevi thought and defining it as religion, they are missing the point that, in fact, *Alevilik* extends far beyond the precepts of the *dedes*; it is a worldview, one that includes Alevi music, dance and the conception of gender relations as reflected in both secular and sacred ritual.

To give a specific example: the question of whether it is possible to 'turn' a *semah* within the confines of a wedding ceremony frequently occurs within the diaspora. There is developing a strong view that the *semah* is a sacred dance, which therefore can only be part of a religious tradition and should not be profaned by being part of a wedding where those present may have imbibed alcohol. This, of course, is new. It is factually the case that in village life there exists a *semah* that is 'turned' in wedding ceremonies, as well as in the *cem*. The link is crucial because it enables both the wedding and the *cem* to become ways of celebrating *Alevilik*, one sacred and the other secular. For this reason, to claim that the *semah* can only be performed within sacred space and, therefore, should not be found at weddings is to miss the point entirely. In the village setting, any celebration or coming together of like-minded persons can give rise to the kind of goodwill for fellow men that they refer to as *muhabbet* or divine love. Eating together, visiting, sharing food after the death of a person – it is the coming together positively and harmoniously as part of a sharing, caring community that constitutes an integral part of what it means to be Alevi. The *semah* reflects this, and that it takes place at a wedding reflects the way in which the divine can be part of everyday life, and not at all a profane expression of impiety.

Yet, it is precisely this that is in danger of being excluded from the teachings of *Alevilik* as the doctrines are being written down and reformulated in order to be taught in schools. To put this simply: *Alevilik* does not begin with a doctrine. Rather, it is the sense that the most important celebratory element in religious thought is the human; that religion, in turn, can help believers to recall the importance of universal humanity. This can be recalled in many ways, even by simply taking a meal with a companion. To celebrate this in a wedding, even if it is the antithesis of a scriptural interpretation, lies at the heart of the Alevi form of religious life. Unless one is familiar with village life, this can hardly be known.

Conclusion

To summarise and conclude, truth claims are made about the Alevis regularly, both by researchers and by those who are associated with the Alevis. These truth claims, although they are almost inevitably made in the diaspora, or at least in urban contexts, often concern not just life in the cities, whether in Turkey or Europe, but the way in which Alevi life is traditionally led in Anatolia. To respond to these in a scholarly way, we need to undertake research in villages, as well as in these new urban contexts. Further, we need to do so in a way that can answer broad questions of population size, distribution and geographical extent, and we need to conduct micro-studies.

Anthropology was once famously characterised as *Small Places/Large Issues* (see Eriksen 2015). In the case of the Alevis at least, this is only part of the answer. We need to look at small places and large issues. But we also need to look at 'large' places and large issues together. I have taken three concrete instances: simplification as a public discourse of *Alevilik*, internal currents within the Alevi movement and the creation of maps. I do not doubt that many more may be chosen. To go forward, we need to research both Anatolia and the diaspora together. Only then will we be in a position to respond convincingly and adequately to the queries that we, as researchers in this field, should be able to respond to, whether they emanate from colleagues in universities, policy-makers, politicians, or the Alevi community itself.

Bibliography

Andrews, P. (1989). *Ethnic Groups in the Republic of Turkey*. Wiesbaden: L. Reichert.

Eriksen, T. H. (2015). *Small Places, Large Issues: An Introduction to Social and Cultural Anthropology*, 4th ed. London: Pluto Press.

Gellner, E. (1969). *Saints of the Atlas*. London: Weidenfeld and Nicolson.

Gezik, E., and Gültekin, A. K., eds (2019). *Kurdish Alevis and the Case of Dersim: Historical and Contemporary Insights*. New York: Lexington Books.

Göner, Ö. (2017). Alevi-State Relations in Turkey: Recognition and Re-Marginalisation. In: Issa, T., ed., *Alevis in Europe: Voices of Migration, Culture and Identity*. London and New York: Routledge. pp. 115–27.

Jenkins, C., and Cetin, U. (2018). From a 'Sort of Muslim' to 'Proud to be Alevi': The Alevi Religion and Identity Project Combatting the Negative Identity among Second-generation Alevis in the UK. *National Identities*, 20(1), 105–23.

Karakaya-Stump, A. (2018). The AKP, Sectarianism, and the Alevis' Struggle for Equal Rights in Turkey. In: Jenkins, C., Aydın, S., and Cetin, U., eds, *Alevism as an Ethno-Religious Identity. Contested Boundaries*. London and New York: Routledge. pp. 53–67.

Melikoff, I. (1998). *Hadji Bektach: Un Mythe et ses Avatars: Genèse et Évolution du Soufisme Populaire en Turquie*. Leiden: Brill.

Özkul, D. (2019). The Making of a Transnational Religion: Alevi Movement in Germany and the World Alevi Union. *British Journal of Middle Eastern Studies*, 46(2), 259–73.

Shankland, D. (1998). Anthropology and Ethnicity: The Place of Ethnography in the New Alevi Movement. In: Olsson, T., Özdalga, E., and Raudvere,

C., eds, *Alevi Identity: Cultural, Religious and Social Perspectives*. Istanbul: Swedish Research Institute in Istanbul. pp. 15–23.

Shankland, D. (2003). *The Alevis in Modern Turkey*. London: Routledge.

Shankland, D., and Çetin, A. (2005). Ritual Transfer and the Reformulation of Belief amongst the Turkish Alevi Community in Europe. In: Langer, R., Motika, R., and Ursinus, M., eds, *Migration und Ritualtransfer: Religiöse Praxis der Aleviten, Jesiden und Nusairier zwischen Vorderem Orient und Westeuropa*. Frankfurt am Main: Peter Lang. pp. 51–72.

Shankland, D. (2010). Maps and the Alevis: On the Ethnography of Heterodox Islamic Groups. *British Journal of Middle Eastern Studies*, 37(3), 227–39.

Shankland, D. (2012). Haritalar ve Aleviler. *Alevilerin Sesi*, 160, 12–25.

Sökefeld, M. (2008a). *Aleviten in Deutschland: Identitätsprozesse einer Religionsgemeinschaft in der Diaspora*. Bielefeld: Transcript.

Sökefeld, M. (2008b). *Struggling for Recognition: The Alevi Movement in Germany and in Transnational Space*. Oxford: Berghahn Books.

16

CONCLUDING REMARKS:
ALEVI AGENCY AND VISIBILITY

HEGE MARKUSSEN

Introduction

This book offers multidisciplinary approaches to Alevi agency. As such, it situates Alevi communities in Turkey and in the diaspora as actors on the stage of contemporary politics in the countries where they live. The multi-faceted strategies used by Alevis when resisting suppression – that is, the mobilisation of identities and negotiations for minority rights – are motivated and shaped by political and structural changes in Turkey and in the diaspora. Moreover, the contributions in this book clearly demonstrate how the dynamics and diversity of Alevi identity, religion and culture provide, and have for decades been providing, a core set of ideas and practices around which diverse Alevi communities can organise and develop. While current Turkish politics increases polarisation in Turkish society, anti-Muslim sentiments are finding their way into European politics and policy-making. It is crucial to investigate how these societal developments affect Alevi communities, both as hardship and as opportunities for mobilisation. Furthermore, understanding both structural and agency-related factors shaping Alevi struggles may also inform our understanding of how other religious minority groups resist, challenge and negotiate political and social discrimination.

Hand in hand with Alevi struggles for recognition and minority rights goes the quest for visibility. The modern collective history of Alevis is narrated accordingly, whether it consists of stories of a withdrawn rural population becoming urban political pressure groups or of heterogeneous and scattered groups of migrants from Turkey forming European transnational ties in order to raise their voice in matters of domestic and foreign politics. Societal visibility is, however, not only a struggle directed towards the surrounding society. Long periods of invisibility have affected Alevis to the degree that teaching Alevi beliefs and practices within the communities – especially, but not exclusively to the younger generations – in recent decades has been as crucial as providing accurate information to outsiders. Societal visibility, then, also increases with heightened internal awareness of one's history, religion, culture and socio-political conditions. An example of this is to be found in Özkan's Chapter 14, which examines the effects of Alevi TV shows aired in Turkey and Europe on the willingness of audiences to talk about their Alevi identity openly. As such, one might claim that visibility is both a result of and a prerequisite to identity mobilisation.

Since the beginning of the 1990s, research within the humanities and social sciences has been an integral part of the processes of increasing visibility of Alevi traditions and communities. As Shankland also notes in Chapter 15, developments in the study of Alevis cannot be fully separated from developments within Alevi civil society. Still, in the growing field of Alevi studies, researchers from within Alevi communities and so-called interested outsiders cooperate, challenge and complete each other's perspectives from diverse scientific disciplines. Alevi visibility through research is, therefore, also a relevant object of investigation. In this concluding chapter, I revisit some of the themes in this volume from the perspective of visibility in both society and research.

Political and Legal Visibility and the Definition of Alevism

As Dressler points out in Chapter 2, how to define Alevism is highly political. It also has far-reaching consequences for the ways in which Alevis become visible in society and how this visibility is negotiated *vis-à-vis* the state. In Turkey, the question of how Alevism is to be related to Islam has increased in both importance and controversy under the AKP regime. As Borovalı and Boyraz demonstrate in Chapter 3 on the government-initiated workshops on Alevism in 2009, the Turkish government and the Presidency of Religious Affairs (*Diyanet İşleri Başkanlığı*; in short, *Diyanet*) representatives have no ambitions of supporting political or legal visibility for Alevis as religious communities. On the contrary, their persistent manoeuvres in framing discussions on Alevism within a state-sanctioned version of Sunni Islam seems more a strategy of maintaining Alevi invisibility. In this context, there are no prospects for Alevis to succeed in their goals of reforming the *Diyanet*, abolishing compulsory Sunni religious education or receiving official recognition for *cemevi*s as houses of worship. The current situation of Alevis in Turkey is, however, even more worrisome. With increasing political and social polarisation and a president who has repeatedly degraded Alevis in public, Alevis are now receiving a kind of visibility in the country that is potentially dangerous. Red markings on the doors of Alevi homes in Yalova constitute a distressing recent reminder of this.

In Europe, Alevi visibility has been influenced by at least three concerns: the status of religious communities in relation to individual states, the importance of not being understood or categorised as a Muslim community and the utilisation of strong transnational ties and supranational authorities. In Germany, where the majority of the European Alevis reside, Alevi mobilisation has been guided by available structural opportunities for the recognition of religious communities in its quest for visibility and legal rights. As Sökefeld points out in Chapter 7 (see also Sökefeld 2008), this development had not been the original aim when Alevis started organising. Rather, it had been a gradual shift from the recognition of Alevi culture to that of Alevi religion. Interestingly, Özkul demonstrates in Chapter 8 that similar developments in the institutionalisation of Alevism occurred in Australia, despite different political and legal approaches to immigrant communities in the two states. She suggests that, beyond political opportunity structures, the transnational impact from the polarised European and Turkish contexts has an important effect on the ways in which Alevis negotiate and represent their identity.

In Europe, the dominant approach to Alevism is to classify it as a religion of its own, disconnected from Islam. The reasons why this definition of Alevism has gained such a strong foothold in Europe are manifold. In a general sense, one might explain differing views on the nature of Alevism along ethnic demarcation lines. The strand of Alevis understanding Alevism as an Islamic tradition consists mostly of ethnically Turkish Alevis, while Kurdish

Alevis, in the majority in several European countries, approach Alevism as a religion older than Islam and centred around natural phenomena.

Alevis' experiences with Islam *vis-à-vis* their encounters with the Turkish state constitute another reason for distinguishing Alevism from Islam – even in the European context. The Turkish state's active foreign policies and the influence of the *Diyanet* are felt strongly in countries such as Germany, which hold the largest Turkish Sunni Muslim diaspora population. Furthermore, growing anti-Muslim sentiments in Europe also have an impact on how European Alevis relate to Islam. As immigrants from Turkey, a 'Muslim country', Alevis strive to show that they are different from Muslim immigrants and allies with European authorities in the fight against Islamism (see, for example, Arkilic's analysis of the Alevi mobilisation in France in Chapter 9). Even in countries such as Sweden, where both the Muslim and the Alevi population are relatively small,[1] being recognised and receiving state funding as a religion of its own have been crucial for Alevis. For this reason, Alevis in Sweden have sought to establish relations with state authorities outside of the Islamic Cooperation Council, which gathers all state-funded Muslim organisations in the country under the same umbrella.

Dynamic transnational networking constitutes one of the strengths of the Alevi movement. This involves not only strong ties between Alevi associations in Europe, but also with associations and foundations in Turkey and elsewhere. As Özkul, Arkilic and Akdemir demonstrate with examples from Germany, France and Britain (in Chapters 8, 9 and 10), Alevi mobilisation facilitates transnational cooperation, aiming at visibility and legal rights in European countries, but also with ambitions to influence political and legal developments in Turkey. In Germany, legal recognition as a religious community has resulted in the inclusion of Alevism as a subject to be taught in schools and at universities in a number of states (see Dressler's Chapter 2 and Sökefeld's Chapter 7). In pursuit of changing the mandatory religious education in Turkish schools, supranational authorities such as the European Court of Human Rights (ECHR) have been engaged, but unfortunately their

---

[1] Estimates of the Swedish Alevi population range between 7,000 and 15,000 persons (Sorgenfrei 2017, p. 25). Estimates of the number of Muslims or persons with Muslim background range between 150,000 and one million (Sorgenfrei 2018, p. 28).

rulings do not seem to have had any impact on the Turkish government as it continues to ignore Alevi demands (see also Borovalı and Boyraz' Chapter 3). The European Union Commission Progress Reports have repeatedly noted discrimination against Alevis in Turkey on issues of education and the absence of recognition of the *cemevi*s, but to no avail (see Kurtarır's Chapter 13).

Alevi traditions have become visible within another supranational authority – the United Nations' Educational, Scientific and Cultural Organization (UNESCO). In 2010, the Alevi-Bektaşi *semah* ritual found its way into the UNESCO list of Intangible Cultural Heritage of Humanity. As Özdemir discusses in Chapter 12, this was an initiative from the Turkish Ministry of Culture and Tourism, followed up with official identity cards for *zakir*s providing the *cem* rituals with music and the recognition of Dertli Divani as a 'Living Human Treasure'. These acts might appear as recognition of Alevi religious traditions on behalf of the Turkish state, but they are not.[2] Particularly since the 1990s, various Turkish governments have highlighted Alevi traditions as an authentic Turkish Anatolian culture in order to incorporate Alevi visibility into a Turkish nationalist history. Representatives of political parties lining up to underline the importance of Alevi culture for Turkish folklore is a common spectacle in Alevi festivals and public gatherings. Yet, again, it is a form of cultural appropriation and not recognition of religious traditions.[3]

Visible as What? Injustice, Victims and Agents

Traumatic injustice is an essential part of the collective history of the Alevis. From the Ottoman period until today, Alevi communities have been stigmatised and exposed to hate crimes. For those who trace Alevism back to the *Ehl-i Beyt* (the family of the Prophet Muhammad), this understanding of Alevi history fits well with the Shi'a-Islamic martyrdom perspective on early Islamic history. As such, suffering in the face of injustice is a central part of the definition of Alevism. What is striking about the ways in which incidents such as the Maraş massacre, the Sivas arson attack and the Istanbul Gazi shootings are remembered is that they exemplify not only contemporary

---

[2] For a discussion of the absence of Alevi support for the *semah* nomination, see Aykan (2013).

[3] For the content and forms of Alevi festivals in various times and places, see Norton (1995), Soileau (2010) and Salman (2020).

hate crimes, but also structural discrimination when authorities such as the police, fire brigade and municipality representatives enable the atrocities and worsen the consequences. As Çaylı shows in Chapter 4 on the Turkish state's responses to Alevi requests for a memorial museum at the site of the Sivas massacre, the historical legacy of these incidents is still a matter of contention between the Alevis and the Turkish state. When never put to rest, these experiences become nodes for Alevi collective memory conservation, as Akdemir illustrates in the importance of the 1978 Maraş massacre among the Alevis in Britain (see Chapter 10). The military operations in Dersim in 1937–38 count among earlier examples of injustices inflicted on the Alevi population; as Zırh demonstrates in Chapter 5, developments in Dersim still generate political controversies and concerns. The contributions to this volume chose to highlight Alevi agency in the face of injustice and invisibility.

The fairly recent invisibility of the Dersim Alevis in historical and contemporary narratives of Alevis is challenged by Gültekin in Chapter 6. The notion of Alevis as a suppressed minority at odds with the state is complicated with an understanding of Alevis as a majority in Dersim, alongside the Sunni minority. Furthermore, Salman Yıkmış demonstrates in Chapter 11 that changes towards relatively better conditions for practising Alevism with the transition from the Ottoman Empire to the Turkish Republic do not apply to the holy lineage of the Çelebi family, who were formally recognised as the hereditary successors of the saint Hacı Bektaş Veli in the Ottoman Empire but lost all of their granted privileges after the establishment of the Republic.

Visibility through and in Research

Alevi traditions and communities have also gained societal visibility through research. Since the end of the 1980s, when Alevis in Germany started to organise and when the first international books were published,[4] the field of Alevi studies has developed in consonance with the progress of the Alevi movement. Apart from Shankland's early studies of Alevi villages (1993, 1999, 2003) and valuable historical studies by Kieser (2001), Dressler (2005,

---

[4] Among the earliest international publictions were Kehl-Bodrogi (1988), Mandel (1989) and Vorhoff (1995).

2013) and Karakaya-Stump (2019), among others, there has been a dispro-portionate focus on Alevi civil society and Alevi-state relations – in both Europe and Turkey. There exist major achievements in this focus of research, and this book partakes in the development of this field with its emphasis on Alevi political agency.

Unfortunately, this has also created some problematic blind spots in our understanding of Alevi communities. First and foremost, Alevi studies have created 'the Alevi': an ageless and genderless person diversified along other demarcation lines, such as rural-urban, lay-leadership and traditional-con-temporary. Studies of internal transformations of identity, religious practices and leadership related to migration and urbanisation have stayed within these borders of binary oppositions – and the contexts of these studies have also been communities related to Alevi associations and foundations (see, for example, Markussen 2012).

A small number of studies on Alevi women has been published (Özmen 2013, Okan 2018, Poyraz 2018, Akdemir 2020). Some of these studies deal in various ways with the idea of Alevi women being more liberated than other women living in patriarchal contexts. There is an apparent need to deal with this narrative, relating these discourses to women's lived realities. Studies of Alevi women that go beyond this discussion are scarce, while studies focusing specifically on Alevi men or masculinity are yet to see the light of day.

Lately, the field of Alevi studies has witnessed a rising interest in Kurdish Alevis, with a special focus on Dersim (Gezik and Gültekin 2019; see also Gültekin's Chapter 6 in this volume), as well as on the Kurdish Alevi population in Britain, with a welcome emphasis on generationally related ways of being Alevi (Jenkins and Cetin 2018, Jenkins 2020, Cetin 2020, Yilmaz 2020).

Alevi visibility in research, however, has been limited. Alevi studies is a rather isolated field of research, although it has been informing theoretical fields such as ritual studies with, for example, the concept of ritual transfer by Langer et al. (2006) and studies of transnationalism and migrant perspec-tives on social movements. Apart from Boyraz (2019) and Karakaya-Stump (2018)'s recent contributions on Alevis' struggle for equal citizenship, Alevi studies have not influenced the field of citizenship studies, even though this is a struggle at the centre of attention.

Moreover, significant – and, so I would claim, more devastating – is the fact that the study of Alevis or Alevism has not had noteworthy impact on the general understanding of modern Turkey. Alevis come to surface in the historiography of modern Turkey only as victims of oppression and hate crimes and occasionally as rebellious groups (notably the 1937–38 Dersim rebellion and the 2013 Gezi demonstrations). Especially when it comes to the relationship between religion and politics, which often is understood as an underlying dynamic in the development of modern Turkey, it is noteworthy that studies of Alevis' experiences with long-term engagement in religio-social identity politics in and outside of Turkey have not succeeded in broadening this narrow window of analysis.

Bibliography

Akdemir, A. (2020). The Construction of Gender Identity in Alevi Organisations: Discourses, Practices and Gaps. *Ethnography* [online]. May 2020. [Viewed 30 March 2021]. Available from: doi: 10.1177/1466138120924435

Aykan, B. (2013). How Participatory is Participatory Heritage Management? The Politics of Safeguarding the Alevi Semah Ritual as Intangible Heritage. *International Journal of Cultural Property* [online]. 20, 381–405 [Viewed 30 March 2021]. Available from: doi: 10.1017/S0940739113000180

Boyraz, C. (2019). The Alevi Question and the Limits of Citizenship in Turkey. *British Journal of Middle Eastern Studies* [online]. 46(5), 767–80. [Viewed 30 March 2021]. Available from: doi: 10.1080/13530194.2019.1634396

Cetin, U. (2020). Unregulated Desires: Anomie, the 'Rainbow Underclass' and Second-generation Alevi Kurdish Gangs. *Kurdish Studies* [online]. 8(1), 185–208. [Viewed 29 March 2021]. Available from: doi: 10.33182/ks.v8i1.541

Dressler, M. (2013). *Writing Religion: The Making of Turkish Alevi Islam*. Oxford: Oxford University Press.

Dressler, M. (2005). Inventing Orthodoxy: Competing Claims for Authority and Legitimacy in the Ottoman-Safavid Conflict. In: Karateke, H. T., and Reinkowski, M., eds, *Legitimizing the Order: The Ottoman Rhetoric of State Power*. Leiden: Brill. pp. 161–73.

Gezik, E., and Gültekin, A. K., eds (2019). *Kurdish Alevis and the Case of Dersim*. New York: Lexington Books.

Jenkins, C. (2020). 'Aspirational Capital' and Transformations in First-generation Alevi-Kurdish Parents' Involvement with Their Children's Education in the UK.

Kurdish Studies [online]. 8(1), 113–34. [Viewed 29 March 2021]. Available from: doi: 10.33182/ks.v8i1.545

Jenkins, C., and Cetin, U. (2018). From 'Sort of Muslim' to 'Proud to be Alevi': The Alevi Religion and Identity Project Combatting the Negative Identity among Second-Generation Alevis in the UK. In: Jenkins, C., Aydin, S., and Cetin, U., eds., *Alevism as an Ethno-Religious Identity: Contested Boundaries*. Oxfordshire and New York: Routledge. pp. 105–21.

Karakaya-Stump, A. (2019). *The Kizilbash Alevis in Ottoman Anatolia: Sufism, Politics and Community*. Edinburgh: Edinburgh University Press.

Karakaya-Stump, A. (2018). The AKP, Sectarianism, and the Alevis' Struggle for Equal Rights in Turkey. *National Identities* [online]. 20(1), 53–67. [Viewed 29 March 2021]. Available from: doi: 10.1080/14608944.2016.1244935

Kehl-Bodrogi, K. (1988). *Die Kızılbaş/Aleviten: Untersuchungen über eine esoterische Glaubensgemeinschaft in Anatolien*. Berlin: Klaus Schwarz Verlag.

Kieser, H. L. (2001). Muslim Heterodoxy and Protestant Utopia: The Interactions between Missionaries and Alevis in Ottoman Anatolia. *Die Welt des Islams*. 41(1), 89–101.

Langer, R., et al. (2006). Transfer of Ritual. *Journal of Ritual Studies*. 20(1), 1–10.

Mandel, R. (1989). Turkish Headscarves and the 'Foreigner Problem': Constructing Difference through Emblems of Identity. *New German Critique* [online]. 46, 27–46. [Viewed 29 March 2021]. Available from: doi: 10.2307/488313

Markussen, H. I. (2012). *Teaching History, Learning Piety: An Alevi Foundation in Contemporary Turkey*. Lund: Sekel Förlag.

Norton, J. D. (1995). The Development of the Annual Festival at Hacıbektaş, 1964–1985. In: Popovic, A., and Veinstein, G., eds, *Bektachiyya: Etudes sur l'ordre Mystique des Bektachis et les Groupes Relevant de Hadji Bektach*. Istanbul: The Isis Press. pp. 191–223.

Okan, N. (2018). Thoughts on the Rhetoric that Women and Men are Equal in Alevi Belief and Practice (Alevilik) – to Songül. In: Jenkins, C., Aydin, S., and Cetin, U., eds, *Alevism as an Ethno-Religious Identity: Contested Boundaries*. Oxfordshire and New York: Routledge. pp. 69–89.

Özmen, F. A. (2013). Alevi Women and Patriarchy. In: Dönmez, R. Ö., and Özmen, F. A., eds, *Gendered Identities: Criticizing Patriarchy in Turkey*. New York: Lexington Books.

Poyraz, B. ed. (2018). *Hakikatin Dârına Durmak. Alevilikte Kadın*. Ankara: Dipnot Yayınları.

Salman, C. (2020). Diasporic Homeland, Rise of Identity and New Traditionalism: The Case of the British Alevi Festival. *Kurdish Studies* [online]. 8(1), 113–32. [Viewed 29 March 2021]. Available from: doi: 10.33182/ks.v8i1.547

Shankland, D. (1993). Alevi and Sunni in Rural Turkey: Diverse Paths of Change. Unpubl. Doctoral Dissertation, Cambridge University.

Shankland, D. (1999). *Islam and Society in Turkey*. Huntingdon: Eothen Press.

Shankland, D. (2003). *The Alevis in Turkey: The Emergence of a Secular Islamic Tradition*. London: Routledge.

Soileau, M. (2010). Festivals and the Formation of Alevi Identity. In: Markussen, H. I., ed., *Alevis and Alevism: Transformed Identities*. Istanbul and Piscataway: The Isis Press and Gorgias Press. pp. 91–108.

Sorgenfrei, S. (2018). *Islam i Sverige – de första 1300 åren*. Stockholm: Myndigheten för stöd till trossamfund.

Sorgenfrei, S. (2017). Aleviter. In: Larsson, G., Sorgenfrei, S., and Stockman, M., *Religiösa minoriteter från Mellanöstern* [online]. Stockholm: Myndigheten för stöd till trossamfund. [Viewed 30 March 2021]. Available from: https://www.myndighetensst.se/download/18.457bad0515f1c30d5b62c7c8/1508243249324/MENA_låguppl_inledning.pdf

Sökefeld, M. (2008). *Struggling for Recognition: The Alevi Movement in Germany and in Transnational Space*. New York: Berghahn Books.

Vorhoff, K. (1995). *Zwischen Glaube, Nation und neuer Gemeinschaft: Alevitische Identität in der Türkei*. Berlin: Klaus Scwarz Verlag.

Yilmaz, B. (2020). Language Attitudes and Religion: Kurdish Alevis in the UK. *Kurdish Studies* [online]. 8(1), 133–61. [Viewed 29 March 2021]. Available from: doi: 10.33182/ks.v8i1.512

INDEX

Printed in the USA
CPSIA information can be obtained
at www.ICGtesting.com
JSHW052030231023
50693JS00005B/38